BORIS YELTSIN

BORIS YELTSIN

A POLITICAL BIOGRAPHY

Vladimir Solovyov and Elena Klepikova

translated by
David Gurevich
in collaboration
with the authors

WEIDENFELD AND NICOLSON
London

First published in Great Britain in 1992 by
George Weidenfeld and Nicolson Limited
91 Clapham High Street, London SW4 7TA

British Library Cataloguing-in-Publication Data
is available on request.
ISBN 0 297 81252 1

Printed in Great Britain by
Butler & Tanner Ltd,
Frome and London

CONTENTS

"What are you talking about—'destiny'!
Politics are destiny."

NAPOLEON

"I'll never let you back into politics!"

GORBACHEV TO YELTSIN, 1987

ACKNOWLEDGMENTS

THIS BOOK is a product of our three trips to Russia in the last year and a half, between the spring of 1990 and the fall of 1991. We are grateful to those who communicated with us there, whether in person or by phone or by mail: their names, whenever we were allowed to use them, have been included in the text or the footnotes.

After one of us was interviewed on Russian TV about our project, we were deluged with additional information until our departure for New York. Back in America, we found piles of letters from Russian émigrés who had met Yeltsin, in response to our inquiry in a Russian émigré paper. Unfortunately, our Moscow schedule became so overloaded that we had to cancel our scheduled trip to Sverdlovsk, where Yeltsin had spent most of his life prior to his departure for Moscow in the spring of 1985 at Gorbachev's behest. We managed to reach Sverdlovsk on the phone and interview a dozen people who knew Yeltsin well; we also received some invaluable materials from Sverdlovsk in the mail.

On the other hand, perhaps it was better that we never made it to Sverdlovsk, where a local travel agency is already conducting Yeltsin Memorial tours. There, we were expected to meet with a local fan who proposed to take us to see Yeltsin's ex-schoolmates and colleagues, who were to tell us the most heroic, sentimentalized anecdotes concerning their famous friend.

We talked to enough persons like that, ones who were eager to build a Potemkin Village of history and sing hosannas to the leader, but we also talked on the phone to those left out of that group—whether because they were too talkative or too critical. Yeltsin himself has nothing to do with this idolatry and may not even know of the Sverdlovsk myth-making industry.

He did insist on seeing our manuscript—something we would have never dared ask him to do—and was upset that it was still missing a few chapters, especially the one describing the August coup. The request was stated in a rather jocular form: "Am I President of Russia or not? Don't I have a right to know what's been written about me?"

We do not think that this curiosity was purely egocentric. After all, our biography was not the only one: Pavel Voshchanov, his press secretary, showed us the manuscript of a book by ex-Reuters reporter John Morrison, who asked Yeltsin to write a foreword. But, unlike Morrison's, our book was written in Russian. Besides, Yeltsin turned out to be familiar with our work. What happened was that several years earlier, chapters from our "Kremlin" books, published in the West, had been translated back into Russian and reached Russia in pirated editions. One of them, the description of Gorbachev, was a Samizdat bestseller for a year. Yeltsin, along with his close assistants—Valentina Lantseva, Lev Sukhanov, and Valery Bortsov—had read our descriptions of the Kremlin leaders. "It was as if you'd been there!" Yeltsin commented. "Too bad we didn't know what you knew." Well—we were flattered.

We do not know how attentively Yeltsin was reading the manuscript, which accompanied him on his shuttles between his "White House"—the Russian President's headquarters—and his Kremlin office. We barely managed to rescue it on our last day in Moscow—it was a working copy, with corrections and insertions and translator's notes. Yeltsin's request to read it caught us unawares, and we did not have a chance to make a copy. (A copy in Moscow! As if it were New York, with a copy shop on every corner!) Yeltsin's younger daughter, Tanya, assured us that "Father read it from beginning to end"; according to Pavel Voshchanov, there were hardly any negative remarks. Yeltsin was surprised to see so much material unearthed about him: more than he had used in his autobiography. We let him in on some of our sources and kept silent about others. We are grateful to Tanya Diachenko-Yeltsina for her corrections and suggestions.

We postponed the chapter on the Three Days in August until our last trip to Moscow in October 1991; we wanted to interview as many participants and witnesses of this historic event as we could, and clarify the role of Gorbachev in it. What we found out surpassed all our expectations.

After an entire month spent practically camping in the corridors and offices of the new center of power, we decided to add a post-putsch chapter, which would point the book toward the unpredictable Russian future. Yeltsin was used to being in the opposition and ready for drawn-out trench warfare with the Kremlin, when, as a result of the failed conservative coup, power fell into his lap. He had neither a detailed blueprint for governing nor the skill for it on such scale—hence the quasi-stupor of the new Russian leadership in the first weeks after the putsch. The Moscow White House that we found was a hive of quarrels, intrigue, and infighting—deprived of a real, identifiable enemy, the democrats plunged into an internecine settling of scores. Even the "Sverdlovsk mafia" that Yeltsin had recruited from among his native Uralites was far from united: one might think Yeltsin was a beautiful heiress the way its members were vying for his attention.

The euphoria of unexpected triumph had gone up in smoke, replaced by the fear of another coup. An impatient society expected Yeltsin to perform miracles of New Testament magnitude; when none took place, many began asking: how are democrats better than Communists?

Perhaps worse, some answered, recalling an old Indian tale of a beggar whose bleeding wounds were besieged by flies. When a good Samaritan tried to chase the flies away, the beggar protested: "Leave them alone, sir. They have already had their fill; they do not bite hard or often. If the new, the hungry ones come, they will torment me much worse till they are sated."

Yeltsin performed his feat of demolition—he did away with such seemingly indestructible monoliths as the Soviet Empire, the Party, the KGB—but did he, a construction engineer by training, have any energy left to exercise power, to build a new edifice? The old system lay in ruins; the new one, the replacement, was yet to be created. The country disintegrated apace, its economy plummeted, political anarchy broke out—society panicked. Unlike Gorbachev, Yeltsin did not have time for maneuvering: Gorbachev, by clinging to power, wasted both his own time and Yeltsin's. Both leaders maintained telephone contact, still settling old scores, still subverting each other's power, of which Gorbachev had very little left. As the Union fell apart, he became like King Lear after he divided his kingdom among his daughters. As Machiavelli would say, to reign he lacked only a kingdom. In the meantime, journalists and investigators still kept trying to find out Gorbachev's involvement in the failed coup, while he insisted on a closed-door trial and set up his own commission of inquiry.

One morning we arrived at the Russian White House to learn that Yeltsin had just called Gorbachev at the Kremlin and demanded that the highest governing body of the disintegrating Union should consist only of the Republican Presidents, with the President of the Union playing the purely symbolic role of their coordinator. Gorbachev would not agree to such a drastic reduction of his power. The same night, Yeltsin spoke agitatedly on Moscow TV and warned Gorbachev that if the latter tried to limit Russia's rights, there would be a "counterstrike."

The counterstrike came after we left Moscow. After the Ukrainian referendum's vote for independence, Yeltsin met in Brest, on the Polish border, with the leaders of two other Slav Republics. The three declared the formation of a commonwealth of independent states; several days later it was joined by most other ex–Union Republics.

Was this something Yeltsin had planned long ago? Or a political improvisation? Or an eleventh-hour last resort? Regardless of the genesis of the Commonwealth or its future, the move of the center from Moscow to Minsk dealt a deadly blow both to the Kremlin and to Gorbachev the politician.

Every Yeltsin adviser we spoke to in Moscow told us that it was time to finish Gorbachev off. Yeltsin, however, seemed to hesitate, then, as if afraid to be rid of his bitter enemy and be left face-to-face with an ungovernable country. In order to become a fully empowered ruler of Russia, Yeltsin still had to overcome the revolutionary in himself. He had had enough inner force to turn from a Communist into a democrat, but would he have enough strength—or time—to turn from a destroyer into a creator? It would be a late political debut; he had not attained power until the age of sixty, when he was already physically and emotionally exhausted. The material was begging to be turned into a chapter.

The copy shown to Yeltsin also lacked the latest additions, about fifty pages long, made on the basis of the material we had collected on our last trip—including some of a rather personal nature. In one case, our source—who for a time had been close to the Yeltsins—later asked us to omit certain details. Thus he helped us rid ourselves of our own doubts; we already suspected we had gone too far in our reportorial doggedness— we had intruded into an area we had no business to be in. We regretted dropping some of the tidbits, but we decided to make the sacrifice: they did not have a direct bearing on the political portrait of the Russian President.

A few hours before our departure, in the middle of the night, we got a call from the Yeltsins. After a long discussion, we agreed to delete two absolutely reliable stories that had to do with Yeltsin's worries about his fatherly duties. The stories portrayed him as a complex person: hot-tempered yet easily mollified; tolerant yet somewhat old-fashioned on certain issues. "Unlike us, Father is monogamous," one of his daughters told us. We will confess we felt sorry to be omitting these stories as well, but we felt we should: they involved other people, completely innocent and entitled to their privacy. It has never been our intention that our book cause anyone anguish; therefore we decided to keep the word we had given to the Yeltsin family.

We also thank them for the permission to publish the snapshots from the family album. Other pictures were provided by Valentina Lantseva, the director of the Press Center at the Presidium of the Russian Supreme Soviet; by *Rossiya* weekly editors Alexandr Drozdov, Andrey Dyatlov, and Gennady Shalayev; by Yuri Feklistov, the staff photographer for *Ogonyok* magazine; by Yeltsin's former secretary Tatyana Pushkina, and reporter Yuri Kozyrev. In gathering material we received substantial assistance from Moscow journalists Artyom Borovik, Evelina Guret-skaya, Sergei Kozyrev, and Feliks Medvedev; Yevgeny Muslin from Radio Liberty; Ilya Levkov, the publisher of the Russian-language Liberty Publishing House in New York; and Albert C. Todd, Professor of Slavic Languages and Literatures at Queens College, CUNY.

Finally, we thank the people who believed in this book before we started working on it: our indefatigable agent, Heide Lange—this is our third book with her—and her assistant Douglas Stallings. Our translator, David Gurevich, a novelist and essayist, who spent much time and energy to create an American equivalent of a book by two Russian authors about a Russian politician. Our editor, Neil Nyren of Putnam's, who came to believe in our book on the basis of a six-page proposal. We would like to express our appreciation for the valuable suggestions which he made upon reading the manuscript. We particularly wish to acknowledge the talented stylistic editing by Fred Sawyer of Putnam's, who brought the English translation to the closest possible proximity to the Russian original. We are grateful to PIK publishers in Moscow for their gracious permission to quote and paraphrase Yeltsin's memoirs, *Confession on an Assigned Theme*.

At the risk of sounding frivolous, we still would like to thank Charlie and Prince Mishkin, our two feline friends—their gentle playfulness was a great source of help and diversion on the all-too-scarce breaks in writing this book.

INTRODUCTION
Hercules' Thirteenth Feat

INTRODUCTIONS ARE often added after the book has been completed—out of lack of confidence or last-minute anxiety over one's literary child. The author may reshuffle the sequence of events to forestall the criticisms of readers, fill in gaps in the text, or compensate in some other way for omissions or shortcomings in the rest of the book. Extraordinary events interrupted our work when it was in full gear, however, with over half the book already written, so this introduction represents a break with tradition in that it was written *in medias res.*

Had we known what would happen in Moscow on August 19, 1991, we might not have undertaken this project, which was risky to begin with. For, according to Priestly, there is nothing more difficult than describing a bullet in its flight. This is an apt description of the dizzying career of our hero—Boris Nikolayevich Yeltsin. And how could we anticipate the turn of events that would cause the bullet to accelerate to the speed of light— what biographer could keep up with it?—to say nothing of radical changes in the book's format midway through writing it, and the addition of new chapters, with the tight deadline unchanged.

In short, we attuned ourselves to the wild rhythm of Yeltsin's life, to the abrupt shifts of its gears. We could guess that, as we worked on the book, his life could—and would—take new hairpin turns. It was not just Yeltsin; it was the entire country, whose only predictable quality is its utter unpredictability. We had not ruled out the possibility of a hard-liners' coup, but we were sure that it would put an end to Yeltsin's political career. Like so many, we were taken unawares by the reverse turn in the August putsch, which not only failed to eliminate Yeltsin, but put him center stage in Russian and world history. We must be honest about it: with all our respect for Boris Yeltsin, we could not foresee that under such exceptional conditions he would summon all his will, courage, intelligence, and cunning to defeat the conspirators and save Russia.

All of this despite the fact that by then we had studied his biography in detail and realized that we were dealing with a man of truly heroic stature. Moreover, as writers, we felt somewhat ambivalent: after all, the age of heroes is long gone, and our book ran the risk of reading like a parody, for the modern reader is generally more responsive to complex, contradictory natures than to consistently heroic ones. So in order to avoid canonizing Yeltsin in his lifetime, we still had to come up with a devil's advocate.

By August 19, 1991, Yeltsin had already overcome many seemingly impossible obstacles and invincible enemies, but on that day he faced alone the military repressive mechanism of a superpower, aimed at him personally. It was as if Hercules, weary after his twelve feats, were promptly told to accomplish the thirteenth one, surpassing all the twelve previous ones put together.

"Don't worry, Dad. Now it all depends on you alone."

With these words Yeltsin's younger daughter, Tanya, sent him off as he was getting into his car. It was in Usovo, a village outside Moscow, where the Russian cabinet of ministers had gathered when they learned of the coup. They decided to go to Moscow, to the "White House" on Krasnaya Presnya, and from there to call an emergency session of the Russian Parliament. Yeltsin had to wear a bulletproof vest—everyone understood that from now on he was the putschists' main target, as well as the freedom fighters' last, however faint, hope. On the way to Moscow, they passed endless columns of tanks and armored troop carriers, moving in the same direction.

WE HAD conceived a book about Yeltsin a year earlier, when we came back to Russia after thirteen years' absence. We hardly need explain the reason for our return: we went as soon as political émigrés were allowed back in. It was not the first time we had seen Yeltsin; we saw him a year earlier, in New York, during his first visit to America. The very first time, a fleeting glimpse, took place about fifteen years earlier in Sverdlovsk, which one of the authors visited with a delegation of Moscow writers. At that time, on a very superficial level, Yeltsin stood out among other local *apparatchiks,* perhaps solely in a literal sense: he was taller and more athletic. Had this coauthor possessed a gift of clairvoyance, he would of course have tried to make the acquaintance of that provincial function-ary—at the time it was an easier task. It would also have saved us the laborious task of gathering material on the fifty-four years of Yeltsin's life in the Urals that we needed desperately for our chapter on the compara-tive lives of Gorbachev and Yeltsin. (On Gorbachev, by contrast, we had more material than we needed, left over from our previous book, *Behind the High Kremlin Walls,* in which Gorbachev featured prominently.)

As journalists, we closely followed Yeltsin's stormy career in Moscow from overseas—his ups and downs, his involvement in scandals, his pe-riod in political limbo, and his miraculous Lazarus-like revival. We do not wish to pat ourselves on the back, but, in order to explain the genesis of this book, we have to note that we saw him in a positive light even at the time when the Soviet papers first splattered him with mud, then joined hands in a conspiracy of silence. At the same time, the Western media wrote off Boris Yeltsin as a clown, a demagogue at best; at worst he was considered a Russian chauvinist, even a fascist. But it was not until we returned to Russia and failed to recognize the country where we had been born and spent thirty-five years each—that's how radically it had changed—not until then did we realize that we could not tell its story without telling about its hero—the man it had chosen. We needed another trip, to give a more concrete shape to our initially vague concept of a political portrait of Boris Yeltsin against the background of revolutionary Russia. In June 1991 we sent a letter to our literary agent; two weeks later Putnam's accepted our proposal and we sat down to sort out twelve thick files—the Yeltsin Files.

Calling the Soviet Union on the phone consumed much of our time and energy. First, it was hard to break through; second, it was summer—the dead season, when it took a lot of luck to catch people at home or in the office. Nonetheless, we managed to take a number of interviews by phone and discuss our meeting with Yeltsin's aides and advisers.

To be honest, the latter did not seem terribly important, since we already had abundant material, primarily transcripts—published both clandestinely (as Samizdat) and officially, mostly in provincial papers—of Yeltsin's numerous interviews, talks, and press conferences. We took the trouble to count: we had on record 7263 answers that Yeltsin had given in response to questions asked him from 1986 to 1991. Unlike Gorbachev, who is given to monologues, Yeltsin is a "dialoguer": question-and-answer is his favorite format, and the sharper, the more provocative the questions, the more he loved fielding them. Considering his openness, unusual for a Soviet politician, it seemed that in these 7263 answers he had already told everything of himself that he remembered and considered necessary—to say nothing of his autobiography, published all over the world.

The problem was not how to avoid repeating what he himself had said. We had many important details that he had either forgotten or reinterpreted in what seemed like a subjective and tendentious manner, or preferred to omit for tactical reasons—he was, after all, a working politician who wished to keep his cards close to his chest. Here we had to deal with complex ethical issues. For example, should we mention his illness, which he took pains to deny or at least camouflage? Also, despite our positive view of Yeltsin, our fascination with his political career—in contrast to Gorbachev's—we were not about to compose a panegyric. Rather, we planned to create a many-sided, balanced, and objective portrait of a politician in the context of Russian reality, so contradictory and unpredictable. We planned to analyze that reality as well (especially in the third part of the book, where Yeltsin is elected by popular vote, pressed into service by history, and becomes inseparable from it—completing his transformation from an *apparatchik* into Russia's leading politician).

Finally, if people write biographies of Marcel Proust, the most autobiographical writer in history, who created a seven-volume lyrical epic about himself, how could Yeltsin's 7263 answers plus his autobiography get in our way? Especially since his book ended as of spring of 1989, that is, long before Boris Yeltsin became the first freely and popularly elected leader in Russian history.

We had a different problem. Although our book was conceived with a Western audience in mind, we had no desire to go out of our way to please it. We were writing about a man whom the West still treated with wariness and distrust, considering him—as opposed to Gorbachev—an intellectual lightweight and a power-hungry Bourbon. Yeltsin's first trip to America was a resounding failure. Although by then he was already the head of the political opposition in Russia, and its most popular politician (while Western favorite Gorbachev was steadily losing popularity), he had to practically fight his way to the White House gate. When, in the spring of 1990, Gary Kasparov, the world chess champion and a democratic activist, told Brent Scowcroft that Yeltsin would soon become the Russian President and should be taken seriously, President Bush's national security adviser laughed.

The Western public, from political leaders to the media to the man in the street, had long since put their money on Gorbachev, and resisted changing horses in the midstream of Russian politics. It did not matter that a new political star had risen in the Kremlin firmament while the old one was in decline; that Yeltsin won one victory after another by democratic means while Gorbachev clung to power by the tried-and-tested Kremlin method of intrigue. We regarded this Gorbophilia/Yeltsinophobia as a case of double standard, of political myopia, of the West betraying its own democratic principles, and as contempt for the will of the Russian people, who expressed frequently and unequivocally that for most of them Gorbachev was an impostor and Yeltsin was their preferred representative.

It was easy to assume that given these circumstances, our book would be perceived as biased; this is why we wanted to use the foreword to affirm its objectivity. To us, the true bias lay in Western Gorbocentrism, which preferred to view an enormous country through the eyes of one of its statesmen—especially one with a plummeting popularity rating—and his even less popular wife. We had long been American citizens, yet we never ceased being Russian, and we made our political choice along with our people. Our book on Yeltsin and Yeltsin's Russia was conceived to counterbalance the endless stream of paeans to Gorbachev that for the last six years the media had poured on Western audiences. Gorbachev's biographies alone number over a dozen, forming a genre, or, rather, a branch of publishing. We wanted to use the foreword to state that, in contrast to the biographies of the official Kremlin leader, our book would be about the leader of the Russian *people*.

The three days in August made this kind of foreword redundant.

On Sunday, August 18, expecting many Muscovites to be returning home from their dachas, we took turns dialing Moscow—our exhausting daily routine. Except for a direct hit or two, it took us from an hour to an hour and a half to complete each call; the message came through loud and clear: "All international circuits to the country you are calling are busy now." Every time we managed to break through this telephonic Iron Curtain, we listened on and on to the long signals, in desperate hope that someone thousands of miles away would pick it up. We were already dialing by heart: 292-6065 for Valentina Lantseva, 205-6422 for Lev Sukhanov, 298-0258 for Lev Shemayev, and, finally, 250-8777 for Yeltsin himself. None of them, of course, had an answering machine.

It was nighttime in New York, while the sun was coming up in Moscow. Out of despair, we called a Moscow friend—bingo! Connection! He gave us this astounding bit of news: "We have a coup here. Gorbachev's under house arrest. A junta has taken over."

"What about Yeltsin?"

The line went dead before he had a chance to answer.

This was the unexpected end of our telephone vigil and the beginning of the TV one. Not much can be said about the latter: the whole world was watching. And being a part of the world—watching the events from the sidelines, from the safe distance of thousands of miles—made us uncomfortable, though God knows it was not our fault.

It looked as if it were all over. The end of all hopes. Moscow was occupied by the Army—martial law was announced—medieval night had descended upon the land.

There is no need to pretend: our project was on our minds, too. There it was, on the desk: a red fake-leather file (Soviet-made) with white laces, containing the opening chapters on Yeltsin and Yeltsin's Russia—obsolete, no longer needed. In the last chapter finished before the coup, we had described his Herculean feats, his triumphs, his records. He was of a pioneer breed: much of what he had accomplished was the first of its kind in the history of the Communist Party, in Soviet history, even in the thousand-year history of Russia.

Later, our editor, impressed with Yeltsin's election as President, called us to suggest that we open the book with that event.

"What if something else happens in the meantime?"

He agreed that with Russia—and Yeltsin—one could expect anything.

We have probed deeply enough into Yeltsin's life to perceive him as a tragic figure in Russia's equally tragic history, and now we were plainly afraid for his life: after all, Yeltsin—not Gorbachev—was the putschists' enemy number one.

A few hours later we saw Yeltsin climb a T-72 tank in front of his "White House" on Krasnaya Presnya, which, at the junta's orders, was to be stormed any minute by the Alpha Group of specially trained KGB commandos. Alpha boys are experienced in storming palaces: almost twelve years earlier, on Christmas Eve of 1979, when Soviet troops invaded Afghanistan, Alphas had stormed the President's palace and butchered Hafizullah Amin, his family, and his court.

Standing atop the tank, Yeltsin addressed thousands of his supporters and called for resistance to the junta.

In his excitement, our editor called us again. The book now had a new opening: the Tank Speech.

Then familiar voices came over the radio and TV: our Moscow friends Artyom Borovik and his wife, Veronika Kilchevskaya, were reporting from the besieged White House. The attack was about to begin. Yeltsin had warned the world: there was little time left. His supporters designed a secret plan to evacuate him, but he categorically refused to leave the building. The Moscow White House was the last bulwark of democracy, and in that hour of decision its defenders were unanimous: they would never surrender.

Later it turned out that it was Veronika Kilchevskaya who called John E. Frohnmayer, the Chairman of the National Endowment for the Arts, on Monday night, and asked him for Bush's phone number—for Yeltsin. Veronika had met Bush in the early '70s, when he was American Ambassador to the UN and she was six years old, but that is another story. Thus, Frohnmayer and Kilchevskaya together established a direct link between the Moscow White House and Kennebunkport, Maine, where the US President was vacationing. Bush was already awake: he had been awakened at five to midnight and informed of the coup. Later, the two Presidents, Bush and Yeltsin, talked on the phone several times.

We recalled our last meeting with Veronika and Artyom in Kropotkinskaya, a privately owned Moscow restaurant. Artyom is the editor-in-chief of the tabloid *Top Secret,* circulation 4 million, in which he had published chapters from Vladimir Solovyov's futuristic novel, *Operation Mausoleum,* and now planned to issue it in book form. The novel, originally published in 1989 in New York, described something very familiar—an overthrow of Gorbachev in a coup d'état led by the KGB chief.

However, after the book had been written, its author visited Moscow twice and consequently took a more optimistic view. He asked Artyom, just to make conversation: "Can the country be turned around?"

"Absolutely!"

"When Gorbachev had his own capital occupied last spring by troops to prevent pro-Yeltsin demonstrations—wasn't that a farce?"

"It was a show of *force*," Artyom said. "What if force had really been used, and Gorbachev had been replaced by an Ivan the Terrible?"

"An Ivan the Terrible—today that really sounds funny."

"From New York it does. Here, after they execute the first thousand or so, no one will be laughing."

We quote the conversation verbatim from the tape that we made, thinking to use it later in the accounts of our Russian trip. When we heard Veronika and Artyom's voices from the Moscow White House—besieged, but unvanquished—we felt a little ashamed of our spectator's optimism.

Despite the barricades, despite the handful of tanks that crossed over to Yeltsin's side (he used one of them to make the speech), despite the several thousand demonstrators forming a live barrier around the White House, despite the coup's denunciation abroad, democracy in Russia seemed doomed, its hours numbered. The bulwark of Russian liberty resembled the ancient Masada—both were defended not out of hope but out of despair.

We had an odd, unexpected, perhaps unjustified feeling that there was something superficial, theatrical, even TV-like, about the Moscow events. There was a "hey-boys-and-girls-let's-put-on-a-*Coup*-show" quality: the announcement of the emergency; tank columns on the streets; a priest blessing the White House defenders while next to him an instructor was coaching them in using Molotov cocktails; even Yeltsin atop a tank perversely reminded us of the textbook image of Lenin atop the armored car in 1917. After all, coups and revolutions are not everyday events and are not meant to be perceived as routine. And, in our TV age, any ocular reality is perceived as a show.

While we were still in New York, we were wrong about the genre of the program: we thought it was a tragedy but it turned out to be a farce, which is traditionally much shorter. This farce of a putsch lasted less than three days and ended as suddenly as it started. Instead of thousands dead, only three. Six, to be precise: three from each side. Three Moscow White House defenders: Dmitry Komar, Ilya Krichevsky, and Vladimir Usov; and three men involved in the putsch: one of its organizers, Minister of the Interior Boris Pugo; Gorbachev's military adviser, Marshal Sergei Akhromeyev; and Gorbachev's Party aide Nikolai Kruchina.

The first three died fighting the tanks; the others were alleged suicides: one shot himself ten minutes before arrest, one hanged himself in his

Kremlin office, and one threw himself off a terrace. From Moscow, however, came unofficial reports that these men had been murdered at the orders of the main conspirator, the one behind the stage, the Ninth Man (in addition to the eight-man junta), the one mentioned by Yeltsin—not by name—in his nighttime interview as he was awaiting the storming of the White House. All six dead seem like an illustration of Jefferson's maxim that the tree of freedom must be from to time nurtured by the blood of patriots and tyrants.

Thus we had an additional reason to go to Moscow: to try to learn at least something about this mysterious putsch. Call it what you like—"velvet revolution" or "conspiracy of the damned"—it pushed Russian history out of an impasse and served as a catalyst for an inevitable disintegration.

We were less interested in the actors who performed this tragicomedy on the historical stage than in its directors, who, understandably, could not have been numerous. Parallels with the past were no help, though we discussed a few historical notables like Nero. In any event, the questions tormented us like no headache could.

It turned out that Foros, the luxurious Black Sea estate where Gorbachev had spent three days incommunicado, was not so easy to cut off from the rest of the world. According to the director general of Signal Enterprises, responsible for presidential communications, one would have needed to disassemble and remove tons of equipment, for Foros is one of the main switchboards for running the country and houses numerous autonomous communication systems. Even if all of them had been disabled, there was another, top secret one, and the President needed to have only a pen and paper in order to get in touch with Russia and the world. According to this expert, the failure to communicate was voluntary.

It was much easier to isolate Yeltsin, yet he stayed in touch as if nothing had happened, maintaining regular contact even with foreign leaders. In the course of the three days, he spoke to the plotters several times, and, when the putsch failed, he recommended that they go to Foros to see Gorbachev. Strange as it may seem, they heeded his advice. The general opinion was that they went to ask for the President's apology, although Alexandr Podrabinek, the editor of *Express Khronika,* believes that at that moment they looked for the most part like "victims of a deception who had panicked and were dashing to talk things over."

However, their plane was followed to Foros by another one, containing Yeltsin's people, who brought Gorbachev, his family, and the plotters back to Moscow the same night.

What transpired during those few days at Gorbachev's Crimean villa is no less mysterious and exciting than what was occurring in Moscow's seats of power—the Kremlin and the White House. Why were the men who had dared to stage a coup d'état suddenly struck by paralysis? What became of their determination? What had frightened them at the last moment? Well-schooled in following orders, they all acted like novice pilots who had lost contact with ground control. And, even if, as was possible, this bomb of a show had had an incognito director operating behind the scenes, what stopped him at the last minute?

One theory maintains that the putsch bore the unmistakable imprint of Gorbachev's vacillating, half-measure executive style. To us, this seems like an overly structured, a priori explanation based on assumptions about one man's personality. It cannot serve as convincing evidence.

But even the sensational debacle of the putsch did not write finis to a series of improbable events. Gorbachev became a secondary figure while Yeltsin moved to the forefront, which caused consternation abroad and panic within the disintegrating Empire. Yeltsin underwent a striking political metamorphosis: from Gorbachev's nemesis to Gorbachev's regent. Yeltsin's figure, his size alone, were impressive, and now he had an immense country behind him—we of course mean Russia, not the Soviet Union, which somehow seemed to disappear.

FOREIGN GORBOMANIACS and Gorbophiles, including George Bush, were appalled when at the session of the Russian Parliament, immediately following the coup's collapse, Yeltsin, in plain sight, came up to the podium where Gorbachev stood, and, pointing his finger, forced him to read the transcript of the meeting between the plotters and the ministers. It was as if Gorbachev had become a puppet in Yeltsin's hands, following Yeltsin's orders, disbanding the Communist Party and then the Soviet Parliament, appointing Yeltsin's protégés to all the key positions, and recognizing the independence of the Baltic states, which Gorbachev used to oppose vehemently.

If Yeltsin was indeed wielding such power, what did he need Gorbachev for? What forced Gorbachev to take orders, and why was Yeltsin using him as a proxy rather than take direct action? To us, ardent cat lovers, this reminded of a cat-and-mouse play, and we even caught ourselves feeling sympathy for Gorbachev, so lost and humiliated. Perhaps he was caught in the trap he had set up himself; still, you couldn't help feeling sorry for him.

As for Yeltsin, we now eyed him with mixed feelings, trying to guess what was behind the façade of his sly, arrogant smile. Was it the victor's triumph? Secret knowledge that he could not yet share but only hint at with his expression? The relationship between the two Presidents, the Soviet and the Russian one, hardly made one think of dual power.

Back in liberated Moscow from his Crimean imprisonment, Gorbachev offered Yeltsin the highest Soviet award, the Gold Star of the Hero of the Soviet Union. Yeltsin turned it down: "The people defeated the putschists; real heroes manned the barricades."

This was not false modesty; not even the modesty that conceals pride, but, rather, the realization of being at one *with* the people, as well as one *of* the defenders of freedom. Each did his job. Yeltsin could not alone have defended the democratic gains, but victory would have been impossible without him, too, whatever you wish to call him in this context—the leader? The standard bearer? The banner itself? In fact, he was more like the center of gravity.

It is doubtful that tens of thousands would have rushed to defend the Moscow White House if Yeltsin had not been there (or if Gorbachev had been there). Nor would the putschists have selected the White House as their chief target, sending troops and preparing to storm it, if Yeltsin had not been there. Even if Gorbachev was innocent as a lamb, even if his participation in the coup was an indirect one (after all, the leaders were his personnel choices)—the August 19 putsch was directed against Yeltsin, whom the putschists planned to remove, not against Gorbachev—and implemented by Gorbachev's own people. As for Gorbachev, according to Acting President Gennady Yanayev, he was soon to return to his Presidential duties.

The Guinness Book of World Records tells of a man who has been struck by lightning twenty-two times and survived. This is a good image of Yeltsin, who, as a symbol of liberty, attracted both enemy and friendly forces with equal power.

Yet behind the symbol there was a human being—Boris Nikolayevich Yeltsin—who refused the title of Hero of the Soviet Union because he was convinced he had already been sufficiently rewarded by his deed. Whatever lies ahead of him, by defending democracy in Russia, he has already accomplished his thirteenth *Opus Herculeum*. Our editor was right: the Speech from the Tank in front of the Moscow White House was Yeltsin's apogee. How then should we view his past triumphs as they recede into the past, fading away under the onslaught of new, extraordinary events?

As his biographers, we were feeling a little lost. By placing Yeltsin's Ural background in the middle of the book and opening our story with his tumultuous Moscow rule, we had already decided against the traditional chronology; but now, when those quarrels, intrigues, and scandals seemed to have taken place fifty, not five, years ago, who cared about their details? Finally, we realized that no matter how rapidly the book needed to be completed, Russian history, wildly accelerating, would leave us behind anyway, and to try to chart its hazardous twistings and turnings would merely be frivolous on our part.

After the putsch was over, we finally began reaching our Yeltsinite contacts, trying to set up an itinerary. In response, Lev Sukhanov, one of his closest aides, exclaimed, "That's a month from now! We haven't any idea what will happen tomorrow."

Yeltsin had spent the last five years as a battering ram aimed at the Communist Party and the KGB, the two principal bulwarks of the world's last empire—and at the Empire itself. His labors had not been in vain; the anachronistic edifice collapsed within hours, right after the failed coup. *Etiam periere ruinae*—the very ruins were destroyed.

Boris Yeltsin's historical mission has been completed. The titanic role he played was a destructive one; we are not sure he has enough strength left for constructive activity. He is accustomed to being in the opposition; even when he became Russian President he anticipated carrying through his reforms both in opposition to the Kremlin and under its benevolent aegis. Now that the Kremlin was no longer the center of imperial power— only the towers and the churches remained—Yeltsin had absolute power over the disintegrating country. The irony is that he strove for power but never really expected it to fall into his lap. Nor did he expect to find himself alone, without a superior to oppose or a rival to defend himself against. The main result of Yeltsin's victory over the putschists was that he found himself tête-à-tête with the nation he had saved from dictatorship.

When the dust had settled, we reread the pages we had written just prior to the coup. Now we were comparing Yeltsin to Hercules, but when he first took on enemies that outclassed him in every way and who seemed invincible, he was more like Don Quixote, and his Sancho Panzas, only a handful but irreproachably loyal, would have agreed. From Don Quixote to Hercules—Yeltsin grew stronger in combat; he was being created and reinforced by obstacles thrown in his path; and popular support was crucial to his victory.

The following are his accomplishments. We move them from the middle of the book to the foreword.

He was the first Kremlin dissident, surpassing reformers like Khrushchev and Gorbachev by breaking with the Kremlin, by voluntarily leaving the highest Party positions, and by turning down all privileges and entitlements. The crucial difference was that Khrushchev and Gorbachev were reformers, even revolutionaries, but within the Kremlin, whereas Yeltsin was the first to head a popular revolt *against* the Kremlin. To that end he first had to demystify the Kremlin. Ignoring the euphemisms that the nomenklatura had invented during the seventy years of its supremacy, he was the first to call things by their proper names, employing the power of a naive truth like Andersen's little boy crying out that the king was wearing no clothes. Yeltsin's merciless attacks revealed the nudity of the "kings" of totalitarian socialism: the Army, the KGB, the Party and its General Secretary. He laid bare their impotence, the lack of justification for their claim to absolute power, in those three days in August. The system shook, then collapsed. When in 1987 he challenged the Kremlin for the first time, he was fifty-six. What other prominent political leader has acted so decisively, so rapidly, so late in life, as Boris Yeltsin?

But before he could bring down the system, he first had to expose the Communist bogus utopia, to show beyond question how the Party had illegally seized power, and to transfer politics from the back rooms of the Kremlin to the democratic arena. Yeltsin's popularity, repeatedly reaffirmed at the ballot boxes, was unparalleled, especially if we compare it with the showings of Khrushchev, Brezhnev, Andropov, Chernenko, or Gorbachev. Finally, as we mentioned, Yeltsin was the first leader in Russian history to be elected by popular vote. He was not selected by the ruling mafia, he did not claw his way up by means of intrigues, and he did not inherit the throne or lead a palace coup.

Boris Yeltsin was the first Soviet politician after Trotsky who dared criticize the Party's General Secretary in public and then call openly for his resignation. In other words he introduced into Soviet political life the notion of impeachment, nonexistent in the Soviet Constitution. After Stalin murdered his rivals—more imaginary than real ones—Yeltsin was the first to form and head a political opposition inside a one-party system. Finally, he left the Communist Party in a demonstrative manner—again, first among the Party aristocracy (a year later he was followed by Eduard Shevardnadze, the ex–Foreign Minister).

Yeltsin was the first Soviet leader to make a comeback from political limbo and to restart his career outside the ruling Party mechanism— through a direct appeal for grass-roots support.

He was the only person among the ruling elite who conceived the radical idea of Russia leaving the Soviet Union, which he set out to implement by breaking the back of the Kremlin's administrative system and putting an end to the atavistic, useless Soviet Empire.

In addition to grand-scale victories and innovations, Yeltsin has also chalked up a number of smaller ones. (They look small when compared to the cataclysm of 1991, but at the time they required courage and revolutionary thinking.) For example, he was the first Soviet politician to remove Lenin's picture from his office. When visitors came, he would point at the wall: "There's only a nail left," he would say with a sly grin.

He was also the first among several hundred Central Committee members to vote against the resolutions of Gorbachev's Politburo, thus destroying the illusion of unanimity in the Party. It is an important part of his character: he is not afraid to go it alone, even if he is defying the entire world.

Finally, he revolutionized traditional Party and political vocabulary. He was the first to use "subversive" words in his speeches such as "opposition," "split," "pluralism," "multiparty system," "alternate thinking in the Party" (a.k.a. dissidence), "totalitarian socialism," "factionary struggle"—and, of course, the ultimate taboo, the ticking bomb of the word that made the nomenklatura's knees grow weak—"de-Partization."

With his unique political intuition, he was first to realize that the rules of the game had changed, that the Communist State and its Party/police base were rotten to the core, that the Empire was coming apart at the seams while Gorbachev continued to play his Kremlin games and gradually turned from a reformer into a retrograde. Once Yeltsin realized all this, he began to act accordingly. As a result, he shifted the political balance of the country, radically and irrevocably. Not only did the failed anti-Yeltsin putsch lead to his triumph, but it also crowned his four-year battle with the monstrous edifice of the Socialist Empire. Having played out his heroic role in Russian history, Yeltsin came to power exhausted, on the verge of a breakdown. As we studied his life, we had—and still have—the uneasy feeling that fate chose him for a tragic part in history.

HISTORY RERUNS its dramas as farces. If the putschists had not existed, someone should have invented them. Karl Marx, by now out of fashion, believed that history bids farewell to its past by parodying itself. The farcical August putsch cast a shadow upon the revolution that it brought about, lending it, despite the victims, a touch of its own ludicrousness. Heroization ran parallel to de-heroization; myth accompanied irony; and the significance of persons and events seemed to fluctuate according to one's momentary perspective.

For example, the new Defense Minister, Shaposhnikov, who at the time of the putsch commanded the Soviet Air Force and later crossed over to Yeltsin's side, declared that if the conspirators had attacked the White House, he would have bombed the Kremlin—the plotters' nest—to smithereens. Does one attribute that statement to courage or saber-rattling bravado; to daring or barbarism?

The farcical elements of the putsch did not belittle its significance, but humanized it and prevented it from becoming a saga filled with heroes and evildoers. It failed because it was headed by petrified bureaucrats, not intrepid villains. It was a throwback to Brezhnevism, not Stalinist terror. It was like an inoculation, causing a bit of fever instead of a mortal disease. The Magnificent Eight—or were there nine?—of little Pinochets involuntarily rendered the nation a service by lancing a seventy-three-year-old boil. For whatever ordeals await the former Soviet nations, anything is probably better than a battered, creaking pseudo-empire based on an anachronistic ideology and massive, inhuman punitive institutions. If we distance ourselves from current frustrations and anger, the bumbling putschists will be seen to deserve praise, not opprobrium, from grateful future generations. Perhaps the descendants of those who are passionately tearing down the Communist idols will reuse the pedestals for monuments to the putschists.

ACCORDING TO Alexis de Tocqueville, a revolution erases its own blueprint in its course. The Russian Revolution went further. Instead of just erasing the original, it kept obliterating the successive blueprints that it created. One is tempted to characterize the Russian Revolution as never-ending. More precisely, it is like a cycle of revolutions and counterrevolutions, the difference between the two depending on one's point of view. In any event, the monstrous pendulum set in motion by Lenin still cannot seem to stop. With minimal imagination or unorthodox thinking, we should reclassify Lenin—from the student of Marx to one of Foucault.

The 1917 Revolution marked the beginning of a chain of experiments that is still going on in Russia, and that continues to make abrupt shifts with each new ruler, and the current epoch of Russian history is no exception. We will gain a better understanding of Boris Yeltsin if we view him against the background of his predecessors—all of whom reacted almost as violently against the past as did Yeltsin.

It should be noted that every Soviet ruler with the exception of Lenin and Yeltsin instituted their changes within the mossy, corrupt framework of the Soviet system. Kremlin rule is characterized not by consistency but by breaks in tradition; it is a system of ideological and political zigzags, and sometimes the pendulum swings are dizzying.

Take any Russian leader. Beginning with Lenin, each moved in a direction opposite to that of his predecessor. Then, beginning with Stalin, who was more of a monarch than a revolutionary, every ruler, except Yeltsin, followed, in a sense, in the footsteps of his predecessor's predecessor.

Moreover, each new Russian ruler was an impostor, a usurper. Lenin was brought to power by the Bolshevik Revolution; Stalin, by massacring Lenin's Old Guard; Khrushchev, by eliminating Stalin's heirs such as Malenkov, Beria, and Molotov; Brezhnev, by overthrowing Khrushchev in a palace coup; Andropov, by a police putsch against Brezhnev's minions; Chernenko, by a gerontocrats' revolution; the gerontocrats were removed once and for all by Gorbachev and his comrades. In methods of taking power, and in the essence of its rule, each new stage was a sort of mini-revolution vis-à-vis the preceding stage.

Total: seven revolutions in seventy years.

Yeltsin continues the tradition, but with substantial differences.

• He is the only one in this series who has been popularly elected; his power "grab" from the Gorbachevite putschist team was based on the popular mandate.

• Having taken power democratically, Yeltsin has been the first and so far the only ruler to prove his dedication to democratic principles through deeds, not words. This is why there is hope that while he is alive and while he holds the highest executive power Russia will stay the democratic course.

• It is true that the cyclical nature of Soviet history offers little reason for optimism. It is probable that Russia will make its habitual about-face again, the way it did after Lenin—after Stalin—after Brezhnev—after Andropov—after Chernenko—and now after Gorbachev, too, for, regardless of Gorbachev's personal fate, his epoch has ended. Boris Yeltsin's arrival on the political scene has ended Soviet history. The Soviet Union no longer exists, and its territory is occupied by new, independent states, including the one led by Yeltsin: Russia. For the first time, Russia is a democratic nation.

Under Yeltsin, as under Lenin, Russia moved in a radically different direction. But while the socialism of Lenin-Khrushchev-Brezhnev-Andropov-Chernenko-Gorbachev was absolutist—sometimes enlightened, sometimes far from it—Yeltsin's Russia took the untried, civilized path of Western democratic development. With Yeltsin's revolution, Russia has finally broken out of the old, vicious, repetitious pattern.

We would be happy to see our theory refuted.

And replaced by another, a funnier one.

For example: humorist Vladimir Voynovich, in response to Chernenko's coming to power, offered his own interpretation of Soviet history—bald and hairy rulers succeed one another.

Lenin—bald
Stalin—hairy
Khrushchev—bald
Brezhnev—hairy
Andropov—bald
Chernenko—hairy

Gorbachev—bald
Yeltsin—hairy

Now the reader can easily determine what kind of ruler will replace
Boris Yeltsin.

PART ONE

A POLITICIAN
IS BORN

A BULL IN A CHINA SHOP
(1985–1987)

BORIS YELTSIN spent less than two years as the Moscow First Party Secretary: December 24, 1985, to November 13, 1987, yet in this short time he made more of a splash than any of his predecessors had in decades. We can only speculate about what kind of city the Soviet capital might have turned into had he stayed at the helm of the Moscow Party for another year or two.

"With the kind of perestroika we have in Moscow, we'll run out of jail cells for all those we plan to lock up." Thus spoke Yeltsin at the height of his reformist campaign, according to a reliable source—Vayno Vyales, the leader of the Estonian Communist Party at that time. An anonymous letter from Moscow, published in the spring of 1987 in a New York émigré paper, said: "Our Tsar's [i.e., Gorbachev's] form of rule is emulated by his right-hand man, Boris Yeltsin, the First Secretary of the Moscow Party Committee, who uses the only method available to him—dismissals."

On April 11, 1986, Yeltsin met with Party propaganda cadres in the Political Enlightenment House. In the course of the five-hour meeting he received hundreds of notes from the floor, including these:

"You have Napoleonic ambitions! You are biting off more than you can chew! Stop playing Gorbachev's hatchet man—go home to Sverdlovsk before it's too late."

Or: "Khrushchev tried to send us up the river, too—how far did he get? You're no smarter than he was. We've always stolen and we won't stop."

We received a typed transcript of this meeting from a writer with a liberal reputation and a well-known name that we will not disclose—he was our guest in New York and spoke off the record. Referring to Yeltsin, he used an old proverb: "A new broom sweeps clean."

Out of thirty-three district Party Secretaries, Yeltsin replaced twenty-three—several of them twice, since the new appointees turned out to be

31

no better than their predecessors. "Six of one and half dozen of another," he joked. One of the fired Secretaries later jumped out of a window. Yeltsin was upset: it added to the repeated accusations that he was purging the cadre. True, he replaced 60 percent of district bosses, but, he pointed out, Gorbachev replaced even more—66 percent of Party Secretaries across the country. In the City Committee proper, Yeltsin dismissed 40 percent of Party functionaries, as well as 36 percent of City bureaucrats and 44 percent of the union bosses. Comparable figures for Gorbachev: 60 percent of Cabinet members and 70 percent of Party Central Committee department heads.

So Yeltsin was no more ruthless than Gorbachev. Then why all the fuss? Was it a case of a double standard—one criterion used for the nation's ruler and another for his local viceroy?

It was Gorbachev who had summoned Yeltsin from Sverdlovsk to take over the top Moscow job. Gorbachev inherited his original team from his mentor, Yuri Andropov: Prime Minister Ryzhkov, KGB Chief Chebrikov, Party Deputy Chief Ligachev, and Foreign Minister Shevardnadze. Yeltsin was Gorbachev's only personal choice.

Another personal pick was Alexandr Yakovlev, though he had been summoned to Moscow from Canada, where he was the Soviet ambassador, even before Gorbachev came to power. Yeltsin, however, came to Moscow a mere month after Gorbachev's inauguration. In that context, those who subsequently accused Yeltsin of ingratitude and even treachery had a point. Of course, a wise mentor prizes his disciples for just that: ingratitude; he calls it independence. When Yeltsin turned from Gorbachev's comrade into his rival, a Moscow wit said, paraphrasing Voltaire, that if Yeltsin had not existed, Gorbachev should have invented him. On the other hand, can we demand of such a pragmatic and power-hungry politician as Gorbachev that he also possess moral altruism?

Both Gorbachev and Yeltsin are the same age, both came to Moscow from the provinces, but Gorbachev made the move in 1978, and had ample time to master Kremlin intrigue and put on some Moscow polish. He could even pass for a Muscovite, save for his excessive talkativeness and southern accent.

Most of the Kremlin elite were ex-provincials, too: Ligachev from Siberia, Shevardnadze from Georgia, Ryzhkov—like Yeltsin—from the Urals. One way or another, they all took root in Moscow and blended into the Moscow—the Kremlin, to be exact—scene. They were adaptable and knew how to change direction according to the way the political wind was blowing. Yeltsin did not; even in Moscow he remained a country bumpkin—an ill-mannered upstart.

The contrast was especially vivid since Yeltsin was not like the other leaders, cloistered behind the Kremlin walls. His job always kept him in the public eye. He was different by nature, too: sociable, noisy, effusive, a bit of a showoff, with none of their behind-closed-doors style. In his new job, he took buses and the subway, showed up unexpectedly at factories and stores, and held marathon press conferences, fielding hundreds of questions. Yeltsin often gave the impression of being sincere but naive; his replies were widely bandied about and he became the butt of popular jokes. Someone asked him about his schedule. "I work from six A.M. to midnight," he said. "Four hours of sleep. From six to eight I improve myself." The Moscow intelligentsia had a picnic with "self-improvement."

Yeltsin never hid his provincialism; on the contrary, he gloried in it. There was a sly edge to his rustic simpleton image. Not that his sincerity and openness were a ruse; rather, they seemed a style. A deliberate tactic? Perhaps.

At a meeting with propaganda cadre Yeltsin was asked where he shopped for shoes. He stood up, took off his size 12 shoe, and held it up before the audience.

"I'll tell you in confidence," he said. "I didn't get my shoes in Moscow. I bought them in Sverdlovsk. Locally made, at the Ural Shoe Factory—just twenty-three rubles. I recommend them—very sturdy, will last you a five-year plan."

It is unlikely that he was being facetious—calculating, perhaps: by that time Muscovites had heard plenty about the Gorbachevs' being outfitted by Yves St. Laurent and the like.

Yeltsin's was a new style, unusual for Moscow. It appealed to some; it disturbed others; it intimidated many. Some were angry. If style makes the man, then the man who arrived in Moscow was something completely different from other Kremlin insiders—a stranger, an outsider whose outward bravado bespoke something deep and substantial. Among his Kremlin colleagues, even among lower-ranking *apparatchiks,* Yeltsin was a maverick, yet it did not seem to bother him.

If he was career-minded, his career was not made in the Kremlin's smoke-filled rooms, Chicago-style, but in the streets of Moscow—hence the many accusations of populism. In the street, in buses, in the subway, in dismal lines outside stores—wherever he appeared, suddenly, unheralded, he remained a yokel, insisting on his provincialism, defending and emphasizing it. It was as though he knew that his career would soar beyond the capital, that soon Moscow's wide boulevards would not be spacious enough to accommodate his ambitions.

The local elite, both the Party and the intellectuals, failed to inculcate Yeltsin with Moscow patriotism, or, more precisely, Moscow chauvinism. It might even be called Moscow-centrism, since it defines Russia as Moscow with numerous faceless provinces and colonies as its dominions.

The conflict is more social than geographic. Moscow is one big Potemkin Village, a façade showing foreigners the kind of Russia that exists nowhere but there. Hence, until recently it was always better-supplied, which led to the daily swelling of its population. In the winter, every morning, two million people arrive in Moscow from out-of-town, and in the summer the figure climbs to three. Naturally, the city's services—public transport, stores, hotels, even toilets—cannot deal with this flood, and hostilities break out, Muscovites calling out-of-towners "locusts," while the visitors label the locals "parasites."

Five years later, control of the city would pass—formally, at least—to democratically elected candidates headed by Gavriil Popov. Obeying popular demand, they tried to cordon Moscow off. With every purchase buyers had to show their internal passports with a Moscow stamp-of-residence. Back in Moscow after thirteen years, we took it personally: our American passports did not have a stamp from Moscow or any other city. The new law hit the inhabitants of nearby villages and small towns the hardest. They threatened to cut off supplies to Moscow, and we, though ex-Muscovites ourselves, instantly empathized with them despite the assurance of our Moscow friends that the provincials wanted to starve the capital.

Later Popov and others will become Yeltsin's allies against Gorbachev, but when Yeltsin took over the city, their positions differed widely. Yeltsin's was broader and more democratic. He was not in a rush to join the ranks of the "patriots."

"Out-of-towners are grabbing all the goods," people complained. "Why don't you help us?"

"We can't wall Moscow off the way they did eight hundred years ago," he said. "Limiting access won't help. The capital is the capital. Some people are lucky enough to come here once in their lives. I repeat: we should assume that in reality there are eleven or twelve million of us rather than the nine on paper."

Another source of overpopulation and resulting social tension were the *limitchiki*—a cheap labor force hired outside Moscow by the most important (in the government's opinion) plants and factories and lured to the city by the promise of a residence permit. In just one decade they accounted for an increase of 700,000 in Moscow's population. Waiting for permits, they crowded dormitories and barracks, adding to the housing crisis of a city in which a million people already live in communal apartments. Impoverished and desperate, they often turned to crime.

Still, in the apartment-exchange business a room in a Moscow communal apartment is worth a two- or three-room apartment out-of-town. Moreover, the exchange has to be blessed by a dozen permits from local authorities. We learned this first in 1975, when we tried to move from

Leningrad to Moscow: the amount of red tape doubled the distance. A few years later it was easier to move from Moscow to New York.

Moscow snobbery—what Yeltsin calls the Moscow syndrome—encompasses an entire world-view, and it would be a simplification to reduce it to mercantile considerations like the availability of hard-to-get goods and career opportunities. This world-view also includes an irresistible, blind instinct that echoes Chekhov's *Three Sisters*—"To Moscow! To Moscow!"—and the words of General Panfilov, whose infantry division fought to the death to stop the Nazi army outside Moscow in 1941: "Can't retreat any farther—it's Moscow behind us!"

Not every leader was Moscow-centric. Field Marshal Kutuzov surrendered the city to Napoleon in 1812, and Lenin, according to Trotsky's memoirs, was prepared in case of military defeat to surrender the entire European part of Russia and retreat with his Bolsheviks behind the Urals.

Yeltsin, a man of the Urals, even after he became the Top Muscovite, never caught the virus, but he did rid himself of Moscow-phobia, a mixture of anti-Moscow bias and big-city envy. The Muscovites are often arrogant; the provincials embittered. We have often witnessed fights, in lines and in buses, between the Muscovites and the out-of-towners who had come to the capital to shop.

Ironically, almost every Moscow-hating redneck dreams of leaving his or her provincial nest and moving to Moscow. This is even more characteristic of provincial *apparatchiks* who profess to despise Moscow—until they are transferred there. Yeltsin had already turned down a few Moscow-based offers, including that of a ministerial position. He seemed to prefer to be a king in his own small domain (and the Sverdlovsk Region was not that small) than a pawn in the palace.

According to Yeltsin, on April 3, 1985, he received a call from Vladimir Dolgikh, a Central Committee Secretary. Acting on Gorbachev's behalf, Dolgikh offered Yeltsin the position of the head of the Construction Section of the Central Committee. Yeltsin turned it down, perhaps more for strategic reasons than local patriotism: The Sverdlovsk Region was the third in the country in industrial production, and Yeltsin's two predecessors in the job, Kirilenko and Ryabov, had been transferred to higher positions in the Central Committee.

The next day it was Ligachev, Gorbachev's de facto right-hand man, who called Yeltsin with the offer to move to the capital. Yeltsin began to argue, but Ligachev reminded him that it was a Party decision and protest was useless. A week later Yeltsin started his new job, and two months later he was a Central Committee Secretary—the job he had been shooting for.

Six months later, again contrary to his wishes, he was transferred to the

Moscow Party Office. Again he was reminded—this time by Gorbachev himself—that as a Party member he was subordinate to its discipline. Gorbachev calculated correctly; if anything, he underestimated Yeltsin. He had wanted an obedient tool to help institute reforms, but he got far more than he bargained for. More than any other Russian city, Moscow was an Augean stable of corruption, thievery, and nepotism and clearly needed a Hercules for a major cleanup. Yeltsin—tall, strapping, with a confident stride and physical stamina, with tireless vigor and a short fuse—fit the bill. Although he started his undertaking eagerly and without delay, he never got a chance to finish the cleanup, for he was saving his strength for the remaining eleven labors.

Perhaps this is all hindsight; what Nabokov described as smuggling the present into the past. Also, in retrospect, one might note the political aspect of the supercleanup assigned to Yeltsin. His predecessor was Victor Grishin, one of Gorbachev's two rivals in the battle for power fought over Chernenko's coffin (Romanov was the other one). After Gorbachev's victory, Romanov was summarily ejected from the Politburo, and the seventy-one-year-old Grishin was next to be axed.

In a curious footnote, the Politburo member to follow Grishin on his way down was Vladimir Dolgikh—by Kremlin standards relatively young at sixty, businesslike, reform-minded, untainted by intrigue, and innocent of any plotting against the victorious Gorbachev. But Grishin planned to make Dolgikh his Prime Minister upon victory, and Dolgikh's name, among those of other members of Grishin's future cabinet, was on a piece of paper that was later taken from Grishin and passed to Gorbachev—who was not on the list at all! Gorbachev's vindictiveness is less a factor here than the centuries-old principle of undivided power that goes back to Machiavelli. Accordingly, everyone installed by Grishin during his eighteen years at the helm had to be removed from the Moscow Party machine. It is curious how, in this case, the interests of perestroika serendipitously matched Gorbachev's own personal motives.

So it is no wonder that, initially, no matter what Yeltsin did on his new job, everyone said he was carrying out Gorbachev's orders under the General Secretary's aegis. In a way it was true; for a while the two men desperately needed each other. Gorbachev was Yeltsin's shield, and Yeltsin was Gorbachev's sword. But this tactical union was not meant to last.

The shakeup of the staff was the easiest and the quickest of Yeltsin's Herculean deeds—it took him a week to send Grishin's men packing. Solving the capital's vital problems was much more of a challenge. Yeltsin described some of the problems as he addressed Moscow propaganda employees in the spring of 1986 in the following speech:

*

Moscow's population is currently 8.7 million people (over the projected 7.6 million in 1990). Of these, 2.5 million need apartments. About a million live in communal apartments. Twenty-eight thousand live in shacks that should be razed immediately. We are about to demolish the Lagutenko housing project.* I'm talking about housing with kitchens of 3.5 square meters. We have many ample-bodied women in this country. A woman like this enters the kitchen—there's no room for the husband.

The historical face of Moscow has been vandalized. Since 1935, 2200 important architectural monuments have been destroyed. Many others are in a sad state and are used for the wrong purposes. The church where Pushkin got married† is an office belonging to the Ministry of Energy. I went there yesterday with Minister Mayorets** and he finally agreed to move the office elsewhere.

Transportation is in bad shape. Sixty kilometers of subway lines need to be built. The rolling stock is worn out. There were 2000 accidents in 1985. We're 5000 drivers short, too. In 1985 for the first time the subway operated in the red. As a result, there was no allocation for social and cultural needs.

Here—I just got a note from the floor. "They say Yeltsin rides the subway, but we never saw him. How can you raise the problem of transport? Where did you get your impressions—from the window?"

What can I tell you? I haven't seen you either. Maybe it's because there's too many people in Moscow. Also, I'm a recent arrival to Moscow—an unfamiliar face.

I made it a rule to visit the stores at least once a week. Unfortunately, people start recognizing me. Somehow they find out my routes. They clean the mess, put on fresh uniforms, get the hard-to-get stuff from under the counter. We got to do something about it—I don't need these snow jobs.

Stores are crowded all day long, even late at night. We have to provide the goods not just for the nine million Muscovites but for two or three million guests as well.

The former City Council banned open-air kiosks under the pretext that they are an eyesore. What kind of logic is that: go hungry but look pretty? Can't we build a bunch of pretty-looking kiosks for the summer?

*"Simplified" apartment housing—no elevators or terraces, low ceilings, tiny rooms. Built in the '50s and named after the designer, Vitaly Lagutenko.
†The former Great Resurrection Church at Nikitsky Gate.
**Anatoly Mayorets, the Minister for Energy and Electrification.

We have a problem with soft drinks in Moscow.* And we still produce cheap port. We must keep reducing alcohol production and the number of places that sell it. In the first quarter of this year the sales of alcoholic drinks fell 30 percent. Still, drunks have been seen on the street again lately. It shows that we relaxed in our fight; we thought that the evil had been conquered. Meanwhile the anti-alcohol campaign is in its first stage, and we must not relax yet. We chased drunkenness from the street into people's homes. No wonder burglary statistics are up. No wonder the slogan "Let's Turn Moscow into an Ideal Communist City"† sounds like an insult. We have to revise our criteria of what "ideal" and "Communist" really mean.

I visited many Moscow farmers' markets. What prices! A measly bunch of parsley costs fifty kopecks or even a ruble. A kilogram of meat is eight rubles.** But we can't put a ceiling on prices: we tried it and it didn't work. The vendors simply move to another city. We must fight the markets with our own retail outlets. We must build a co-op store near every market. It doesn't matter if sausage in these stores costs eight rubles. At least it will smell like meat.

We're getting too conservative here. City authorities were pulling the wool over people's eyes: "Everything's fine, we're the best in the world, let's not advertise our dirty laundry to the world." Whoever still feels this way should clear out his desk and leave.

The City Council is nothing but red tape. There's a big shuffle going on, the staff's being reduced. The Party Committee sets a good example. For example, we reduced the number of Secretaries from seven to six.

By the way, Moscow is a sister city with all the socialist capitals, as well as with sixty-four countries. That's why Promyslov†† couldn't find time to work—he was always gadding about and signing agreements.

I have here three hundred more questions. Let's take a break for about twenty minutes, have a drink of water, and then I'll take a look at your notes.

[after the recess]

I'd like to stress that 90 percent of these notes are anonymous. And that

---

*The speech was made in the heyday of Gorbachev's anti-alcohol campaign, which was a failure: alcoholism did not decline, and the government lost its monopoly of alcohol production. Moonshine production tripled; in this way, people got drunk and made money at the same time. The government's losses from the campaign ran into billions of rubles.

†Brezhnev promoted this slogan in the early '70s.

**Early 1986 prices. Since then they have become stratospheric.

††Vladimir Promyslov was the Mayor of Moscow for twenty-two years, from 1963 to 1985. His frequent trips abroad resulted in this joke: Promyslov stopped over in Moscow on the way from Washington to Tokyo. We met him only once, when he let us swap our Leningrad apartment for one in Moscow.

comes from you—propaganda employees! Didn't we agree to be upfront with each other? I'll answer the anonymous notes—but this is the last time.

They say that Muscovites have it too good.
This opinion is widespread in the provinces. When I lived in Sverdlovsk, I used to think so, too. But it turns out that Muscovites live worse than the rest of the country. Look:

- *Capital Spending:*
  1965—Moscow was in the 5th place nationwide
  1975—Moscow was in the 12th place nationwide
  1985—Moscow was in the 44th place nationwide
- *New Apartment Construction:*
  1975—Moscow was in the 22nd place
  1985—Moscow was in the 58th place
- *Day Care Centers:* 33rd place
- *Birthrate:* 65th place
  (average for the USSR 19.6 per 1,000; for Moscow, 13.6)
- *Average Life Span in Moscow:* 1983—70 yrs
                                  1985—68 yrs

What were your major problems on your job?
The main problem was unfamiliarity with the people and the lack of manpower. And people are used to working slowly. Right now we can't afford it.

As a Central Committee Secretary, you traveled around the country. How does the level of Moscow industry compare to other cities?
The technological level of Moscow industries is much lower. I visited the Dynamo Plant, for example. It's a shame how run-down it is.

On services.
In three months I visited twenty-nine factories. Only two directors were paying attention to services. I've seen a design firm that has four separate cafeterias—for four different hierarchy levels! I went to the director's cafeteria, the one for himself and his close subordinates—it had everything, down to an imported baby-blue toilet bowl. Certain leaders have distanced themselves from the masses. We have to fight that.

On research institutes and design firms.
We identified thirty-nine institutes that have done no research in years. We cut off the funds to fifteen and closed them down. Thirty thousand

research workers who have failed recertification will be assigned to factories. The professional level of researchers and instructors is down. Mediocrity breeds mediocrity.

There's widespread drug abuse in Moscow.
We're not trying to hide it. We have registered 3600 users. They wouldn't register voluntarily. So the question is, how many of them are really out there?

What about Danilov, Oktyabr District's Second Secretary?
He has been fired and censured. He got himself a palatial apartment, with a personal fireplace and a personal chimney that goes through the entire building. We can't have such robber barons in the Party! We must maintain the integrity of all Party members.

How many Party members were dismissed between the 26th and 27th Party Congresses?
About seventy to ninety thousand nationwide; twenty thousand in Moscow alone.

Do you receive ordinary people, too?
Yes, I do. A few days ago I received a young woman, a saleslady and mother of two. We talked for about two hours. She told me in detail about the bribe system in our retail trade. In the last few months we have arrested eight hundred retail executives in Moscow. We keep digging but we still can't reach the bottom of this barrel of filth. But we must see it through. We try to break up the criminal rings, to identify the ringleaders, to replace them with honest people, loyal to the Party, and then proceed to go deeper. It's a long, hard job, but we're determined to clean up this mess.

What do you do in your spare time?
I don't have much. I read. Once in a while I go to the theater, mostly as part of the job.

What kind of human traits do you like and what kind do you hate?
I value honesty, integrity, and character. I hate crooks and apple-polishers. I remember a comrade who delivered a report on his work at the Moscow University. He was praising his performance a bit too excitedly. We had our doubts and ran a check. The real statistics were way lower. Now this comrade has a long way to go before he recovers his reputation.

In three years you'll have to report on all the promises you made.
I'm getting ready. I intend to spend these years fighting.

One shouldn't speak too soon. Yeltsin did not have much time left:
eighteen months later, the omnipotent, self-confident, hard-driving Moscow Boss turned into a rejected outsider.

He was an outsider in Moscow even prior to his downfall and this was
both his weakness and his strength. Not for nothing did he frequently use
the word "fight." All his life he sought obstacles to overcome—and
Moscow was a nonstop obstacle course.

Question-and-answer meetings became one of his most effective forms
of combat. The format fit his dialectical mind; he is, as Nietzsche put it,
"a man of question marks." Moscow snobs loved to mock his Ural
provincialism, his rough peasant manners, his naiveté and simplicity, his
"self-improvement from six to eight A.M." But Yeltsin had the last laugh,
since even the arrogant Moscow intellectuals were soon taking him seriously—more as an opponent than a partner.

As Yeltsin answered thousands of questions—he replied to three hundred at the House of Enlightenment meeting alone, of which we quoted
just a few—he also honed his rhetorical skills and trained himself in the
give and take of democracy. He did not dodge a single question, no
matter how difficult or insulting. He vowed to be sincere, and in those
days, when glasnost had been proclaimed but tongues were still tied, this
was something new. Perhaps a person is better judged by his questions
than by his answers, but for a man who thinks as he speaks, rather than
thinks in advance, the questions directed at him become the questions he
aimed at himself.

In that first long question-and-answer session, Yeltsin's replies still
abounded in Communist orthodoxy, Party demagogy, administrative
usages, propaganda clichés, and dated slogans. All the more startling,
then, are the psychological and political metamorphoses that he underwent later. When he first arrived in Moscow, he was not quite a politician
yet, but he was no longer a Partocrat. However, in his political thinking
he was already far ahead of his epoch and its chief spokesmen. This is the
root of his conflict with Gorbachev—a worshiper of compromise, half
measures, and the golden mean. Soon Gorbachev would lag behind the
changes he himself had initiated; he would delay making decisions while
Yeltsin would move beyond the same changes. Soon their conflict would
acquire additional psychological, even psychoanalytic nuances. What did
Gorbachev feel when he learned that Muscovites use a *yelts* as a unit of
progress in glasnost and perestroika? Hadn't it been he, Gorbachev, who
put the two initiatives on the map?

Boris Yeltsin's name was quickly on everyone's lips. Stories circulated of his incognito voyages by bus and subway, of his sudden appearances in stores and cafeterias, of his standing in a long line for pastries that ran out just as his turn came. He mentions some of these stories in his memoirs:

At a store, Yeltsin discovers bags with delicacies in the manager's office. "Who are these for?"

"These are pre-ordered."

"Can anyone pre-order?"

Silence.

He finds out that "pre-orders" are distributed hierarchically: District Soviet, Foreign Ministry, Party District Committee, other city authorities. The bags vary in size, in assortment, and in quality. Just what Marx predicted: from each according to his ability, to each according to his need. And as one moves up the career ladder, the needs rise accordingly.

Yeltsin checked the paperwork on the supplies of delicacies to Moscow and discovered that the incoming figure for each kind was several thousand tons higher than the figure for consumption, after the adjustment for the usual loss in transit. Why? He can't find out. The cover-up is impenetrable.

But one day he got lucky.

As he was leaving the store after one of his routine checks, a young woman ran after him. "I have something to tell you . . . it's really important."

It was the saleswoman whom he mentioned during his House of Enlightenment meeting. He immediately gave her an appointment. This led to the uncovering of the retail mafia and eight hundred arrests.

However, his "raiding" style was running its course. For Yeltsin's six-foot frame became easily recognizable; salespeople were tipped off and erected Potemkin villages—the old Russian tradition of pulling the wool over the boss's eyes. And his mixing with the people—for some reason especially his rush-hour rides amidst bleary-eyed blue-collar workers in packed subways and buses—began to irritate other Politburo members. All of this would escalate into his future conflict with the Kremlin elite. The bubble of Politburo impatience would explode, and this would be one of the comrades' main grievances: "Comrade Yeltsin sought cheap popularity."

"How come no one else tried to seek it?" he said angrily later. "They think it's so easy—one subway ride and you've got it? Why is it that even those who don't remember what popularity is never got the urge to do it? Sure, ZIL limos are more comfortable: no one tramples on your feet, no one shoves you in the back or pokes you in the ribs. The car goes fast, no stops, green light all the way, all the cops salute—sure, that's nice."

As Moscow Party Boss, Yeltsin was a Politburo member, though without voting rights. Had he behaved, he would have made full member in a few years. ZIL armored limos, popularly called "coffins," and nonstop green lights provided for them (the rest of the traffic was blocked off), were but one of the perks against which he would later crusade and which would yield him the greatest popularity among the common people with their suppressed egalitarian aspirations.

For the moment he was fighting the privileges only of low-ranking Party functionaries, but reports of his campaigns made Kremlin Olympians fear for their own perks. Moscow's art crowd, too, had special resorts, restaurants, clinics, and even tailors. Afraid to lose these tiny advantages, they resented Yeltsin and dubbed him the neo-Bolshevik. This is one of the reasons (we'll deal with others later) why years later the Soviet liberal intelligentsia allied themselves with the Party bigwigs in attacking Yeltsin. Strange bedfellows indeed.

But the intelligentsia had a long way to go to catch up with the Party mandarins. According to Yeltsin, the latter had already built themselves a shining Communist future; its benefits were spread out among two dozen or so people: Politburo members and Central Committee Secretaries. This mini-Communist society was run by the KGB's Section Nine, which specialized in perks: food packages with exotic items at half-price, junkets across the country in personal planes, imported drugs, and the inanely luxurious dachas. After Gorbachev had one built especially for himself, he passed his old one on to Yeltsin. As Russians say, a fur coat off the master's back.

On his first visit to his new dacha, Yeltsin recalls, he was greeted by the senior guard, who introduced the help: three chefs, three waitresses, chambermaids, more guards, and a gardener with his own staff. Then, a tour of the house.

On the first floor: a huge marble lobby, beautiful rugs, a fireplace, and elegant furniture. A number of rooms, each with a color TV. A giant glassed-in terrace. A full-sized dining hall with a table long enough to feed a soccer team. In the back, a restaurant-sized kitchen with an underground freezer. A screening room and a pool room. Bathrooms? Yeltsin, used to an ascetic lifestyle, lost count.

He was led up a wide marble staircase to the second floor. Another hall, another fireplace, and a door leading to the greenhouse. Further, a study, bedrooms, cut glass chandeliers antique and modern, precious rugs, oak parquet floors, more bathrooms. It looked more like a hotel for nobility than a house for one family. The Yeltsins, unused to such luxury, did not know what to do with themselves; they felt out of place. Eventually they refused the dacha.

Besides the dachas near the capital, there were ones in the Crimea, in the Caucasus—all over the country, all of them plush. In one, the owners and guests were driven by car to the beach—the whole two hundred yards, noted Yeltsin.

None of this was personal property; it all came with the job; when an unfortunate person lost his Kremlin position, he lost all his privileges and was reduced to the status of an ordinary mortal. Imagine how hard one must strive to get to the top, and how one must fight to stay there.

Here, too, Yeltsin was an exception: he did not value the privileges bestowed upon him, and this freed him from depending on them. On the contrary, he perceived them as chains he had to shake off as soon as possible; they galled him not just for reasons of style or personal taste, but for what they stood for. He was the only Soviet ruler who had ever made it to the top of the mountain, then hurried down back to the valley—of his own free will. That was his main breach of age-old Kremlin tradition: one could make the descent only by dying or being expelled. Great power automatically called for great slavery, and no Kremlin slave could simply shake off the chains of privilege. Yeltsin was the only person who ever considered it possible.

In his personal life, Gorbachev was the exact opposite of both his protégé, Yeltsin, and his mentor, Andropov. The contrast played an important part in the Gorbachev-Yeltsin duel.

To Gorbachev, nothing was ever enough. He was the one to propose that Politburo members' salaries, already sky-high, be almost doubled. He expanded, up from Brezhnev days, dacha construction for the Kremlin elite, and first of all for himself. He built himself a house on the Lenin Hills and a new dacha outside Moscow, renovated Khrushchev's dacha outside Pitsunda on the Caucasian Black Sea coast, and erected a super-modern palazzo in Foros in the Crimea, where a few years later he would be held captive during the half-baked coup launched by his closest comrades. Gorbachev was the first Kremlin ruler to order his suits from international couturiers, for which he was dubbed a Gucci Communist; the same went for his spouse, popular in the West and hated by her own people, who blamed her for all that was wrong with Soviet life. According to Yeltsin, however, Gorbachev loved la dolce vita himself and was no stranger to creature comforts. In patronizing Gucci, Pierre Cardin, and Yves St. Laurent, the Gorbachevs were curiously oblivious to the popular reaction to their high-flying life-style. Yeltsin's antiprivilege campaign understandably hit the spot with the Soviet people.

It had become commonplace for the intelligentsia to blame the Russian people for their egalitarianism; to call it the source of almost every woe that befell Russia. But the people had a good case: they were the ones who fed the hordes of the Party—and other—parasites. In Moscow alone, 40,000 persons were supplied with "special packages." Nationwide, the size of this huge feeding trough was unimaginable. Yeltsin called it "teasing the people on a giant scale." And now, as glasnost had done away with so many fears, popular hatred began to come out into the open, focusing on the Kremlin. Here's one of many jokes we heard:

"I had a dream: the entire Kremlin was afire, and Politburo members were hanging from the towers—"

"And?"

"I don't remember what's next."

"Too bad. Great opening."

Shortly upon his arrival, it fell upon Yeltsin to declassify the Kremlin— the first such effort in the seventy years since the Bolsheviks moved in.

ACCORDING TO Yeltsin, he did not adopt egalitarianism out of belief in some sort of ideal, primitive form of equality or in search of cheap popularity, but: "As long as our lives are so poor and miserable, I cannot eat sturgeon and caviar; I cannot speed away in a limo, ignoring traffic lights and people leaping out of my way; I cannot take imported miracle drugs, knowing that my next-door neighbor has no aspirin for her child. I would simply be ashamed to do that."

It was this feeling of shame that distinguished Yeltsin from his Kremlin colleagues. As he exposed the Kremlin's dolce vita existence, he did not exaggerate anything—more likely, through his lack of information, he seriously underestimated its extent.

Everything in the Kremlin's orbit was special. There were so-called Civil Defense Objects under the Kremlin and under the Central Committee building on the Old Square—air raid shelters, bunkers, tunnels— virtual palaces, with the help to match: 170 people in the Central Committee's maze alone, and in the Kremlin's even more, though we were unable to obtain a specific figure. A special Wing 235 under the aegis of the Civil Aviation Ministry serviced the Kremlin elite, with a pecking order of its own: full Politburo members flew Ilyushin 62s, while Candidate Members and Secretaries made do with Tupolev 134s. In either case, a jumbo jet was used for one person and his five bodyguards.

Special dachas, sanatoriums, hotels, schools, restaurants, the Sunny Kindergarten, famous all over Moscow—even its own furniture factory that provided furnishings for the apartments of the elite—we could go on and on. No wonder Yeltsin's crusade against privilege was so popular.

As his popularity soared, so did the Kremlin's displeasure. He challenged them himself, and they had no choice but to accept the challenge.

It is something of a wonder how a man of his nature, his habits, his life-style, and his principles found himself on the Party Olympus. Yeltsin believes that the ancient machinery, well oiled and carefully programmed to pick the same type of rulers over and over again, somehow got jammed and failed in his case. There is no question that he was of a breed different from that of the other Kremlin bigwigs, and his revolt is the best proof of it. But it is doubtful that he would have dared to revolt in Brezhnev's Politburo, to say nothing of Stalin's; an anti-Gorbachev rebel was himself the creation of Gorbachev's epoch.

What happened? Was Yeltsin more Catholic than the Pope? Or was Gorbachev out of touch with his own principles, unexpectedly finding himself left behind by the epoch to which he lent his name?

Yeltsin was the only desperado in Gorbachev's Politburo. Some other members were, up to a point, businesslike and conscientious in their desire for reform. Alexandr Yakovlev, Gorbachev's chief adviser on glasnost and perestroika; Foreign Minister Eduard Shevardnadze, who, like Yeltsin in Moscow, had conducted a merciless anticorruption campaign in his native Republic of Georgia; Nikolai Ryzhkov, the assiduous Prime Minister, also from the Urals. With the exception of Gorbachev, none of them had a particular penchant for high life, though none would turn down a perk, either. This attitude went back to Andropov, who, in his brief reign, tried to teach a few lessons to the elite who had gone out of control under Brezhnev. He demanded, if not asceticism, then at least a brief period of fasting for the Kremlin nabobs, and promoted men who behaved halfway decently. Gorbachev was a different person then, too, and behaved more modestly. He started changing only after becoming General Secretary; perhaps the change was caused by Raisa—a vain, limited woman.

Why, then, did Yeltsin and the Politburo not see eye to eye?

Yeltsin's conflict was not with the Politburo but with its leader— Gorbachev himself. Gorbachev was not simply envious of Yeltsin's growing popularity; the town was just not big enough for the two of them. Their rivalry could be defined in equal part as personal and political. It began during the decline of Gorbachev's revolution, when he lost control of the changes he himself had set in motion. Gorbachev, a psychologically stable man, suddenly developed an idée fixe: whatever happened, Boris Yeltsin was to blame. Soon, every conversation with Gorbachev would sooner or later turn to Yeltsin.

Everything about Yeltsin irked Gorbachev, including Yeltsin's criticisms, even when they were not directed at Gorbachev, and his popularity, which rose in direct ratio to Gorbachev's own loss of esteem among the masses. Yeltsin seemed to attract love. Gorbachev's fears were not imaginary: comparing the two leaders became commonplace on the street.

Did Yeltsin realize where things were heading or did he hope that in the days of glasnost he could get away with covert and overt attacks on the General Secretary? Undoubtedly, every such attack was reported to

Gorbachev. It is also possible that many of these attacks were a fiction; it was then that Yeltsin began to be mythologized as the People's Defender, Advocate, and Hero. It makes no difference what was true and what was not: the important thing was that the Yeltsin myth was being born, while Gorbachev became the butt of an increasing number of jokes:

GORBACHEV CALLS Stalin for advice.
Stalin says, "Execute half the Central Committee and paint the Kremlin blue."
"Why blue?"
"I knew you'd have a problem with the second issue."

*

A SOVIET dog on glasnost and perestroika:
"The leash is three meters longer, the bowl has been shifted five meters away, but you can howl to your heart's content."

*

A BUS stops near a liquor store, and the passengers push for the exit.
"Calm down," the driver says. "The next stop is at the end of the line."

*

A DRUNK stares at Gorbachev:
"Sorry, Mikhail, couldn't recognize you without Raisa."

*

RAISA AND Mikhail are in bed. She stares at him for a long time and then asks, "Mikhail, have you ever thought you would be sleeping with the wife of the Secretary General?"

*

ALL THE Communist leaders are riding in the same train. Suddenly the tracks end. What to do?
Lenin: "Declare another working day and have workers and peasants lay down more rails."
Stalin: "Shoot every peasant in sight, then bring in the prisoners from the camp and have them build a railroad."
Khrushchev: "Take the rails from behind the train and lay them out in front."
Brezhnev: "Close the curtains in the car and rock it back and forth" (to create the illusion of motion).

Gorbachev: "Get everybody out of the train and yell, 'No rails! No rails!'"

*

IT WAS at the height of this orgy of anti-Gorbachev humor that Yeltsin got involved in an episode that was aired around the world and generated accusations that he was sympathetic with the cause of Pamyat, the most radical wing of Russian chauvinists. The odor of these charges lingers to this day.

According to witnesses, it happened around 6 P.M. on May 6, 1987, when he had another six months to go in office—you will see later how dates are of special significance. A crowd formed on Manezh Square, near the Kremlin—at first a few hundred, but then the crowd grew to almost a thousand. They unfurled red banners and placards with rather innocent slogans, many of them opaque to the uninitiated:

Down with the Saboteurs of Perestroika!
Recognize the Historical and Patriotic Society Pamyat!
We Demand a Meeting with Gorbachev and Yeltsin!
Stop the Construction on Poklonny Hill!*
Restore Poklonny Hill!

Each slogan was duplicated: some were turned toward the old university building, others toward the Alexandr Garden and the Kremlin wall. Sounds of snickering and shouting about "Zionists" and "bureaucrats" were heard in the crowd, but the organizers quickly removed the hecklers lest they compromise the rally. The police surrounded the crowd with a tight line along the perimeter to prevent acts of violence on the part of the demonstrators and to protect them from hostile passersby.

After an hour the crowd moved from the Manezh toward Soviet Square, the seat of the City Hall. As if following unspoken directions, they marched in a well-organized manner, holding aloft their banners and placards. They were escorted by the police, who became nervous as the crowd swelled. Moscow Mayor Valery Saykin came out several times to beg the demonstrators to disperse quietly, but they insisted on their original demand: a meeting with Gorbachev and Yeltsin.

In those days, despite the supposed constitutional guarantees, rallies were permitted only on national holidays: May Day and November 7, Revolution Day. The authorities, at least the local ones, unused to unplanned and unsanctioned rallies, panicked. Besides, Pamyat was notori-

---

*Poklonny (Bow) Hill was a subject of heated discussions as the suggested location for the Victory Over Hitler monument.

ous for its slogans that sounded like they originated in the age of pogroms, and the consequences of their rally in the center of Moscow could
not be predicted. When Yeltsin got a call on the hot line from nervous
officials at the Internal Affairs Section, he acted without delay, sending
Saykin back to the demonstrators to inform them of his consent to meet
them at City Hall, Moscow Party Committee headquarters, or the Political Enlightenment House.

In that day, the decision was highly unorthodox. A standard modus
operandi would have been to call for extra police plus soldiers and plain-
clothes cops, disperse the rally, and arrest the organizers.

"I chose to act differently," Yeltsin recalls. "I told them I'd meet them.
Ever since, my ill-wishers—that's putting it mildly—have accused me of
being friends with Pamyat. No doubt they would have preferred it if I had
had the demonstrators clubbed."

The demonstrators picked City Hall, since it was nearby, and marched
up Gorky Street (now renamed Tverskaya Street), a major thoroughfare.
Traffic was blocked off. Policemen followed along on the sidewalks.

Meanwhile, a crowd of onlookers, more numerous than the Pamyat
mob, formed outside the building. About a hundred broke through the
police line to enter the building with the Pamyat supporters. Pamyat had
to post its own guards to keep nonmembers out.

Inside, in the Marble Hall, Yeltsin attempted to address the crowd and
reply to their questions, but the demonstrators were in a state of frenzy.
Yeltsin sensibly stepped down from the podium—they would have
stormed the stage. The discussion lasted for about two hours. Afterward
the demonstrators folded their banners and slogans and took them to the
nearest police precinct.

What follows is an excerpt from that discussion. Each side spoke its
own lingo. The Pamyat people employed euphemisms to parry accusations of anti-Semitism and chauvinism. Yeltsin, though speaking sincerely, expressed himself in the Party phraseology, open-minded
statements mixed with propaganda clichés: at that time Gorbachev's
glasnost was only fourteen months old.

DMITRI VASILYEV (Pamyat): You must set up a procedure for the
common people—not just their deputies—to come talk to you. It is next
to impossible to get through your staff. No materials submitted ever reach
you. Your chief of staff, Tolstov,* is a horrible man. Second, there are
shameful goings-on on Poklonny Hill. Third, the enemies of perestroika

---

*Yuli Tolstov, a Jew particularly hated by Pamyat, got his job under Grishin (Yeltsin's predeces-
sor). Yet Yeltsin knew him for a long time through his brother, the director of a large factory
in Sverdlovsk. The Tolstovs' father was executed under Stalin.

are stepping up their activities nationwide. With direct contact, we could fight them together. Fourth, the sobriety campaign is being waged on a primitive level . . . An avalanche of cosmopolitanism—all those rock groups and their rock philosophies—has flooded the media. The names of Alexandr Nevsky, Suvorov,* and other Russian commanders are fading into oblivion. Why use glasnost to disseminate cosmopolitan Western culture in our media? Then there is distorted information about us; we're called Nazis, chauvinists, anti-Semites. No—we're patriots! And we back the Party's politics.

VLADISLAV SHUMSKY (Pamyat): An individual threatened us when we stood on the Manezh . . . We demand that construction on Poklonny Hill be stopped . . . You and Gorbachev are our only hope . . . There is insufficient public opposition to alcoholism and drug addiction. Rock 'n' roll and drug addiction are one big plague. We're being accused of being against everything new. We're not against the new; we're against the harmful. Art must be based upon Communist morality, while rock 'n' roll is Americanization and computerization of the individual.

VALERY YEMELYANOV (Pamyat): It is time we put an end to rotten liberalization; the publications of Nabokov, all that praise for Tarkovsky,† who left our country and died abroad. I even suggested that boxcars with the soil from different areas of the country be brought to Poklonny Hill. The Arch of Triumph** should be returned, too.

YELTSIN: I don't want to deal with your overly emotional comments right now. And I categorically reject the charges that all meetings with me are "court audiences." About three times a week I meet people—on the street and in stores. On May Day I went to the Lenin Stadium—a thousand people came to talk to me. These are not court audiences. It is true that there are no regular scheduled contacts with groups like yours. But we're developing a schedule of meetings with journalists, managers, and other categories. I get between 150 and 200 letters a day, and since I work eighteen to twenty hours a day, I cannot see all of them . . . Right—we don't have an organized system of monitoring public opinion. This is a serious drawback nationwide. We should have such a system.

Now—about monuments. We've gone over this dozens of times. Following the General Development Plan of 1935, 2200 historical monuments have been destroyed. We have placed 9500 monuments under

*Alexandr Nevsky and Alexandr Suvorov—famous Russian troop commanders in the thirteenth and eighteenth centuries respectively.
†Andrei Tarkovsky, a prominent Soviet film director *(Solaris, Stalker),* left the USSR to work in the mid-'70s in the West, where he died in 1987.
**As part of its program to restore Moscow to its former condition, Pamyat demands the return of the Arch of Triumph, erected to commemorate the victory over Napoleon, from Kutuzov Avenue to its original location near the Belorussky Station.

protection. In the next five-year plan, we'll double the volume of restoration work. If memory serves me right, we have 1585 monuments in critical condition, and we plan to restore them . . . Now, Poklonny Hill is a tough issue. We want to have the best monument in the world; on the other hand, war veterans want to see it before they die. We did remove the tower cranes. As for the rest, we're not sure. Let's sit down and talk. . . .

Now, about perestroika, glasnost, congressional and plenary resolutions. You must admit progress has been made. Mouths have been muzzled for a long time. Even now, many mouths are open, but bodies are still standing at attention. We're having a hard time with perestroika, too. We must learn how to function in a democracy. If someone sabotages this effort—out with them! We should know their names, but they are mostly silent types; they do their deeds in silence. We support the renovation of our society in all its aspects.

About recognizing Pamyat—there is much public speculation about you. Many say bad things about you. But you provoke this with your remarks verging on anti-Sovietism. We will consider recognizing you— but only as a truly patriotic organization.

This two-hour meeting with Pamyat created Yeltsin's reputation as a man who supports and encourages Pamyat's Great Russian brand of aggressive nationalism and anti-Semitism. Naturally, the Moscow intelligentsia, who already had enough reason to be displeased with him, were the first to sound the alarm and feed their lines to the Western media. While Yeltsin never met with Pamyat activists again, he had a hard time repairing the damage. Moreover, Pamyat and its ideologues launched some of the most vicious, below-the-belt attacks on him, from accusations of betraying the Russian people to rumors that he is really a Jew whose real name is Baruch Elkind and he is married to a Jewish woman; in fact, his wife, Naina Yeltsin, is Russian, born in a Russian village—but does it really matter?

The ethnic or religious characteristic of Jewishness has been turned into an ideological label, a political stamp; Jews are no longer born Jewish, they are designated as such. To Pamyat, all of their ideological foes, whatever their origin, are Jews, from poet Yevgeny Yevtushenko to politician Boris Yeltsin, who, according to them, was a "super-Jew" because he advocated the breakup of the Soviet Empire. To them, a Jew is not an enemy, but an enemy is always a Jew.

Such an expanded interpretation is convenient to identify an ideological or political foe according to his or her ethnicity, but it is not cost-free: if Yevtushenko and Yeltsin are "Jews," what do you do with real Jews? This labeling weakens and dilutes the anti-Semitic charge, deprives it of its sense and objective, and ultimately turns against its advocates, like a boomerang in an inept hand. In part, it is the anti-Semites that made anti-Semitism no longer fashionable—the main reason, though, is that fear of Jews has been replaced by far more urgent issues. Still:

"Boris Nikolayevich, ours is a Russian country. Why do you kowtow to the Jews?"

"What do you call kowtowing?"

"Well, you're conducting an erroneous policy."

"I have never singled out an ethnic group. I think that each nation, each people, should have equal rights. You, too, should rate people, whenever you can, by other criteria than nationality entries in their passports."

This last exchange is from Yeltsin's call-in question-and-answer session by phone, held with the help of *Komsomolskaya Pravda* on March 11, 1991. We are not quoting this to protect Yeltsin from empty accusations and insinuations, but, rather, to show how a Jew or a person sympathetic to Jews is defined by Russian chauvinists: if your policies are "erroneous," you must be either "nice to the Jews" or a Jew yourself.

Neither attacks of Moscow fascists, nor his own rebuttals, nor his impeccably internationalist policy, nor his clearly pro-Western, pro-democracy views, not even Yeltsin's gradual Americanization as a result of his trips to the United States and his general ideological evolution—none of this succeeded in eliminating the stigma of that meeting with Pamyat. Three years later, after so many cataclysms in Russian history and Yeltsin's life, David Remnick, *The Washington Post*'s Moscow reporter, wrote a piece called "The No.1 Nationalist"—plainly influenced by the Moscow intelligentsia—in which he linked Yeltsin, now the Russian President, with Pamyat lunatics "with their black T-shirts and 'Kill the Yids' placards."

The only new evidence provided by Remnick that Yeltsin's liberal views are suspect was Yeltsin's uncharacteristic evasiveness when queried on anti-Semitism at a meeting with Muscovites. Apart from that, Yeltsin has made a number of unambiguous statements on the issue. He even proposed that a special commission be established to safeguard the rights of Russian Jews. At his meeting with the delegation of the World Jewish Congress, he agreed that the Soviet Jews are entitled to their own holiday—as the Russian Orthodox are entitled to celebrate Christmas. Two months after the article in the *Post,* a writer for *Forbes* contrasted Yeltsin with Gorbachev, observing that the latter, "afraid to antagonize extremist groups like Pamyat, has failed to speak out against anti-Semitism."

Six months after Yeltsin's meeting with Pamyat he would be removed from the job of Moscow Party Boss. At that Party meeting, Yuri Prokofyev, his replacement on the job (true, by then the job would have lost all political or administrative importance), would rub in the memories of Pamyat: "Speaking of Comrade Yeltsin's political literacy: I witnessed his meeting with Pamyat. You know who those people are. Comrade Yeltsin invited them to City Hall and spoke to them, conceding one Party position after another. To whom? To these neurotics who emulate pre-Revolutionary Jew-baiting reactionary Black Hundreds."

Pamyat's dubious intentions are undeniable, though its role as aggressive nationalists is much exaggerated, as is the danger it represents. Its importance is blown out of proportion not only by the Moscow intelligentsia, many of whom are Jewish (and to a mouse, a cat is the most dangerous of the beasts), but by the Western media and by Yeltsin himself. Otherwise he would not have agreed to meet with Pamyat. The authors contributed to the exaggeration campaign when we emigrated to the States and published half a dozen pieces in both Russian- and English-language papers about the so-called Russian Party. Later, when we talked about the relatively insignificant role of Russian jingoists in the current political struggle, our Moscow friends beat us over the head with our own earlier arguments.

It is not that we have distorted this role since first writing about them fifteen years ago, but times have changed, and our subjects have failed the test of democracy. To their own surprise, and that of their liberal opponents, the rabid protectors of the Motherland received so few votes that they were disqualified from participation in most elected bodies. It turned out that they do not function well in a democracy, and that totalitarian conditions are the only fertile ground for their nationalist games. This was exactly the situation in which we wrote about these borscht patriots, whose love of Russia turned into hatred for its alleged enemies—the Jews.

This has happened before. On the eve of the 1917 Revolution, with a more fluid political balance of forces, the nationalist-chauvinists still lost ground and received fewer votes than the Socialist Revolutionaries, the Constitutional Democrats, the Bolsheviks, or the Mensheviks—or anyone. In addition to a totalitarian environment, they also needed secret backers—the Tsar's secret police before the Revolution, the KGB in the stagnation years of Brezhnev and Andropov.

By the late '80s, the heyday of glasnost, Pamyat was reduced to an ideological minority, a marginal political group, less popular among the population than, say, Jean-Marie Le Pen in France. Yeltsin made an error in receiving Pamyat's maniacs; not merely a tactical one in terms of his future political career, but also an error of judgment. He overestimated Pamyat's influence, and a mountain was made out of a molehill. Of course they had to be received, but it should have been done by one of his aides, who could have determined that what Pamyat leaders needed was a referral to a psychiatrist.

Much later, with Pamyat practically off the political map, the Moscow *Independent Paper* published an essay written by New York–based cultural critic Boris Paramonov. The piece, daringly titled "Shit," was a convincing social psychoanalysis of the Russian fascists. Paramonov views anti-Semitism as a shameful emotion that normal people tend to hide, and considers the Russian anti-Semites' childlike shamelessness in advocating their ideas a kind of neurosis. He compares it to the way children treat their own feces—as something valuable, since it is a product of their effort, their "creativity," a kind of thoughtful, worklike activity that brings them closer to the adult world. Hence his diagnosis of their infantile, unsublimated, pregenital psyche; their cultural regression to primitivism and savagery.

Discarding the author's yen to *épater,* his conclusions have merit. Consider Yeltsin's opponents in City Hall: Dmitry Vasilyev, Pamyat's official leader, claimed that Adolf Eichmann was Jewish and had purposely destroyed six million of his co-religionists to enable the rest of them to prosper—in keeping with the Jewish theory of "branch-lopping," designed to save the tree.

The audience at the meeting also included Valery Yemelyanov, who had penned a book called *De-Zionization,* published in Russian by Yassir Arafat in Damascus. Suspecting his own wife of working for Mossad and spying on him for "world Zionism," Yemelyanov murdered her with an ax. The court found him insane, and he had spent several years in an asylum prior to his audience with Yeltsin.

To such people, the Jews were the universal scapegoat, responsible for all the world's evils, but especially for all the calamities that had befallen Russia in its thousand-year history. Now it turned out it was the Jews, not the Tatars, who kept ancient Russians in slavery for centuries; Jews plunged Russia into chaos in the early sixteenth century—never mind that there were no Jews in Russia in those faraway days. Great Russian poets who died violent deaths—Pushkin and Lermontov in duels, Yesenin a suicide—those were also the Jews' victims. Trotsky, not Lenin, was responsible for the evil of the Revolution, just as Stalin was but a puppet in the hands of Lazar Kaganovich. Perhaps Paramonov is right, and psychoanalysis is indeed a proper tool for understanding Pamyat.

How did Yemelyanov manage to have his book published by Arafat when he did not have a chance to publish it in Russia? (He could nowadays: Gorbachev's glasnost provided fertile soil for "a hundred flowers to bloom," as the Chinese say—and that includes some *fleurs du mal,* both Baudelaire's and Pamyat's.)

An earlier book of ours, *Yuri Andropov: A Secret Passage Into the Kremlin,* contained a chapter called "Russian Nationalism: The KGB's Ideological Stake." Andropov was hardly an anti-Semite, but it was a political stake in his Big Game—a trump, more precisely—though only at certain times and for a limited duration. Once he won the game and took over the country, he discarded nationalism. However, the links between the Russian Party and the KGB that we traced in our book remained. In the midst of the political chaos of Gorbachev's days, the wild dog of Great Russian nationalism was unleashed onto the political stage, but it did not live up to its own expectations, having offended far more people than it attracted, and so it was put back on a leash, to wait for a more propitious moment. It remains unmuzzled, however, and can howl and bark to its heart's content.

The political defeat of the Russian nationalists took place in the early '90s, with democracy on the rise. In the spring of 1987, which many liberal intellectuals saw as "Springtime for Pamyat," things looked different. The Russian Party, which, amidst the broad spectrum of political groups, most depended on its secret supporters, was manipulated by its KGB handlers particularly actively. It is hard to imagine that at the time when street democracy was barely getting under way, Pamyat would undertake a mass rally right in the city center without the knowledge or sanction of the authorities, or, at least, an encouraging wink from them. A few years later, in Moscow, we heard Pamyat's followers complain of having been used and discarded by the powers-that-be. In particular, we were told that the demonstrators' demands to meet Yeltsin, and their steady refusal to negotiate with Mayor Saykin, had been specifically ordered by their sponsors.

What about the panicky—as Yeltsin thought—call he received from the Internal Affairs Section, subordinated directly to the KGB? How panicky was it? Why would law-enforcement officials panic over a rally of their own protégés? It is hard to avoid the conclusion that the KGB played matchmaker in the meeting between Yeltsin and Pamyat. In the light of subsequent setups that the KGB arranged for him, this one should be considered the first and the most successful. Their calculation was flawless: the meeting did enormous damage to Yeltsin's reputation, and he was compromised internationally for years to come.

The timing of the trap into which Yeltsin naively stepped is also important. By then the successes of his year-and-a-half rule of Moscow were becoming evident. One hundred sixty enterprises were transferred to a regime of economic self-sufficiency, and by the next year their number was expected to exceed a thousand. The import of a *limitchik* slave-labor force—80,000 a year—was stopped, causing labor productivity to double. Five hundred new stores opened, as did regular open-air markets. The corrupt Grishin's guard were sent packing, and for the first time about two thousand executives were elected rather than appointed.

Under Yeltsin's aegis, *Moskovskaya Pravda* became one of the most daring papers in the country. In the Politburo, Gorbachev frequently complained about its editor in chief, Yeltsin's protégé Mikhail Poltoranin. "Circulation's rising," Yeltsin jocularly shot back, "how about your Afanasyev?" Victor Afanasyev was editor in chief of Gorbachev's *Pravda,* whose circulation was indeed tumbling despite the fact that Communists were forced to subscribe to their Party's paper.

Finally, Yeltsin was the first Moscow Boss to pay serious attention to the environment. One of Moscow's key problems was that, with its population growing steadily, it lacked room to expand. Its green belt was only twice the city's territory (the ratio is 4:1 for Tokyo and 6:1 for New York). A 500-meter-deep layer of atmosphere over the city and a layer of ground of the same depth were analyzed from a satellite; the results showed exceptionally high pollution levels. In response, Yeltsin's team developed a plan to remove 140 factories from Moscow and convert surface public transportation, which accounted for half the pollution in the city, to a cleaner type of gasoline.

Not all Yeltsin's changes in the city could be deemed positive, though. Once he realized that his innovations were being sabotaged, he was ruthless in fighting back. His newspaper, *Moskovskaya Pravda,* published a special phone number that vigilant citizens were encouraged to call to report corruption and thievery. Naturally, many, especially the intelligentsia, perceived this as an appeal to informants and a throwback to Stalin's days.

The same *Moskovskaya Pravda* began publishing items exposing bribe-takers, "mafiosi," slackers, and other "enemies of progress." Set in black obituary frame, overdramatized and sensationalized in Western tabloid style, the lists read like battle reports—clearly aimed to touch a public nerve.

Yeltsin's naive use of his Sverdlovsk methods under Moscow conditions was dubious. For example, he initiated "Sanitary Fridays," forcing well-qualified professionals to help clean the city. Insisting on what he called social justice, he referred his critics to the redundance of white-collar workers and the acute shortage of street sweepers. Naturally, white-collar workers bristled at being handed the broom and sent out to the sidewalks. Yeltsin rejected Moscow's traditional rules and insisted on his own, imported from the Urals, where mores were simple and the gap between rulers and masses was not as wide.

In the middle of this intense activity, in spite of—or, perhaps owing to—the evident success of Yeltsin's measures, a conflict with Gorbachev was brewing. It burst into the open in the spring of 1987, and Yeltsin's fate was sealed behind the Politburo's closed doors.

According to Mikhail Poltoranin, who was appointed by Yeltsin to edit *Moskovskaya Pravda* and removed from the job following his pa-

tron's demise after the newspaper ran a series of articles on Moscow
organized crime, he got a dressing-down from Mayor Saykin (a Yeltsin
protégé, too). "What are you trying to do? Yeltsin's here today and gone
tomorrow—but you'll still have to work with us." Another of Yeltsin's
subordinates, Yuri Belyakov, his right-hand man in the Party Committee,
was even more direct. "It's time you chose whose side you're on." Yeltsin
himself admitted there was nothing he could do about Moscow's "mafia"
and said to Poltoranin, "I know they're digging my grave."

Yeltsin was on the ropes and he knew it. In this context we gain a better
understanding of the Pamyat setup. It was not enough to condemn Yeltsin in Doublespeak from the Party podium; he also needed to be vilified
in common Russian, and his contact with Pamyat presented an opportunity.

Yeltsin was getting into more scrapes at the Politburo, whose sessions he
regularly attended, though without the right to vote. He thought it was time
to declare open war on privileges enjoyed by the nomenklatura—the top
functionaries. Gorbachev disagreed, realizing that such a war would
eventually reach the doorstep of the most privileged person of all—the
General Secretary himself. Yeltsin grew increasingly irritated by Gorbachev's smugness, by his Politburo speeches—long, polished, and, as Yeltsin
thought, empty. Perestroika was spinning its wheels, while its chief trail-
blazer showed little concern. A genuinely explosive debate was replaced by
a fake one, diluted by panegyrics to the Secretary General. What other
forum was there for the situation that Yeltsin regarded as critical?

Yeltsin asked to see Gorbachev. Their talk lasted over two hours and
yielded no results—their positions were too far apart, and their ambitions
were diametrically opposed.

In his autobiography Yeltsin describes how on September 12, 1987,
without consulting his family, he wrote Gorbachev a letter. He sealed the
envelope and handed it to his aide. The mail route between Moscow and
Pitsunda, the Black Sea resort where Gorbachev was on vacation, functioned smoothly, and several hours later the General Secretary was reading the letter from his fractious protégé:

> . . . I have always tried to voice my viewpoint, even though it was at odds with
> that of others. This has led to an increasingly undesirable state of affairs. More
> exactly, with my style, my straightforwardness, and my background, I have
> discovered I am ill-equipped to work at the Politburo . . . I am aware that I am
> causing problems. I also realize this is not easy to resolve. But it is better to
> admit the error now. Given the composition of the current Politburo, there will
> be more difficulties involving myself that will be an obstacle in your work. With
> all my heart I would like to avoid that.
> Another reason why I want to avoid it is that, despite your tremendous

efforts, the struggle for stability will lead to stagnation, to the same (rather, similar) kind of situation that we have already had. This must be prevented. These are some of the reasons and motives that urge me to submit this request. It is not done out of weakness or cowardice.

I hereby request to be relieved from the duties of the First Secretary of the Moscow Party Committee, as well as of the Candidate Member to the Politburo of the Party's Central Committee. Please consider this request official.

I believe there will be no need for me to address the Plenary meeting of the Central Committee with this request directly.

Respectfully, B. Yeltsin

Yeltsin spent several sleepless nights waiting for an answer. Finally, tired of waiting, he went to the alumni reunion of the Ural Polytechnical Institute. Now he needed the reunion more than ever before. Relaxing among his friends and fellow Uralers, he became loose-tongued: "I'm so happy to see you . . . I've never been as lonely as I am in Moscow . . . I'm used to working in the Urals; everything was more simple, more open: tell the truth, fight for what you believe . . . Here it is more complicated. Another year and a half, two years like this—and you'll see my obituary in the papers."

According to Yeltsin, after Pitsunda, Gorbachev called him and suggested they meet—but later. A week passed, then another—an invitation never followed. A regularly scheduled session of the Politburo discussed Gorbachev's speech for the seventieth anniversary of the Revolution. When his turn to speak came, Yeltsin recalls, he made a few critical remarks. Then, unexpectedly, Gorbachev fled the room. He was missing for a good half hour; others maintained a dejected silence, not knowing what to do. When he finally came back, instead of responding to Yeltsin on issues, he launched into an insulting, hysterical tirade. Everything came under attack including Yeltsin's personality and his allegedly being spoiled by Moscow popularity.

The rest were silent, taking no sides. The battle was between the two men, and at that stage the Politburo wanted no part of it. Even Yegor Ligachev, Yeltsin's—according to Party lore—chief antagonist, held his peace.

Having listened to Gorbachev's remarks, Yeltsin rose to say that he refused to comment since the attack was subjective and expressed in an unacceptable form.

Afterward, Gorbachev tried to ignore Yeltsin, though they had to see each other at work at least twice a week. Gorbachev avoided handshakes and greeted Yeltsin with a silent nod. Thus Yeltsin was becoming a pariah, an outsider banned from the General Secretary's compliant team.

His fate was sealed; his days at the Kremlin were numbered.

CRIME AND PUNISHMENT, KREMLIN STYLE
(October 21–November 18, 1987)

HISTORY HAS little regard for the intentions of those who set great events into motion. Who could imagine that the assassination of the successor to the Austrian throne by a Sarajevo conspirator would lead to a four-year European slaughter, the demise of three empires, and two Russian revolutions; that the revolutions would change the balance of world forces and thus define most political conflicts throughout our century? Least of all could this have been foreseen by Gavriil Princip himself, an obscure Serbian nationalist. Lenin, too, whether avenging the execution of his terrorist brother or spying for the Kaiser, probably never foresaw in his wildest dreams that he would shake the world, or even one-sixth of it—Russia.

By all standards what took place in Moscow on the morning of October 21, 1987, was insignificant. Not one shot was fired; even the hothead who set the wheels in motion hardly believed that his four-minute speech would have consequences not just for his own political career but for the entire country as well.

Yeltsin had not prepared a speech, and until the last moment he hesitated whether he should ask for the floor. His eventual decision to do so had little to do with strategy or tactics, but, rather, with his emotions; the same impatience of the heart had failed him so many times before—but in the end, oddly enough, worked in his favor. He walked to the podium as if it were the gallows; indeed, the execution immediately followed the speech. It was a "civic execution," the stripping off of civil rights, but it could have turned into a real one, or a general slaughter, which was avoided by a miracle.

Outside observers in Moscow and abroad could not help noting a certain resemblance between the Kremlin gallows of '87 and the Moscow show trials of the late '30s. However, unlike Zinovyev, Kamenev, Bukharin et al, Yeltsin survived.

Yeltsin's biography needs no dramatization—it is already chock-full of dramatic events that began in the very first days of his life. At his baptism, the drunken priest dropped him into the font and forgot to take him out; had it not been for his mother, who saved him, Gorbachev would not have had such a serious rival, nor would the Russian people have had their hero and defender. Apropos of the role of incident in history: If, according to Pascal, the shape of Cleopatra's nose was of such historical importance, then a village priest's alcoholism collided with a mother's vigilance to have a considerable long-term impact on Russian history.

The authors do not believe in historical determinism: a person plays a more important role in history than an incident—or else we would not be writing biography (this is our third, preceded by books on Andropov and Gorbachev). On the other hand, beginning with the Party Plenum in October 1987, Yeltsin's life has increasingly followed the course of history of his country, while Gorbachev's has reflected mostly the history of the Kremlin; the two histories take separate courses; they rarely overlap.

One of these overlaps was Yeltsin's unprecedented rebellion—in essence, a rude popular intrusion into the sleepy routine of Kremlin life. It dumbfounded the Kremlin Olympians by violating the historical tradition that "the people are silent," as Pushkin put it in *Boris Godunov,* and that the ruler speaks and acts on their behalf. Yeltsin's breach of tradition was at the same time a breach of the code that led to a scandal in a "good family."

In 1987 the Soviet Union was still off-limits to those who had left for political reasons, ourselves included (we had to wait for another three years to pay a visit—as tourists—to our geographical homeland). On the other hand, the door out of Russia suddenly opened, and a steady stream of our friends—mostly writer colleagues whom we had not seen since we left Moscow—poured into New York. Under Brezhnev and Andropov they wrote, as Russians say, "for their desks," not daring to attempt to publish their work. Gorbachev legitimized them, brought them to the Kremlin court, and made them his most loyal supporters. Loyal they would remain, long after he lost the popularity of the masses and the trust of the nomenklatura.

In the olden days, when the Gorbachev-Yeltsin conflict was still young, our Moscow guests were solidly in Gorbachev's corner and denounced that "disturber of the peace," Yeltsin. All reproached him for receiving Pamyat, and some criticized him for not being a "team player"—for arguing with the captain (Gorbachev) in the middle of the game. Many said that he was no intellectual, a boor, that he banged his fist on the table. He interrupted others while they spoke; he was intolerant and even cruel—an *apparatchik* fired by him had jumped out of the window. Their final argument was, *Leave the good well alone,* which they illustrated with an old joke. A man tried to tell everybody that the new ruler was wrong and that two times two was four, not five, as the latter claimed. To which the prudent citizens said, "Shut up, you fool, or else it will be 'two times two is nine' again." In short, each new arrival brought a long list of grievances against Yeltsin.

However, our Moscow friends told us of five different versions of Yeltsin's escapade at the Central Committee's Plenum. What he did was so unexpected and outrageous that long before the content of his four-minute speech became known, rumors were circulating about what had prompted him to deliver it.

Some said that Yeltsin's act had been prearranged with other disgruntled Central Committee members and had their support, but at the last minute they backed out and remained silent, while some of them soberly assessed the situation and quickly defected to Gorbachev's side.

Others told us in confidence that the arrangement had been a sham; that the Kremlin rulers had actually decided to get rid of Yeltsin, sick of his obstinacy and constant harassments. They concocted a false plot against themselves and lured Yeltsin—a naive straight-shooter, inexperienced in Kremlin intrigue—into it, promising that his speech would be the signal for further discussion of perestroika. They set him up.

According to the third version, Yeltsin himself was a false conspirator. The Kremlin establishment felt power slipping away, the earth trembling, and popular discontent growing. So they decided to quietly assign the role of the leader of the opposition to one of their own in order to keep popular grumbling under control. And who was better suited for the part than Boris Yeltsin—always malcontent, unwilling to go along with the rest, contradicting everyone, and pushing through no matter what. Not for nothing was he nicknamed the Bulldozer.

The fourth version disclosed that Yeltsin was incurably ill, had nothing left to lose, and thus dared this démarche.

Finally, some hypothesized that Yeltsin had gone insane. What normal person would risk his career—if not his life—and confront the closed ranks of the Kremlin leaders singlehandedly? And at the Plenary meeting, of all places!

The rumor of terminal cancer did not check out, but some of the Kremlin elite liked the one about psychological instability; after all, they had to explain Yeltsin's revolt somehow, both to the Russian people and to themselves. Moreover, such an explanation followed an old Russian tradition. The Russian Emperor himself pronounced the philosopher

Pyotr Chaadayev mad, banned the publication of his work, and placed him under house arrest for the rest of his life (twenty years). It was the most famous case of a person declared mad for his philosophical, religious, or political beliefs, but it was far from unique. No wonder it was used as a plot by Russian writers. In Griboyedov's classical comedy *Woe of Wit* and Chekhov's story *Ward Six,* the heroes are truth-seekers and champions of justice. The former is pronounced mad by the society he had infuriated with his barbs, while the latter is simply locked up in an asylum.

Stalin pooh-poohed such refined punishment of suspected heretics, preferring to murder them, but in Brezhnev's era the use of psychiatric asylums against dissidents moved from literature to life, reaffirming the major function of literature in Russian reality. Not only does literature reflect Russian reality, but it also has a crucial—though sometimes unexpected—effect on it. Under Brezhnev, asylums soon filled with patients bearing fantastic diagnoses such as "truth-seeking obsession." Among them was a certain Ilyin, a failed assassin of Brezhnev; General Grigorenko, a champion of the rights of ethnic minorities; Joseph Brodsky, the future Nobel Prize winner; Vladimir Klebanov, the founder of the first independent union in the country; the dissident Bukovsky; and many others, famous and obscure. Yeltsin could easily have ended up joining the club. Official speakers began mentioning his emotional instability, political immaturity, distance from reality, superiority complex, reckless adventurism—all the qualities that Soviet psychiatry routinely recognized as symptoms of political insanity. The condition was diagnosed; opinion was readied; the tactic had been used many times before.

But the calculation misfired. It is easy to declare a normal person mad when everybody lives in an asylum, but patients can gradually get better and cease to believe medical charlatans. In this case, society itself was recovering; it did not buy the story of Yeltsin's sickness and came to his defense. Glasnost, much touted by the Kremlin, turned against them this time. The Yeltsin affair was not unique in that regard, but it turned out to be the most vivid, the most incontrovertible evidence of the political atavism of Yeltsin's persecutors. With all their talk of stepping into an era of "new thinking," they did so with one foot only, while the other was hopelessly mired in the swamp of the previous era. The Kremlin show, "The Political Destruction of Boris Yeltsin," was played out according to the old script and with the old sets. But history, in order to avoid repeating itself, turns tragedy into farce. In a farce the hero does not die; instead, he ridicules the plots against him. This was the secret of Yeltsin's survival.

Although comedy is a parody of tragedy, none of its characters, including the hero, suspects it. The hero himself is unaware of the happy ending of the intrigue that has been set into motion to punish him, to make him a victim. He takes it at face value. In response to Yeltsin's four-minute speech, a chorus of twenty-six members of the Kremlin areopagus spent several hours vilifying him. Less than a month later the scene was replayed at the Moscow Party Plenum, with a different cast of characters, but with the same antagonists—Gorbachev and Yeltsin. Finally, when the mass media were activated to step up the campaign, the persecutors achieved their objective: the victim felt that he had been hunted down, annihilated.

But the director and the cast of the Kremlin show failed to account for the audience, on whom the show had an effect opposite to the one desired. It was the audience, no longer hypnotized by fear, who turned potential tragedy into farce. The contradiction between the concept and the result gave birth to the Kremlin Theater of the Absurd, along the lines of Beckett and Ionesco.

Eighteen months later, after the episode had spawned conflicting versions, wild rumors, and myths, the Party finally dared to publish the transcript of the secret Plenum. Its most salient feature was the immense gap between the initial impulse and the events that followed. In the fable a mountain gives birth to a mouse, but in this case the mouse produced a mountain.

To illustrate this point, we are going to reverse the sequence of events, first giving the reaction to Yeltsin's speech and then the speech itself.

Of the entire cast of this drama/farce, we will quote only the most famous ones.*

GORBACHEV (chairing the meeting): Some kind of new stuff coming up here. Are we talking about the secession of the Moscow Party organization? Or, perhaps, Comrade Yeltsin decided to submit the issue of him leaving the Politburo, and at the same time remain the First Secretary of the Moscow Party Committee? It seems like he's spoiling for a fight with the Central Committee. That's how I see it—though maybe I'm making this sound more critical than it is.

(At this point Yeltsin leaps to his feet and attempts to protest, but Gorbachev cuts him short):
Sit down, sit down, Boris Nikolayevich . . . Comrades, those wishing to speak raise your hands.

YEGOR LIGACHEV (Yeltsin's chief Kremlin antagonist, not counting Gorbachev): . . . I categorically deny Comrade Yeltsin's statement . . .

*The speeches of the Kremlin leaders are close, literal translations, with no cosmetic or stylistic touch-ups. If sometimes they seem devoid of either logic or sense, they were. In official translations, Gorbachev & Co. often sound much better than they did in the original.

Nikolai Ryzhkov (the Soviet Prime Minister, a friend of Yeltsin's since Sverdlovsk, where Yeltsin was Party Boss and Ryzhkov director of the largest factory in the city): How could this happen? I'm sitting here, thinking how could this happen. Comrade Yeltsin and I come from the same city. I've known him for years, before he was made regional Party Secretary . . . I don't think it's accidental . . . Boris Nikolayevich, you've been headed this way for a long time . . . I think the moment he was transferred to the Moscow Party organization he began developing political nihilism. He began to like it when various radio "Voices" began quoting him. "What Yeltsin said . . ." All sorts of publications, too—"what Yeltsin said . . ." Quoted all over the place. This is a fact, we have it documented. So it seems like some kind of isolated stance, some distance from the entire Politburo, from political leadership. I think Comrade Yeltsin liked it a lot. I think that's what led to him developing oversized ambition—and that's that.

Vitaly Vorotnikov (Russia's Prime Minister): You know, it's like you had some kind of mask on your face. I feel a sort of constant discontent, a sort of alienation. He wasn't like this when he worked in Sverdlovsk. Here, he put on a mask. Not happy about anything, some kind of dissatisfaction with everybody and everything.

Victor Chebrikov (KGB Chairman): You don't really like Muscovites, Boris Nikolayevich. If you loved this city, you would never allow yourself a speech like this from this podium . . . The word I want to use is *slander*. It fits your speech well . . . Imperialism is panicking, looking for ways how to prevent us from conducting perestroika, how to really prevent us from conducting perestroika, because it realizes that perestroika strengthens us, that it bolsters us from all sides. And in this difficult time, this crucial time, when we must be all as one and preserve our unity as the apple of our eye, as Vladimir Ilyich Lenin said in his testament—at this time we begin speeches that do not prove anything, we begin demagogy, we begin to indulge in slander, instead of reuniting, tackling the unresolved issues, and march on bravely toward our objective that we set at the last Party Congress.

Alexandr Yakovlev (Gorbachev's most pro-Western aide, hailed in the West as the father of glasnost and perestroika): Perhaps Boris Nikolayevich thinks that he spoke his mind here at the Plenum in a brave and principled manner. In truth I don't think his speech was either. If so, then the speech was politically erroneous and morally dissolute . . . Of course, personal factors played a part. As has been said here, it is the awe of pseudo-revolutionary phraseology, the awe of his own persona. It always dims a politician's view. But the most important thing is that he did not understand—I repeat—what takes place around him. That, I think, is the most important thing. And without that, it's very hard to

work. He thinks it's revolutionary, but in fact that is profoundly conservative. Ultimately, what we heard here, to my greatest regret, was the most
direct statement of surrender in the face of difficulties that a man encounters, the most open expression of what happens when a man decides to
set his ambition, his personal character, and private follies above Party
and social matters.

EDUARD SHEVARDNADZE (Minister of Foreign Affairs. Three years
later he would leave his post. Six months after that he would leave
the Communist Party and organize an anti-Communist one): . . . I would
not dramatize Comrade Yeltsin's speech, but I would not simplify it
either . . . Various terms have been used here—for example, conservatism.
I would add: primitivism. But most of all—it is, perhaps, the most
focused assessment—irresponsibility. Irresponsibility in the face of the
Party, the people, the friends and colleagues in the Politburo . . . I didn't
want to use this word—perhaps my speech is too big on emotion—but in
a sense this is the betrayal of the Party. Perhaps I've put it too strongly,
but I can't say it differently.

ANDREI GROMYKO (who loyally served six Kremlin leaders from Stalin
on—and changed his political credo correspondingly): . . . he has his own
incorrect views . . . Therefore I think that the Central Committee will act
correctly if in connection with Comrade Yeltsin's speech it will resist all
the attempts to sway us, to cast shadows on the course of our perestroika,
to shake the confidence of the Party and the people in our success.

MIKHAIL SOLOMENTSEV (Chairman of the Party Controlling Committee): This is what I think: Maybe you decided that at the Central Committee Plenum there will be people who will support you, who will follow
you, and agree with your conclusions? But now you see the maturity
displayed by the Plenum participants: no one supported you. And I'm
sure no one will. Your hope for support was in vain. Your speeches—not
the one here, of course—but the ones you make for newspapers, your
interviews—they get coverage. But not in *our* newspapers, though I don't
read all the regional papers . . . Your coverage, unfortunately, comes
from the West. We learn about it on the radio. It goes through a different
kind of media. Why do your speeches attract them so much? They attract
because they are against our general line. Which is what the enemy needs.

The other day, at the session of the Supreme Soviet, there was a remark
about the interview you gave, when you gave the number of prisoners in
our country. Where did you get these numbers? Why do you think you
can play with these numbers, that you can provide, so to speak, fodder
for reporters, and carry it all over the world? Who needs this? Do our
people—our Party—need it? No, this is needed by our ill-wishers, by our
enemies. You can't do things like that. This is what they call a stab in the
back, or a rabbit punch. When they had fistfights, even then you could

not use a rabbit punch. And this is no fistfight; this is politics. And what politics! My impression is that Comrade Yeltsin has a kind of anger that kept snowballing all the time . . . Comrade Yeltsin keeps to himself, distances himself from the collective. Why? Who hurt your feelings, old man? Why should you, as we say, put at somebody; why make a face? Why? For what reason?

YELTSIN: It's a tough lesson today for me, of course—all my life, since childhood, and as a Party member, too, including my jobs in the positions where I was trusted by the Central Committee, Party Committees—

GORBACHEV: Boris Nikolayevich . . .

YELTSIN: Yes.

GORBACHEV: Are you so politically illiterate that we must teach you the ABCs of politics today?

YELTSIN: No, there's no need anymore.

GORBACHEV: And after all this you accuse the Politburo of ignoring the past? Isn't this what you said in your speech today?

YELTSIN: By the way, about the speech—as I—

GORBACHEV: It's not "by the way." We had to delay the discussion of the main presentation because of your escapade.

YELTSIN: No, I mentioned the presentation first—

VOICES: He thought only of himself.

Of his unsatisfied ambitions.

GORBACHEV: I agree. And that's how the Central Committee members see it. Aren't you satisfied that the entire city of Moscow revolves around your persona? You need the Central Committee to take care of you, too? To coddle you? It's amazing how one could develop such an oversized ego, such conceit to set one's ambition above Party interests—above our cause! Especially now, when we're in such an important stage of perestroika! You had to inflict this discussion on the Central Committee! I consider your actions irresponsible. The comrades correctly assessed your escapade. Tell me, in principle, how do you feel about criticism?

YELTSIN: I told you how I feel about it politically.

GORBACHEV: Tell me how you feel about the remarks of your comrades from the Central Committee. They said a lot about you, and they must know what you think. It is up to them to make a decision.

YELTSIN: With some objections, in general I agree with their assessment. That I failed the Central Committee and the Moscow Party organization with my speech today. It was a mistake.

GORBACHEV: Do you have enough strength to carry on with your job?

VOICES: He can't!

We can't leave him in such a job.

GORBACHEV: Wait, wait, I asked him a question—

YELTSIN: I can only repeat what I said: I request to be released from the candidate membership in the Politburo, and, correspondingly, from leading the Moscow Party organization.

GORBACHEV: Personally, I see it as lack of respect toward the General Secretary . . . For the two and a half years that Comrade Yeltsin assessed so negatively we have followed a correct course. And the main plus of this two-year period is that the Party has a well-planned policy that by now is well tested in many regards. And reality proves it. Comrade Yeltsin may not like it, but we have not spent these two years in vain. We have not! Look what he's saying! I already received the transcript. Here's what he said: in these two years the people did not get anything in real terms . . . By the way, this is Comrade Yeltsin's style, and we've had some personal talks about it—not just at Politburo meetings. So it's not the first attempt, now on the Central Committee level, to impose his assessment on the crucial issues of our policy. And from a negative position, too; mostly a leftist one. He must have wanted to provoke a fight among us, so that we made a mess like, for example, the one that Comrade Khrushchev made, and split society apart instead of uniting on the basis of perestroika . . . And now, Comrade Yeltsin, you got what you deserved. The Plenum participants have made a politically correct assessment of your position.

Of twenty-seven speakers at a Party Plenum that may well be called historical, only Georgi Arbatov, director of the US-Canada Research Institute, dared mumble something in Yeltsin's defense, and in return was immediately cursed by the next speaker. Two weeks later, on the seventieth anniversary of the Bolshevik Revolution, in keeping with Party protocol, Yeltsin—at bay but not yet cast out of the Communist Eden—climbed atop the Lenin Mausoleum, ignored by his Politburo comrades: his scandalous speech had, after all, almost messed up the celebration.

Of those on the podium, only two people, both foreigners, supported him in that difficult moment. One was Fidel Castro, who hugged Yeltsin three times and said to him something in Spanish; Yeltsin did not make out what it was, but the friendly sentiment was hard to mistake. The other one was Polish general Wojciech Jaruzelski, whose role of the Savior of the Motherland has been steadily replacing his reputation of a dictator. He also gave Yeltsin a triple hug and said to him in the flawless Russian that he had learned in Siberian exile: "Hang in there, Boris!" All of this in front of Gorbachev & Co.

However, at the next Party tribunal, when Yeltsin was being removed from the job of Moscow Party leader, he had not one brave supporter.

In his autobiography Yeltsin describes how, two days after the Red Square celebration, he was hospitalized with a heart attack and nervous exhaustion. Rumors of his death spread all over Moscow. He was alive,. however, though very ill. He stayed in intensive care, as doctors kept him alive on IV support and injections. The patient's condition was so serious, they said, that any excitement would be dangerous. Then, two days after he was admitted, the phone rang in his ward. It was the *Kremlyovka,* the special line linking the Kremlin elite.

The call was from Gorbachev. "Boris Nikolayevich, could you come by my office for a while?" His tone was unruffled, as though he were calling Yeltsin at the dacha. "Maybe we'll hold a Plenum of the Moscow Party Committee, too."

"I can't," Yeltsin told him. "The doctors won't even let me get up."

"That's okay," Gorbachev said jauntily. "The doctors will help you."

Still subordinate to Party discipline, Yeltsin began to pack. The doctors, who had just forbidden him to get up, obeyed the will of the Kremlin and pumped him full of tranquilizers. His head was swimming; his knees buckled; his speech was slurred. His wife, Naina Iosifovna, demanded that they leave him alone. This quiet woman, a nervous wreck because of her husband's persecution and illness, now lashed out at KGB Colonel Yuri Plekhanov, the head of Section Nine, personally responsible for delivering her husband to Gorbachev.

"This is sadism," Naina said to the doctors and Plekhanov. "How dare you disturb him? Your job is to take care of him, and now you're killing him with your cowardice!"

"I think they would have dragged me out of the grave to the Plenum if they were so ordered," Yeltsin joked later.

He was sore at the boss, not at the subordinates:

"I'll never understand it," he said later. "Through all my years of work, I can't remember one case—whether it was a worker or a manager—in which someone was dragged out of the hospital to be fired from his job. That's impossible . . . However poorly Gorbachev treated me, this was an inhuman, immoral deed . . . I just didn't expect it of him. What was he afraid of? Why was he in such a rush? Did he think I would change my mind? Or did he think he would have an easy time handling me in this condition? Did he plan to finish me off physically? I can't comprehend this cruelty."

The show went on: same script, new cast. The old actors—the Kremlin elite, headed by Gorbachev—installed themselves in the Presidium, vigilantly watching the audience.

Pseudo-decisiveness and pseudo-revolutionary spirit, exaggeratedly excited perception, grand ambition, rigidity, demagogy, political immaturity, Big Boss syndrome, political adventurism, pretension to infallibility, intolerance, impatience, mistrust of colleagues, wrathful speech, personal ostentation, self-contradiction, lack of ethics, high treason—Yeltsin's ex-colleagues sweated to outdo one another in the severity of their charges. In its inspiration and viciousness, this chorus, twenty-four strong, exceeded its Kremlin predecessor. The conductor, though, remained the same: Gorbachev made both the introductory speech and the concluding one. Pumped full of drugs, Yeltsin comprehended little of what was going on, but he sensed that the wolves, sicced on by their leader, were ready to tear him apart.

The Party-meeting routine also required that the victim repent. According to the witnesses, he was hard to recognize; he impressed them as being mentally disabled—a different person altogether. His face was swollen, his voice was hoarse, he paused often to catch his breath. He spoke absentmindedly, losing his train of thought, breaking off in the middle of a phrase and starting another one. His mumbling incoherence was in keeping with the ideological and aesthetic context of Absurdist drama: ". . . my deed was simply unpredictable . . . I give you my honest Party word that I surely harbored no designs, and my speech had no political agenda . . . One of my main qualities came into play—my ambition, of which they spoke today. I tried to fight it, but, unfortunately, in vain . . . As a Communist, I lost my leadership image . . . I'm very guilty regarding Mikhail Sergeyevich Gorbachev personally, whose authority is so high in the Moscow organization, in our country, and in the whole world."

This is not from Orwell's *1984;* it is from Gorbachev's *1987.*

IT IS time to turn back from the consequences to the original act. (We have actually followed the course of events: both Yeltsin's fellow citizens and Western observers had to wait for *a year and a half* for the publication of Yeltsin's speech, for which he had been subjected to Party ostracism, public persecution and insults, and, finally, removal from the two high positions he had occupied—Candidate Member of the Politburo and the leader of the Moscow Communists.)

Wait a minute! Didn't he himself ask to be relieved from both jobs? Isn't this where it all started: Yeltsin wanted to quit, but they would not let him, and cast him out in shame? Reliable confirmation arrived on the evening of October 31, ten days after the Central Committee Plenum, when the Teletypes at the Moscow papers ran an item from TASS that Yeltsin had himself offered to resign at the Plenum in protest against the slowdown of perestroika. Yet nineteen minutes later the Teletypes were busily tapping out another TASS release, which "categorically" recommended against printing the previous one.

The unwritten but still binding Kremlin code did not provide voluntary descent from the breathtaking political heights of the Politburo. It was as though such a descent would cast doubt on the absolute status of membership in the Kremlin oligarchy—and, by extension, on the oligarchy itself. It was as if a god voluntarily left Mount Olympus in favor of life on Earth. Yeltsin's act was an unprecedented, brazen breach of the Byzantine ceremonial code that for many centuries has been a substitute for political life in Russia. That is why TASS would not print its own release on Yeltsin's request to resign; that is why the Politburo, headed by Gorbachev, decided to reshuffle the incident and alter the reason for Yeltsin's fall—not voluntary resignation, but Party punishment.

Punishment presupposes a crime; yet the crime had never been made public, and Moscow hummed with rumors, each more bizarre than the other—up to Gorbachev's suspecting Raisa of being attracted to Yeltsin and acting out of jealousy. Gorbachev's jealousy was in fact impersonal, though no less painful: he was jealous of Yeltsin's popularity, and the entire subsequent history of the enmity between the two Russian leaders is in a sense a male rivalry that both of them carefully cloaked in ideological euphemisms.

In the winter of 1989, Yeltsin would return to politics, to run for a seat in the Soviet Parliament. Rather than running in his hometown, where his victory was guaranteed, he chose Moscow, where his enemies would stoop to anything to discredit and destroy him. Yet it was important for Yeltsin to win the city back from his chief rival. Besides, combat was his element, resistance stimulated him, and he had always gotten everything and everywhere by himself—why settle for a walkover when you can mix it up? Yeltsin had enough reasons to be nominated in Moscow rather than in Sverdlovsk; it was important to win a rematch where he had lost—in the capital.

For a moment, though, let us return to rumor-filled Moscow in the fall of 1987. Since the Kremlin refused the demands that Yeltsin's speech be published, different versions of the speech began to circulate in print around the world—from Moscow Samizdat to émigré papers, from *Le Monde* and *Die Zeit* to London's *Observer* and *U.S. News & World Report*. In many versions, Raisa Gorbachev played a prominent part, though in a more, shall we say, believable context than the sexual-jealousy tales.

A Samizdat version of Yeltsin's speech accused the Kremlin's First Lady of (a) being paid for a sinecure as Deputy Chairman of the Cultural Fund—to the tune of 780 rubles a month, four times the average Soviet salary, (b) stepping aboard a Navy ship in Murmansk that she visited with her husband and posing for photo reporters among the sailors—a flagrant violation of a Russian naval tradition according to which women are not allowed aboard a military ship. A few months later *Le Monde* would publish another version of the heretical speech featuring Madam Gorbachev in a different context: ". . . I must ask the Politburo to protect me from the petty harassment of Raisa Maksimovna, from her almost daily phone calls and lectures."

Whether Yeltsin mentioned Gorbachev's wife in his speech or not, rumors of her haranguing him fell on receptive ears. She was widely resented from the moment she first appeared in Gorbachev's inner circle. An adviser half-jocularly suggested that Gorbachev's popularity would rise if he got a divorce. We heard this remark much later, in the spring of 1990, on our first visit in Moscow after the thirteen years' absence. Most of the street talk we wrote down was far nastier:

"She plays him [Gorbachev] like a fiddle. Him, he's got no spine—just enough to fight Yeltsin."

"He's taking his monkey everywhere. 'Ah, Roman ruins!' She should see the ones in Moscow . . ."

Was it Raisa's personality? Or the general attitude toward women in Russia, where, according to the old saw, "a chicken is no bird and a woman is no person"? Or was she a scapegoat for her husband's sins?

Gorbachev came in for his share of barbed wit as well, in an invented version of Yeltsin's speech that made the rounds in Moscow. The Gorbachev cult, which had been created by his comrades, drew special fire. Other high officials flayed in this manner were Foreign Minister Shevardnadze, who spent too much time flying around the world instead of bringing the boys home from Afghanistan; KGB Chairman Chebrikov, for increasing corruption; and, of course, Yeltsin's presumed number one enemy, Yegor Ligachev, for his Stalinist administrative methods. All the versions dealt with the privileges of the nomenklatura:

> Comrades, I find it hard to explain this to a worker—why in the seventieth year of the dictatorship of the proletariat does he still have to stand in line for sausage that has more starch than meat in it? Why do our tables here groan with sturgeon and caviar and other delicacies that we get without difficulty in places from which the same worker is barred? How do I explain this to veterans of the Great Patriotic War, or ones of the Civil War—how many are left, anyway? Have you seen what they can get with the so-called "holiday order"? I saw it; they delivered me one. How do I react when I hear people call it "crumbs from the masters' table"? You know whose table they're talking about? How can I look them in the eye? They risked their lives to win power and hand it to us. Could Comrade Ligachev advise me? I think, comrades, that all these "troughs," as people call them, are leftovers from the era of stagnation, through which all of us have lived. It is time we put an end to this practice.

Yeltsin did not say anything of the kind in his speech. But these publications—first Samizdat, then in the Western media—were not forgeries in the accepted sense of the word. They were samples of popular political writing. Without access to the actual text of the speech, people composed their own, inserting the longstanding complaints in an imitation of Yeltsin's style. They were creating, not a speech for their hero, but the hero proper. Yeltsin could do nothing to confirm or correct the myth of himself in the making, for he was gone—slandered, vilified, and spat upon; banished along with his speech. It would take him another year to resurface from political oblivion with the aid of the provincial media. By then the legend was complete, replacing the real Boris Yeltsin. "Each period has its greats," Helvetius wrote. "If there are none, it invents them." An invented, idealized, larger-than-life Yeltsin assumed a life of its own; a people's defender and a desperado. Later the real Yeltsin had no choice but to conform to this folk myth.

It was not as though the myth and the real Yeltsin had nothing in common; they did—quite a bit. No other member of the Kremlin elite qualified for mythmaking. Fair or not, the Yeltsin myth was being created on an ascending curve, while the popular image of Gorbachev was sinking. The real Yeltsin, back in politics, had to catch up with his own legend. Something happened to him in the meantime. When he read the transcript of his speech, published in the spring of 1989 for the first time, he was shocked: he had thought it sharper and more provocative.

The editors of *The Central Committee News,* which published the transcript, may have done some polishing, omitting personal attacks and softening some of the phrasing. Or Soviet society may have made gigantic democratic strides since, extending the limits of the permissible. Or perhaps the imaginative versions of the heretical speech, having beaten the official publication by a year and a half, had, in the minds of the Russian people, supplanted the original. The force of the original had faded and no longer satisfied even the author, who now, like everyone else, preferred the myth. Paradoxically, the invented texts turned out to be more true to the essence of Yeltsin's Kremlin revolt than the original.

In any event, while Yeltsin was in exile, condemned to silence, rumors created a myth that was bound to take concrete form when, heeding the popular call, he returned to politics to catch up with his fame. In his subsequent speeches and interviews he dealt with the topics attributed to him by his anonymous "coauthors"—from the "masters' table" to Raisa's political vanity. He had to play the political role that *demos* had written for him. Gorbachev and his Kremlin pals, by suppressing the speech, encouraged the making of the Yeltsin myth—a live person became a nationwide symbol of—rebellion? Despair? Hope?

Here are substantial excerpts from the speech that ended Boris Yeltsin's Communist Party career and turned a new leaf in Russian history:

> . . . I think that what was said at the congress regarding the progress of perestroika in the last two to three years—two years—almost—have passed, and

now we're talking about another two to three years—all of this befuddles the people and the Party. We know our people, and we sense that they perceive perestroika in waves. It started with high enthusiasm—it soared. This enthusiasm stayed in high gear, including the January Plenum of the Central Committee. Then, after the June Plenum, somehow people started losing faith. This concerns us a great deal. Of course, two years were wasted on developing all the documents that never reached the people, and they are worried that they never got anything to show for this time.

This is why I believe that perhaps we should be more careful when we announce the time frame and the actual results of perestroika in the next two years. They will be very, very hard, and we realize it. Even if we need to revolutionize radically—and we do—the activity of the Party—yes, the Party—and its committees, well, it will take longer than that. After two years we run the risk of finding ourselves, shall we say, with the Party's reputation lowered considerably.

I must say that the constant appeal to adopt fewer resolutions, when in reality more documents are being adopted—locally these resolutions begin to be treated superficially; there's less faith in them. Paper keeps mounting. We issue appeals to close down idling research institutes. In Moscow, I'd like to point out as an example, there were 1041 institutes a year ago. After a great deal of effort, of working with State Committees, we closed down seven—but the total rose to 1087 because in the interim new ones were created. Of course this runs against the Party line, the Congress resolutions, and the appeals that we keep making.

Another question. It's a hard one, but this is a Plenum. The Central Committee members are the most reliable, confidence-inspiring group of people, and I can and must say—also, I'm speaking as a Communist—everything that I have carried around for a long time.

I must say that in the last seventy years we have learned some hard lessons. We have had victories, which Mikhail Sergeyevich has noted, but we also had to draw lessons from bad, heavy defeats. These defeats formed gradually; they happened because we had no collegiality, because we had different groups, because the Party's power was concentrated in one hand, and because he—this man—was isolated from all criticism.

Something else concerns me. It's still not too bad here in the Politburo, yet one thing has grown—what I'd call paeans that some Politburo members—permanent members—sing to the General Secretary. I don't think it is permissible now. Exactly now, when we are developing more democratic forms of communication—forms based on principles—and of comradely relationships with one another. To criticize face to face, eye to eye—yes, we need that. But to fall for this constant praise, these kudos—that may become a norm again, and we can't allow that. We just can't.

I realize that, unlike in the old days, it does not lead to far-reaching, impermissible violations, but we have the first signs of such attitude, and I think they should be nipped in the bud.

And the last thing I want to say.

[pause]

I don't think I'm doing too well in my Politburo job. For various reasons. Could be my inexperience, could be other things. Could be a lack of support from certain parties, especially, I would stress, from Comrade Ligachev—all this has led me to decide to ask you to relieve me from the duties of Candidate Member of the Politburo. I have already submitted an official request in writing; as for my duties of the First Secretary of the Moscow City Committee—well, it is for the Plenum of the City Committee to decide.

This is the speech that caused such a furor among Communist believers and led them to close their ranks and launch a deadly assault on Yeltsin.

What rankled them most of all?

A negative assessment of perestroika? But it contained so much hedging and half-concealed praise that it could be ignored. In any event, by the Kremlin code, it was not worth a scandal.

Could they have been offended by a personal attack on Ligachev—one Siberian attacking another? But Ligachev was no Gorbachev. Even if, as Western Kremlin-watchers believed, he was number two in the Party, number two is closer to the rest than to number one. Gorbachev had thrown comrades to 'the wolves in the past, and was unlikely to rush into battle for Ligachev, who was politically over the hill and headed for a fall.

It was this explanation—conceding to conservative pressure, Gorbachev had to sacrifice one of the most ardent champions of reform—that acquired currency among Western Kremlinologists and reporters. Paradoxically, the world's sympathy shifted from Yeltsin to Gorbachev. Boston Sovietologist Marshall Goldman's article in *The New York Times* was entitled, "After Yeltsin, Gorbachev?" The accompanying drawing showed a man sawing off the branch he was sitting on.

"Mr. Yeltsin was mercurial, unsophisticated, and not terribly subtle," Goldman wrote. "Yet his policies and actions were precisely those that Mr. Gorbachev was seeking to stimulate in others. In other words, he was Mr. Gorbachev's point man.

"That is why it is disturbing that pressure from conservatives and nomenklatura was such that Mr. Gorbachev found it necessary to sacrifice one of his most outspoken supporters. If Mr. Gorbachev holds to his reforms, it is hard to see how he can escape a similar fate."

Time has shown that not only has Gorbachev easily avoided Yeltsin's lot, but—more important—he has never been at risk, though the West reacted to anything happening in the Kremlin with profound concern for his political career. We are interested less in Goldman's error per se than in the source of this legend—that the sacrifice of Yeltsin was inevitable, and even, according to *The Chicago Tribune,* justified, in order to save Gorbachev's reform.

A week before Goldman's piece, *The New York Times* ran an item by its Moscow correspondent, quoting the reactions of liberal-minded Moscow writers to Yeltsin's fall. One of these remarks—"Today Yeltsin, tomorrow Gorbachev"—sounds like a direct inspiration for Goldman's piece. Another writer went even further by saying, "Let us hope that this was only a temporary defeat, one caused more by the erratic personal behavior of Yeltsin than a change of heart by Gorbachev."

We have seen the ease with which the so-called liberal players on Gorbachev's team—Shevardnadze and Yakovlev, for instance—washed their hands of Yeltsin. At a press conference a few days after the October Plenum, Yakovlev did not bat an eye at discounting the rumor that Yeltsin had voiced discontent with the Gorbachev cult of personality in the making and the snail-like pace of perestroika as "pure fantasy." Gavriil Popov, later Yeltsin's ally and successor as the Moscow Boss (the real power has shifted to the Mayor's office), at the time a progressive professor of economics at Moscow University, accused Yeltsin of "authoritarian conservative vanguardism" and likened him to Leon Trotsky—in the context of Soviet history, a politically charged label.

A year and a half later, at a meeting at Columbia University, Yeltsin would say, "The only thing I share with Trotsky is that both of us criticized the General Secretary—he was the first one to do so in 1927, and I took the risk to do it sixty years later."

Yeltsin was also likened to Robespierre, Napoleon, and Mussolini. The Moscow intelligentsia was running out of labels: "Jacobin," "sans-culotte," "populist," "windbag," "power-hungry extremist," "neo-Bolshevik," "Trotskyite."

The making of Yeltsin's image in the West was not exactly dictated, but was undoubtedly influenced by the Moscow intelligentsia, who have better access to Moscow-based foreign correspondents than any other group, and are the main sources of quotes. We know this from experience. When we formed our press agency in 1977, Western reporters poured into our tiny apartment on Red Army Street and raced one another to transmit our releases. Unsurprisingly, Gorbachev's glasnost made it safe for the intelligentsia to deal with the media, and the links between the two thus became stronger. The intelligentsia acquired a worldwide audience; its opinions, addressed to the West, bounced back to Russia in Russian-language broadcasts by the Voice of America, the BBC, Radio Liberty, and the Deutsche Welle. "The people," to quote Pushkin again, "were silent." The Yeltsin affair ended this; now people spoke out. Then the intelligentsia, in its attempt to silence the popular support of Yeltsin, stepped in where the Party had failed.

Why did the intellectuals join the Party chorus? Even Academician

Sakharov, their honor and conscience, gave Yeltsin a kick or two. How could this curious division of forces—Yeltsin and the people on one side, and the Party and the intellectuals on the other—come to pass?

It is much easier to understand the quarrel between Yeltsin and the Party elite. He initiated the breakup: He rebelled when he realized that the talk of democracy had deteriorated into idle chatter, that democracy was impossible above all within the Politburo, where everything was decided behind closed doors by a few men who had usurped power. For no one had authorized them to make decisions: not the people, not the Party, not even its Central Committee. Yeltsin challenged the Politburo when he realized that the country's highest ruling organ still remained a tightly knit mafia—that nothing had changed. According to their corporate code, they had to close ranks against a traitor and, casting decency aside, resort to Stalinist techniques to nail Yeltsin to the cross.

The intellectuals' position in this conflict was more complicated. They were the main beneficiaries of glasnost and perestroika; as such, they closely allied themselves with the powers-that-be, taking an unequivocally pro-Gorbachev stance not only against the conservatives but against Yeltsin-type radicals as well. They had benefited from Gorbachev's reforms, from freedom of expression to regular trips abroad (so regular that many literary lions of perestroika were spending more time abroad than at home). Gradually, the perestroika intelligentsia became a nomenklatura in its own right and assumed a defensive stance against any further changes that could endanger its special status and privileges and bring it down to the hoi-polloi level. This was exacerbated by mutual alienation between the people and the intelligentsia: now the people saw it as the nomenklatura's ally, rather than the leader in the struggle against it. And the intelligentsia felt the first rumblings of fear of the irritated, hard-to-control masses. The intelligentsia's refusal to accept Boris Yeltsin was born out of its parochial guild interests and cloaked in ideology: "dictatorial behavior," "demagogy," "populism," "flirting with Pamyat anti-Semites." Yeltsin seemed unaware of the complex reasons for his falling-out with the intelligentsia. Perhaps he simply did not want to endanger his relationship with this influential part of society. He merely acknowledged the existence of bad feelings: "My relations with the intelligentsia followed a rocky road. Someone spread a myth—somehow they tied it in with my personality—that I'm a leader of the Stalinist type, which is a bold lie, if only because with all my guts, with all my being, I'm against what happened in those years. When they took away my father one night—I was six then and I remember it well."

It is a simplification to reduce the conflict between Yeltsin and the intelligentsia to the latter's fear of losing their perks should Yeltsin triumph in his crusade against the privileges of the Party establishment. This fear was unfounded, as Yeltsin has stated his position clearly: "I am for the material support of culture, especially its noncommercial aspects, its administrative bodies, and their staff"; more specifically, "securing living space and normal living conditions for cultural workers, especially creative workers in the arts and sciences."

This, of course, needs to be done in moderation; as Charles the Ninth put it, horses and poets should be fed but not sated.

How Yeltsin will deal with the intelligentsia has yet to be seen, but opposing him used to be the only common ground for Russian nationalists and pro-Westerners. In the case of the latter, one must take into account a certain amount of snobbery and arrogance typical of the Moscow intelligentsia, despite the past persecutions or perhaps because of them. They even felt closer to a Moscow *apparatchik* like Gorbachev, who curried favor with them, than to a rustic like Yeltsin, who cared for people's welfare.

Hertzen noted how far the intellectuals were removed from the people. Several decades later, Chekhov—who, like Hertzen, was an intellectual from head to toe—wrote, "I do not believe our intelligentsia—hypocritical, hysterical, false, ill-bred, and lazy; I don't believe them even when they suffer and complain, since the intelligentsia's worst oppressors come from its own ranks."

Pre-Revolutionary publicist and cultural critic Mikhail Hershensohn wrote a phrase for which he was roundly damned by his colleagues: "The way we are, not only should we not dream about merging with the people—we should fear the people far more than the worst oppression of the authorities, and we should bless the same authorities whose bayonets and jails protect us from the popular fury."

It is understandable that after the Revolution, during seven decades of being alternately cosseted and bludgeoned, most Soviet intellectuals learned to finesse the art of physical and social survival, of dodging the stick and grabbing the carrot. In so doing, they have often turned their backs on ideals and social progress, and become parochial and meretricious. The Yeltsin affair was a "reality check" for whatever bonds existed between the masses and the thinkers, a bond that was not exactly false but was exhausted by the two years of glasnost and perestroika. The intelligentsia stood by Gorbachev while the people followed—or, more precisely, led—Yeltsin. The Party's diatribes were not enough to banish Yeltsin; the curses of the intelligentsia were needed to bring his political career to an end—forever, it seemed. The intelligentsia and Yeltsin parted ways on the basis of their principles. The intelligentsia's monopoly on access to Western media contributed to Yeltsin's unfavorable image in Europe and America, which was still more fair and balanced than they would have liked it to be.

Because of their highly developed instinct for self-preservation, the intellectuals quickly grasped the real cause of the Kremlin scandal. They saw that Yeltsin's quarrel was not with Ligachev and other conservatives but with Gorbachev himself. So they launched a campaign against the man who had cast doubt on the results of Gorbachev's perestroika and who drew a direct parallel between paeans to Gorbachev and Stalin's cult of personality. Yeltsin knew what he was doing; by drawing fire, he violated the Kremlin's principal axiom: the General Secretary is above criticism. Kremlinologists were wrong: the threat to Gorbachev's autocratic power had come from the reformist wing rather than from the conservative one.

Gorbachev purged the Kremlin of retrogrades and gerontocrats quickly, easily, and painlessly, thus accelerating a natural change of Kremlin generations. This was the third such change in Soviet history. The first took place when Stalin murdered Lenin's Old Bolshevik guard; the second, when Khrushchev removed the most fossilized Stalinists. Unfortunately for him he did not finish the job, and the remaining ones brought him down. The third purge was begun by Yuri Andropov, cut short by his death, and finished by Gorbachev, his protégé and a fellow Stavropolian, following a brief interlude with Chernenko, the briefest and most ephemeral of all reigns.

And then, with all the old codgers swept out, the Politburo seemingly staffed with allies for the first time in the Party's years at the helm, an uprising occurred in its innermost sanctum! Only two and a half years earlier, Gorbachev and Ligachev summoned Yeltsin from the Urals to make him a section chief, then a Central Committee Secretary, and finally the leader of the Moscow Communists. And now, instead of gratitude, rebellion! In his two years as General Secretary, Gorbachev had lost the knack of dealing with criticism, so he had good reason to be aghast.

Paradoxically, Gorbachev's struggle against the conservatives ended with the ouster of a reformer.

In his story "How the Two Ivans Quarreled," Gogol wrote: "For a long time I simply would not believe it. Ivan Ivanovich has quarreled with Ivan Nikiforovich! Such worthy men! After that, is there anything solid left in this world?"

It was not the first time that the fate of Russia was decided in a duel between two political opponents: Stalin and Trotsky come to mind, and, like Gorbachev and Yeltsin, they were the same age. In the autumn of 1987, Yeltsin's fall, like that of the stone that looses an avalanche, led to the chain reaction of cataclysms within Soviet society, its ideological split and political fragmentation, thus creating the basis for a transition to a multiparty system.

The Kremlin's public attacks on its critics had backfired before, creating heroes such as Pasternak, Solzhenitsyn, and Sakharov. And the longer and more doggedly the Kremlin fought Yeltsin, the more it reinforced his image as a victim and a hero. The voluntary participation of the intelligentsia in the anti-Yeltsin campaign was something new—in Pasternak's case they had helped but only because they were forced to. The meetings of "perestroika's executives" with formerly sympathetic audiences now ended in bitter arguments and further alienation. At one such meeting Vitaly Korotich, editor in chief of the leading progressive weekly *Ogonyok,* infuriated the audience by shunning direct answers to questions about Yeltsin.

Later, Yeltsin would be interviewed by an *Ogonyok* reporter. Korotich took the material to the Central Committee, which banned publication. Word of the incident quickly spread across Moscow, and Korotich was asked why he had failed to publish the interview. He could simply have told the truth. Instead he went into vague explanations, claiming that the interview was of no interest. Yeltsin had been evasive, Korotich claimed, and the readers would have been bored.

Yeltsin was less angry with the Kremlin's ban than with Korotich's explanation: ". . . the editor chose to assume the responsibility and cover up for the Central Committee. Why? Did he not realize that it's immoral to deny the right to speak to a person who thinks differently—even if the difference is from the General Secretary's thinking? No. He hemmed and hawed instead of telling the people what really happened. If he was so afraid, he could have kept silent. It would have been more honest."

Yeltsin had some allies in the artistic milieu. At the Sovremennik-2 theater, during a show called *Hercules' Seventh Deed,* an actress suddenly abandoned her lines to accuse the audience of indifference toward the New Hercules, banished for trying to clean up the Augean stables of Moscow. Police and KGB agents dispersed pro-Yeltsin rallies, including the one at Moscow University's law school, Gorbachev's alma mater. A wave of riots swept over Sverdlovsk, whose citizens stood up to defend their persecuted son. Signs in post offices warned that communications addressed to Yeltsin would no longer be delivered. Yet flyers and posters appeared on the walls all over the city. For example:

Citizens! The resignation of one of the most loyal partisans of glasnost and democratization will clear the way for Party bureaucracy and saboteurs of perestroika and increase political and ideological oppression of progressive forces.

Citizens! The country is at a watershed—our silence will play into the hands of enemies of perestroika!

Citizens! Yeltsin is from Sverdlovsk—one of our own! Send the Government collective protests against his resignation!

Support and reinforce the democratization of the country.

Protest!

The Kremlin was not afraid of the people's reaction; it still considered them firmly under its thumb. But commentaries on the Yeltsin affair that appeared in the West were another story. Allusions and analogies varied but ran along the same lines, from the Moscow trials of Zinovyev, Kamenev, and Bukharin to the anti-Khruchschev conspiracy in the fall of 1964. Some recalled Hitler's orders to execute Ernst Röhm in June 1934, and Stalin's orders, a few months later, to kill Sergei Kirov, one of his closest aides. The two tyrants were competing in treachery and terror. Someone recalled Rubashov, the Bukharin-inspired hero of Arthur Koestler's *Darkness at Noon.* Of course there was a difference: Stalin had his enemies, real or imaginary, executed; Khruchschev sent them into retirement (which was later done to him); Brezhnev preferred to name his opponents ambassadors to socialist countries, far from Moscow and the West.

A few months before his downfall, Yeltsin met with a TV team from CBS. Seated in his office in front of a row of telephones, one of which was a direct line to Gorbachev, he joked with Diane Sawyer about his attitude toward criticism: "To say I love criticism like I love a woman would be nonsense."

But, he said, he was squarely putting his faith in the new outspokenness as a measure of progress: "For me to express myself this way in the Brezhnev era, I could have been fired," he declared with a smile. "I would have lost my job."

Yeltsin thought a new era had arrived; it had indeed, but it was not enough to poke fun at the old one. Yeltsin himself had caused a temporary return to the old days by his new-style rebellion. Gorbachev did not have him executed, or put out to pasture, or named to a distant ambassadorial post. By leaving Yeltsin in Moscow, Gorbachev turned his foe into a folk hero, a symbol of the latent opposition. At the October Plenum, Yeltsin acted as the Cassandra of perestroika; the role that followed would be that of Gorbachev's Nemesis.

Western reaction to Yeltsin's persecution startled the Kremlin. Despite the fact that the speeches of his accusers stylistically and sometimes literally resembled those of the trials of old, his enemies failed to notice the resemblance. In general, the Kremlin was never conscious of its actions until they were reflected in the mirror of world opinion. In this case the reflection was ugly, and the Kremlin immediately set out to stem the damage.

"No one asked for his blood," said Georgi Arbatov, the Kremlin's spokesman for delicate situations. "We're still learning democracy, the culture of political discussion. Unfortunately we are often creatures of our old habits."

Another Central Committee member echoed Arbatov: "We're still learning democracy. Unfortunately, we haven't made the grade yet."

Gennady Gerasimov, a Soviet Foreign Affairs official, spilled the beans—perhaps on purpose: "You remember the monologue of Brutus on why he killed Caesar—because he was ambitious." Presumably, only the General Secretary is allowed to have ambition.

Gerasimov, however, laughed off a suggestion that his allusion to the assassination of Julius Caesar proved a group conspiracy. Was he afraid that a literary/historical metaphor would take him too far?

In another spin-control measure, the Kremlin quickly named Yeltsin First Deputy Chairman of the State Committee for Construction (Gosstroi), a politics-free job with the rank of minister. In a satirical hit song, a Yeltsin character sang, "A proud mason, I'm leaving for Gosstroi." To Soviet audiences, the reference to a *Free*mason was obvious.

To tell Yeltsin the news, Gorbachev phoned him at the hospital to which Yeltsin had returned after trial number two. It was a sign of benevolence: Gorbachev could have packed him off to retirement or an ambassadorship in Africa. Yeltsin agreed immediately. At the end, Gorbachev warned him: "I'll never let you back into politics!"

This was no surprise. There were no comebacks after being kicked out of the Politburo. As Gromyko, that old Kremlin fox, once said, "Our Politburo is like the Bermuda Triangle: once you're out of it, you disappear."

It is odd that Gromyko, after a lifetime of dealing with the West, never understood what the Bermuda Triangle was: people disappear *in* it, not outside. Even if this was a gaffe, the meaning of his words was clear: *There is no life after the Politburo.* And Gorbachev did all he could to drive this home to Yeltsin.

Thus, at the age of fifty-six, the Party career of Boris Yeltsin came to an end and his political career began. But Gorbachev did not take into account the transition of his country from a controlled democracy to a spontaneous one. The revolution he had started from the top was on its last legs; the revolution from the bottom was under way, and it picked a different leader, though the leader himself was still unaware of it.

Gorbachev had beaten Yeltsin. But it was a Pyrrhic victory.

JOSEPH AT THE
BOTTOM OF THE WELL
(November 1987–March 1989)

ONCE, TALKING to close friends, Yeltsin blurted out, "I'd walk all the way back to Sverdlovsk if I could."

At no other time or in any other place did he feel as dejected as during those days in Moscow. His Party career was finished. He had been humiliated and broken psychologically, and not just by his enemies. For he had renounced himself, repented, and begged forgiveness from his tormentors. Whether they had sincerely believed this sacrifice was necessary or had merely bowed to Kremlin protocol, either way, why couldn't he have left walking tall, after having refused to confess to nonexistent errors? What was he afraid of? It is true that the Party tribunal that condemned him was formally a throwback to the old days, but attitudes had changed. Nothing Yeltsin could have said would have gotten him executed or even imprisoned. It was like the title of Nabokov's novel *Invitation to a Beheading*—a civic, political one, of course. He was free to turn down the invitation. He had been pressured, but no one would have grabbed him and dragged him to the Moscow Plenum straight from intensive care. What, then, prompted Yeltsin, a rebel of unimpeachable courage, to obey Gorbachev's command to leave his hospital bed? Party discipline? A loss of nerve? Had his resistance been undermined by illness and drugs?

Here is how Yeltsin himself explains it—an explanation that does not fully satisfy his biographers.

> I was very sick; I was bedridden. I was ordered to show up at the Plenum in an hour and a half. I don't know to this day what kind of medication the doctors injected, but, frankly, I was completely tuned out from reality . . . They admitted later that they had given me some kind of knockout shots. You understand, I just was not in a condition to refute the lies they poured on me at the Plenum. Normally, I would've fought back right away, without waiting to be given the floor at the end. But . . . physically I was not in fighting shape . . .

A few words about Yeltsin's health. Outwardly, he seemed to have few problems: a tall, muscular ex-athlete with an easy gait and the stamina of a workhorse. But his face gives him away. Sometimes it looks heavy and swollen, his eyes closing to narrow slits, as though he were hung over. It is possible that this lent credence to the rumors, spread by his enemies, that he is a victim to the classical Russian vice of drunkenness.

When you listen to him talk about his health, you are struck again and again by obvious contradictions. On the one hand he boasts a weight lifter's strength and an impeccable athletic shape; on the other, he complains of heart attacks, unbearable headaches, constant insomnia, nervous breakdowns, and even blackouts. What is the truth?

Yeltsin inherited the health of a folk-tale hero. All his grandfathers and great-grandfathers lived past ninety, while his mother, Klavdiya Vasilyevna, who still lives in Sverdlovsk, is eighty-four. But from his youth on, Yeltsin did not take good care of this heritage, and eventually wasted it away primarily through physical and emotional stress. He attacked his work with the zeal of a workaholic, sleeping but a few hours a day—to his superiors a solid asset.

All of his free time he spent exercising—again, he went overboard. As a teenager he talked his classmates into joining him on a hike to look for the source of the Yayva River. They crossed wild taiga forests and finally found the source—a hydrogen sulfide spring, at the foot of the Urals. On their way back, they got lost. They happened on a cave, walked through a long subterranean maze, and eventually found themselves in a completely unknown place. When they ran out of food, they ate nuts and berries and roasted mushrooms. They waded through a swamp; when they ran out of water, they picked wet moss, wrapped it inside a shirt, then squeezed out the shirt and drank the liquid thus crudely filtered—in effect, swamp water. By the time they finally returned to the river, all of them had typhoid. They found a flatbed boat and drifted downriver. During the ride, one by one they began losing consciousness; that included young Boris, who was now delirious. Finally they somehow moored the boat near a railroad bridge, where they were rescued at the point of death. This "hike" lasted not just a few days or weeks, but a full four months, and the whole city thought the adventurers were dead. Their survival was a miracle. Boris spent three months in the hospital recovering from typhoid. Later, he would include the episode in his memoirs.

At school he was on several athletic teams—skiing, boxing, decathlon, wrestling—but was especially fond of volleyball. He was missing his left-hand thumb and index finger, but that was vintage Yeltsin: taking on whatever activity seemed to be proscribed for him.

Yeltsin was a child when World War II broke out. Boys of his age, too young to be drafted but who wanted to fight the Nazis, ran away, were taken off trains and sent back home. Boris and his friends put together crude firearms and even built homemade cannon. Finally, they decided to steal some grenades and take them apart in order to learn their design. Boris volunteered to sneak into a former church used to store munitions. One night, Yeltsin recalls, he got through three rows of barbed wire. He cut through the window bars and safely crawled outside with two grenades. Again he was lucky: the guards had orders to fire without warning. The boys went to a woods forty miles outside the city, to disassemble the grenades. While his friends prudently stood back, Boris smashed a grenade with a hammer, unaware that one should first pull the fuse. He was the only one hurt in the explosion. He regained consciousness at the hospital. Gangrene had developed and two fingers had to be amputated. Only eleven then, this mishap became a challenge. He concentrated on volleyball and developed his own technique for returning the ball. With his wild leaps, he achieved incredible saves. Later, his passion for volleyball would almost cost him his life and would forever undermine his health. This is how he remembers it:

In college, he practiced six to eight hours a day while studying for his exams at night. He worked hard to be an A student and qualify for a higher stipend, which was still tiny. Boris could barely make ends meet, and had no money for warm clothes. He counted on his physical fitness, underestimating the fierce Ural cold.

At first he ignored a head cold; it led to tonsillitis. He ignored that, too—he was too busy practicing for the tournament and cramming for exams. Physical and nervous stress aggravated the illness and led to complications in the form of rheumatic fever, which, as they say, licks the joints but bites the heart. With his pulse beat at 150 and severe general fatigue, he landed in a hospital. Stay for four months or so, the doctors said; we just might bring your cardiac activity back to normal. A few days later, aided by friends, he tied together several bedsheets and shimmied down from the hospital's top floor. He went to stay with his parents in Berezniki, 225 miles northwest of Sverdlovsk.

This was a good chance for him to rest, to regain his health; but he always believed in fighting fire with fire. Instead of sparing his heart, he decided to train it for overload. Swaying in the wind, his heart pounding, he would make it to the gym, and even go out onto the court. He would collapse, and his friends would take him back to the bench. Getting back in the game was all that counted for him, and he achieved it, but he paid a price.

"To be honest, the risk was enormous," Yeltsin admitted later. "I could have permanently damaged my heart."

This confession is only half true. In fact, Yeltsin gradually developed a rheumatic valvular heart disease. Victims of heart disease can carry on for years without noticing it, feeling moderately well and performing their usual tasks. After his rheumatic attack, the twenty-two-year-old Yeltsin, too, felt quite healthy and was in top athletic shape: he played in the national championship games through the summer. The disease at this stage is called "compensated," and this condition can be maintained for years if one keeps to a moderate regimen and avoids exhaustion, which leads to deterioration and decompensation.

A word to the wise should suffice, yet Yeltsin would not give up his stressful, intense life-style. Although as a construction engineer he had to give up much of his volleyball obsession and other strenuous exercise, the rest of his routine—backbreaking work, sleepless nights, psychological and emotional stress—can only be described as self-destructive. Yet he would not have it any other way. "It is better to burn for ten years than to smolder for fifty," he said.

In the summer, he often visits resorts for cardiac patients, especially Kislovodsk, in the Stavropol Territory, where Gorbachev started his career. Yeltsin first went there in 1961, and the last time, quite recently, in April 1991.

In the mid-60s he abused himself particularly badly. He developed congestive heart failure and shortness of breath, his legs began swelling—the heart disease at this stage is considered decompensated. Special resorts do not do much good at this stage; direct medical intervention is needed. Yet Yeltsin, who spent those years working 'round the clock, as he admitted, initially refused to see a doctor, and his condition deteriorated.

We will never know how he would have ended up had he not been picked for Party work in Sverdlovsk in 1969. That meant automatic access to quality medical care—just one of the nomenklatura's privileges he would be crusading against two decades later. A long course of treatment in the so-called special hospitals restored his health, reversing the disease to the compensation stage, though he remained under the observation of the specially assigned doctors. Yeltsin, though rarely mentioning his disease, nevertheless blames it for actions he regrets—including his repentant speech at the Moscow Plenum.

With his heart condition, he did not expect to live to be sixty, but despite the political and psychological drama of late 1987, he managed to pass that age Rubicon. Without accounting for his fragile health, many of his assertions seem contrived and overly dramatic—for example his description of Gorbachev's call to the hospital and the subsequent summons to his trial.

The call to the hospital does not speak well of Gorbachev. Yet Yeltsin's perception of the call as an attempt to finish him off sounds a bit far-fetched—until one considers the disease that Yeltsin prefers to conceal. For when Gorbachev phoned, he knew about Yeltsin's heart—he had to. And the bedridden Yeltsin knew that Gorbachev was aware of the diagnosis.

While at the Construction Ministry, Yeltsin was visited one day by a couple of KGB agents. They described to him in a calm, confidential manner what could happen to him in the period of a week. No ax-swinging, gun-toting thugs, no poison or car accidents; the hi-tech era had dawned on the KGB; they were determined not to fall behind the rest of the world.

"Let's say you're walking through the crowd, and someone points at you a little gadget that emits a powerful signal, with a frequency between seven and eleven cycles per second. Now, that kind of frequency can easily stop your heart. If you don't have a specially equipped ambulance on hand, it's all over for you. That's the way it is, pure and simple: everybody knows about your heart condition."

It is because Yeltsin's foes are aware of his medical history that we, after some hesitation, take the risk of writing about it, though Yeltsin himself prefers to conceal it.

Whatever his medical condition, Yeltsin's decision to head from the hospital to the Plenum still indicated a loss of nerve. Perhaps it was the leftover—from Stalin's day—fear of the General Secretary, the awe of the position, no matter who occupied it. On the other hand, Lev Shemayev, who at one point had been Yeltsin's intimate, explained to us once that close combat is not Yeltsin's forte, and Gorbachev is as well aware of this flaw as he is of Yeltsin's heart condition.

Yeltsin himself has a veiled explanation of his Galileo-like recantation, though he uses as an example a certain marshal, rather than himself, and sets the story at another Party Plenum, in more recent—freer—times. According to Yeltsin, after he, in a breach of Party unity, voted against nominating Yegor Ligachev as a People's Deputy—the only man present to do so—the Marshal came up to congratulate him.

"What about you?" Yeltsin asked him.

"I'm against, too."

"But why didn't you raise your hand? You risked death hundreds of times during the war! How can you be afraid after that!"

The Marshal no longer depended on anyone; he was retired; he had everything. What was there to be afraid of?

The Marshal explained. "I closed my eyes and I told myself, Now I will raise my hand—I'll try to vote against. I keep raising it and raising it, but it just won't—"

The fear, Yeltsin said later, the fear does exist, but it is of a different kind—as if produced by a different gland. And that fear held the Marshal to his seat like a nail, Yeltsin added.

The explanation applies to his own recantation at the Party Plenum. One should give him credit: he was the first to overcome that fear. The irony is that he could not have done without it: the same fear emboldened him, making him *un poltron révolté,* a coward who rebelled.

Our purpose in returning to that story is not to cast yet another stone at Yeltsin, but to explain the popular sympathy he gained in its wake—sympathy for the underdog. Decades of State terror had failed to stamp out mercy and empathy among the people; and this was how the people originally treated Boris Yeltsin—not as a hero but as a victim. He was someone they could relate to. After all, they had a common enemy—the Kremlin.

He received a stream of letters and telegrams of sympathy, too numerous for him to read them all; unopened, they were stacked up in a large wooden crate in his apartment, till the crate was filled to the top. Now it is one of the Yeltsins' most cherished possessions. In his state of physical and nervous breakdown, this deluge of support saved his life and career.

A Russian proverb without an English equivalent applies here: "One beaten man is worth two unbeaten ones." Yeltsin was "beaten," hence one of the people, to be relied on and trusted. Cast out of the Party Palace, he returned to the people—one of whom he has always remained—and did so of his own free will. He challenged the Kremlin first by giving up his privileges and siding with the people, who, for the first time in seventy years, emerged politically and regained their voice; the Great Mute had spoken. The revolution from above—the Kremlin—had exhausted itself, and the new one from below—the anti-Kremlin one—needed its own Robin Hood. Having succored Yeltsin at that crucial moment, the Russian masses proceeded to mold him into a hero and a leader after their own image. No longer did Yeltsin have a choice; the time of doubt was behind him.

But for now he was still at the bottom of the political well called the Construction Ministry. He had to get back to the top, but the path would be unique for a Soviet politician. It is doubtful that Yeltsin himself had an inkling of that path when he reluctantly began his ministry job.

He could have done worse than the Construction Ministry, though—even in Gorbachev's time, to say nothing of Stalin's, Khrushchev's, or Brezhnev's. Gods do not forget fallen angels, and Gorbachev occasionally phoned Yeltsin at the hospital. Knowing of Yeltsin's disease, he guardedly mentioned retirement. It is doubtful that Gorbachev was moved by humanitarian reasons—he was looking for a new status for the heretic of the Kremlin. The doctors joined their Kremlin patron in sug-

gesting that Yeltsin seriously consider retirement. Bear in mind that both
Yeltsin and Gorbachev were fifty-six at the time, though the latter was in
far better health.

Although Yeltsin consulted his wife, the decision was his own: for him,
retirement was equivalent to suicide. "I can't move to a dacha to grow
cucumbers and radishes. I'll howl at the moon; I'll die of boredom. I need
people, I need work—otherwise I'll be gone. I told the doctors I disagreed."

The conversation was instantly reported to Gorbachev, who called
back with an offer of a ministerial job. Yeltsin agreed right away, especially since he was a builder not only by training but by heredity. His
father, Nikolai Ignatevich, was a construction worker, who, despite his
fourth-grade education, came up with improvements that eventually
saved the State millions of rubles. This did not improve the Yeltsins'
finances; according to Andrei Goryun of Sverdlovsk, who has collected
a great deal of biographical data on Yeltsin, in the '30s Nikolai Ignatevich and his two brothers had but one coat that they took turns
wearing.

By the time Boris Yeltsin graduated from high school and decided to
enroll at the Construction Department of the Ural Institute of Technology, his father, after taking special courses, was a "master," in charge of
a construction site.

Ural family mores are traditionally rigid, and we will return to the
harsh treatment that Boris received from his father and that led him to
rebel against paternal authority. His father, incidentally, supported his
decision to become a builder, but his grandfather—his mother's father—
decided to give him a test of his own. He summoned Boris to his village
and told him to build a small *banya,* a bathhouse, in his own backyard.
Otherwise Grandpa would not approve of Boris's decision to enroll in the
construction program. Here is Yeltsin's version of the episode:

"You'll build the frame, the roof—you'll do it all yourself, from beginning to end," Grandpa "encouraged" the young man. "The only thing I'll
do is arrange for the forest authority to give you a plot for wood. The rest
is all yours—chop down the pine trees, clean the moss, dry it, haul the
logs in—that's a three-kilometer haul, by the way. You'll dig the foundation and do the frame from beginning to end, up to the roof. That's it.
I'll keep my distance."

He did indeed—he would not raise a finger to help his grandson.
Needless to say, in a '40s Russian village, John Deere machinery or its
equivalent were unknown, and Boris sweated for an entire summer building the bathhouse. After Grandpa's test, official exams were a cinch,
though he did not have much time to prepare for them.

Upon graduation, Yeltsin worked on many construction projects: the

Ural Chemical Plant, a reinforced-concrete factory, workers' dorms and clubs, residential housing, schools, kindergartens. He spent fourteen years in the construction industry until in 1969 the Party regional committee invited him to head its construction section. Seventeen years later he was summoned to Moscow to fill a similar position at the Central Committee. And now, over two years later, after a dizzying Moscow debut and a humiliating fiasco, he was back in his old profession. In a circular way, the bathhouse builder and construction worker had made it to the Minister of Construction.

His immediate superior, Yuri Batalin, was a fellow townsman, a friend, and, like Yeltsin, an alumnus of Ural Polytechnical. On Yeltsin's first morning at the new job, the staff formed a line to greet the exiled politician. Yeltsin was touched: this reception was like an extension of the flow of sympathetic mail. Yet he was also confused—he could not get rid of the impression he was being taken for someone else. "The kind of opinion they formed of me was perhaps a more favorable one than is justified."

Although the job fit his professional résumé, it was far from exciting: 80 percent was dealing with red tape. A conscientious worker, he quickly mastered his duties, performing them with ease and speed; yet they left him with plenty of free time that he had no idea what to do with. He became restless. He was tied to regular hours; no more emergencies or backbreaking loads. It could not but depress him. He, who hated weekends and missed his work, was now sentenced by Gorbachev to a horrible punishment—leisure. There is a saying about Yeltsin's type: "The more I rest, the more I rust." He missed high politics, from which he had been ousted by the Kremlin mandarins and into which—as Gorbachev made irrevocably clear—he would never be allowed again.

Tanya Pushkina, one of his secretaries, told us that Yeltsin was turning into a nervous wreck waiting for a call from the Kremlin. What was he hoping for? That Gorbachev would ask him to come back?

Calls from the Kremlin were rare and not quite the kind he had expected. According to his assistant Lev Sukhanov, who is with him to this day, after a call from Gorbachev Yeltsin "clenched his teeth and paced the room like a lion in a cage. I kept trying to comfort him. It's not worth getting upset over it, I said. He was so vulnerable, so thin-skinned."

A couple of times a week, Yeltsin would go home for lunch, avoiding the ministry cafeteria. It just so happened that one day while he was away he got a call from Prime Minister Nikolai Ryzhkov. Tanya knew how much Yeltsin cared about calls from the Kremlin and gave him the news the moment he walked in. Yeltsin tensed up and, without saying a word, strode into his office. She could hear him slam the door inside.

A few minutes later he called her on an intercom and asked her to come into his office.

"I will very much appreciate it," he hissed, "if in the future you will refrain from giving me the news in the reception room. Give me at least a chance to take off my overcoat."

On another occasion—again in a foul mood—he summoned her to his office and, without saying a word, vaguely nodded to the side while rolling his eyes upward—what could he mean by that? It turned out he was asking her to close the window (rather, the top-corner section that Russians use for airing the room). He had called her in just for that. She bears the grudge to this day: "He's tall enough to reach it by himself."

When she began working for him, he was in a state of total depression: political, psychological, and physical. He took everything hard, and, looking grim, withdrew into his shell for days. Sometimes, during a conversation, he would grab his chest and ask her to call a nurse, who would give him a painkiller shot. The medicine that he kept in his desk and carried with him no longer helped.

"Sometimes I would walk in and see him bent over—as if life just gave him another hard knock. He would raise his head—he had such a heavy look in his eyes, as if he were suffering from a headache. One had better not come close—he could throw anything at you in such a state. And when left by himself—I could hear him even through a double door, slamming his fist on the table or on the wall. The walls shook, really— with his huge fists it was like an earthquake."

Down on his luck, Yeltsin was no epitome of fairness. He did not— could not—conceal the pain, the desolation of having been doomed to pencil-pushing for the rest of his life. He grumbled, he nitpicked, he took it out on his family and his co-workers. One thing he did not do was use foul language; nor did he allow others to use it in front of him.

Outside the office he was friendly, even intimate, asking Tanya questions about her personal life and chatting humorously of his own. One hot summer day he even took his family by car to visit Tanya, who lived in a suburb, and they all went for a swim in a river nearby. In the office he was a stickler for etiquette and demanded the same of his subordinates. "You do not keep your hands in your pockets when you talk to someone," he chided Tanya.

On occasion, Yeltsin was simply tactless. He repeatedly asked Tanya to ask another typist to dress more appropriately for the office. "What does she wear a stupid skirt like that for? Tell her to put on something decent." It was an ordinary skirt, Tanya comments: a fashionable checked pattern, with flares at the hips—but it was too frivolous for his taste.

Yeltsin's conservative taste went beyond clothes: he was old-fashioned in all his ways. "They don't have people like that in Moscow anymore," a co-worker told us. "Siberian blood, Ural toughness—he's cut from a rock, not a touch of city slickness to him."

"Hard to take," "peevish," "hot-tempered," "changes his moods constantly," "overbearing"—these are the words we heard about Yeltsin from his ex-secretaries and assistants. Yet, oddly enough, they recall him in a nostalgic, even loving manner. "He criticized me," Tanya recalls, "but he taught me a lot, too—first of all, how to work." Another co-worker added: "He could throw fits, yet it was not a game where he'd just put you down. He calmed down quickly, he could not bear a grudge. He always came first to make peace."

Although Yeltsin's domestic behavior had dictatorial traces, his "subjects" tried to please him—perhaps more out of pity and love than out of fear. Having an old-fashioned dad like Yeltsin had its faults—the daughter who still lived with them complained that because of him she had no personal life—but on the other hand one gets an impression that, with his unorthodox politics and unpredictable behavior, he brought color, energy, and excitement to his household, which included his sons-in-law.

Yeltsin paid a good deal of attention to his appearance, aware that his height, his bearing, his powerful voice (of which he was very proud), and his well-groomed appearance were all components of his popular image. Before departing to make a speech at a meetings or a rally, he would change in his office and then present himself to Tatyana Pushkina: "How do I look?" His suits were always an excellent fit.

Tatyana would joke: "You'd kill 'em even in Paris."

He also had a woolen knit pullover that he wore only in his inner circle—Tanya or Sukhanov. When visitors came, he would ask them to wait and quickly change to a suit. His wife, Naina, was his wardrobe mistress; later, when Yeltsin went into an election blitz, she would iron his suits and keep his shirts clean—he went through several in one day—to make sure he looked perfect in public. In Russia, a place with few services available, it was enough to drive anyone to exhaustion.

Once, Tanya recalls, he was putting on a fresh shirt, brought by Naina, and stabbed himself on a needle she forgot to take out when sewing on a button. He reacted with humorous indignation: "I can't believe it! The woman I live with left a needle in my shirt!"

Before he left for work, it was up to Naina or his daughters to make sure that his mane of hair was set in place and would not fall over his forehead. Once, according to Tanya, an American delegation visited the Ministry. Yeltsin had just come in out of the shower after playing tennis. For him, it was inconceivable to be seen by foreigners with his hair wet and bedraggled. His secretary had to quickly get a hair dryer and arrange his hair in an upsweep.

His attention to his appearance was in sync with his growing popularity. He enjoyed being recognized on the street—it was such a contrast with his dreary job at the Ministry.

Yet the cloud had a silver lining. For the first time his stormy life entered the point of calm that everyone needs at some time to take stock of the past and to consider future possibilities, if such are in store. Now Yeltsin had more than a mere two hours in the morning to work on himself—he had days, weeks, months. Could this have been the time when the retired, exiled *apparatchik* turned into the first Russian politician of a new, pro-Western democratic type?

There was only one way to rise from the bottom of the well back to freedom, to social and political commitment, *per aspera ad astra:* through glasnost, which by now had spread beyond its inventor's—Gorbachev's—control and kept gaining ground against his will. When Gorbachev threatened he would ban Yeltsin from politics, he clearly overestimated his own capabilities.

Slowly but inexorably Yeltsin was coming back. First, he lifted the gag imposed on him and gave a few interviews: to *Construction Daily* (in keeping with the nature of his job), to *The Moscow News* (though it was published only in its German-language edition), and, finally, to the Moscow correspondents of BBC, ABC, and CBS (instantly relayed back to Russia through the Western radio stations). Now he was legitimate again.

About that time, *Moskovskaya Pravda*'s former editor in chief, Mikhail Poltoranin, removed from his job the same time as Yeltsin, gave an interview to *Corriere della Sera,* in which he detailed the anti-Yeltsin 1987 conspiracy. Also at that time, various versions of Yeltsin's speech—the one that had started his demise—were circulated in Moscow. When asked by Dan Rather whether he had criticized Raisa Gorbachev in his Plenum speech, Yeltsin categorically denied it. Yet he spoke against Ligachev in guarded but not uncertain terms. And he looked confident on TV—more a victor than a loser.

"A fight is always a fight," he said to Western reporters confidentially. "You attack, you go on the defensive, and sometimes you get knocked out. I've been through it all . . . I'm an emotional person. I take everything to heart, especially if something goes wrong."

This was a coming out, but not yet a political comeback: the gag order was still in force. Yeltsin badly needed a nationwide audience, and the only tiny chance to break through to it was the 19th Party Conference, due to open in the Kremlin on June 28, 1988, and scheduled to be televised throughout the land.

The Kremlin did everything to keep Boris Yeltsin away from the conference. Local Party cells nominated their delegates according to lists passed from above. Yeltsin was a Minister and still a Central Committee member. Even by formal standards, his delegate status was a given, especially since his candidacy was promoted by grass-roots Party organizations across the country. Yet the next confirmation stage—on the city/regional level—was an impassable barrier.

Even in his native Sverdlovsk the Kremlin was putting the heat on the local Party Committee. At the same time, the committee felt the pressure from the local workers, who threatened to strike if Yeltsin were denied a delegate's seat at the conference. The committee was caught between a rock and a hard place: disobeying the Kremlin orders meant losing their cushy jobs, but a work stoppage in the Sverdlovsk region, which in industrial development ranks third in the country, would damage the national economy, already in a permanent state of crisis, to the tune of billions of rubles. Nonetheless it looked like someone up at the Kremlin was prepared to accept the losses as the price of keeping Yeltsin away from the conference.

At the eleventh hour Yeltsin was called to Petrozavodsk, the capital of the Karelian Autonomous Republic, on the Finnish border, and nominated as the Karelian delegate—though he had never even belonged to the local Party cell! Yeltsin's biographers, as well as Yeltsin himself, are not sure if this option was stumbled upon serendipitously or whether Gorbachev became fearful and relented, allowing political common sense to win over his emotions.

The latter should not be ruled out. Not every conference delegate is assured a chance to speak. Yeltsin bombarded the Presidium with demands to give him the floor, but days passed, the conference was nearing its end, and he still had not been allowed on the podium. On the last day, just before the recess, the chairman announced that after lunch the conference would proceed to adopting resolutions. Yeltsin realized he was not getting the floor: Gorbachev, the master of the conference, feared his unpredictability. Then Yeltsin decided to storm the podium—which was not so easy for a number of reasons.

During the conference Yeltsin was not in top physical shape. Having been pumped with tranquilizers in November 1988, and, as he thinks, given knockout shots, he was released in this condition from intensive care into the hands of the Party tribunal. Yeltsin grew wary of doctors, especially the Kremlin ones. It may sound like persecution mania, but it was not unfounded. "You violated your Hippocratic oath," he reproached them at the time. "We've got our own Hippocrates," they replied.

Now, fearing that this "Hippocrates" would go to any lengths to prevent him from speaking at the conference, Yeltsin decided, not for the first time in his life, to gamble his health rather than his political career. He stopped taking the powerful hormonal medication prescribed for him.

His condition deteriorated sharply. His face became bloated; his movements grew hesitant and poorly coordinated; it took a major effort of will to concentrate on his task—breaking through to the podium.

Another problem was that the Karelian delegation, of which he was a member, were assigned seats in the bleachers, so to speak—the top tier, a meter from the ceiling, while the doors to the main floor were guarded by KGB agents. However, the latter recognized Yeltsin and let him pass without problems. Holding high a delegate's red ID, Yeltsin confidently headed straight for the podium, along a lengthy aisle.

The room grew silent. A Tadjik delegate stopped in the middle of his presentation. The eyes of millions of TV viewers were on Yeltsin; a great nation held its collective breath. He walked on, straight at Gorbachev, stamping his feet into the carpet. Reaching the Presidium, he went up a few steps, and, looking Gorbachev in the eye, said, "I demand the floor. Or else let the entire conference vote on it!"

After a momentary confusion, Gorbachev finally said, "Take a seat in the first row."

The Politburo members whispered among themselves. Then Gorbachev called the head of the Central Committee's general section and talked to him in a whisper, too. The latter left, and instantly one of the Party clerks approached Yeltsin: "Boris Nikolayevich, please come to the Presidium room. They want to have a word with you."

"Who's 'they'?"

"I don't know."

"That's not good enough. I'm staying right here."

The clerk left and the Politburo members exchanged more nervous whispers.

The clerk came back to tell Yeltsin that a Politburo member had been assigned to talk to him. Yeltsin rose and quietly walked down the aisle, from time to time quickly glancing at the stage, trying to determine which Politburo member had been assigned. The delegates in the first rows whispered, "Don't leave the hall!" Yeltsin, knowing the Kremlin ruses so well, guessed that he was being lured outside and would not be admitted back in. A few meters before the exit he paused to cast another glance at the stage: all were in place, no one had stood up to leave. The reporters next to him were also cautioning him not to go. Finally, the clerk ran up to him again: Gorbachev would give him the floor if he first returned to his Karelian delegation.

Clearly, the Politburo was running scared. There was no telling how far they would go to muzzle him. When Yeltsin realized this, he turned back from the exit and took a seat in the front row, directly opposite Gorbachev, who had no choice but to let his enemy speak. Yeltsin recounted the episode in minute detail.

That day Boris Yeltsin broke new ground: his storming of the podium established the tradition for the new Soviet parliamentarism.

By the standards of the day his speech was unusually brave and radical. First he replied to his critics on the subject of the interviews he had given to foreign reporters. He had had no choice, since the interviews he had granted to *Ogonyok* and *Moscow News* were banned from publication. He explained his incoherence at the Moscow Plenum, where he had been removed from the position of Moscow's First Secretary: he was sick, had been bedridden, he said; he had been summoned to the Plenum an hour and a half before it opened. He had been drugged by the doctors. He did not refer to Gorbachev by name, but instead unleashed a barrage of criticism on Ligachev, who by then had become everybody's scapegoat and was drawing the fire meant for Gorbachev.

The Party was lagging behind perestroika, which it had itself initiated, Yeltsin said. Delegates for Party conferences were still appointed from above rather than democratically nominated. He spoke against the leaders and the institution of autocratic leadership, reminding the audience of the damage it had caused the country in the past—again, without mentioning Gorbachev by name. He mentioned the privileges of the nomenklatura—his *bête noire*—still naming no names. He called for holding general, direct, secret-vote elections for all positions, from top to bottom, including for the country's leaders. He still did not name Gorbachev, but the reference was clear. He suggested that the holders of high positions limit themselves to two terms, with incumbents being reelected only with proof of solid achievements in the first term:

In a number of countries, when the leader steps down, he takes the rest of the leadership with him. In our country, we're used to accusing only the dead, who cannot respond. Today we are told that Brezhnev alone was guilty of stagnation. Where does that leave those who spent ten, fifteen, or twenty years in the Politburo—and are still there? They just kept voting for different programs. Why were they silent when one person, prompted by the Central Committee *apparat,* made decisions for the Party—for the country—for the socialist way? In the seventy years that we have held power we still have not resolved the key issues—how to feed and clothe our people, how to provide them with services, how to solve social problems. This is what perestroika was meant to resolve, but we keep leaning on the brakes, which means that each of us does not work enough—does not fight enough—for it. Also, one of perestroika's main problems is that it is confined mostly to statements. As a result, in the last three years we have failed to solve a number of tangible problems pertaining to the well-being of our people, to say nothing of initiating any revolutionary transformations.

As we implement perestroika, we should not be setting deadlines for the year 2000. At the moment, many do not care what they will get then, or if they'll get anything at all. We should set ourselves goals for every two to three years—a goal or two—and reach them for the people's benefit. We should not disperse our efforts in all directions, but focus on one, and commit everything—resources, research, manpower. Then our people will truly believe that perestroika is under way, that it yields results, that it's irrevocable—then the people will solve other problems faster. The people's faith could be swayed at any moment. As long as they were under the spell of words, it worked. But if things go on like this, we risk losing both control and political stability.

Again, Yeltsin spoke not just as a critic, but as a Cassandra as well. The speech, aimed at the nomenklatura, was cutting, principled, and prophetic—Gorbachev's fears of giving him the floor had been well grounded. But its sensational impact lay in the closing phrases. Undoubtedly Yeltsin had done his homework, calculating the effect down to the last detail and rehearsing the speech in advance. Very likely he even timed himself to stay within the rigid time limit—speakers were interrupted in midphrase if they exceeded it.

Actually, Yeltsin needed to be interrupted. He had prepared the speech in strict secrecy, and no one, except his older daughter, who had typed it at home, knew its contents.

Done with the main subjects, Yeltsin suddenly said, "Comrade delegates! I have a delicate question. I'd like to address you regarding my personal political rehabilitation following the Central Committee's October Plenum."

The audience stirred; became noisy. Yeltsin paused—and that's when he was interrupted.

"If you feel my time is up, then I'm done." He collected his notes and turned around, ready to step down.

Now the audience forgot they were delegates to a Party conference. They felt more like a theater audience, eager to know, what's next? This was what Yeltsin must have been aiming for: viewer curiosity. Even his sworn enemies must have been curious, at the expense of all other feelings.

Many demanded that Yeltsin be given extra time. Remember that the whole country was watching this superbly orchestrated performance. Gorbachev had no choice but to submit to the will of the majority. Or was he himself curious what was on Yeltsin's mind?

"Well, Boris Nikolayevich, continue . . . people are asking you to," Gorbachev said, to the sounds of applause. "I think, comrades, we should remove the lid of secrecy from the Yeltsin case. Whatever Boris Nikolayevich feels he should say, let him do so. And if we—you and I—feel such a need, too—then we'll do it later. Go ahead, Boris Nikolayevich!"

Gorbachev has many flaws, but he knows how to look like a winner even in the worst circumstances. It was easy to be fooled into forgetting that, along with his Kremlin colleagues, he had done all he could to keep Yeltsin away from the conference and then to keep him from speaking.

One should also remember that at the time, the Politburo Commission on Rehabilitation of Victims of Stalinism was working in full swing, finishing the work started by Khrushchev during his "thaw." Trotsky, Zinovyev, Kamenev, Bukharin, Rykov, and other former "enemies of the people" were being posthumously returned to history from their political limbo. Yeltsin applied that campaign to his own case:

"Comrade delegates. We're now used to rehabilitation after fifty years; it has had a positive effect on our society. But I would like to ask for political rehabilitation in my lifetime. I consider this a matter of principle, and a proper one in terms of pluralism of opinion, of freedom to criticize, and of tolerance of one's opponents—all of which have been proclaimed by previous speakers."

Yeltsin stumbled over the word "pluralism," which was brand new in the Russian political vocabulary. Later, Soviet TV made a point of replaying this blooper several times, but that could no longer harm Yeltsin: he was already the toast of the town. The conference changed the nature of his popularity: from a martyr he was turned into a victor.

"You know that the Plenum branded my October speech 'politically incorrect,' " he went on. "I'm extremely upset by what happened and I request that the conference rescind the Plenum's decision. If you deem it possible to do so, this will rehabilitate me in the eyes of the Communists. This is not just a personal whim—it would be a democratic act in keeping with the spirit of perestroika. I think it would help perestroika and reinforce confidence in it." With these words, he returned to the bleachers and the Karelian delegation.

Yeltsin's request for political rehabilitation was turned down. Moreover, after the recess he was assaulted again by the pack of accusers, led by the baton of an invisible conductor. The accusations remained the same; there is no point in rehashing them. The accusers added that Yeltsin had driven a Moscow district Party Secretary to suicide, though the man had jumped out the window six months after his dismissal, when he was already working at the Ministry of Metallurgy.

A highly emotional man, weakened by the effects of refusing to take the medicines he depended on, Boris Yeltsin summoned all his will to make his speech calm and dignified, but the effort drained him, and he had no energy left to listen to the deluge of slander that now broke over his head. Perhaps he felt that his third trial was under way, and that he was doomed to be tortured for the rest of his life. It was a moral torment that turned into a physical one: he was burning inside, his head was swimming, and he was about to black out. Service staff took him to a doctor who gave him an injection, but the suffering lasted for many days thereafter; tormented by doubts, he could not sleep.

The assault on Yeltsin on the last day of the conference was a milder version of the two previous trials, and there were substantial differences. This time it happened live, in front of TV audiences that numbered in the millions. Yeltsin himself was behaving differently. He withdrew his previous recantation, and, like Galileo, declared to the entire country and the world, *urbi et orbi:* "Still, it turns!"

And yet, as Yeltsin addressed the conference—in reality, the country and the world—his aim was limited: to justify himself in front of his Party comrades, not for his alleged sins, but for his recantation. He still underestimated the colossal changes that the Russian people had undergone in the three years of glasnost—in their political maturity, in learning democracy, in expanding their freedoms. He was still appealing to the Party elite; he did not try to appeal to the masses, nor dared to. His Party-nomenklatura past still haunted him; regardless of his personal qualities, the *apparatchik* in him, alienated from the people, was still alive.

In a way, Yeltsin was propelled into national politics against his will. The Construction Ministry, where he continued to work, received telegrams and letters—just as he had received them at home after the 1987 Plenum—but this time the volume was several times higher. The mailman delivered sacks—hundreds and thousands—of missives from all over the country, an expression of nationwide support. Besides sympathy, people offered honey, herbs, and raspberry jam. They had seen his sorry physical condition. Yet they did not confine themselves to moral support; they demanded that he not weaken, not surrender. Many letters contained the question, "Boris Nikolayevich, tell us: what should we do?" People were entrusting Yeltsin with their personal destinies. Yeltsin could not reject this nationwide mandate, nor had he the right to.

On November 12, 1988, the anniversary of his removal from the Moscow Party Secretary position, Yeltsin held a question-and-answer meeting—his preferred mode of communication—with the students of the Higher Komsomol School. There were 320 questions, and he answered every single one of them. It is an article of his faith that no question, no matter how rash or insolent or even hostile, should go unanswered. The meeting lasted four and a half hours, and its full transcript was fifty-five pages long.

The central media ignored the event, but excerpts began appearing in provincial papers—Ufa, Sverdlovsk, Kursk, Kazan, Syktyvkar, Yakutsk, Perm, Omsk—and then, in Samizdat copies, found their way back to the capital. Since he had faced a young audience, they appeared primarily in youth-oriented papers. His answers hinged on the questions asked, just as he himself now hinged on the demands and tasks entrusted him by the masses, who were shaping him as a politician. The questions he was asked were an indicator of the political evolution of the entire society, just as the answers were a good indicator of Yeltsin's own evolution. Russia had entered a stage of dynamic, dizzying transformations, leaving the Kremlin far behind. Yeltsin himself could hardly keep up with the changes—yet keep up he did.

Are you happy with your work at the Construction Ministry?
No, I'm not! I've worked for seventeen years in the industrial sector, and as a Party worker a little over that. I've always worked with people. It was interesting, dynamic, alive. Now I've been turned into an *apparatchik,* cloistered in my office. Eighty percent of my time goes for paperwork.

Can you comment on the item in the Communist Party's program that the country has entered the stage of well-developed socialism?
We can no longer dogmatically impose Lenin's every statement onto today's reality. We can no longer present ourselves as an abstract entity removed from the rest of the world, from the objective process of its development.

You're always speaking out against special rations for, as you put it, "starving nomenklatura."
I'm against social elites. We mustn't have "special" Communists, ones who have everything while others have nothing. My wife shops in regular stores—we get by. We eat regular sausage, though it pains us to look at it.

Do you have an ideal?
If you're talking about women, my wife is one.

At the October Plenum, did you criticize just Comrade Ligachev or someone else as well?
Someone else as well.

What can you tell us about the fact that Comrade Gorbachev is building a dacha in the Crimea and receiving royalties for his book in Switzerland?
The dacha has been built. I doubt he had enough personal funds for construction. I will not go into the royalties issue.

You're no less popular in the country than Gorbachev. Could you lead the Party and the State?
When we have alternative elections—why not give it a try?

This was something new: Yeltsin took a shot at Gorbachev. He must have realized that the full transcript of the meeting would be on Gorbachev's desk within hours. By declaring himself Gorbachev's political rival, Yeltsin allowed more than a peek at his cards. He gambled: at that stage he was risking more than he could possibly win. All the obstacles placed later in his political path go back to this premature challenge.

Gorbachev accepted the challenge, though he preferred evasive maneuvers and back-room plotting to a head-on confrontation with Yeltsin. They belonged to two different schools of combat, though in the course of their contest they learned from each other. Their situations differed, too. Gorbachev had the machine of the State backing him, while Yeltsin was pushed into the arena by the people, who had awakened from a long political torpor. By all standards, they were in different weight categories, Yeltsin being the lightweight. Yet they had no choice but to engage in battle—their fans and spectators demanded it.

The first round took place at the election of People's Deputies. Yeltsin decided to run a month after his meeting with the youth, on December 13, 1988. At first glance he was committing all his resources and willpower to a trivial objective—to be elected one of 2250 People's Deputies, who would later elect the Supreme Soviet, a year-round Soviet parliament, out of their own ranks.

In adopting a new election law, the Kremlin took pains to protect itself. Only two-thirds of the deputies were to be elected; the remainder were automatically nominated on the slates of various organizations—from the Central Committee (100 seats) to the Academy of Sciences (30 seats) down to the Philatelist Society (1 seat). The entire Kremlin team, headed by Gorbachev, was pushed through as the Kremlin list, but even such progressive academicians as Andrei Sakharov and Georgi Arbatov did not dare try their luck in a popular election, but instead chose to be nominated on the Academy's list. On the positive side, that decision precluded a race between Sakharov and Yeltsin, who would otherwise have run from the same district. The confrontation of two democratically minded politicians was a part of the design concocted by the election organizers, especially since they knew about the friction between Yeltsin and Sakharov.

Yet even the candidates elected through direct vote were subject to a complex, cleverly designed system of discarding, which in most districts—especially where glasnost had not yet reached—guaranteed victory to the local Party elite. These were the first democratic elections in Russia in seventy years, but this brand of democracy was limited, rationed, and guided by the Kremlin. It had as much to do with democracy as monopoly has to do with free enterprise, but Yeltsin had to participate—he simply had no other door into politics.

Naturally, the entire clever system of discarding candidates who did not fit the Kremlin's plans was activated against Yeltsin—the peace wrecker and the Kremlin's enemy number one. Although hundreds of districts nominated him as a candidate, there was absolutely no guarantee that he would be confirmed by the local authorities who ran the elections. Even before being elected, the problem was to be allowed to run, to be admitted on the slate.

Again, Yeltsin's love of overcoming obstacles manifested itself. He sought obstacles because they created him, tempered and shaped him. He once again followed the path of maximum resistance. Naturally, his best chance to clear the traps and barriers of the election mechanism was in Sverdlovsk, where his election was practically assured. His worst chance was in Moscow, where his path was blocked by the guard dogs of the major State organs, from the Party machine to the KGB. In Moscow, he was facing, as he put it, "a nerve-racking, exhausting game, with totally perverse rules; in this game they hit you below the belt, they jump you from behind—they use all sorts of tricks, normally illegal and quite effective."

Instead of running in his hometown, he chose Moscow. Why?

"It's a question of high politics," Yeltsin explained. "Also, my rehabilitation. All of Moscow will be voting! Way back, someone claimed I did not enjoy the Muscovites' trust. Now is the time to settle that issue."

"Someone" was a figure of speech, of course. In another conversation Yeltsin was more frank: " 'It does not look like the Muscovites have recognized you,' Gorbachev told me. Which is why I want a test—have they or haven't they? Kant said that the ability to vote is the only qualification of a citizen. I believe in the Muscovites' qualification . . . So many labels have been pasted on me . . . But they never bothered to tell people the truth. Thus the elections have to show whether the people are dealing with a political corpse, which is how the *apparat* portrayed me, or a popularly acknowledged politician. Political comebacks have not been a custom in Russia. It is time to change that custom."

Choosing Moscow was not a mere question of prestige, but of honor as well. Yeltsin wanted to exact revenge at the site of his previous humiliating defeat—the loss of the Moscow Party Secretary job. It was the next round of his fight against the Kremlin, and was also the struggle of the people against the Kremlin impostors. Yeltsin's name was no longer his own; now it was synonymous with confronting the nomenklatura, which for the masses, in turn, was synonymous with Gorbachev. Yeltsin was a popular leader; Gorbachev a nomenklatura one. In a sense, both were substitutes, just as in a primitive society a conflict between tribes is often resolved in a duel between their chiefs.

The Kremlin clique did everything in its power to prevent Yeltsin's electoral progress: blackmail, slander, threatening graffiti scrawled on his apartment door—even three car "accidents" shortly before the election. "They're attacking me up front. But I don't believe my physical elimination is possible. They're just trying to scare me off."

Yeltsin may have been right. But every attack brought new supporters to his side. The anti-Yeltsin campaign was backfiring: the more vicious the assaults, the better he did. Without realizing it, his opponents were playing into his hands. The man in the street had long ago stopped believing official propaganda. Mostly he simply ignored it, but more often he formed an opinion opposite to the one promulgated by the media. A few days before the election, Vladimir Tikhomirov, a lathe operator and a Central Committee member (what Yeltsin called "recruited by the *apparat* from the proletariat"), came up with a new set of charges: the Yeltsins were still using nomenklatura doctors; his daughter had parlayed his connections into a huge, deluxe apartment in central Moscow; and, when Yeltsin was Moscow's Party Boss, he would ride his official car on a visit to a factory, then, posing as a common man, would change to a streetcar and ride it for one stop to the factory gate.

By then it no longer mattered which of these accusations were true and which were lies. Public excitement about Yeltsin's candidacy had already achieved its apogee; he could have committed a murder or taken a huge bribe and no one would have believed it. At election rallies, public adoration drowned any criticism. A man who dared mention Yeltsin's responsibility for delays in residential housing was booed off the podium. At another election meeting, the vote was tallied at 510 for Yeltsin and 3 against; the audience demanded the names of the three traitors. Moscow was awash in pro-Yeltsin placards, posters, and pins: "Boris Yeltsin—People's Choice," "Tell 'em, Boris!", "If Not Yeltsin, Then Who?", "Hands Off Yeltsin," and so on.

From the Don Quixote who had challenged the nomenklatura, Yeltsin was being transformed into a Gulliver, whom the nomenklatura Lilliputians were trying to ensnare in a web of intrigue. But they did not stand a chance—Yeltsin was firmly protected by popular enthusiasm.

Gorbachev's instigation of the anti-Yeltsin campaign was an open secret. He was quick to support Tikhomirov, the "tame" lathe operator, and suggested that the Central Committee discuss "Yeltsin's political platform." Caught between the rock of the Kremlin and the hard place of the angry masses, the committee responded with little enthusiasm. At Gorbachev's insistence, a special committee was established to investigate Yeltsin's remarks during the campaign—another throwback to Stalin's day, albeit a feeble one. Naturally, both the people and Yeltsin accused Gorbachev of instigating the rest of the attacks, as well.

(We must admit that there is no direct proof of this, though the suspicions are numerous.)

One way or another, for the first time in Soviet politics a democratic election ran into back-room intrigue. The new confronted the old—even though the stake was as insignificant as electing one of 2250 People's Deputies, a position that gave its holder status and prestige but no real power. Nevertheless, both the Kremlin and the voters took the election seriously. A vote for Yeltsin was a vote against Gorbachev; both sides realized it, which added heat to the contest.

The results were extraordinary, mind-boggling: 89.6 percent of the votes were for Yeltsin, ergo against Gorbachev. This victory, on March 26, 1989, meant not only the end of Yeltsin's political ostracism but also the worst defeat of Gorbachev's career. Gorbachev did not even dare run on a competitive basis in Stavropol, his home turf. Instead he played it safe, placing his name on the nomenklatura list. The prize in the contest was the capital, and Yeltsin won it back, just as he would win the entire country—not the State apparatus but the people. At that stage in Russian history, when the people were moving into the political arena, pushing aside the State, the victory was of paramount importance.

Yeltsin's victory was revenge for his defeat at the hands of the Kremlin a year and a half earlier. It had been achieved by democratic means. He was surpassed by his own image. It was a new Yeltsin: an appointed *apparatchik* had been replaced by an elected representative, while Gorbachev remained just another politico.

It does not matter that Yeltsin was a populist and flirted with the masses; that he sought cheap popularity; all the labels his enemies slapped on him could be true or false. He crawled out of the political well where he had been cast by Gorbachev, and he did so by appealing to the people, rather than through Party scheming. Perhaps it was this election that enabled Yeltsin, prompted by the voters, to dare to identify his main enemy. In most struggles, success hinges on correctly identifying your enemy. Yeltsin's was not Ligachev, whose resignation Yeltsin demanded; Ligachev was no more than a stand-in for the real antagonist—Gorbachev. The spring election of 1989 was a correction of a past error in Yeltsin's calculations. He had originally attacked Ligachev, perhaps hoping to outmaneuver him and with Gorbachev's help take his place—until he realized he could not count on Gorbachev.

"Unfortunately, Mikhail Sergeyevich has shifted noticeably to the right," Yeltsin would say a few months later. "Right now it's not Ligachev on the right wing—it's the General Secretary himself. I get the impression that he led our society into a political maze—but I don't know if he himself knows the way out."

According to Yeltsin, right after the election, before the Congress of People's Deputies, Gorbachev phoned him to set up a meeting. Tense and enervating, it lasted about an hour, as the opponents, facing each other, poured out everything they had stored up for a long time. As the conversation proceeded, the wall of incomprehension between them grew. Russia is in catastrophic shape, Yeltsin said, while the *apparat* keeps playing games and won't surrender an inch of its power. Whose side are you on, Mikhail Sergeyevich? Are you with the people, or with the system that has brought our nation to the brink of disaster?

Gorbachev responded in a brisk, hostile manner. He had not, he insisted, summoned Yeltsin to discuss matters of state. He was interested in Yeltsin's future plans—what exactly was he planning to do next?

I'll know after the Congress, Yeltsin replied evasively.

Such an answer, noted Yeltsin, did not satisfy Gorbachev, who continued his interrogation. How would Yeltsin feel about working in the field of economics? A job on the Council of Ministers, perhaps?

The next day Moscow heard rumors: Gorbachev had offered Yeltsin his old job of Moscow Party Boss, or made him Deputy Prime Minister, or his own deputy—Vice-President. Yeltsin was rumored to have turned down all offers—he was, they said, after Gorbachev's own job.

Gorbachev must have thought that, too, and, as Yeltsin evaded a direct answer, Gorbachev grew more irritated. He thought Yeltsin was hiding something; at the same time, sensing his opponent's nervousness, Yeltsin kept egging him on. It was bluff pure and simple: Gorbachev's former ally was now his chief critic and opponent, but as rivals they were not yet on equal footing. Despite his nationwide support, Yeltsin did not have a constitutional opportunity to challenge Gorbachev for the top job. But the election returns allowed Yeltsin to do a little blackmailing, to keep Gorbachev on his toes. It was a risky game; Yeltsin was running too fast for his own good.

De Tocqueville once characterized elections as institutionalized revolutions. The term exactly fits the first semifree election in the Soviet Union—it was the second revolution in just a few years. The first revolution that Gorbachev had conducted from above was coming to an end. Little by little, the new revolution from below was getting under way—Yeltsin's revolution.

PART TWO

THE PRINCE AND THE PAUPER

Parallel Lives of Mikhail Gorbachev and Boris Yeltsin

BORIS YELTSIN'S election to People's Deputy was unprecedented in Soviet history. It had an almost mystical quality: an *apparatchik* comes back to life after his indisputable political death. Gorbachev was sure that Yeltsin was finished in politics. After Yeltsin had been kicked out in November 1987, Gorbachev personally designated him a political cadaver; in his conversation with the Kremlin Heretic he used a phrase that smacked of Louis XIV's domestic absolutism: "I'll never let you back into politics!"

He was as good as his word, doing everything possible and impossible (thereby radically contradicting the pluralism and glasnost that he himself promoted) to prevent Yeltsin's return from his political grave—a fall from the Party Olympus had always been lethal. We are using funereal metaphors with good reason: Western Sovietologists and journalists, amazed at "Yeltsin's unique political resurrection," began calling him the Lazarus of Soviet politics.

Yeltsin, however, turned out to possess extraordinary political instincts, and was the first to sense that the rules of the game had changed. By announcing perestroika as his political objective, Gorbachev opened the cage too wide, and a *rara avis*—by Soviet standards—called public opinion flew out. Now, in 1989, with the support of this public opinion, and under its pressure, it became possible not only to revive but to create a new kind of statesman—one who did not issue from the Party ranks, but came from the outside, from the masses, and based his career on their support.

Yeltsin was the first among the national leadership to see that perestroika, two years after it was introduced by Gorbachev, was spinning its wheels in the very rut that it had dug; that, with the exception of some democratic shifts in glasnost, economic and—most important—political perestroika had not even gotten started; that Gorbachev, along with his Party team, had no desire to institute reforms, but merely wanted to reform his power base. Yeltsin had always been sensitive to the popular mood, and now he anxiously noted a decline in popular enthusiasm for perestroika slogans, appeals, and directives: they were empty; they merely disoriented and confused the average person.

Yeltsin himself had risen on the crest of this initial enthusiasm when he was Moscow's Party Boss. Still a firm believer in the socialist system and its capacity for change and renovation, he was shocked by the cynical absolutism of the Party bureaucracy that he had encountered in Moscow. His rebellion at the October 1987 Plenum, followed by a Party whipping, was an impulsive, desperate act, seemingly inexplicable in terms of potential long- or short-range benefits—essentially a textbook case of political masochism. Yet it was exactly that: a rebellion, an open protest of a loner against the close-ranked Party clan several hundred strong. It was also an unconscious quest for comrades to share his ideals.

This subdued appeal finally reached the broad masses, though in a distorted, folkloric version (it may be remembered that, despite the growth of glasnost, it took Yeltsin's Plenum speech a year and a half to make it into the Soviet media). When Yeltsin, that "scandalmonger," came up with a new signal—people remembered.

That signal appeared after Yeltsin, in forced political isolation, underwent a crisis of faith. At the age of fifty-seven, when most people tend to ossify in their convictions, Yeltsin launched a total revision of his views and principles. Among Party leadership, his ex-brothers-in-reform, he had felt like an outcast; now, for the first time in his life, he was alone with himself, and he decided to use this time to dig up and take a close look at the roots of his once-solid belief in socialism, in Party authority, in the bright Communist future. It was an exhausting process, which verged on emotional suicide, but eventually he saw that not only were the roots rotten, but that they were fake as well. Digressing into psychoanalysis, Yeltsin described that period of emotional schism, of battle with his own self, in his autobiography.

Now, with his mind clear of doubts, he plunged straight into politics (battle to him) with a new program of popular empowerment: the system of *apparat* socialism was to be scrapped and replaced by grass-roots democracy. While, during the years of perestroika, Gorbachev's strategic ruses were mainly aimed at the utopian, futile goal of changing the system within the system, Yeltsin was already preparing a revolution from the bottom—and he signaled it in his heretical, alarm-sounding speech at the 19th Party Conference in the summer of 1988.

He practically crashed that conference, overcoming the barriers erected by the *apparat;* he stormed the podium in the eleventh hour of the conference, barely winning enough time to state the main theses of his battle plan against the system:

• Establish general, direct, secret-vote elections to the top power echelons, including the post of General Secretary,

• Limit the holders of all elected offices to two terms, with an age limit of sixty-five, without any exceptions, especially for the top echelon,

• Remove the veil of secrecy from the leadership; open up the Party to outside criticism, self-criticism, and pluralism; declassify subjects like the Party budget and Party cliques,

• Cancel special Party privileges, including special food rations for the nomenklatura.

As at the October Plenum, Yeltsin's impromptu speech appeared to be pure masochism—banging one's head against the wall of the Party's autocratic power; again he was a lonely rebel in an audience of 5000 delegates. And again the rebellion was followed by the *apparat*'s counter-strike: public assault with slander and insults, aimed at destroying their enemy's morale. But this time, though Yeltsin himself thought it was all over, for him it was only the beginning. Suddenly, when all seemed lost, he was recognized by his people, who discovered their leader in him. The years of roaming the political desert came to an end.

Curiously, at that time, in July 1988, both Soviet and Western commentators were so caught up in Yeltsin's most dramatic gesture at the conference, calculated for effect—his request for political rehabilitation (he was turned down)—that they overlooked his program of far-reaching social renovation, of the Party's subordination to society, which he delivered in an imperious, declarative tone that brooked no objection. But people recognized this program unanimously, almost intuitively, and gave it instant support: it dovetailed with their vague but powerful yearnings.

Why did the people need Yeltsin as their leader so badly? In the eighteen months of his political exile, the nation entered a power crisis, a crisis of trust in the leadership, in the Party, and in perestroika itself. Gorbachev had given up on specific reforms—especially radical ones, reduced to cosmetic measures—and thus became identified more clearly as the leader of the Kremlin, the Party bureaucracy—the nomenklatura. It was logical: he remained loyal to the class that had given him power. The country was fed up with with his insipid, wishy-washy policies; it was stuck in a rut; the slogans sounded hollow, and in 1988 talk was of the impending economic debacle.

A paradox emerged: the man who had initiated perestroika was now braking instead of accelerating it. The masses were disoriented, confused; they had lost hope for perestroika and the promised reforms—primarily the economic ones. Most important, there was no leader. (There were, to be sure, some spontaneous, futile rallies and mini–speakers' corners set up near the glass-enclosed stands where newspapers are displayed for public perusal.)

A similar situation was described by José Ortega y Gasset in *The Revolt of the Masses:* "In a normal public order, the masses as such must not be active. Their purpose in the world is to be passive, to be influenced by someone; someone needs to direct, represent, and organize them . . . 'A man of the masses' needs leadership." In the defeated, humiliated Yeltsin, the Russian people intuitively recognized their champion. Yeltsin, meanwhile, was suffering from political isolation and looking for support. The recognition was mutual and instant; sparks flew.

The Russian people had not recognized the dissidents, who fought their battles, as their leaders. They ignored Andrei Sakharov, though he was dubbed the "people's conscience and honor." Even the great Russian nationalist Alexandr Solzhenitsyn, if he returned to Russia proudly, "on a white horse"—as he must dream—might fail as a popular leader. After all, his ideological Russophile comrades suffered a political fiasco. The difference between these candidates for popular leadership and Yeltsin was visceral: for the masses, they were "not our kind." Yeltsin was.

Yeltsin and the Russian people had the same tastes, the same experience of having been kicked in the teeth by the system; they had common radical politics and a common enemy: the *apparat,* who had usurped power. Now what was needed was to develop a joint strategy of battling the Party bureaucrats for a share of power. "Hey, Party—We Want to Steer, Too!" was a popular slogan of the late '80s.

Thus began the love affair of Boris Yeltsin and the masses. It took place in the streets and squares, in stadiums and arenas, at huge factory rallies, at demonstrations both planned and spontaneous. In the early spring of 1989 one had the impression that all of Moscow was in the streets, looking for their favorite. A rumor spread that Yeltsin would be making a speech at the Brateyevo Supermarket. Overcrowded buses carried thousands to that store. They were everywhere: on balconies, on the roof of the store, standing on empty produce boxes. Moscow and the entire country were rocked by thousands of rallies to elect Yeltsin as a People's Deputy. Men and women carried sandwich boards, placards, pictures, flyers; every hat featured a Yeltsin button. People came to Moscow from Sverdlovsk, Odessa, Irkutsk, Krasnodar to canvass for him. A month before the election, Yeltsin held two rallies a day; popular support was to him like Mother Earth to Antaeus. Yeltsin and the people talked and talked and talked, turning these street rallies and factory meetings into full-fledged lovefests.

Thus emerged the Yeltsin phenomenon that political observers discussed with amazement and irritation—it was too openly populist for their liking. It was the triumph of spontaneous grass-roots democracy in the face of authority.

For a long time Yeltsin had been perceived as just a supporting player. In his first eighteen months as the Moscow Boss he was not seen as an independent ruler, but as the Moscow viceroy who overstepped his authority. Then he was viewed as Gorbachev's antagonist or even as his nemesis. His political position was defined in reactive terms—never as a positive, constructive one, but always as negative, destructive: anti-Ligachev, anti-Gorbachev, anti-Party, anti-nomenklatura, anti-Kremlin. It was as if Yeltsin did not exist as himself, but as an *anti*-prefix who scored political points at the expense of the errors, flaws, and general unpopularity of the Kremlin leaders. Yeltsin personified negation, and was accordingly labeled as a counterweight to the lawless, hated power of the Kremlin.

In reality, however, the late '80s saw a massive shift in society. Quietly but inexorably Yeltsin became an independent—and positive—political factor that could no longer be summarily dismissed. A splash of grass-roots democracy led to the formation of a second power center. The traditional one was still the Fortress Kremlin, headed by Gorbachev, but Russia outside the Kremlin was Yeltsin's turf. This scattering, this political diaspora, needed a focal point, which came to be personified by Yeltsin. The need was mutual: Yeltsin badly needed popular support, while the inchoate popular opposition needed an influential, authoritative, charismatic leader.

For a long time Gorbachev would not notice (or pretended not to) that he was no longer opposed by a personal foe and rival who was avenging his public humiliation and trying to destroy him, but by the leader of a snowballing opposition. To Gorbachev, Yeltsin was still a whipping boy, convenient for his, Gorbachev's, political self-affirmation; someone who could be still chewed out for "political illiteracy" in the Party's inner circle. While Gorbachev continued to berate Yeltsin for lack of loyalty to the existing system, he was too blind to see that Yeltsin was already outside—and beyond—it!

Only after Boris Yeltsin was elected People's Deputy with 89 percent of the vote did Gorbachev finally realize that Yeltsin was a menace with powerful backing. The official media then switched from calling Yeltsin a "populist" to a "power-hungry extremist"—a de facto recognition of his status as Gorbachev's main political opponent.

Whatever the core of the conflict between the two of them—ideology, politics, even personal ambition—it was clear that beginning with Yeltsin's rebellion at the October Plenum, the confrontation defined Russia's political course. In its intricate combinations and complicated tactics, it resembled a chess game whose every move was followed eagerly by the audience at home and abroad. The onlookers evaluated this match, interrupted at times by truces and temporary alliances, differently. Some thought that Yeltsin's criticism served to correct the Soviet President, keeping Gorbachev's constantly wobbling vehicle on the track of reform. Others believed that Yeltsin was struggling to define his political credo, whose original version—"Democratic Russia"—was too vague and general. Yet others foresaw that the rivals would destroy each other and open the way for the emergence of a mysterious "third force."

However one saw that fierce confrontation, it was obvious to all that it was a naked, classical struggle for power. Gorbachev fought for his personal power, while Yeltsin wanted to hand it over to the people.

It became commonplace to regard current politics in the context of the Yeltsin-Gorbachev contest; such comparative analysis became part and parcel of political thinking. Yeltsin received the more-or-less official appellation of "the main political figure battling the President of the USSR." A typical newspaper cliché was, "Yeltsin leads among the politicians who command the most trust; Gorbachev leads among those who cause the most frustration." Praise and blame usually depended on who was ahead at the moment. If, for example, yet another anti-Yeltsin slander campaign succeeded in lowering his popularity rating, it meant that Gorbachev reinforced his position. Or vice versa. It was an ancient principle: *Ridet Caesar, Pompeius flebit* (Caesar laughs and Pompeius cries).

But their relationship cannot be simplified as that of opposites. Sometimes it was more like a love affair, replete with jealousy, suspicions, and slights. "I think Gorbachev knew how I felt; neither one of us would show it," Yeltsin intimated. It was Yeltsin's impulsiveness and nervousness that sometimes made their relationship seem personal and emotional, for Gorbachev tended to be reticent or even disinterested.

Even when they agreed on strategic issues—at least in the late '80s, it hardly went further—they still sharply disagreed on tactical ones. Gorbachev swore to remain a Communist to his dying breath. When Yeltsin was accused in the media of being "against socialism, not wanting to join us on our march to the bright Communist future," his answer was brusque and typically to the point: "No, I don't. I have no such plans."

Apart from tactics and strategy, from ideological disagreements, from politics in general, much hinged on their personalities, life experience, habits, and life-style. These factors contrasted starkly, and for the most part accorded only on paper. They could be compared to the characters in Pushkin's *Eugene Onegin,* in which friendship ends in a duel. Their initial union failed to hide their differences:

> *They got together; wave and stone,*
> *Verse and prose, ice and flame,*
> *Were not so different from one another.* *

Several crisis-ridden, if not fateful, years in Russian history had to pass, marked with the Yeltsin-Gorbachev battle, now raging, now fading, until in the summer of 1991 the conflict erupted on a world scale. Therefore it is instructive to compare their two lives, focusing on Yeltsin, since less is known about his roots than about those of Gorbachev, one of the most chronicled leaders of recent times.

*Translated by Vladimir Nabokov.

A TALE OF TWO LEADERS
A Comparative Diagram

	MIKHAIL SERGEYEVICH GORBACHEV	BORIS NIKOLAYEVICH YELTSIN
Current Post	President (USSR)	President (Russia)
Salary	4,000 rubles a month (in Dec. 1991, roughly $40)	4,000 rubles a month (in Dec. 1991, roughly $40)
Date of Birth	March 2, 1931	February 1, 1931
Place of Birth	Village of Privolnoye Stavropol Territory 750 miles south of Moscow	Village of Butka Sverdlovsk Region 875 miles east of Moscow
Nationality	Russian	Russian
Social Background	Peasant	Peasant
Height	5'9"	6'3"
Body	Tends to gain weight	Heavyset
Eyes	Brown	Blue
Hair	Bald	Thick gray hair
Body Language	Fidgety	Reserved
Special Marks	Large birthmark on right side of forehead	Missing thumb and index finger on left hand
Biographic Detail Concealed in Curriculum Vitae	During the war was in German-occupied Territory	Grandfather exiled in 1931; uncle arrested for sabotage in 1935; father arrested in 1937
Education	Law School, Moscow University, 1955 Stavropol School of Agriculture (correspondence course), 1967	Ural Polytechnic Institute, 1955 Construction Department
Early Vocation	Party functionary	Industrial Manager
Party Membership	1952–1991	1961–1990

A TALE OF TWO LEADERS (continued)

	MIKHAIL SERGEYEVICH GORBACHEV	BORIS NIKOLAYEVICH YELTSIN
Kremlin Patron(s)	Fyodor Kulakov Mikhail Suslov Yuri Andropov Andrei Gromyko	Self-made man
Tactics	Intrigue, maneuver, compromise	Confrontation
Political Base	Kremlin (nomenklatura)	Russia (masses)
Type of Politician	Reformer	Revolutionary
Political Temperament	Rational	Intuitive
Family	Married, one daughter, two granddaughters Mother lives separately in Privolnoye	Married, two daughters, two granddaughters, and a grandson named Boris Yeltsin. Mother lives separately in Sverdlovsk
Type of Wife	Bossy, powerful, abrupt, dominating; resembles his mother	Motherly, conceding, caring, patient, resembles his mother
Leisure	Contemplative, likes walks in the woods	All sports from tennis to volleyball. Incapable of passive leisure
Health	Radiculitis	Heart disease
Accidents	Not known	Four car accidents, one plane crash
Mode of communication	Monologue: accordingly, verbose and didactic	Dialogue: accordingly, laconic
Behavioral Traits	Diplomatic, evasive, careful, reticent, arrogant, in conversation maintains distance	Rough, abrupt, direct, but always democratic, sometimes sly
Attitude to Self	Hedonist, sybaritic	Unsparing, masochistic
Attitude to Criticism	Smug (until August 22, 1991)	Self-critical (until August 22, 1991)
Traits	Reserved Indecisive Complacent	Emotional Risk taker Rebellious
Military Rank	Colonel	Colonel

Initially, the two histories seem to have a few points of convergence. First of all, they seem to have taken parallel routes from remote villages to the highest seat of power in Moscow. Born a month apart, both come from generations of peasants, with birthplaces almost equidistant from Moscow: Gorbachev to the south, Yeltsin to the east, to Siberia (the mid-Urals, to be precise). Both grew up in two-parent families, a rarity in the generation marked by single-mother households: the fathers died in wars or vanished in the islands of the Gulag.

Both were the only ones in their families to graduate from high school and college. Both married classmates, and almost at the same time moved to their respective regional centers. Gorbachev moved to Stavropol, then a provincial town without gas or indoor plumbing; Yeltsin, to Sverdlovsk,* one of the largest industrial and cultural Soviet centers, six times more populous than Stavropol. Both became Party viceroys of their respective provinces, whose economic development was on different levels (Stavropol was much weaker), and stayed in those jobs for about the same time, until they moved to the Kremlin. In Moscow, both ended up as leaders (Gorbachev of the Party, Yeltsin of the opposition), and soon thereafter Presidents (Gorbachev of the USSR, Yeltsin of Russia). Naturally, both lives were affected by events like the Great Terror of 1937, the Great Patriotic War (World War II), Stalin's death, and the initial liberalization known as Khrushchev's thaw.

There is a superficial resemblance in the personalities and life histories of the two leaders. Both seem to have been sexually inhibited in their student years (Yeltsin went in for sports; Gorbachev for the Party); accordingly, they made faithful, virtuous husbands, without a roving eye. Females prevailed in both families: both had daughters, later granddaughters. Both wanted a son badly (at one point Raisa refused outright to have a second child, while Yeltsin got a grandson, also named Boris Yeltsin, as a substitute). Both have a passion for public activity, yet individually seem somewhat dull: their reactions are drearily predictable and emotionally impoverished, or underdeveloped. Another purely situational coincidence: both were the firstborn in families in which mothers doted on the younger sons—Gorbachev's brother Alexandr, sixteen years younger; and Yeltsin's brother Mikhail, a construction worker, who still lives in Sverdlovsk with their mother in a standard one-bedroom apartment. Unlike his outgoing elder brother, Mikhail is a typical introvert, a man of striking modesty. When strangers ask about his last name, he invariably denies being related to the Russian President.

---

*The city was originally named Yekaterinburg (after Peter the Great's wife), then renamed after Bolshevik Yakov Sverdlov, and returned to its original name in the fall of 1991. We call it Sverdlovsk, as it was called when Yeltsin lived and worked there.

However, the resemblances do not go beyond these superficial coincidences, these overlapping biographical events. In all other categories, where personalities and destinies are concerned, the two are diametrical opposites. Moreover, the common high points in their lives underscore the vivid contrast between their experiences and the efforts they made to achieve their victories.

1931–1949

Both Boris Yeltsin and Mikhail Gorbachev were baptized. However, while both of Yeltsin's parents came to his baptism, Gorbachev's parents, active members of the newly organized kolkhoz in their village, did not dare break the commandments of their new religion—atheism—and so baby Mikhail was brought to the church by his grandmother. While Gorbachev's baptism was a routine church rite, performed according to all the rules, baby Yeltsin started his life with a unique accident, possibly an omen of his future trials and tribulations. The drunken priest lowered him into the tub filled with holy water and forgot to take him out. His parents stood at a distance, and did not come to rescue the baby right away. Finally, the water was pumped out, and the priest said unflappably, "Well, he's got to be a tough one to pass an ordeal like this. Let's call him Boris." (After Prince Boris, a Russian martyr.)

Being born in 1931 in a Russian village is not a sign of good fortune. That year saw the peak of forced collectivization of peasant households and the apogee of mass terror against those who resisted the New Agricultural Policy. Since the better-off peasants resisted enslavement the most, it was decided to annihilate them as a social class.

Almost all of Yeltsin's ancestors, his grandfathers and great-grandfathers, lived and died in the village of Butka, 155 miles south of Sverdlovsk. The year of his birth coincided with catastrophe for his entire numerous family. All nine of them—three generations—lived in the same hut, sleeping on the floor; their relative security—they were hardly well-off—came from backbreaking labor. Still, the head of the family, Boris Yeltsin's grandfather, the village blacksmith and church elder, was classified as a *kulak* (as the new rulers pejoratively called well-off peasants); his house, his mill, and his possessions of any value were confiscated. The family patriarch, by then almost seventy, and his wife, along with a dozen other *kulak* families, were exiled north to remote taiga forests. The old couple lived in an unheated barrack in a place where thirty below Centigrade was a normal winter temperature. Four months later Yeltsin's grandfather died.

Those remaining in the village after the punitive campaign were forced to join the kolkhoz. The new kolkhoz members' horses were taken away, and died that winter in the collectivized stable. When the harvest, reaped with so much toil, was confiscated by the State, down to the last grain, the Yeltsins (they were four brothers: Nikolai, Ivan, Dmitri, and Andrian), along with their fellow villagers, faced death by starvation. But the kolkhoz chairman took a chance—the Party would not have spared him had they known—and allowed the villagers to leave for the town for the winter, to earn a living.

Yeltsin himself does not care to talk about the tragic events that caused such an downturn in his parents' lives. He may believe it was their fate, not his, that was affected; if so, he is wrong—the '30s of his childhood left their mark on him for the rest of his life. It was his mother, Klavdia Vasilyevna, who was willing to talk about the family tragedy. (Mother and son have the same facial features; but his steely character, his large body and oxlike carriage Yeltsin inherited from his father.)

In 1935 fate struck again: his father's brother, Uncle Ivan, was falsely charged with sabotage, sentenced to a long term at forced labor, and exiled to do construction work at the town of Berezniki. Soon, two of his brothers followed with their families. Such was the irony of Soviet fate that it was easier for a felon convicted of sabotage to survive in Berezniki than for a peasant to live off the land.

One can tell how hard the older Yeltsins took forced separation from the land by the fact that in the early '70s they returned to Butka, bought a small house with a tiny plot, and stayed to live the peasant's life that they had dreamed of for thirty years of exile in Berezniki.

Boris Yeltsin, too—by then the Party Boss of the immense Sverdlovsk Region—preferred to spend vacations in his native village rather than at comfortable Party resorts and retreats. He loved working on his vegetable patch, chopping firewood, picking mushrooms, fetching water from the well—being no different from his fellow villagers.

In that, he provided a study in contrast to Gorbachev—also from a peasant background—whose ambition spurred him to break way from his village, to climb the social ladder, to imitate the *apparatchiks* and his ideological mentors. Gradually he broke all of his inherited ties with his fellow villagers and spent all his vacations at luxurious government resorts.

In Berezniki, Yeltsin senior found a job as a construction worker. The entire family settled in a barrack—a drafty, long wooden barn. On one side was a communal corridor; on the other, up to twenty tiny rooms, with one—sometimes large—family per room. The barrack was a child of early five-year plans; a temporary shelter, hastily hammered together near a huge indistrial project under construction. (A chemical factory, one of the largest in Europe, had been built for ten years by the time the Yeltsins arrived in Berezniki.)

Again, Soviet fate struck the Yeltsins; this time it was a direct hit. In 1937 Yeltsin's father, Nikolai Ignatyevich, was arrested and spent several months in jail. After his release he was unemployed for a long time. Boris never dwelt on the circumstances which had labeled his father an enemy of the people. Boris's father was a builder by nature, with an inventor streak, who spent nights trying to design an automatic bricklayer. During the war, Nikolai Yeltsin, a self-taught builder with a fourth-grade education, had refused outright to head the construction of a new factory; he had found defects in the design that had been approved by Moscow bigwigs. The eventual examination by Moscow experts, made at his demand, proved him right. Whether he was railroaded for this "crime" or for something else is unclear, though Yeltsin dates the event in 1937.

Yeltsin's mother worked as a seamstress. Boris's only memory of domestic cheer was the nightly buzzing of her sewing machine in the corner of their tiny room. The family tried to survive and had no plans beyond that. Yeltsin's eighty-four-year-old mother remembers Boris as a mother's little helper: he took care of his little brother and later his baby sister, cooked dinner, fetched water from the well, washed dishes, and hoed the vegetable patch. During the war he stood long nights in lines for a loaf of bread. His mother still keeps a small throw rug little Boris embroidered with a goldfish. He mastered the sewing machine and became a competent apprentice to his mother, going as far as to sew his own underwear. (Fifty years later, on his American tour, he amazed workers in Manhattan's garment district with the skill with which he handled a Singer.) Now, in hindsight, his mother even sounded somewhat surprised that he had never shirked his substantial household duties. Boris developed early on an awesome—for his age—sense of duty to his family and especially to his mother.

Yeltsin's relations with his mother were extremely close in his early childhood, until he was about fifteen: they were both friends and soulmates. As her mainstay, he became familiar with every detail of quotidian family life, especially the feminine side of it. A Russian teenager caught doing "women's work" might have felt ashamed; young Boris displayed nothing of the kind.

For instance, when, at the end of the war, his mother gave birth to his sister Valya, thirteen-year-old Boris cooked dinner and brought it in tin pots to the maternity hospital. Her neighbors in the ward, with whom she shared the food, shook their heads: "A boy cooking like that!"

Every summer mother and son went to do seasonal farm work out of town. They mowed grass and dried and sold hay to buy bread in town. His mother defended him staunchly from his father, acting as a lightning rod for her husband's anger. Thus, in Yeltsin's world view a woman is a kindly, warmhearted influence that softens the masculine world—roughhewn, powerful, and demanding. His early familiarity with a woman's world, his sensitivity to women's practical needs, tastes, habits, and sensibilities, ensured his subsequent success and ease of communication with women in all walks of life.

At the university, he coached the women's volleyball team; when he worked in construction, he always had the closest, friendliest relations, based upon instinctive understanding, with women's crews; later, speaking in the name of millions of Soviet women, he would chide Gorbachev's wife—addressing her as a family member would—for her desire to have a "beautiful, luxurious, and comfortable life" in a society devoid of the bare necessities. The many years spent by the Yeltsins in the barrack, where every intimate detail of twenty family lives was public knowledge, developed his sensitivity toward women—but in a familial, sympathetic sense rather than a romantic one.

The barrack would dominate Yeltsin's life for another ten years, till he left for Sverdlovsk to enter college. It would resurface thirty-odd years later, when, as the Party Boss, he would attempt to eliminate barracks, to erase them from his memory, by moving all of the Sverdlovsk barrack-dwellers into new apartments in just one year. Barracks are a motif in his life worth emphasizing, for they hold some clues to the Yeltsin phenomenon, his so-called populism, and his unprecedented popularity.

Times were hard; comforts nonexistent. The Yeltsins bought a goat; all six—parents, children, and goat—slept together on the floor. Yeltsin's reminiscences about the goat, the children's pet, whose fatty milk saved them from hunger throughout the war, may sound like *Fiddler on the Roof*—an idealized representation of poverty straight out of Sholom Aleichem—but one should keep in mind the bitter Ural winters. One would be hard put to squeeze a single drop of the idyllic out of barrack life, and Yeltsin's childhood memories are devoid of lyrical detail. Not only did their beloved goat feed the children, but it also saved them from freezing: "You press yourself against it, it's warm like a stove."

Lack of warm clothing kept the Yeltsin children indoors through the winter; this aspect of poverty would reemerge dramatically when Boris, already a student, would rely on his vigorous health and attempt to survive a Sverdlovsk winter without a heavy coat. In his childhood memories, the fierce Siberian winter is perceived as an enemy, a tormentor, along with the constant fight for survival and his father's beatings. Even in the matter of climate, Gorbachev was luckier, having the benefit of warmer Stavropol weather, to say nothing of the fact that he spent his first nineteen years in his native village, in his parents' house, with his grandfather, the kolkhoz chairman, and his father, the chairman of the local tractor station.

Yeltsin's father belted him mercilessly, infuriated by the boy's stubborn silences. Yeltsin does not say why he endured his father's punishments, gnashing his teeth, not uttering a sound—the entire barrack would have heard him. Yeltsin senior belted his son, who had kept the household running since the age of six, for every childish prank. The beatings grew more ferocious, as the father could not bring himself to stop. He called these torture sessions education. Another educational measure was to leave the boy standing in the corner, buffeted by ice-cold drafts, all night long.

Yet none of this Dickensian brutality crushed Boris or even depressed him. In a way they were a match: if the father was a sadist, then the son showed an early masochistic bent. First of all, Yeltsin neither loved nor felt sorry for himself, and thus always placed excessive demands on himself. This pathological self-cruelty ran through his entire life, and was noted with surprise by his relatives and co-workers. Obstacles and difficulties excited him, they caused a surge of energy; he could grow and develop only under the cruelest stress. The stronger the pressure, the sturdier he grew. His father's sessions with a belt were exactly the kind of obstacle that Boris overcame successfully and affirmed himself as a result. He endured them till he was fifteen, when he stopped his father's hand, holding the belt, with a memorable phrase: "That's it! From now on I'm educating myself!" That's how he put it, quite seriously: "educating."

Yeltsin rather loved his father. In any event, the only time he has been seen to cry was at his father's funeral—a significant fact. The Yeltsins were typical barrack-dwellers—stern, rigid, blunt, with a he-man behavior code of their own. Any sentimentality, any open show of feeling, was a weakness. Pushkin's lines apply to them: "A stern Slav, I shed no tears."

The pattern of barrack living was spread throughout Russia; some Russians even call barracks their "Little Motherland." The barracks were conceived of as temporary—the authorities called it "emergency"—shelter, meant to last a year or two. They were a feature of the wandering life of trailblazers, pioneers, exiles. Yet, through historical circumstances, this ephemeral, rootless life-style lasted for another twenty to thirty years: generations of Soviets grew up in these places.

Boris Yeltsin is a graduate of the first generation of barrack-dwellers. He could still fall back on Revolutionary heroic pathos and wartime patriotism. No family celebration in his barrack—about a hundred people—was complete without an enthusiastic chorus singing Revolutionary and Civil War songs. At fifty-nine, Yeltsin, trying to answer a Western reporter's question, would use his hands and facial expressions to reproduce the lyrics from a song about Tschors, the famed Civil War commander. The foreigner, unaware of Yeltsin's household icons, was baffled. The barrack is Yeltsin's Motherland, his tradition, his people.

Barrack living is characterized by the absence of privacy. Every detail of domesticity, however intimate, is shared by the entire community. As Yeltsin put it, "Quarrels, secrets, scandals, laughter, tears—the entire barrack can hear, the entire barrack will know." Compared to the openness of the barrack—a hundred souls emotionally naked vis-à-vis one another—the village hut, about which Yeltsin's mother dreamed all those years, or even a tiny room in a thick-walled urban communal apartment, were fortresses of privacy.

In a barrack, things are in plain sight; no act is left unseen and uncommented. Nuances of the personality are quickly eroded, human quirks disappear, as does sensitivity. But the inmates develop an uncanny ability to adapt, a modesty of demands, and an emotional invulnerability. It was here that Yeltsin grew the thick skin that would later stand him in good stead, helping him survive in the extreme situations in which his life would abound.

In times of hardship, the strength of the barrack lay in its closeness, its sense of the needs of others. Yeltsin's mother, Klavdiya Vasilyevna, recalled the return of famine in the first wartime winter. She remembers the ten-year-old Boris coming home from school, moaning, "I am hungry-y-y, I can't go on anymo-o-ore." There was not a crumb of bread in the house. But the whole barrack starved, too; slim comfort that, but it at least provided some moral support. Barrack morals are based on an unconditional egalitarianism, both household and public. It is the simplest formula of survival in the close quarters.

It was in the backwoods of Berezniki—in the lean war years, too—that Yeltsin first confronted social inequality, the elitist underpinnings of Soviet society, carefully camouflaged by patriotic slogans and administrative regulations. According to Klavdiya Vasilyevna, the Berezniki stores, where people exchanged their ration cards for food, had two sections: one for the general population and one for the elite. In the former, one could get coarse flour, rancid butter, and fish—sometimes. In the latter, naturally, mere mortals were not allowed. But little Boris somehow sneaked inside and saw the foodstuff that a barrack-dweller could only dream of: cheese, white bread, and cans of American corned beef. The boy's reaction to the first social snub in his life was somewhat unexpected. Klavdiya Vasilyevna remembered his words well: "Mama, no matter what, I'm gonna become a boss!"

Yet when he became a boss—first of Sverdlovsk, then of Moscow, then of Russia—fighting perks and privileges became the centerpiece of his reformist policy. He was criticized for cheap populism, for flirting with the masses. The critics were wrong. First, he did not need to flirt with the masses—he is part of them, like a branch on a tree. More important, his crusades against elitist socialism, as well as his rejection of personal privileges and perks, stem from an acute sense of injustice inflicted on the people, the same old "snub" that, he felt, had been applied to his entire barrack.

His reaction to the life of privilege sounds naive: "Shameful." But it is utterly pure. It is beyond reproach. Isn't it, indeed, a shame "to swallow imported superdrugs when your next-door neighbor doesn't have aspirin for her baby"? And he feels shame, too, when he sees abundance of food in an American supermarket—shame towards his own people. Not only did Gorbachev, popularly called the Nomenklatura Tsar, never have this feeling, he did not even know what it meant.

The Yeltsin Phenomenon—the way he quickly attracted wide popular sympathy—is rooted in his instinctive solidarity with men and women on the brink of the abyss. Yeltsin attended his first, and most formative, "school of life" in a tightly knit community, and, no matter how high his career would soar, he would never violate the moral code or even the day-to-day routine of communal living. He knows popular tastes and needs, wants, and possibilities from A to Z; he shares a popular "vocabulary" that goes deeper than words. In his innumerable, exhausting speeches in front of audiences thousands strong, he never had to play-act: his audience recognized him as one of their own by his very tone of voice. And one must admit: in talking to people, Yeltsin never played one false note; it was pure straight talk. This is not populism, much less demagogy.

Yeltsin's intuitive sense of the popular "raw nerve" differentiates him radically from Gorbachev. In the course of his social climbing, Gorbachev acquired a nobleman's snobbery and forever lost (as Yeltsin remarked, not gloatingly, but, rather, with genuine surprise) "two-way communication with people." Baffled by Gorbachev's endless gaffes and tactical errors, Yeltsin and his aides never tired of commenting: "He just doesn't sense popular reaction." He shows "total lack of understanding of the laws of human behavior." When the Gorbachevs showed up in front of an audience driven mad by nonstop shortages, he in a British country-squire raincoat and Italian shoes, and she in a stylish fur coat, what could Yeltsin say? "Oh, God—there he goes again!" Gorbachev's sometime sorties outside the Kremlin, when, tightly surrounded by KGB bodyguards, he lectured the man in the street, or when he was flown in his personal plane to a town already embellished for his visit—these had long been the subject of popular mockery. The arrival of the Apostle of Perestroika was sometimes preceded by age-old Potemkinization. For example, when he flew to Lvov, in the western Ukraine, in 1989, the city fathers quickly built a green "wall"—a tight row of potted trees—to block Gorbachev's view of the sewer pipe that was dumping noxious industrial wastes into the river.

And yet Yeltsin can hardly be called a standard product of forced communal living. Like generations of Yeltsins before him, he was tough, rebellious, unbending. He hated the barrack: its leveling, its lack of roots, but the effects of the barrack are nonetheless obvious.

For example, he is not used to privacy, to being by himself, nor is he particularly fond of it. He can be happy among friends in a cramped dormitory cell for four people. His notion of friendship could not be more romantic: even after he became a family man, he spent one vacation every five years with his college friends—one time with eighty-seven of them. As a young engineer with a wife and two young children, he was more comfortable in the rootless ambience of workers' dorms near construction sites than in the relative stability of a city apartment. When, in the summer of 1957, his wife, Naina, gave birth to their first daughter, it was not just a happy father with flowers who came to the hospital; Yeltsin arrived in the company of a bunch of the "guys." And why was he so frightened when he went without his wife on vacation to Kislovodsk, the resort in the Stavropol Territory, and found himself alone in a crowd of idle vacationers? He cabled Naina, who, with great effort, found someone to babysit and flew over. Only then did he calm down—before, "he was so jittery he couldn't even sit down." On his very first construction job he often worked late, sometimes close to midnight; it was as though he were afraid to be idle and by himself—or perhaps was bored by himself.

All his life he was bored by holidays and any form of leisure. Weekends were too long for him: all his life he worked Saturdays. Naina insisted on the Sunday-dinner ritual, to instill a sense of family in the children. Yeltsin did love his wife and daughters and yet they were no substitute for the communal hive of the barrack.

His Sverdlovsk co-workers remember how, after a Saturday at work, he reluctantly headed for his Party dacha. According to the tradition that goes back to Stalin, functionaries were supposed not just to work together, but to relax together as well, in one another's sight, at specially built clusters of dachas. One can sympathize with Yeltsin's Party colleagues when on a Sunday, unable to rest anymore, he proposed that they continue an unfinished meeting from the day before or discuss work-related questions in an unofficial setting.

When teenage Boris fled the jam-packed barrack for the wilderness of the Ural taiga, it was not out of a need for solitude: he never went on hikes without friends. That was how he moved through life: from one crowd to another.

Misha Gorbachev was barely noticed during his nineteen years in his village—a boy with little personality, one like all the rest. Much later, under the reporters' pressure, fellow villagers would make an effort to remember two or three untypical episodes from his life; mostly, they had to improvise. His classmates would rack their brains trying to unearth a single original trait that forty years later would develop into "new thinking." Even in the village school, with its handful—fifteen—of students, Misha Gorbachev merged into the background.

At the beginning of his political career, perhaps his only salient feature was his ideological zeal, which could be attributed to his desire to conceal, aided by the local Party Committee, a black eye in his biography. In 1942 the village of Privolnoye had been occupied by the Nazis. This had to be concealed under Stalin, for anyone who had spent any time in occupied territory was automatically suspect at best. At worst, they had been collaborators. One simply could not launch a career in Moscow with such a background. When Gorbachev filled out a questionnaire required for school admission, he added on some work experience to cover up for the years he had missed during the occupation. This innocent, quite justifiable, falsification helped him enter Moscow University without problems.

By contrast, Yeltsin's life, from the earliest years, abounded in quirks and mutiny. No matter how small the group, down to three persons, he had to be the leader. He would turn the most spontaneous get-togethers into an "organized" shape. Nearly every summer he would "organize" his schoolmates into some sort of trip; later, in college, he would organize all the athletic activities. In this, he showed a well-developed public instinct, hypertrophied at the expense of personal qualities; a quasi-instinctive preference for communal life over private life. Unsurprisingly, when talking about his school years, he rarely uses the first person singular, which one would expect in this kind of narrative, but prefers a generalized impersonal first- or third-person plural ("the guys," "my pals and I").

Hikes and team sports aside, Yeltsin's favorite form of organizing activity was rebellion, such as an entire class protesting a teacher's unjust action. Yeltsin's rebellion was anything but spontaneous; it was well planned, down to the last detail—and, however odd it was in Stalin's school system, justice triumphed. Two years later he did it again, but this time it was far more subversive. At junior high school graduation, with all the parents, teachers, and students present, he publicly denounced an unworthy teacher and demanded her resignation, a genuine act of civil disobedience. It was also impulsive, rash, even suicidal. Forty years later Yeltsin would do it again at the October session of the Central Committee; one might say that he had progressed from a Berezniki school to the Kremlin.

As mentioned, in the '70s, Soviet "mental hospitals" contained patients with surrealistic diagnoses such as "truth-seeking mania." The indestructible human yearning for truth was regarded then as an illness by people whose very existence was based on lies. In a sense, Boris

Yeltsin personifies a Russian truth-seeking type. He keeps repeating, stubbornly and monotonously, as if learned by rote: "For me, the meaning of life never changed since childhood. For me, it is the struggle for truth and justice. And wherever I worked, I fought for truth on my own barricades."

Throughout Yeltsin's life, his rebellions and scandals originated in a sense of wounded justice. Oddly enough, he has nearly always succeeded. Being far removed from the centers of power helped, too: had he grown up in Moscow or Leningrad, his teenage rebellion against the Soviet pedagogical system would have doomed him. But in Berezniki a commission was established that eventually dismissed the denounced teacher.

Thus, Yeltsin encountered the machinery of state, as represented by the Berezniki Party organization, at the tender age of fifteen. For him, it was a positive experience of self-affirmation. Three years later, trying to correct another injustice—he was not allowed to take the graduation exams in advance—he would take a familiar route: district school board, city school board, Party executive committee, city committee. Again, he would win. Such triumphs bred a sense of civic optimism in him.

Yet was young Yeltsin's faith in the justice of Stalin's State so blind and limitless? Did he digest Stalin's persecution of his family—his grandfather, his uncle, his father—in the '30s so easily, so painlessly? Here we run into another Yeltsin improbability: a provincial teenager took to studying Lenin's works by himself, making copious notes in his schoolbook. In an odd twist, by the late '40s, with State terror on the rise again, reading Lenin in the original became a bit dangerous. One was expected to study Lenin in Stalin's interpretation, via Stalin's book *Problems of Leninism.* Many works by Marx, Engels, and Lenin were banned outright; for example, reading Lenin's *Testament,* with its unflattering comments about Stalin, was equivalent to high treason. But student Yeltsin still yearned for answers; he still wanted to understand the mechanism of state and its current policies, and so he kept night vigil over Lenin's theoretical works.

It is doubtful that he found the answers to his burning questions in the Communist gospel. Soon, upon graduating from high school in 1949, Yeltsin had to make some revisions in his autobiography, as Gorbachev had. In one section of the long questionnaire he had to fill out for college entrance, he had to list all his relatives who had been jailed or exiled. The grandson of a *kulak,* the nephew of a saboteur, and the son of a man who had been arrested, would have been barred from higher education. Yeltsin did not mention any of it—just as a year later, Gorbachev, enrolling with a Party recommendation at Moscow University, would conceal the potentially lethal fact that in 1942 he had lived in Nazi-occupied territory.

1950–1955

Any Gorbachev biographer, regardless of affection for the subject, would nonetheless agree that the Soviet leader's years at Moscow University did not exactly form the most attractive part of his story. On the other hand, this is the best-documented period of his life. From the point of view of obtaining information, Moscow University is a much more accessible place than the boondocks of the Stavropol Territory, where he spent altogether forty-two years of his life, and the still-classified Kremlin, where he spent his last days in power. A dozen of his classmates are now scattered around the world: from Vladimir Liberman in Moscow to Lev Yudovich in Germany to Czech Zdenek Mlynar, who now lives in Austria. Together, they draw a contradictory but trustworthy picture of life in a Soviet school in the last years of the Stalin era.

Gorbachev's student years were drastically different from Yeltsin's. It was not merely that Gorbachev went to school in the metropolis of the Stalinist empire, a few kilometers away from His Majesty's Kremlin Palace, while Yeltsin was in the sticks, on the imperial periphery, which Stalin's ukases reached in a sometimes diluted form. Another difference lay in the content of the two young men's educations. However ideologically orthodox the young builder was going to be, he still had to study engineering. The Moscow School of Law was something else completely: for whatever future lawyers studied there, it had nothing to do with the law. As Mlynar noted, instead of teaching young people to think in terms of legality, Soviet law schools weaned them away from it. Students were perceived as the future cadre for the punitive organs—above all, State Security.

That period, the late '40s and early '50s, saw yet another nationwide ideological witch-hunt. The enemy was now called "cosmopolitanism." The idea was to identify persons with dubious ethnic origins and/or pro-Western orientation in academe and among the creative intelligentsia. Moscow University, especially its law school, was one of the prime arenas. Students brought to the campaign the fervor of youth, though they were motivated less by fanaticism, which had disappeared in the early '20s, than by enthusiasm for their careers. Now, vigorous participation in exposing the "cosmopolites," "enemies of the people," and "agents of imperialism" guaranteed the exposers lucrative places in the sun of the Stalin era.

Gorbachev was frenetically active: he was the youngest Party member at the school, Komsomol (Youth Party League) Secretary of the Law Faculty, and a member of the Party Committee of the entire university! (One could join the Party and retain Komsomol membership.) Lev Yudovich recalls that Gorbachev was widely resented by his classmates for his active participation in the "anti-cosmopolitanism" campaign, as well as for his excessive zeal in discussing personal cases.

The farmboy's "straight from the soil," as the current shibboleth went, ideological zeal did not pass unnoticed. Alas, it backfired: Stalin's death destroyed student Gorbachev's ambitious designs. In Khrushchev's era, Gorbachev's aggressiveness and the supporters it had yielded him became a liability. He cultivated an impressive number of influential patrons, but they fell into disfavor, and he along with them: he failed to find a position in Moscow upon graduation. Clutching a Soviet Ivy League diploma in his hand, he had to return to Stavropol. De-Stalinization dealt a severe blow to Gorbachev: when the smoke had settled, he was back to square one.

By contrast, Boris Yeltsin made a solidly pragmatic choice, unburdened by ideology: the Construction Department of the Ural Polytechnical Institute. With 30,000 students, it is one of the largest schools in the country. Naturally, the local Komsomol, Party, and KGB did their best to promote the atmosphere of militant Stalinism—albeit it was in its death throes. Yeltsin, though, seemed to be indifferent to the political passions raging at the institute—partly out of caution, but mostly out of conviction. In any event, beginning with his freshman year, he suppressed his desire for involvement in public issues and his rebelliousness. He was no longer in relatively secure Berezniki, where he had become a veteran of battles with the State. His former teachers recall that Yeltsin shunned ideological, doctrine-laden courses, which constituted almost a quarter of the curriculum, by using every means available, mostly excusing himself for team practice.

His bent toward revolt and truth-seeking now showed itself on a smaller scale, among the student body. He was still fond of organizing protests. Boris Speransky, a former professor, recalls Yeltsin showing up at the head of a student delegation, demanding a longer period of preparation for exams. The professor proposed that he take an exam on the spot, without preparation. Yeltsin did, and got a B—the only one in his transcript—unfairly, he believed. The memory of that injustice would torment him for decades, and he would insert the "damned B episode" in his autobiography. Thirty-seven years later, Speransky, still living in Sverdlovsk, admits, "I should have given him an A. But he truly maddened me."

The same Speransky also recalls that Yeltsin, during the darkest years of totalitarianism, loathed any sort of repression or coercion. Once he sensed them, a revolt was inevitable. In a typical episode, Speransky decided to teach him a lesson in obedience—in front of the class—and suggested that he apologize with a nod of his head.

"[After Yeltsin refused categorically] I grabbed his neck and pressed his head down. 'If you want to make it in this life,' I told him, 'the first thing to learn is obedience.' "

At first Yeltsin seemed to accept defeat at the hands of the much smaller man, but then he suddenly jerked his head upward, and, to a laughing class, the professor's legs dangled in the air.

Anneta Lvov, of Sverdlovsk, a former classmate of Yeltsin's and the closest friend of his wife, recalls young Boris's outspokenness, his perpetual need to voice his opinion. "He was utterly undiplomatic; nothing wishy-washy about him . . . Always firing away whatever was on his mind—however tactless it may have been. Always calls 'em as he sees 'em. It was a torment for him to hold back."

The world of sports, with its insistence on reining in aggressivity and directing it to a specific objective, was a revelation to the eighteen-year-old Boris. He threw himself into sports passionately, at the expense of his studies. Pure, untainted by ideological considerations, sports gave him a chance to show his mettle and to display his most salient qualities: the love of risk, the ability to act fast in an emergency, decisiveness, goal-orientedness, and combative instinct. It also highlighted his organizing abilities. He was charged with setting up all intramural sports. In addition to playing on college teams, he also was a coach. Only his prowess in sports, particularly in volleyball, could satisfy his penchant for leadership and winning. Even with his crippled hand, he headed the school team, and soon was included on the city team, which played the top twelve Soviet teams (college and professional sports were oddly mingled in Russia). By graduation, he almost qualified as a "Master of Sports," which gave him a chance to turn professional. His college friend Yakov Olkov recalls that "Yeltsin was famous all over school. Coeds came to the games just to see him. His fans were legion."

In Yeltsin's view, the worlds of sports and politics have much in common. Athletic competition sharpened the fighting instincts, both offensive and defensive, needed for his future political career. Much later, already in the top echelon of leadership, Yeltsin frequently used athletic terminology in talking about politics. Unlike him, Gorbachev never, either in high school or in college, showed any interest in sports. Accordingly, his politics have always been free of any "game rules" or "sporting ethics"; he preferred diplomatic maneuvers, allowing him to outflank or outwait the rival.

Yeltsin's five-year-long athletic "binge" also involved his masochist streak. While at college, he relentlessly tried to do everything: sports, travels around the country, coaching (four teams at once), even studies. He deliberately overloaded himself, as if testing the limits of his endurance, only to exceed them. He made his own schedule—six to eight hours of practice in the daytime, and studies at night—and stuck to it scrupulously. To this day, he sleeps only three to four hours a night, as his family attests.

On one occasion, he turned his willpower against his health. In his book he described in detail how, after a strep throat and rheumatic-fever complications, he tried to train his already damaged heart to function at the rate he needed to play volleyball. It was an act of pure will—and of masochism.

During his college years Yeltsin was permanently broke: a small monthly allowance from his parents plus a meager stipend were barely enough to buy food. Along with other needy students, he often hired out to unload railroad cars. His friends recall Yeltsin's typical getup: the same velveteen jacket, sackcloth pants, and fake-leather boots. Only when he traveled across the country could he eat his fill.

He made the trip by himself (his friends would not take the risk) in the summer of 1952. In three months he covered thousands of miles. He was spurred by a romantic dream: to see the sea—an emotional reaction perhaps to the claustrophobia of the barrack and Berezniki itself, where every view was blocked by a hillock or woods. But he also needed to feel at home in his country, which he regarded as an extension of his home, of his family. This close kinship, this identification with the State, the country, the people, is vintage Yeltsin.

Stalin's Russia was still a static place, whose citizens were chained to their places by stamps in their passports—and by fear. Yeltsin, however, took off without a kopek in his pocket, traveling primarily on the roofs of railroad cars; in large cities he slept at railroad stations or in parks. Even then, he was never too far away from his "collective," writing postcards to his classmates regularly.

In a sense, Yeltsin's college years were like a sunny interlude between the misery of his childhood and the brutal toil of his career years. He brimmed with energy, vigor, naiveté, jokes. Some of the latter were not terribly sophisticated and had a hooligan streak about them, like kicking the chair from under someone or tying a bucketful of water over the door; whoever walks in first, gets drenched, recalls Yakov Olkov.

But he was a romantic, too—witness his dream of seeing his native land and the sea. Gorbachev, neither in college nor later, had any desire to travel across Russia, preferring tours abroad. Yeltsin created a cult of lifelong friendship with his classmates, extracting a solemn pledge to get together every five years. Again, mark the plural. Yeltsin did not have one close personal friend of childhood or youth; strictly collective-minded, he befriended an entire group, about thirty "guys and gals."

When we read in his autobiography that the next reunion was scheduled for the summer of 1990, we decided to check. It seemed incredible that the Chairman of the Supreme Council of the Russian Republic, with his "extremely" ("extreme" is his favorite word) busy schedule, would find time for a vacation with a group of his classmates. We delayed the question until meeting him in person, but then we unexpectedly received a picture from Anneta Lvov, from Sverdlovsk. The picture was taken on June 19, 1990, on the bank of the Gauya River, near Sigulda in Latvia: Yeltsin looks completely relaxed, even mellow, lying on the grass amidst his friends.

Yakov Olkov, Yeltsin's classmate, also present in the picture, said that young Yeltsin was exceptionally loyal in his attachments and would go to any lengths for a friend. On a female classmate's birthday he brought a basket of flowers—an almost impossible gift to obtain in the bitter Sverdlovsk winter. Yet he did, regardless of the fact that it set him back a few months' salary. "I could cite many more examples like this," Olkov said.

Always a leader, always among people, Yeltsin has been less confident in personal situations, and utterly gauche in love affairs. Friends recall his platonic crush on one of the "gals"; to win her affection, he jumped, fully clothed, in late fall, into a lake. Yet the moment he learned that the girl preferred a friend of his, the infatuation vanished: his idolization of friendship always had an upper hand over his more private emotions.

His youthful chastity, his lack of passion, seem to contradict his impulsive nature. They are the product of his willpower: a self-imposed austerity, a self-denial, even self-mockery; from his early years, he forced himself into a hair shirt. While giving vent to his extrovertedness, drinking in the joy of being with friends, in his private life (if the term applies at all), he was oddly shy and reticent. In the pictures of his student days, noted Goryun, he always stands to the side or even behind his friends' backs. Putting his heart into organizing his friends' weddings, Yeltsin almost missed a chance to have his own.

Even in his own words, his love affairs were diffuse, generalized: he fell in love with the "great, friendly family of students." It took a long time before in this adopted impersonal group he finally singled out one girl—Naya Girin. It was hardly love at first sight; he could experience such ardent passion only toward a community of friends.

He singled out Naya in the bunch by pure instinct. She was "his kind of woman," patterned after his mother: tender, sensitive, patient, quiet, caring, incapable of scenes, she combines the functions of her husband's mother and his best friend. Yeltsin sensed these qualities as early as in their sophomore year; yet as usual he could not bring himself to make a conscious effort to put his private life in order. And, though they did formally declare their love for each other, Yeltsin did not speak of marriage. To sum it up: unlike in sports or in work, Yeltsin had no gift for love.

According to friends, it was hard for Naya to endure the years of uncertainty in their relationship. Especially in the last year of school, when she found out (Boris was, as usual, touring with his team) that they had been assigned jobs in different cities: Boris was left in Sverdlovsk while she was sent to Orenburg, 440 miles southwest of Sverdlovsk, where her parents lived.

For many young couples who had not taken practical steps toward marriage, such a forced separation would have been a disaster. It seems that Naya Girin, left in Orenburg alone with her broken dreams, felt that way, too. Yeltsin was not as upset; he was too busy mastering twelve building trades in one year. He was happy where he lived: in the dorm, surrounded by people. He felt none of the anxiety one would expect from a separated lover; it never occurred to him that he could lose Naya forever. Yet it was not a case of indifference; once again his public interests took priority over personal ones.

He also misrepresented the motivation for their separation in his memoirs, claiming that Naya and he had decided to test their love—just like Tolstoy's Prince Andrei and Natasha—and remember how that ended! His explanation sounded contrived and overly literary, especially to his classmates, who knew the real story. This episode points to a certain retarded development in human terms; a lack of sophistication in his feelings; a desiccation of the entire intimate side of his being. It is his blind spot, a barrenness that is unlikely to ever change.

When they finally were married—in the presence of one hundred fifty "guys and gals"—and settled down in Sverdlovsk, for a long time Yeltsin would not call his wife by name. He addressed her impersonally as *devushka,* which means "young girl" or "miss." To him, she personified his entire group, his beloved classmates, who by then were scattered all over the country. It took him a long time to adjust to family life, which was such a stark contrast with his public disposition. In fact he never did adjust. What he did instead was assume his workaholic life-style, which permitted just one day with the family—Sunday.

This sort of emotional inadequacy is one of the few things that Yeltsin and Gorbachev have in common. Their justifications differ. While Yeltsin responds to personal questions with clichés, Gorbachev is simply helpless and lost; he seems to have no vocabulary to express himself on the subject. He evades details and perceives things in general terms, ignoring nuances. Unlike the impulsive Yeltsin, Gorbachev treats people, even those close to him, for the most part with indifference. Ortega y Gasset noted that, if societies or persons are reduced to serving the State, they too gradually become bureaucratic. Gorbachev's profession—*apparatchik*—exacted its toll. Indifference is bureaucratization of feeling, a paralysis of spontaneous reactions. One should also take into account that in private life Gorbachev is mostly under his wife's thumb—voluntarily, which is why he does not reveal himself spontaneously.

1955–1969

In the summer of 1955 Mikhail Gorbachev returned to Stavropol, where he was to spend the next twenty-three years. He had to launch his Party career (he could conceive of no other) from scratch. In the new era of "thaw" he could not make use of the political training he had received in Moscow. Nor was his legal training any good: he had studied to become a Stalinist Chekist, an old-time KGB man, but by then the title had turned from honorable to shameful.

Gorbachev's first job was extremely modest in the Party's pecking order, even in the provinces—Assistant Chief of the Propaganda Section of the Territorial Komsomol Committee. Never before in the history of the Stavropol Komsomol had a Moscow University graduate, with three years of Party membership under his belt, landed on a ladder rung so low; generally it was the starting point for provincial careerists with only high school diplomas. A year later, he moved up one rung, to become Secretary of the City Komsomol Committee. Yet until 1960, when he first got himself an influential patron, Gorbachev's career promotions were purely routine: he moved into a vacated position. Nothing was required of him but unconditional obeisance and an ability to please his immediate superiors, qualities that he developed very well and which he would later make use of in the Kremlin.

Gorbachev never used his university degree. His sole choice was Party work—the path of least resistance. Such work required little effort; it was a humdrum career of following in someone's footsteps and hoping for a break.

Gorbachev and Yeltsin differ the most in their attitude toward work and professionalism. From the very start of his career in construction, Yeltsin erected hurdles to clear, created difficulties where none had seemingly existed, even though he was routinely handed the toughest projects. He felt the need to strive, conquer, achieve; only resistance gave him satisfaction. He always left a deep, highly visible mark behind him; easy stints and make-work disgusted him.

In Yeltsin's fourteen years of construction work, this attitude delighted some, while irritating and confusing others. Since we could not trace this idealism to any social, monetary, or ideological roots, we turned to his ancestry. Indeed, there is a common line—a genetic code—that runs through generations of Yeltsins: his grandfather, a village handyman and jack-of-all-trades; his father, who treated the prosaic craft of a construction worker with romantic awe; and Yeltsin himself. It is a kind of maximalism that becomes labor ethics, or what he calls "workingman's conscience."

One recalls the idealism of his grandfather who gave his eighteen-year-old grandson a severe test before allowing him to go into construction. By this self-indulgent act of folly, the grandfather could have easily ruined Boris's future by denying him the chance to prepare for college entrance exams. Yeltsin barely made it to Sverdlovsk in time for the exams. But even more curiously, the rebellious and willful grandson considered his grandfather's demand a fair one, and spent the entire summer, without anyone's help or a moment of rest, erecting a log sauna under his grandfather's critical eye. "It was a torment," Boris would later admit.

Immediately after graduation, in his first year at work, Yeltsin did something unique. Unlike his classmates, or all the past and future graduates of the construction department, he did not take a foreman's job at an industrial construction project. He reasoned that he would be unable to be a competent supervisor unless he learned all aspects of the production process. Accordingly, he set himself the task of mastering twelve construction skills in a year. One a month. The task was not merely backbreaking, but ostensibly unrealistic as well: it takes a skilled worker a minimum of six months to master his craft. The laborers next to whom Engineer Yeltsin worked as an equal on the site chuckled and marveled at an obsessiveness that stemmed neither from ideological commitment nor from profit motive. If anything, it was the opposite of the latter: at the time when, planning to start a family, he needed money badly, he refused an engineer's salary.

Nevertheless, it happened the way it always did with Yeltsin: once he promised something, he did it. He worked till he dropped with fatigue, two shifts in a row. By the end of the year the twenty-five-year-old Yeltsin had mastered a dozen skills including those of stonemason, cement layer, carpenter, cabinetmaker, spackler, painter, and crane operator. Only then, satisfied with his acquired competence, did he come to his manager and tell him that he was ready to work as a foreman.

Artur Yezhov, who worked with Yeltsin then, recalls Yeltsin's first day as a foreman. Disregarding his work experience and qualifications, his superiors decided to test his construction skills by ordering him to build a small firing hut. Yeltsin refused categorically: the task was beneath his professional level. That was highly unorthodox. According to the work code of the day, a young specialist was expected to follow orders. As a result, Yeltsin was assigned to the lowest position imaginable.

Impatient to perfect his skills and knowledge, Yeltsin considered the assignment a stinging injustice, the sort to which he had been accustomed since childhood to respond to in one way only: revolt. He spoke at a general meeting in front of several hundred persons, asserting that he was capable of much more and demanding a more responsible job, one commensurate with his training. This was something new in the area of workplace behavior and the Soviet attitude toward work in general, for, by the mid-'50s, catchwords of the early post-Revolutionary years such as altruistic "burning out on the job" and self-denial for "the cause" had come to be perceived as anachronisms and mockeries.

It is ironic that young professional Yeltsin was a living illustration of these outdated attitudes. He won his case, and was assigned to one of the toughest construction sites, one that every expert had refused to oversee.

Thus began Boris Yeltsin's professional career, in a burst of enthusiasm; as his career took off, his enthusiasm kept pace. By the late '50s, his "emergency" hours, from seven in the morning to eleven at night, became routine. He neglected his health, and he admits that his memories of his daughters' early childhood are sparse (Lena was born in 1957; Tanya in 1959). Nevertheless he recalls every detail of complex engineering and construction projects from that epoch.

Hard on himself, Yeltsin showed no mercy toward others. He refused to concede that not all his co-workers were willing to burn themselves out for the common cause. In his very first job, trying to rouse the workers' enthusiasm, he resorted to Draconian measures: high fines and dismissals. It yielded results. In assigning tasks, he was evenhandedly demanding toward friends and strangers alike, refusing to play favorites. People tell of a classmate of his who carelessly damaged a multifiber telephone cable. Yeltsin ordered the man to repair the damage overnight and fired him the next morning. He refused to help his brother-in-law get promoted to an insignificant position. Yeltsin defined the man's level of competence with a typical phrase: "Too early; he's not ready yet."

He developed his own leadership. In striving for efficiency and discipline, Yeltsin purged his work-related communications of every human element. He deliberately cooled relations; at a new job, he refused to greet his underlings: his somewhat primitive method of insisting on the subordination that would enable him to issue orders and make heavy demands. In his work, he was a fanatic, meting out punishment to those who plodded along, uninspired. Later, this would be denounced as managing by order, but, according to Yeltsin, it was the only method that worked back then. People usually say about bosses like Yeltsin: he was rough, crude—but fair.

No one, even his closest kin, could use him as a source of clout. "I remember it well," said Anneta Lvov. "It was November of 1961. Freezing cold. We just moved into a new apartment—a very plain, modest place. My father was paralyzed; very sick. Inside it was as freezing as outside—they had not installed all the radiators. I called Naina right away: Please talk to Boris, we need a radiator badly. The next day I got my sled and went over to his site—he was a construction manager then.

"He stepped outside onto the porch. He looked glum—there must have been some inner struggle going on. 'If your father wasn't sick,' he said, 'there would be no radiator for you. Here's an invoice, pay for the radiator—but it's the last time. Tomorrow someone will ask for a windowframe, then a door—you can't run a business like that.'

"I loaded the radiator onto the sled and headed back home. But he was right. He never asked his bosses for anything personal. His friends requisitioned things on his behalf; they practically forced him to move into a new apartment. He felt very guilty about it."

Yeltsin's engineering career advanced apace. There were no gaps, delays, or upsets; it proceeded in a straight line, from construction foreman to the manager of a large construction company. At thirty-two, he had thousands working under him. By that time Gorbachev had barely crawled out of the Komsomol bog in which he had napped for far too long. He was helped out by his first powerful patron: Fyodor Kulakov, sent from Moscow to head the Stavropol Party organization.

Yeltsin, by contrast, was a self-made man. He created himself according to some sort of design that only he understood. No patronage, connections, shortcuts—he was intolerant of easy ways out. His impressive résumé reflects years of backbreaking effort. Moreover, in his work he was not used to subordinating himself to someone else's will and orders: he was used to taking responsibility. Now, he remembers with surprise that he had never been anyone's deputy: "I'd rather be a mere construction manager than deputy manager of a construction division; a manager of a construction division rather than a deputy company director." The strong suit of Yeltsin the politician—his decisiveness in a crisis, his willingness to take risks—was developed on the construction sites of his youth.

It is puzzling: this labor fanaticism, this toiling till exhaustion—what was the point? Was it money? The Yeltsins always lived modestly, settling for the bare necessities. According to Rosa Alexeyeva, Yeltsin's sister-in-law, in the late '50s, when his work load was the heaviest, when Yeltsin worked like a maniac, when his wife fell asleep over the supper that had grown cold, as she waited for him to come home—he still could not provide for the family. Consequently, Naya could not take time off to be with her baby daughters—she had to combine her engineering job with family duties. As for Yeltsin, he had neither time nor energy left for his family. If Naya talked him into going to the movies, it would be the last show, and she had to come and tear him away from work.

The Yeltsins never saved a ruble. Relatives and friends were amazed by the modesty of their domestic needs, even when the head of the family

earned, in his own words, a "sizable salary" as the director of the construction company. It was from the same relatives, by the way, that Boris
Yeltsin, already the Party Boss of the entire Sverdlovsk Region, had to
borrow money. When the Yeltsins moved to Moscow, they furnished
their apartment with the beat-up furniture they had brought from Sverdlovsk.

In Moscow, the Yeltsins have always lived modestly, which befits their
tastes and needs. Yeltsin's salary and his wife's small pension are their
only income; there are no privileges, no perks. They find luxury tasteless,
burdensome, depersonalizing—they are not comfortable with it, though
one cannot say that they have had a good taste of it. Still, Yeltsin pays
a great deal of attention to looking respectable (a decent suit, always a tie,
a well-starched white shirt, and shoes color-coordinated with the suit). In
his two years as Minister of Construction, according to his secretary, "He
never bought anything." Finally—along with other Ministry workers—
he was issued a ration card to buy standard Soviet shoes; it could not have
been more timely.

In the summer of 1989 the Yeltsins were stuck in hot, suffocating
Moscow, with no dacha to go to on weekends. So Minister Yeltsin began
to think about buying a car for family outings with his grandchildren.
Yet, as he soberly calculated one afternoon in his typist's office, he could
hardly afford such a luxury—"unless my in-laws help out." When he was
elected People's Deputy, he automatically lost his Minister's salary. His
wife, to whom he diligently handed over his salary, declared that after two
weeks they would starve. Exactly, confirms his secretary: he had enough
money left for only two weeks. Despite his jocular bravado about taking
a janitorial job, for two shifts back-to-back—180 rubles a month—he was
worried about his temporary inability to support his family.

Becoming President of the Russian Republic did little to change the
Yeltsins' habits—not that it meant much more money, either. His salary
had grown substantially, to 4000 rubles from the 800 rubles he got in 1989
as a Minister. However, with adjustment for inflation, it was the same
money, if not less. Whether he was the Party Boss of Moscow or Minister
of Construction or Russian President, his wife has always shopped in the
regular stores, standing in line with the rest of Moscow. Their daughter
Tanya, who still lives at home, says quite sensibly, "You can catch
Mother at home from twelve to six. But not all the time. She has to go
shopping, too."

When we arrived in Moscow, it took us three days to reach the Yeltsins
on the phone. It turned out, Tanya explained, that "because of all that
putsch business we lost the phone bills. So they turned off the service."

They do not have a secretary or a housekeeper, and Naina Iosifovna's
time is divided among three telephone lines, household chores—of which

there are always plenty—and trips to the dacha in Usovo, where she also shops and cooks by herself. She also picks up her eleven-year-old grandson, Boris, at school. To this day, the Yeltsins' house is so vulnerably open, so accessible to strangers, that in approaching them we felt uneasy, as if we were violating this private-citizen democratic simplicity that they treasure so much.

The Yeltsins' nondescript three-bedroom apartment houses two families: Yeltsin, his wife, and Tanya, with her husband and son. There are two Boris Yeltsins in the household—the President and his grandson. Little Boris sleeps on the couch in the living room. When there are guests, or the family stays up late watching TV, the boy goes to sleep in his parents' room; then, sleepy, he is carried to the couch. The living room is furnished with Sverdlovsk-made furniture, objects of family pride: "much better quality, and sturdier, too, than Moscow-made junk." And they still remember how much they paid for it.

Yeltsin's study is a small room that most people would find confining. It contains an armchair, a desk, and a bookcase, but no room for a small couch. Yet, like his wife, Yeltsin has always been content with the bare necessities. In short, his is hardly a presidential residence. Yeltsin received it in 1985 when he came from Sverdlovsk to take a rather modest— compared to today's—position as Central Committee Section Chief. "By Soviet standards they're doing decently," remarks his former assistant Valya Lantseva. "Of course it would make sense for them to move to a larger place, but Yeltsin does not have time for that. He doesn't have time for things personal."

Compare the Gorbachevs' royal—by Soviet standards—five-room apartment. After they moved from Stavropol to Moscow, enterprising Raisa Maksimovna furnished the place with hard-to-get Finnish furniture, decorated it with expensive Bukhara rugs, antique china, and Western-made gadgetry. What a vast gap in demands, in taste, in life-style . . .

One struggles to comprehend Engineer Yeltsin. He always worked at specific construction goals, be it a water tower or a cement factory, performing narrowly circumscribed professional duties. Whence his social commitment verging on asceticism, or, as an ex-colleague of his put it, his "joy in killing yourself for the common cause"? Why was he so enthused when their crew carpenter agreed to work overtime, and rewarded that carpenter with a hard-to-find transistor radio that he had obtained with such difficulty for his own family? Why was he so willing, when his family was in financial straits, to spend his own money on public needs—for improvement in the women's locker rooms, for example? According to Sverdlovsk journalist Andrei Goryun, for a long time Yeltsin helped a woman worker he barely knew support her family after she had been unjustly fired on a false accusation. He supported her until she was reinstated. Later, in Moscow, when he was already Party Boss, a fellow reformer ran into him at the farmers' market. Yeltsin was loading the trunk of his car with bags of fruit, on his way to visit a children's home. With fruit prices at the Moscow market sky-high, how much of his monthly salary did that represent? All of these acts were mechanical, routine, far from publicity-motivated. Few people knew about them and no one talked about them.

Yeltsin evaluated a builder's efforts from the point of view of public utility and good citizenship. He undertook his tasks voluntarily, and performed them with inspiration, investing routine jobs with public spirit. Some of his colleagues saw this as a contradiction, if not a paradox. He saw his numerous construction projects, as he would later see the Sverdlovsk Region, then Moscow, and finally all of Russia, in personal, subjective terms. He could never draw the line between the personal and the public in the accepted sense of the two words. He perceived his projects in domestic terms—a hole in the roof of the lathe shop was like a hole in the roof of his own kitchen; he simply could not distinguish between the two. Moreover, he was more likely to repair the lathe shop.

WE, HIS biographers, are dealing with a human configuration that we do not claim to understand. Boris Yeltsin may arouse admiration or hatred as a politician, but his psychology remains opaque. Valentina Lantseva, his closest aide for years, said that he is "so very simple, so uncomplicated." But we felt somehow that simplicity was being confused with wholeness of character; the two are not identical. We tried to localize the "Yeltsin type" geographically: the free-spirited Urals have long supplied Russia with roughhewn, practical-minded diamonds-in-the-rough. In his tireless, religious obsession with work, whether as foreman or Party Boss, whether in the opposition or as a national leader, he has acquired a heroic image that seems too good to be true. In order to see Yeltsin up close, as he is, one must constantly downplay his heroism.

When, in the spring of 1985, Yeltsin was transferred to Moscow, he left behind good memories of himself, and fellow Sverdlovskites would later be the first to support him when the attacks on him were at their most violent. This hardly implies, however, that he was a saint on all of the countless jobs that he had in the thirty years after graduation. He had many battles, and he was not always in the right. It would be an exaggeration to say that his path was strewn with corpses but there were some.

A thirty-year-old story, still remembered by Sverdlovsk old-timers, tells us that Yeltsin was not always scrupulous and independent on the way up. According to Goryun, in the early '60s Yeltsin allegedly worked hard to rekindle a friendship with Boris Kiselev, a college friend of his, several years his senior. Kiselev was by then very successful, heading the construction department of the Sverdlovsk Regional Party Committee. No one in the region's construction industry was promoted without his say-so. On Yeltsin's initiative, the former friends began socializing family-style, visiting each other's houses—in short, moving toward a closer friendship. As a result, Yeltsin's career took off. But after Yeltsin became a high Party official, he quickly cooled toward his friend, ignored him, and even made derogatory remarks about him. Did he resent the man whose influence he once had had to win by apple-polishing? Or was being the protégé of a college chum an insult for a man as proudly independent as Boris Yeltsin?

Another case provided by the same Goryun did not seem convincing, and we could not confirm it by a third party. Yet Goryun insisted he had the testimony of several witnesses.

It goes back to the early '60s, too. Boris Yeltsin, heading a construction division, was quickly outgrowing routine promotions. He wanted to move faster, and there was only one way: the old propaganda song-and-dance that goes back to Stakhanov days—setting a record. One of the crews under his command did just that, doubling its productivity. It was a simple stunt: the "progressive" crew received supplies ahead of others, often at their own expense. The glory reflected on Yeltsin as well: he was promoted to chief construction engineer. Now he took a dim view of anyone who refused to praise his "record."

Yeltsin's immediate superior, Construction Director A. L. Mikunis, viewed the triumph skeptically, ignoring the record-makers and refusing to report their string of successes to his superiors. At a Party meeting, when the discussion moved to the "progressive" crew, he was silent: "Then Yeltsin spoke. It is no longer possible to find out exactly what happened afterward—eyewitness accounts vary—but after the meeting Mikunis had a heart attack from which he never recovered, and soon died. Yeltsin moved into his old boss's office. Soon after that he lost all interest in the 'progressive' crew—a big boss does not get much credit for bringing about the nonstop operation of a handful of workers."

Perhaps it is unfair to charge Yeltsin with driving his superior to a heart attack, but there is a credible element here. Yeltsin, motivated by the desire to serve the general cause rather than by a taste for personal aggrandizement, considered human beings means to an end. The fact that he treated himself with equal pragmatism ("usefulness is the main criterion") hardly justified such an approach toward others.

His joining the Party had a similarly utilitarian basis, especially since, unlike Gorbachev, he signed up at a mature age, with considerable work and administrative experience under his belt. The Party card was a pass to the next rung of his career. It is unlikely, though, that Yeltsin was

hypocritical about it: Party membership suited his civic-minded temperament. Also, at the time, the Party was the only outlet for political activity;
there were no other ways for further professional growth and career
promotion. How could this dynamic, ambitious man stop on a dime and
retire into himself? Of more interest is this: what took him so long to join?

By then Gorbachev was already a seasoned Communist. From the
Party standpoint, though, despite a superficial resemblance, the two men
were complete opposites. Gorbachev was of course a Party prodigy—few
people join so early, at twenty-one, and while still in college. Yeltsin, on
the other hand, was joining too late; at thirty, from a career standpoint,
he was overripe.

The Parties that Gorbachev and Yeltsin joined were identical in name
only. The Party Gorbachev joined in 1952 was Stalinist; the Party Yeltsin
joined in 1961, the heyday of reform and liberalization, was a Khrushchev
one. By then, both men were formed professionally: Gorbachev an *apparatchik,* Yeltsin an industrial manager—a Partocrat and a technocrat.
Finally, a long-awaited point of convergence: both Gorbachev and Yeltsin were made Party Bosses of their respective native regions. Gorbachev
made the grade six years earlier: he became the Party Secretary of the
Stavropol Territory in 1970, at thirty-nine, while the forty-five-year-old
Yeltsin took a similar job in Sverdlovsk only in 1976.

1969–SPRING 1985

When Yeltsin, using Party clichés, talks about the date when he moved
"from economic to Party work," he is clearly wrong. For the nine years
he spent as the First Secretary of the Sverdlovsk Region, he remained a
manager, master of a huge estate, an area of 80,000 square miles. His
inspection trips across his domain demonstrate his managerial fervor.
Every year he visited the towns and large villages of the region—all
sixty-three of them. Those were no junkets; they were working trips, tests
of endurance. Yeltsin met with experts and made spot decisions. Staying
on top of problems, examining them in detail, was the only way he could
confidently rule his domain. From the sidelines it seemed that he was
constantly racing the clock, living on the cutting edge of the possible; it
looked like never-ending forced labor. But it was self-imposed; he neither
knew of any other way of life nor wanted one.

Even when he visited Moscow to see the Central Committee or Brezhnev personally, Yeltsin went with an economic agenda; he avoided court
intrigues and claimed no Kremlin patron. Perhaps he did a bit of scheming, but it was for the cause, for Sverdlovsk—never for himself. Once, he
managed to outmaneuver Brezhnev, by now senile, and cajole him into

signing, without even looking at, the authorization to build a subway in Sverdlovsk.

On another occasion, taking advantage of the doddering General Secretary's incompetence, Yeltsin talked him into designating the Sverdlovsk Region part of the so-called Non-Chernozem Zone. At that time, in the late '70s, the Kremlin made yet another last-ditch effort to at least reduce the growing unprofitability of agriculture—which had been in the red since time immemorial—by making major investments in the Northern European part of the USSR, officially termed the Non-Chernozem Zone. *Chernozem* is a term for fertile soil, and really applies to the south.

The inclusion of the Sverdlovsk Region, way to the east, into the zone was quite fishy. That did not bother the insouciant General Secretary, and it disturbed the Sverdlovsk Boss, Yeltsin, even less. By that ruse Yeltsin managed to ease the food crisis in his region, where farming is a marginal industry and cannot feed the population.

It was this chronic lack of foodstuffs that induced Yeltsin to seek barter deals with the Stavropol Territory, one of Russia's breadbaskets. This was their first introduction—over the phone. Yeltsin offered lumber and steel from the Urals, while Gorbachev was ready with Stavropol bread and meat. Both headed their respective Party Committees, though, as Yeltsin, wounded by what he perceived as General Secretary Gorbachev's arrogance, would note later, their domains were not comparable: Sverdlovsk was far ahead of Stavropol in economic might.

But neither economic performance nor business acumen made a provincial *apparatchik* a winner in the Grand Kremlin Stakes. In 1978 the fates cast both Yeltsin and Gorbachev in similar dramatic situations.

That year, at different times, both Gorbachev and Yeltsin stood on their respective railroad platforms, awaiting the train carrying the powerful guest from Moscow. But only one of them—Gorbachev—got to see the General Secretary.

On September 19, 1978, a special train carrying Brezhnev and his aide Konstantin Chernenko to Baku, the capital of Azerbaijan, made an unscheduled stop at a station of a small resort village called Mineralny Vody. On the platform, they were met by the KGB Chairman, Yuri Andropov, who was taking the waters in the nearby resort of Kislovodsk, in the Stavropol Territory, and his protégé, the Territory's First Secretary, Mikhail Gorbachev. The brief encounter decided Gorbachev's destiny: by the end of the year he was in Moscow. Since the meeting itself was briefly noted in the Soviet media, this must be regarded as an historic occasion: on September 19, 1978, four successive Soviet leaders—Brezhnev, Andropov, Chernenko, and Gorbachev—met at the small station of Mineralny Vody.

Yeltsin, too, came out to the platform to greet the General Secretary, who was passing Sverdlovsk en route to the Far East. But Brezhnev did not deem it necessary to see a man, who, unlike Gorbachev, was without political potential. The train rushed, without even slowing down, past the dumbfounded host and his Sverdlovsk courtiers.

It seems that Yeltsin was in general not very sensitive to the court etiquette that Gorbachev had successfully set out to master upon his move to Moscow. Soon, Gorbachev had a chance to share his newly acquired polish with Yeltsin and teach the Siberian hick some manners.

In the late '70s, Brezhnev's Kremlin sycophants, out of ideas on how to stroke their Methuselah-like boss's vanity and reap political dividends for themselves, decided to launch an informal but notable nationwide campaign to immortalize his name. The Ukrainian city of Dnepropetrovsk, where Brezhnev had begun his Party career, was turned into a sort of open-air memorial; marble plaques on the buildings celebrated every stage of his life of achievement.

Then came Sverdlovsk's turn to join the chorus: in the '20s, Brezhnev had gotten his first land surveyor job there. Moscow "researchers" found the building where the great event had taken place, and, referring to the Kremlin's directives, demanded that First Secretary Yeltsin convert it into a museum. Yeltsin, not versed in the court games of toadying and brown-nosing, ignored the demands, for the first time in his life disobeying the Central Committee. This was not an act of rebellion: he just did not take the order seriously. He was not alone. Outside the Kremlin, Brezhnev, who had long ago stopped attending to State affairs and was rapidly sinking into senile epicurean folly, was perceived solely as a butt of numerous jokes. Yeltsin even quipped to the Moscow messengers: "How about the font in which he was baptized—you're sure you don't want to have it gold-plated?" The Brezhnev Museum never materialized.

Yeltsin was called on the carpet in Moscow. Passing from one high office to another, he finally arrived at that of the Central Committee's Secretary on Agriculture, Comrade Gorbachev, with whom he had had previous economic dealings. But this time Gorbachev was not interested in Sverdlovsk's agricultural woes. He asked Yeltsin cautiously, "Do you disagree with the Central Committee?" And, casting a meaningful look, said, "You should draw conclusions, you know . . ." He said it twice. This was not a reprimand; it was a clever way to caution Yeltsin, who had committed a flagrant violation of Kremlin etiquette.

Shortly thereafter, Yeltsin became involved in another building controversy—though of a much different kind. Of all the things he has done in Sverdlovsk, the one he has been blamed for the most—some consider it a crime and demand that he be punished—was the destruction of the Ipatyev House. It was in the cellar of that house that, following Lenin's personal orders, Nicholas the Second had been executed along with the members of his household—wife, children, maids of honor, and even the family doctor. Although, unlike in the case of the Brezhnev Museum, Yeltsin did follow Moscow's orders, he was the one later held responsible. The history inevitably surfaces in every anti-Yeltsin campaign. Here is an excerpt from an article published in 1990: "The Ipatyev House was spared in the Civil War; it endured the era of Stalin's cult of personality and Khrushchev's voluntarism. The only comparison that comes to mind is the destruction of the Christ the Saviour church in Moscow. Russia has cursed Kaganovich* for eternity—what about Yeltsin? How can this chameleon of a functionary still be elected to office, enjoy popular trust, and reach for the Crown of Monomakh?† How low have we fallen! Haven't we learned anything? Please, Russian people—open your eyes!"

There is a certain paradox: Russia's future ruler, at the time the Kremlin's viceroy in Sverdlovsk, destroyed the last traces of the last Russian Emperor. Neither he nor any other provincial satrap would ever have dared decree such a momentous act without the Kremlin's direct instructions. In fact, an instruction was secretly issued by Brezhnev's Politburo following reports that Ipatyev House had turned into an informal shrine.

The reports were exaggerated, of course; in any case, there was never any mass pilgrimage. Sverdlovsk is more than a day from Moscow by train—not a location popular with tourists, to say nothing of advocates of monarchy. Vladimir Solovyov visited it in the '70s (Yeltsin already headed the local Party Committee), and, naturally, was curious to see where the House of Romanov, which had ruled Russia for three hundred years, had met its end.

Asked how often he had to take visitors to the Ipatyev House, the cabdriver replied, "Not too often. Locals don't care at all. Mostly *your* kind." He gave Solovyov a certain look.

"From Moscow?"

"Moscow, Leningrad—don't matter. From all over. But all of them Jews. Why *you* people are so interested in *our* Tsar . . ." He sounded genuinely curious, not sarcastic.

It was absurd to label Ipatyev House a hotbed of monarchism. But fear spreads fast, and the Kremlin rulers, well aware of the illegitimacy of the power they had usurped in 1917, from time to time tried to concretize one of their fears. This time it was that of the restoration of the monarchy.

---

*The church of Christ the Saviour in Moscow, built 1837–1883, was destroyed at Stalin's personal order, yet Russian chauvinists place the blame on Lazar Kaganovich, a Jew, who at the time was Moscow's Party Boss, in a sense, one of Yeltsin's predecessors in that position.
†The informal name of the Russian ancient crown. Grand Prince Vladimir Monomakh was one of the first Russian rulers.

Yeltsin could not disobey a direct Kremlin order. He was given a deadline: in three days the house was to be destroyed. One night heavily guarded bulldozers and excavators pulled up to the house. By morning not a trace of the historical building remained. Every brick, including ones from the foundation, had been taken to the city dump. In order to completely erase the memory of the horrors that had taken place there sixty years ago, the site was carefully paved with asphalt. Now it is a part of the highway.

In carrying out the Kremlin's orders, Yeltsin was utterly indifferent to the barbarous destruction of a historical monument. Subsequently he was vague on facts and dates, and could not even remember the name of the street where the house was—amazing, considering his excellent memory.

An interesting detail: for sixty years the Kremlin had ignored the reports of individual pilgrims to the Ipatyev House. Then, all of a sudden, the Kremlin stirred, and sent a secret cable to Sverdlovsk demanding that the house be razed within three days.

We would like to venture a theory that we consider as good as true. We bear personal, if involuntary, responsibility for the events that took place that night in Sverdlovsk; like Yeltsin, we stand charged and plead not guilty.

In early 1977 we broke away from official literature to form an independent information agency, Solovyov-Klepikova Press. The subject of our first press release, distributed among the Moscow-stationed foreign journalists in Moscow, was a literary/political scandal in Leningrad: Vladimir Toropygin, the editor in chief of *Aurora* magazine, and his deputy, Andrei Ostrovsky, had been fired for publishing a poem by Nina Koroleva, in which she voiced sympathy for the executed Tsar's family—especially the Tsarina and the young Prince.

> ... *And in that year when the flame flickered*
> *on the thin banner,*
> *in that town the Czarina with her child*
> *did not smile.*
> *And I suffocate in impotence*
> *I have no power to save them—*
> *I am privy to misfortune and violence*
> *and I am privy to malice.*

Commenting on the scandal, we wrote in our release that "while Western readers might find it difficult to understand why someone should be punished for showing pity toward an executed woman and her young son, Soviet readers are still astonished that such a poem could slip by the censor's knife and see light."

The release was first covered by *The Christian Science Monitor* and by David Shipler of *The New York Times*. Shipler asked our permission to do a piece on the scandal and to mention us at the end as the source. Several days later a separate piece by him on our agency with our pictures made page one—and once again mentioned the ideological crime-and-punishment in Leningrad. By now the story was aired day and night by Western Russian-language radio stations: the Voice of America, Radio Liberty, and the BBC, whose reporter Kevin Ruane spent days and nights at our apartment. Koroleva's "monarchist" poem was heard all over the Soviet Union. Some of our sources told us that a Politburo meeting held at this time discussed the growth of monarchist sentiment in the country—with the report by KGB Chairman Andropov.

Now, a word about the chronology of these events. The first report about our agency and the story about the dismissal of *Aurora* editors was published by *The Christian Science Monitor* on April 27, 1977. The next day, *The New York Times* ran a more detailed item. At the same time—late April and early May—our story, translated back to Russian, began coming back to Russia through Russian-language programs, routinely taped by the KGB. They are also heard by the Kremlin leaders, who rely on them for information on their own country more than on the subordinates' sycophantic reports.

In any event, in early May, the "monarchist" poem was being aired so often that Politburo members, despite their senile amnesia, could learn it by heart. Their horror of a relatively innocent little piece seemed to match that of Macbeth being scared by Banquo's ghost—an overly literary hyperbole, perhaps, but how else does one explain to a sane reader the Kremlin maniacs' reaction to a lyrical epitaph to an executed mother and child?

A mere two months after the broadcasts, Yeltsin received a secret order to raze the Ipatyev House—which he did on the night of July 27, 1977.

As the Russian nineteenth-century poet Fyodor Tyutchev wrote:

It is not given to us to predict
The response our words will provoke . . .

How could we guess the unexpected consequences of our first press release, either short-term—the destruction of Ipatyev House—or long-term—the accusations that Yeltsin followed the Politburo's orders? Did he have a choice?

We should, however, note Yeltsin's executive zeal: once the orders came in, he wasted no time; the necessary paperwork was done later—and backdated. It is likely that Yeltsin, a goal-oriented industrial manager, did not realize that the Politburo's orders might not be enough, and additional legal justification for his action was required. Yet later it turned out that, even in Brezhnev's Russia, some niceties needed to be observed. For example, it turned out that the Ipatyev House was officially protected as a historical and architectural monument. Before it was destroyed, it had to be removed from the protected list. This was done in a special act of the Sverdlovsk City Council dated August 3, 1977, a week after the house was gone. And it took the same City Council another six weeks to issue an official decision to raze the house—on September 21. To endow this shameful timetable with an appearance of plausibility, the official documents were made out to show that the house was torn down not in one night, as had been the case, but in the period from July to September 1977.

All the documents pertaining to this act of vandalism are still classified; even the writer Eduard Radzinsky, who has devoted years to investigating the circumstances of the execution of the Tsar and his family, could not determine the exact date when the house was destroyed. It took our Sverdlovsk source, too, a great deal of effort to supply us with these dates. It shows that Yeltsin clearly jumped the gun in following the Kremlin's orders, and later had to cover up his excessive zeal by manipulating the truth.

Despite this episode, however, it is important to remember that Yeltsin has always been indifferent to ideology. Party old-timers in Sverdlovsk, like F. M. Yelokhin, describe him dismissively: "As a Party man, he was a zero." Even when he became First Secretary, "it was essentially the same." Whatever position Yeltsin occupied, he remained a builder, a manager, an administrator, and even his—in Sverdlovsk—unequivocally command-administer style had nothing to do with ideological fervor.

If he started out treating the Sverdlovsk Region like a cost-conscious estate manager, upon his appointment to Moscow he expanded this attitude to the Moscow level, and then to the entire country. He would be the first Soviet politician to remove publicly (at the 19th Party Conference) the veil of secrecy from a classified subject like the Party budget. Like a new master speaking on behalf of an impoverished nation, he demanded that the Party lords account for "where the Party money goes—and that's hundreds of millions of rubles." Later, in early 1991, Yeltsin, upon becoming the ruler of the Russian Republic, would be the country's only leader to call for prosecuting Party tycoons for their financial misdoings. He would make an anxious, emotional, despairing appeal on the TV screens: "Where does the Russian Federation's gold go, and how? In a little over a year, two hundred tons of gold, as well as a lot of diamonds, vanished abroad. This gold disappeared from the national—the Russian—gold reserves. For what purpose? Where is it? Who is responsible? What did it pay for? No one knows. No one . . ."

In Sverdlovsk, too, the industrial sector was his principal arena, where he focused his energy and where he fought pitched battles with his Moscow overlords. In his job as First Secretary, he did not buck the trends of his time or question the legitimacy of the political system. He followed his superiors' orders—destroying the Ipatyev House, for example—with mechanical obedience, like a disciplined Communist. He did not bother to contemplate the meaning of the order, and erased it from his memory the moment it was executed. Later on, in hindsight, he would claim a seer's pain over the barbarous act. Yet until 1990 his attacks were against the hierarchy of power—be it the school system or the Kremlin—without disturbing its ideological basis, which he considered unimpeachably right and rock-solid.

As a First Secretary defending his region's interests, Yeltsin engaged in a direct confrontation with Moscow on a few occasions. In the late '70s he took a risk, shifting his construction resources from industrial projects (which the government called for) to residential ones. Instead of doing it over the ten-year period specified in the government plan, he razed all the barracks and moved several thousand families into new, modern apartments within one year. By the end of the five-year plan, "twenty-five percent of Mid-Ural families celebrated a housewarming." According to Yeltsin's Sverdlovsk ex-colleagues in construction and Party work, this rosy figure conceals an appalling amount of backbreaking effort and "almost devilish manipulation" by their boss, for at that time, because of the economic crisis, residential construction had collapsed.

WHEN YELTSIN sometimes says that he used the almost unlimited power of the First Secretary "only for the people's good, and never for my own benefit," it might sound like another election slogan, but he means it. Whether working as an engineer, a Party functionary, or a politician, he has always consciously served the people, sacrificing himself and his personal interests to the general good. Moreover, the heavier the sacrifice, the higher his satisfaction. Of course, the effectiveness of the sacrifice was a factor, too: "I made the wheels of the economy spin faster."

Since Yeltsin always believed in hands-on management, he spent little time either in his enormous office in the Sverdlovsk Party Committee building (now proudly displayed to tourists) or his own apartment, which was in the building informally called the Old Bolshevik House (all the tenants were purged in the '30s). Yeltsin felt like a legitimate master—a lord of the manor in the region that was third in the country in industrial production. He liked getting into the nuts and bolts of every form of manufacturing, without relying on experts. This led to an enormous work overload, noted by all of his ex-colleagues. For example, the Sverdlovsk

Region, where the ground is covered with snow two hundred days a year, has always been in chronic need of food. Yeltsin was always on the lookout for new ways of feeding his subjects, and, as a result, became an expert in agriculture.

Some of Yeltsin's ex-colleagues charge that he has always been a dictator, that he has never been in favor of governing democratically. When discussing specific issues, and already knowing the answer in advance, he used storm trooper tactics on his opponents. Yeltsin made all the responsible decisions, especially the ones that potentially meant trouble with Moscow, by himself. His advocates claimed that he brought a high degree of competence to every issue discussed. However, unlike many provincial Secretaries of the period, he did not govern by fiat out of ignorance or arrogance. Yeltsin's maddening pressure on his subordinates had one objective: that they perform with maximum efficiency.

Sverdlovsk still remembers how Yeltsin personally forced through the emergency construction of the highway between the city and the northern part of the region, which had had no paved roads. The highway was divided into a number of sections. Each district boss was responsible for his local stretch. On the day the construction was scheduled to be finished, Yeltsin drove all the local bosses along the highway in a large bus. If, on a given section, the road was not finished, Yeltsin personally, in front of everybody, had the local boss taken off the bus and left in the middle of nowhere. Getting back to town was the man's own problem.

To be sure, these were brutal tactics, management with an iron fist—but that was the only way Yeltsin could get what he wanted within the existing system: "They obeyed, they listened, and as a result the factories were run better." He treated people exclusively as cogs in a machine and allowed no personal, human feelings in his work relations.

Yeltsin also tried to lay claim—for the cause, naturally—on the free time of his Sverdlovsk Party colleagues. Their lunches often turned into working lunches—"informal exchanges of opinion on general issues," as he diplomatically put it. In the Committee's cafeteria, he made sure that the Secretaries, Bureau members, and section chiefs were seated close to his table; in the thirty to forty minutes allotted to lunch, they managed to resolve a whole array of issues. Presumably, they had time to eat, too.

Of course Yeltsin firmly believed in *mens sana in corpore sano:* in winter, the entire Party Committee went skiing. Twice a week, Bureau members and their families went to the volleyball court to play Yeltsin's favorite sport. One imagines that at least some of them had different ideas for their leisure; or, if exercise was inevitable, they would rather have jogged or played tennis instead of playing a team sport like volleyball.

Yeltsin never bothered with such trivia as personal likes or preferences, yet it was not out of crude egoism or the love of tyranny; somehow he was firmly convinced that his communal fervor and selfless love of labor had to be shared, as selflessly and enthusiastically, by all his subordinates, who would thus inevitably turn into comrades-in-arms and fellow believers.

Later, after Yeltsin moved to Moscow, he further cultivated his habit of using his subordinates to what he considered selfless and exalted ends. Take his Minister's job in 1988–89, from which he began his inroads into politics: first taking part in the 19th Party Conference, then his election to a People's Deputy. Not for a moment did he doubt that his staff secretary, Tatyana Pushkina, should devotedly work overtime on his political campaigns.

At Yeltsin's "request," she would take a train from her suburb to be at her job at seven, in order to type yet another draft of his speech or his notes prior to yet another conference or congress. When she tried to slip out for lunch, Yeltsin would invariably remark in a jocular, chiding tone: "Lunch again? How can you have lunch every day?" He often missed lunch, wrapped in his work and politics, and naturally assumed that those around him—his personal and ideological comrades—should work on the same emergency schedule. In the evening, in the by now empty Ministry building, Tatyana would still be working, and when, about ten, she rose to go home, Yeltsin cast a meaningful look at his watch: "Leaving already?"

Naturally, Yeltsin's secretary, like her indefatigable boss, should work Saturdays voluntarily—as well as holidays. She remembers one holiday evening that she spent bent over her typewriter—it was the eve of March 8, Women's Day, generally celebrated in Soviet offices with a great deal of pomp. On that particular day—and it was already long over—neither Yeltsin nor his assistant Lev Sukhanov remembered to wish Tatyana a happy Women's Day: the election was close, and both were working around the clock. Finally, a call came from Yeltsin's wife, part of whose job was to correct her husband's social gaffes. "Tanya? Why are you still there?" Then Naina called her husband on his personal line. She must have reminded him of the holiday, because minutes later Yeltsin was running out of his office, pulling a ballpoint out of his pocket—*a present*—and wishing his secretary a happy Women's Day!

Thus, in the spirit of heroic self-effacement, Tanya worked two years for Boris Yeltsin. They parted ways for "purely financial" reasons. In his new job at the Supreme Soviet, Yeltsin could offer her a meager 200 rubles a month; finally she dared to bring him down to earth and tell him that this was not enough to live on. Once again, her boss tried to remind her of her civic duties: "I'm fighting salary raises for the nomenklatura, and now you want one, too." Tanya had to draw a picture for him. How could 200 rubles be enough when a pair of boots for her teenage daughter cost 160? "It's like this: either she walks barefoot or we starve," she said. Despite the pathos of his speeches, Yeltsin was not aware of the prices of essential goods, for his wife took care of the practical side of his life.

Tatyana Pushkina is still a Yeltsin fan, but she cannot help recalling the two years of selfless toil for him without a bit of frustration and hurt.

She is an example of Yeltsin's habitual insensitivity, of his abstract view of individuals. Like many born leaders, he looks his best in a close-up, at a public function, on the podium, atop a tank, on the TV screen—as a leader of the people. When he addresses the masses, he finds precise words that go straight to the heart. Yet in personal close contact, Yeltsin is oddly disappointing. His bluntness, abruptness, and sincerity impress one as residual teenage aggression. His willpower, his obsession with self-improvement, seem psychologically infantile. His combative temper is often ill-aimed and hence makes no sense: whom exactly is he angry at?

One of his closest co-workers said, when asked to characterize him as a person: "Yeltsin is a big, abstract 'something.' It's not a good idea to try to dwell on nuances when talking with him—he won't understand, and will get bored, too . . . You know, he thinks on a grand scale, in general notions. His relations with others are on some level that transcends humanity. He never has time; he is horribly short of time. Many people get hurt . . . He has an incredible amount of energy that propels him forward, in a straight line . . . If I were him, I'd try to do something human for my family, my friends—all those wonderful people around him—I would give them a little rest. With him, it's like being tied to the tail of a rocket—you can only burn out, nothing else. I've been with him for three years and I'm on the edge—over the edge, really. I don't think he's aware of it . . . You know why women like him? They think they can be safe behind his broad back. Myself, I doubt it. But that's the image he projects."

Another Yeltsin co-worker, who was with him for two years: "He's very hot-tempered. Of course, he's seething with emotions. But he knows how to keep them in check. All these emotions, these passionate outbursts—it's all about politics. Fall in love with him? You must be joking: you can't even have normal human interaction with him, to say nothing of romantic stuff. You simply can't have your feelings in tune with his."

A journalist who had worked with Yeltsin confessed that "you don't get much pleasure out of close contact with Yeltsin. He is just not that kind of person."

*

FROM THE very beginning, Naina was her husband's wife and mother; with years, the maternal element grew. A former Sverdlovsk classmate said that for Naina, "Boris was a younger son. She took complete care of him, thoroughly sheltering him from reality." "Who were the elder children, then?" we wondered. "Why, her daughters, of course: Lena, and then Tanya."

When the daughters grew up—a fact that passed unnoticed by their father—their stormy private lives forced Yeltsin to take a closer look at his family problems. More important, he had to acquire some tolerance and shed his typical—at the time—puritanism. Somehow, both daughters were in a rush to leave the family and get married. In neither case did it quite work out.

Lena, the older one, "leaped to the altar at eighteen, straight from high school, over her father's sharp objections. Her husband turned out to be a notorious skirt-chaser; she was unhappy," and ultimately came back home. Tanya, the younger daughter, struck out on her own when she entered Moscow University and moved into the dormitory, where she also had her share of broken affairs. Yeltsin was extremely upset over the failures in his daughters' private lives. Yet their second marriages turned out to be lasting and happy ones—and they are the ones that he later described in his autobiography, omitting the previous ones that had caused him so much frustration.

In his autobiography, Yeltsin sidesteps his private life. While he does not have much of one, it cannot be said that he has none at all. What he has is owing to Naina's efforts. It did not take her long to see that by nature her husband was doomed to be a political animal; that home and family would always be his bottom priority. According to a close friend in Sverdlovsk, Naina never tried hard to drag him into family concerns: "family life just bounces off him." Private life simply could not accommodate Yeltsin's persona, nor did he value privacy and stay at home for too long. Within the family he felt a kind of emotional claustrophobia; it seemed to curb his public temperament, which drove him to the Great Outdoors of public service, and, later, to politics. As a family man, Yeltsin is a disaster.

Not surprisingly, in his memoirs his wife and daughters do not come across as individuals. As he tries to retrieve them from his memory, he finds them to be familiar strangers. He sees them—or, rather, shows them to the reader—through the rose-tinted glass of stale clichés of family bliss.

Naina Yeltsin, however, is a very real human being. Unlike her husband, with his passion for public life, she is an intensely private person, who cherishes family values and her ties with her relatives and friends. In Sverdlovsk, she worked for many years as an engineer and highly valued the independence of her career. Being her husband's comrade in his political struggle holds as little appeal to her as do the official duties of Russia's First Lady that she has had to perform on occasion.

LET US return to Sverdlovsk, where Boris Yeltsin is the First Secretary of the Party Committee. One can hardly call the working relations he established from the start with his fellow *apparatchiks* democratic. They were authoritarian: Yeltsin demanded, pressured, imposed his own views, and governed from the position of tight control and accountability. His sternness and rigidity toward his subordinates constituted a conscious policy. Yeltsin knew that such a rarefied, pure-business ambience would provide a less favorable milieu for the viruses of corruption and bribery that raged through the entire Soviet power structure at the time. As his former co-workers and friends confirm, no one would have dared ask the new First Secretary for any favors.

When later, in Moscow, Yeltsin made combating social inequalities the centerpiece of his opposition program, he was accused of playing to the mob. Critics failed to take into account his Sverdlovsk experience in fighting Party privileges. In general, Yeltsin perceived injustice in a socialist society in acute, personal terms. It was a "shame" or "disgrace" for a Party leader to insist on privileges. While still in Sverdlovsk, Yeltsin closed down the special stores and canceled all special rations. He let the special hospital alone for a while, but its doors were now opened to retirees and old Party members. He would have closed it, too, had it not been for his transfer to Moscow. Even now a few old *apparatchiks* living in Sverdlovsk cannot find a kind word to say of Yeltsin, who took away their privileges and benefits.

While his method of running the Party machinery was far from democratic, Yeltsin insisted on democratic forms of communication with various groups of the population. This dialogue was his personal innovation, but now it was on the level of a First Secretary. He began holding meetings from the very beginning of his rule. These were large audiences: a thousand, even two thousand people. He met with principals, schoolteachers, artists, sociologists, scientists—no group influencing public opinion, or whatever passed for it in Sverdlovsk in those days—was neglected.

These meetings, in which both sides exchanged their views on a variety of subjects, including current politics, were held at Yeltsin's own initiative, not that of the Party. The primarily economic duties of First Secretary did not satisfy his public temperament and his political yearnings. The meetings filled the gap, and it was in the course of them that he developed his lively, spontaneous, dynamic style of addressing crowds, one that years later, under glasnost, would astonish Moscow audiences.

For the moment, in the era of political stagnation, Yeltsin chose a highly individualistic form of questions and answers, not dodging a single question, no matter how pointed or politically risky—something no other Party leader of the period dared to try. Sergei Demyanenko, who now lives in Moscow, recalled seeing Yeltsin in 1981 at a meeting with Sverdlovsk students. It lasted about five hours. Hundreds of questions were asked, and Yeltsin fielded every one of them. His answers were short and to the point; they suggested confidence between the two sides, and their directness and openness were unthinkable in those days. The air in the auditorium was relaxed, but the temperature of the discussion was many degrees higher than usual: no one had expected a Party Boss to show himself so independent of ideology, so firm in his opinions, so informal in his style. "I, a young student," Demyanenko recalls, "thus formed a very distorted opinion of Party Secretaries: I began to think of them as better than they actually were."

Another Sverdlovsk citizen, Andrei Goryun, first met Boris Yeltsin in November 1981 at the meeting of social scientists, organized by the regional Party Committee. Such meetings were routine, and Goryun had expected to hear the standard ideological dogmas, Party formulas, and bureaucratic Newspeak. What actually happened left the audience wide-eyed.

"A tall, snowy-haired man stepped up to the podium," Goryun recalls, "dressed in a well-cut suit that showed off his athletic build. He began to speak. With the very first phrases, people held their breath. Many grabbed their note pads, trying to write down every word. What was he saying . . . This meeting was the first time I learned the truth about this country. Perhaps not the entire truth, perhaps a minuscule part of it—but it was a revelation to me."

In Sverdlovsk, Yeltsin is remembered not merely as a "good tsar" who took care of his people. As far back as the early '80s, the masses throughout the entire region, i.e., through his Party domain, perceived him as a charismatic leader. His popularity was immense. When, in November 1987, his former subjects learned of the scandal in faraway Moscow—that Yeltsin had been removed from the First Secretary job—a huge rally in his support was held in Sverdlovsk's central square; an unprecedented event. When, in early 1989, Yeltsin ran for People's Deputy, citizens of Sverdlovsk participated ardently in all the stages of his election campaign.

It is worth recalling that through the six years of so-called glasnost, not once did Gorbachev risk running as a candidate anywhere in the Soviet Union—not even in his native Stavropol, where he had left behind mixed memories. Unlike Yeltsin, who, as First Secretary of the Sverdlovsk Region, took his job as a creative challenge, constantly searching for new forms of management within the dying system, the First Secretary of the Stavropol Region ruled his domain in a passive, undistinguished manner—just like many other obscure Party functionaries across the land. In Khrushchev's day Gorbachev would have been kicked out for poor economic performance, lack of initiative, and bureaucratic complacency. But by then Brezhnev had given up on reform and on agriculture; he decided it was more profitable and less troublesome to spend hundreds of millions of dollars on importing grain rather than invest this money at home.

Still, Gorbachev was lucky with his bailiwick: it included the country's main resort area, with numerous spas and dachas. It was a unique opportunity for a humble Party Secretary to make friends, or even rub shoulders, with the country's masters. It was here, playing host to high Kremlin guests, that Gorbachev won his Kremlin patrons: Fyodor Kulakov, Mikhail Suslov, and the most important among them, Yuri Andropov, then chief of the KGB. Stavropol's famous resorts paid off handsome dividends.

Gorbachev's early prominence among his fellow provincial satraps showed in the most sought-after gift that the Kremlin could bestow on an *apparatchik:* travel abroad. In 1966, even before he was made First Secretary, Gorbachev and wife spent a few weeks driving around France in a rented Renault. This was followed by trips to Belgium (1968), Italy (1972), and West Germany (1975), to say nothing of less prestigious trips to East European countries.

By comparison, Boris Yeltsin, who spent nine years heading one of the most important economic regions of the Empire, was never awarded a trip to the West by his Kremlin bosses, though he did dream about it, given his intellectual curiosity and interest in international politics. He was hardly the Kremlin's pet. They set him inflated target figures for industrial output, then demanded that he meet them, and kept calling him on the carpet. Almost every year Party auditors swarmed to Sverdlovsk. Neither a cynic nor a Machiavellian plotter, Yeltsin believed naively that government awards and perks are issued on the basis of merit. He did not get to travel to the West till 1986, when he went to West Germany as a Soviet delegate to the Congress of the local Communist Party.

Gorbachev made it to Moscow seven years ahead of Yeltsin. Two years after his arrival, with his clout, he was included in the gerontological Politburo. He was twenty years younger than the average age of his colleagues, and thirty-two years younger than the oldest of them, Arvid Pelshe. His willingness to go along was rewarded with trust and influence, which he used wisely. Everyone was his benefactor: Brezhnev, Andropov (a lot), and even Chernenko, who briefly occupied the driver's seat that should have been his, Gorbachev's. The system of patronage made Gorbachev into the darling not only of his mentors, but of political destiny itself: what others had to fight for dropped into his lap.

Gorbachev was a graduate of the Kremlin school at the time of its political decadence. He was a top student; he graduated summa cum laude; but his degree was as much of a sham as his previous ones—from Moscow University's Law School and from the Stavropol School of Agriculture. The Kremlin school does not teach to govern, but, rather, to pretend that you govern. Instead of enterprise, it teaches obedience; instead of originality, clichés; instead of sincerity, hypocrisy. Gorbachev learned these Kremlin lessons well, for what others were there?

This is one of the reasons why, after Chernenko's death, the Kremlin's gerontocrats, led by Andrei Gromyko, overcame their pathological fear of youth and consented to name Mikhail Gorbachev their leader, "first among equals." In six years, they had grown used to him; he suited them; and, though different in age and biography, in his essence he seemed to belong to their older generation. He did not seem likely to rock the boat; he seemed a typical product of the Party bureaucracy, even-tempered, reasonable, and given to concessions. He had no trouble adapting to his epoch and assuming its protective coloration. He was truly a man for all seasons: a Stalinist in Stalin's day, a Khrushchevite in Khrushchev's, a Brezhnevite in Brezhnev's, and an Andropovite in Andropov's.

According to Yeltsin, if another candidate than Gorbachev had been proposed for the highest office in the country, then he, along with other provincial satraps, would have declared war on the Politburo at the Central Committee Plenum. We find this hard to believe; it is a case of selective memory. Yeltsin transfers the Party and public mores of mid-1989, when he was working on his memoirs, to the era of four years earlier, when those mores were quite different. The issue of the new Party leader was decided behind closed doors, at a Politburo session, with only a few men participating, while the confirmation at the Plenum of the Central Committee, which by then had several hundred members, was a rubber-stamp procedure. Like all his predecessors, Gorbachev was unanimously confirmed. The Central Committee members would have voted just as unanimously for any other candidate proposed by the Politburo.

When in April 1985 Yeltsin was urgently summoned from Sverdlovsk to Moscow at Gorbachev's personal recommendation, the call was hardly a case of patronage. It was not as though Yeltsin had finally found himself the most powerful patron in the country. It was a uniquely active period in Gorbachev's career; it was Gorbachev himself who badly needed people like Yeltsin: hardworking, high-principled, incorruptible idealists. As a Central Committee Secretary, Gorbachev had firsthand knowledge of the talent pool of provincial *apparatchiks;* he knew that precious few of them were like Yeltsin.

Yeltsin moved to Moscow reluctantly. He felt somewhat slighted. The job he was being offered—section chief—was lower in status than the Central Committee Secretary position that a regional First Secretary could traditionally count on. It was not just Yeltsin's sense of justice that was hurt; he defined himself pragmatically, as a productive unit, and correctly believed that a Party Boss of his caliber, with his rich experience and knowledge, could have been used more rationally and effectively. This was his first, though veiled, conflict with Gorbachev.

According to Anneta Lvov, Yeltsin's wife took the move as a domestic catastrophe. To the Yeltsins, Sverdlovsk had become a family estate. Surrounded by relatives and friends, they were solidly rooted in the community. Naina had worked for twenty-nine years at her company, she had made it to Chief Engineer—and now, two years before retirement, she had to quit and follow her husband to Moscow. There, she would find a job based on her professional résumé, but, in the words of the same Lvov, Yeltsin put his foot down. She, too, realized that without help from their relatives and friends, their life was not going to be easy. Three families—older Yeltsins and both of their daughters with their respective families—moved into a three-bedroom apartment. Only two years later did the older daughter, Lena, move out to an apartment of her own. For the time being, Naina Yeltsin had to look after her three little grandchildren, cook for the huge extended family, and take complete care of her "youngest," who in Moscow had even less time for his family than he did in Sverdlovsk.

So, by one means or another, Gorbachev attained the position of General Secretary, and almost immediately Boris Yeltsin moved to Moscow. The parallel lines of their lives finally crossed. From now on they would flow interdependently, inseparably. The interdependency was underlined by the conflict that has marked their relations.

Later, Yeltsin would repeatedly say that, not only did he regret moving to Moscow, he considered it a major mistake. If Gorbachev had ever spoken as openly, he would probably have admitted that inviting Yeltsin to the capital was *his* worst blunder: it is doubtful that he could have found such a formidable rival.

But what is the point of second-guessing? History does not recognize the subjunctive mood. Despite their opposite qualities, fate brought the two leaders together, placed them in the same political harness, and their rivalry, their reciprocal denial and repulsion, their principal antagonism, became a major motive force in Russian history in the late '80s and early '90s.

PART THREE

THE SCHOOL OF DEMOCRACY

MR. YELTSIN GOES TO
WASHINGTON
(Summer–Winter 1989)

No government can be long secure without a formidable opposition.

DISRAELI

Now WE come to a period of time in which Yeltsin was passive rather than active. From a subject, he turned into an object; he let his destiny slip away; he became a pawn in other people's games. This chapter could well have been without a hero at all, but for an obscure professor from Siberia who decided to sacrifice his own political ambition for Yeltsin's.

This is what happened.

Yeltsin had waged an electoral campaign that was without precedent in Russian history; equally unprecedented politicization of Moscow voters led to a landslide—almost 90 percent of the vote. Now he was a People's Deputy, an equal among 2250 others. Yet this triumph was of no practical value.

The newly elected deputies were there to elect a permanent Supreme Soviet out of their number and then to return to their hometowns and villages. Yeltsin ran—and failed. He ran on the Russian Federation list: twelve contenders for eleven seats, and he turned out to be an odd man out; he received more than half the vote, but fewer votes than other Russian delegates. Along with other democratic deputies like Academician Sakharov, Economist Nikolai Shmelev, future Moscow mayor Gavriil Popov, historian Yuri Afanasyev, and social scientist Tatyana Zaslavskaya, he found himself excluded from the country's highest legislative body. He was out of business—he was out, period. All the effort, all the time and energy that went into the campaign had been wasted.

This setback revealed two things. First, Gorbachev's parliamentary system was rigged cleverly enough to keep out of the Supreme Soviet all those who had triumphed over lies and plots to be elected deputies. Second, one third of the delegates who made up the new legislative organ had been appointed, not elected. Another third were the deputies elected by means of intimidation and blackmail of voters, and sometimes through bald deception. After all, it was the first time a semi-free election was held, and fear of the KGB and the Party outside Moscow was very much alive. These Kremlin manipulations and calculations delivered the deputies from whom the Supreme Soviet could be selected. Yuri Afanasyev, the Director of the Moscow Institute of History and Archives, called the composition of the Supreme Soviet "Stalin-Brezhnevite," but it was most definitely a Gorbachev tool, obedient to its creator and master.

Another of Afanasyev's phrases was more to the point: he talked about an "aggressively obedient majority" of deputies. In Yeltsin's case the majority turned out to be more aggressive than obedient; it is unlikely that Gorbachev had deliberately planned Yeltsin's loss, which was followed by a wave of civil-disobedience: demonstrations, rallies, demands for Gorbachev's resignation and even threats of strikes. All that made Yeltsin cheer up and even gloat: another Gorbachev attack on him had boomeranged. Now Yeltsin was impatiently waiting for his opponent as Yeltsin himself put it, to "fight his way out of the corner into which he painted himself." This was a political scandal that, in the explosive atmosphere of the day, could have far-reaching, unpredictable consequences. The act of tripping up Yeltsin seemed like an egregious snub of the unequivocally expressed popular will.

"Yet, as always in Russia, there turns up one person who figures a way out of the most impossible situation," Yeltsin comments. "This time the deus ex machina was personified by Alexei Kazannik, a deputy from Omsk."

What Kazannik, a professor at the University of Omsk, did was to concede his seat—in favor of Yeltsin. Gorbachev instantly confirmed the substitution, thus avoiding a political crisis.

Poor Kazannik—the Siberian kamikaze's political career was nipped in the bud. Yeltsin's own attitude toward this selfless act smacked of exploitation: he accepted Kazannik's sacrifice as due and inevitable, though it was not quite voluntary and Yeltsin knew it. Public pressure had been applied to People's Deputy Kazannik—but to Yeltsin such pressure was normal, especially since it was Yeltsin himself who had originally suggested that Kazannik be included as the twelfth member—as an alternative candidate.

This is how Kazannik explained his action to Yeltsin: "Tell me, Boris Nikolayevich—what should I say to my voters? They know there's six million Muscovites behind you. If I stay, my voters will kill me."

Yeltsin accepted the sacrifice without a second thought and entered the Supreme Soviet.

When Yeltsin first knocked on the door of Soviet politics, it was slammed in his face; when he forced his way in, he was neutralized by two Gorbachev tools: the Congress of People's Deputies and the Supreme Soviet.

For convenience, we will merge the "small" and "large" Kremlin Parliaments, since, apart from legalistic and quantitative differences, they are alike.

Under Stalin and his successors, the powers-that-be had a tacit understanding with the Russian people: the Supreme Soviet, its elections and sessions, were pure fiction. It was common knowledge, and no one had any illusions. This fiction, and many others like it, comprised a mythological structure that for seven decades functioned more or less well—from the Kremlin's point of view.

Gradually, however, the edifice developed a multitude of very real cracks, whose existence was, in turn, ignored as a fiction. The cement of ideology crumbled; the corpse, made to look like a live person, began disintegrating—just like Lenin's mummy.

The new Kremlin lords, headed by Gorbachev, saw clearly the disintegration of the old matrix and took emergency action—glasnost/perestroika—to reconstruct the former bonding of the molecules of state. Part of the scheme was to create a new Parliament that would look more democratic than its predecessor.

Thus, instead of becoming a new, authentic political apparatus—a legislative basis for a reformed State—the Parliament turned out to be a forum for glasnost. It was just like the media—another Hyde Park Speakers' Corner that could not influence the existing order. The selection of the "small" Parliament out of the "large" one showed that the entire structure had nothing to do with democracy. It is not just that the secret-vote system blackballed a popular candidate like Yeltsin, who had made it to the "small" Parliament despite the system and thanks to the political altruism of a fellow Siberian. It is more interesting to see not who was rejected but who made it upstairs—without a major effort on their part. The list includes Gorbachev; his second-in-command in the Party, Ligachev; the new Moscow Party Boss, Zaikov; and KGB Chairman Chebrikov. All of them blithely sidestepped the rigors of an electoral campaign and entered the Parliament on the Central Committee slate through the back door. This while a popular favorite, a number one (at least in the Russian Republic) candidate, was barred by the system while less popular figures—widely hated, like Ligachev, or steadily losing popularity, like Gorbachev—glided in.

The Siberian professor's semi-voluntary sacrifice actually distorted the picture by making the cruel, unfair election system, which provided a safety net for unpopular politicians and tossed the popular ones overboard, look more benign. That Yeltsin was smuggled into the Supreme Soviet served to reinforce the Potemkin façade of glasnost rather than the cause of democracy. It is far more significant that neither Sakharov nor Shmelev nor Popov nor Afanasyev nor Zaslavskaya was elected.

The Supreme Soviet became a branch of the Moscow Circus, with Gorbachev a skilled animal-tamer. He brought along his college pal Anatoly Lukyanov: when Gorbachev became the Chairman of the Supreme Soviet, Lukyanov was his deputy; when Gorbachev became President, Lukyanov became Chairman. It was later learned that between the two of them, Gorbachev and Lukyanov personally designed the makeup of the Supreme Soviet, from its members' names to the Chairmen of its two Houses and Parliamentary Committees. Yeltsin, as a professional builder, got to chair the Committee on Construction and Architecture. It was somewhat like his old job, but on the Parliamentary, rather than Ministerial, level—that is, with a skeleton staff, a minuscule budget, and no executive power. Gorbachev was apparently still trying to keep Yeltsin out of politics.

He partially succeeded. At the beginning, Yeltsin was buried in an avalanche of incoming and outgoing memos and papers, of complaints and inquiries. He did manage to bring over a few of his close aides from his Ministry, including the loyal Lev Sukhanov. But if Yeltsin, fresh from his electoral triumph, was still hatching Napoleonic schemes, he had to give them up. Although electors perceived him as an alternative to Gorbachev, Yeltsin backed out of the race for Chairman of the Supreme Soviet. Without a doubt, he would be defeated squarely, not by Gorbachev personally, but by his "aggressively obedient majority."

Later, Sukhanov told us that they had considered having Yeltsin run for Chairman of the Nationalities Soviet, one of the Supreme Soviet's divisions. But, mindful of the ease with which fellow deputies had blackballed him at the election to the Supreme Soviet, he had to reject that idea as unrealistic. The Committee on Construction and Architecture was Yeltsin's only option.

It was owing to Yeltsin's efforts that the sessions of the Congress, and later of the Supreme Soviet, were broadcast live on television. "For ten days running," Yeltsin recalls, "the entire country was glued to their TVs, watching heated congressional debates. Politically, those ten days gave people more than the seventy years of millions of Marxist-Leninist politicians. By the time the Congress closed, the people had changed from what they were when it had opened . . . It was as though the entire nation—well, almost—woke up from hibernation."

The TV debates gave birth to new heroes who pushed Yeltsin backstage. Somehow his rally-addressing style did not fit the parliamentary format. There was also a psychological factor. Unlike Yeltsin, an old pro whose vanity had already been satisfied, his deputy colleagues were making their debut in the political arena. They seemed to vie passionately for the viewers' attention; they outdid one another in breaking the old taboos. One successful speech off the podium brought a speaker instant national fame and political stardom. Even academician Sakharov confessed that after one of his speeches at the Congress of People's Deputies, he "in one hour gained the support of millions—the popularity in our country that I had never had."

This was the Nobel Prize–winner speaking. What about ordinary mortals like Alexandr Obolensky, a Leningrad engineer who nominated himself as an alternate candidate for Chairman of the Supreme Soviet? He knew he was no match for Gorbachev—but what a precedent to set! Another Leningrad deputy, the yet-unknown Anatoly Sobchak, who would be the Mayor of St. Petersburg, made his name by drawing clever parallels and—at the time—shocking assaults on Prime Minister Nikolai Ryzhkov, bringing the Prime Minister to tears in front of an audience of millions of TV viewers. (Rumor had it that Sobchak was aiming for Ryzhkov's position and trying to prove himself to Gorbachev.) The attack dealt a fatal blow to Ryzhkov's reputation. What kind of a Prime Minister is he, people reasoned, if he cannot even hold back tears? From then on, his nickname was *Plaksa* (Crybaby).

To the audience's untold delight, ex-KGB Investigator Telman Gdlyan exposed corruption in the Party's upper echelons. He went as high as Ligachev, the Party's number two man and a personal foe of Yeltsin's. Yet Gdlyan's real target seemed to be Gorbachev himself: Gdlyan had information about a 160,000-ruble bribe that Gorbachev had taken when he was the Party Boss of the Stavropol Territory. (He never dared to make the information public.)

The most courageous and colorful speech was given by a man who needed no publicity. Yuri Vlasov, several times Olympic weight-lifting champion, already had plenty of publicity. Later, people would joke that it took the strongest man in the world to challenge the authorities.

While the Congress was in session, twenty peaceful Georgian demonstrators demanding independence were beaten to death by soldiers. Deputies launched an inquiry: who had given the order for the crime? As he would do later with similar massacres in Baku, Vilnius, and Riga, Gorbachev claimed ignorance: he was out of town, he was asleep—he always had an alibi.

> Under no circumstances must we allow [Vlasov said] the leader of the State to be unaware of the facts of this case. If it is true that he knew nothing, what kind of leader is he? Nor can we allow similar ignorance on the part of Politburo members. Keep in mind that no one has answered insistent inquiries from at least a dozen deputies; then again, silence is an answer in itself. But I'm not talking about an important fact being concealed from the Congress; I'm talking about adding to the Constitution an article about impeachment—about stripping the Chairman of the Supreme Soviet of his authority for having concealed the truth from the people. It is of paramount importance for our future. The head of the government must be fully cognizant of whose side he is on: his "corporation"—or the people.

Yet Vlasov did not limit himself to challenging the President and his power. He also lashed out at the KGB, an attack that was equally unprecedented:

> In order to limit the power of the *apparat,* the people must control one of the most powerful elements of its support base. With one hand the KGB protects the people from external enemies, yet with the other, a much stronger, hand, it performs a certain very special function . . . In our first steps on the path of democratization, when every attempt is being made to crush it, a force like the KGB plays a unique role. It is subordinate to the *apparat* alone . . . The KGB is not a service—it is a true underground empire that up to now has not opened its secrets—only its graves.

Yet the true hero of this TV show became Academician Sakharov, who had sorely missed politics in his Gorky exile. With all the differences between them, Sakharov and Yeltsin were both ingrates as far as Gorbachev was concerned: he had returned Sakharov from Gorky to Moscow, and he had invited Yeltsin to Moscow from Sverdlovsk. Now both were Gorbachev's main critics and opponents: Yeltsin at rallies, Sakharov in the Congress. Yeltsin was popular among the people; Sakharov among the intelligentsia. In a sense, the two were rivals, though Yeltsin would not admit it.

Sakharov, however, recalls a rally in Luzhniki, in which Yeltsin beat him to the punch, grabbing the microphone first and saying the things that he, Sakharov, had planned to say. The Academician found himself unable to "redeploy" and later confessed that his speech had been a fiasco. He was particularly hurt because it was his birthday—"it put me in a bad mood." Sakharov did not conceal his wounded vanity: he was upset by playing second fiddle at the rally, which turned into a show of support for Yeltsin. In general, Sakharov was wary of Yeltsin; he considered him a lesser figure than Gorbachev, and his popularity, a factor of Gorbachev's "antipopularity."

Outdone at rallies—Yeltsin's natural element—Sakharov got his revenge in the Congress, where he could outshine any other speaker, including Yeltsin. Although in its essence and outcome the first Congress of People's Deputies belonged to Gorbachev, it could be called Sakharov's for the frequency and import of his speeches. Sakharov practically stormed the podium; he would loose his verbal cannonade before he got the floor, violating every rule of decorum. Deputies who disagreed with him booed him, called him names, and chased him off the podium. Gorbachev once even turned off his mike. Still, nothing could block Sakharov's youthful irreverence, passion, and fearlessness. His speeches were courageous and principled, especially the ones on the war in Afghanistan, the massacre in Tbilisi, and the need to limit presidential powers. And yet, if Gorbachev sometimes lost control of the deputies, he retained his role of animal-tamer in his private political circus; Sakharov was doomed to play the jester, to entertain the public, rather than influence the course of events.

This was another reason for Yeltsin's withdrawal: he was already too familiar with the role of entertainer, which he had played at Party meetings, when he spoke the truth—and was thought to be trying to shock people. He wanted to be useful—not to amuse. Long before others, Yeltsin grasped the essence of the "guided democracy" that characterized Gorbachev's parliament.

Of the 280 million Soviet citizens, Gorbachev was the principal beneficiary of his creation dubbed "Parliament." Not only did he manipulate the Congress of Deputies and the Supreme Soviet, inventing and overcoming nonexistent problems, but through live broadcasts—which he at first opposed—he also enjoyed a nationwide audience for his performances, and later, via satellite, an international audience as well. Since his majority, both in the Congress and in the Supreme Soviet, was assured, neither Yeltsin nor Sakharov nor anyone else threatened his power. The new system could absorb any opposition member, and, through ostensibly democratic means, turn him to its use. The very presence of both Yeltsin and Sakharov among the deputies, to say nothing of their speeches, easy to counter with the "aggressively obedient majority," was trumpeted as evidence of Gorbachev's democracy in front of both local and international audiences.

Of course, real democracy had not emerged yet. It was still the age of glasnost, when one could tell the truth and criticize, but neither truth nor criticism could rattle the throne or the courtiers surrounding it. The masses were allowed to voice their grievances, but barred from decision making; they could grumble but not act—not yet.

The first Congress of People's Deputies was coming to an end. Finally, the debate was closed. Lukyanov leaned over to Gorbachev and, grinning, whispered in his ear. The remark could not be heard by the deputies, but, with the microphones plugged directly to TV equipment, it was heard clearly by millions of viewers. There was relief in Lukyanov's voice: "Well, Mikhail—it's over!"

His relief was short-lived. The deputies insisted that the debate go on. Gorbachev had no choice but agree. He was apprehensive about the Moscow deputies, feeling safer with provincial ones, so he gave the floor to a deputy from Orenburg. The latter, however, declared the formation of the Interregional Deputies' Group. A frightened Gorbachev instantly turned off the cameras, and the astonished viewers were jolted straight into a soccer game in progress.

Since Gorbachev's democracy was a controlled one, it was logical that he be the de facto TV producer, too. He could turn off the in-house microphones—he did it once with Sakharov—as well as in nationwide broadcasting, as he did now. What frightened him so?

Democratic-minded deputies, convinced that Gorbachev's tamed democracy could not be dislodged by individual effort, decided to join forces. In late July 1989 they formed the so-called Interregional Group, with five co-chairmen: Yuri Afanasyev, Gavriil Popov, Victor Palm, Andrei Sakharov, and Boris Yeltsin. At the outset it included 256 deputies, and by September the number grew to 362. While strictly speaking it was not yet an opposition party, it was a collective, organized body of opposition to the Kremlin.

The very term "opposition" had to be avoided: it had been taboo since Stalin's days, as was opposition itself. But the upper nomenklatura could not be fooled: they immediately grasped the dangerous idea and attacked it with all the might of their propaganda machine. The Group was denied room for meetings and printing presses for their publications. It was dragged through all the levels of Soviet verbal mud. Members were called "fractionists," "revisionists," and "powermongers." And, of course, "oppositionists"—still the leading curse in the official vocabulary, and, to the powers-that-be, like a red rag to a bull. Gorbachev's political perceptiveness was immediately apparent: he instantly felt the danger and turned off the cameras.

But it was too late. The opposition was formed: the first one since Stalin's day. While still a minority in Gorbachev's Parliament, it steadily gained nationwide popularity. And Boris Yeltsin, elected its first leader (the position was to be rotated among cochairmen), played a major part in the process. Finally, everything was in place: from a leader of the de facto opposition he had turned into the leader of the de jure one.

The opposition was a fact that the Kremlin leaders would not acknowledge. They would not acknowledge it, but they feared it.

Now united, Yeltsin and his comrades were looking for a way out of the political dead end into which they had been driven by Gorbachev's half-free, half-controlled Parliament. Yeltsin gained personally, getting out of the bureaucratic trap of the Committee on Construction and Architecture, where he was wasting his strength. As the leader of the Parliamentary opposition, he now needed international recognition. It was a formidable challenge. The game now shifted into an arena that Gorbachev dominated—his reputation abroad was at its highest. Nonetheless, Yeltsin played a "foreign card."

MUCH HAS been written about Boris Yeltsin's foreign trips, a good deal of it false. What follows is not speculation; it is re-created directly from Yeltsin's little-known interviews and speeches, as well as from conversations with the people (including ourselves) who accompanied him or met him during his trip to the United States.

Yeltsin almost took his first foreign tour in his new job as the leader of the opposition shortly after the Congress. Along with Soviet and German political scientists and economists, he was invited to attend a round-table discussion on the problems of East-West relations in West Germany. Yeltsin had already visited the country twice, once as a guest of the West German Communist Party congress in Hamburg in May 1986. It was shortly after the Chernobyl disaster, and he impressed journalists with his sincerity and the accuracy of his information (bear in mind that that was before glasnost).

On this trip to Germany, Yeltsin planned to speak out in favor of German unification—since the Kremlin opposed this, it was to be his political trump. But when all the travel documents were ready, Yeltsin got a call from Yevgeny Primakov, one of Gorbachev's top men in the Supreme Soviet, later Gorbachev's special envoy during the Persian Gulf War, and after the coup the head of a newly formed counterintelligence service. He informed Yeltsin that the travel permit had been denied.

If Yeltsin had gone, he would have created a sensation: a Soviet politician speaking out for a united Germany! One need only look at the reaction of East German papers two months later, when he finally did make the statement during his first trip to America. The official *Neues Deutschland* accused him of joining the "campaign of hatred" waged by the American media against East Germany. "What can you expect of a

Communist who, in spite of his people's great efforts in perestroika, calls Communism a pipe dream?"

That summer, while actively working in the Parliament on behalf of his Interregional Group, Yeltsin became increasingly interested in the legal status of minority opposition in the US Congress. With the naiveté and ardor of a rookie politician, he grilled the visiting columnist Jack Anderson, on the details and working conditions of Democratic congressmen under a Republican President. Anderson failed to grasp the seriousness and urgency of Yeltsin's queries and brushed him off with a joke: he proposed that the Soviet and American caucuses launch a joint attack on the Congress and the Supreme Soviet.

Yeltsin was professionally interested in America long before his controversial trip in September 1989. He converted to democracy—both in conviction and in action—after his fall from the Politburo and the subsequent crisis of faith. He waged his entire electoral campaign in the spring of 1989 in keeping with grass-roots tactics: rallies, meetings, and a non-stop dialogue with the people. At the 19th Party Conference, more than a year before his American trip, he put forward a coherent package of democratic reform in the Party and in the country, including the necessity of introducing general, direct, and secret-vote elections. As Ortega y Gasset appropriately put it, "The stability and prosperity of democracies, regardless of their type and degree of evolution, depends on a minuscule technicality: electoral procedure. Everything else is secondary." We are not sure that Yeltsin is familiar with the Spanish philosopher's works, but his intuitive grasp of the main prerequisite of democratic rule shows that his conversion was a substantial one.

Yeltsin understood that one cannot construct a democracy guided by one's instincts alone, and quickly adopted a model to emulate—an American one, which he knew in theory only. Considering his age, Yeltsin was exceptionally receptive to new ideas, with an intellect capable of evolving. His enemies called it "omnivorousness." Soon he grew enthusiastic about "democracy in America." Yeltsin accepted the American political model unconditionally for reasons of both common sense and expediency, he said. Rather than wait for Russia to develop its own democratic institutions, "We decided it was best to learn from the US, where democracy has existed for two hundred years."

Once again, Yeltsin acted like a cost-conscious manager, trying to cut down the costs of manufacturing such an important, direly needed product—democracy in Russia—in the shortest time possible. He and Yuri Vlasov immediately introduced into Soviet political parlance the notion of impeachment. He proposed to limit the President's term to four years and divide legislative functions between two elected Houses, similar to the House of Representatives and the Senate. Now he treated as gospel the opinions and forecasts of Soviet development made by American Sovietologists and politicians. A day before his election as a People's Deputy, Yeltsin expected to win in a landslide—"that was the American forecast," he said. After brushing aside the possibility of a civil war in the USSR as a canard planted by Soviet reactionary propaganda, Yeltsin quoted US Sovietologists' predictions that such a hypothetical civil war would kill 5 to 7 percent of the population.

Thus Yeltsin had become a passionate Americaphile long before he stepped ashore there. "Learn from the Americans" became more than a motto; it was a substantial part of his platform. On the other hand, he was a little embarrassed that his outspoken pro-Americanism was second-hand, and the embarrassment made him even hungrier for direct experience. By now a trip overseas was urgent.

He had learned a lesson from the ukase that had blocked his trip to Germany, so he planned his American trip carefully and thoroughly, with a number of backup contingencies in case of another rejection. Originally, the host would be the Esalen Institute (a Soviet request), and the Rockefeller and Ford Foundations agreed to be included in the host list.

According to Gennady Alferenko, the Soviet-side coordinator of the East-West Exchange Program, who organized the trip and accompanied Yeltsin in America, finding an American sponsor to finance it was no easy task. Both American government circles and US public opinion were dominated by Gorbachev, and the leader of the anti-Gorbachev opposition was a persona almost as non grata in America as in the upper reaches of the Soviet *apparat*.

Thanking James Harrison, the director of the Esalen Institute, for the invitation, Alferenko added, "When we discussed whether Yeltsin's trip was feasible (we send twenty Soviets to the US every month in our program), we thought: why cannot Yeltsin—a Soviet citizen—be included in the program? James Harrison was the first American to take real responsibility. I was surprised that many American organizations were afraid to sponsor the trip and assume full financial responsibility. They were afraid to offend Mikhail Sergeyevich Gorbachev."

The trip's organizers did everything to emphasize that Yeltsin was going as a private citizen. Harrison labeled it tourism: "discovery of America and familiarizing himself with the country." Also, Yeltsin was going to deliver lectures in several American universities. Besides Alferenko, he was accompanied by his aide Lev Sukhanov; Supreme Soviet Deputy Victor Yaroshenko; and Pavel Voshchanov, economics columnist for *Komsomolskaya Pravda*.

Not only did the Soviet authorities refuse to acknowledge Yeltsin as the leader of the Parliamentary minority, they even refused to honor his People's Deputy status. When Parliament went into recess, many deputies traveled abroad at state expense—not so with Yeltsin's delegation, though it included two deputies. They were not acknowledged as a delegation, not allowed to exchange a single ruble, and handed exit visas only a few hours before departure, which made them sweat a bit.

Since the Soviet authorities would not honor his status, Yeltsin was determined to obtain it through the offices of the American President. Even before the trip, he knew that it was customary for a democratically elected government to receive foreign opposition leaders. While still in Moscow, he put out feelers to be received by President Bush and Secretary of State James Baker, but could not get a definite answer, so he dreamed up a strategy to "coerce" the US administration into recognizing him as the leader of the opposition.

According to Lev Sukhanov, Georgi Arbatov, Director of the US and Canada Studies Institute, lent Yeltsin a hand by sending over a few of his researchers to brief him "on Americana and political etiquette." It was also important that Yeltsin develop his own behavior pattern, his own manner of expression in front of American audiences. This was a potential drawback: the two trips to Germany, plus trips to Cuba and Nicaragua, comprised his entire international experience.

Many US reporters mistook Yeltsin's spontaneous, easygoing behavior in America for lack of political manners, basic ignorance of political etiquette. Yet his democratic simplicity, sometimes dipping into familiarity—"call me Boris"—with the most diverse audiences, his effusiveness and sincerity in the public discussion of political issues, were not a show of political naiveté, or even, as some reporters thought, the result of his irrepressible temperament—they were a conscious tactic.

"At best naive, at worst dangerous"—this phrase, which became a cliché in Washington political parlance, requires an explanation. Strictly speaking, by the time Yeltsin came to America, he was no political babe in the woods: he had won two heated electoral campaigns and taken part in a Parliamentary opposition movement; he had come up through the school of grass-roots democracy, through meetings and rallies where he perfected his style of dealing with audiences.

In preparing for his trip, uncertain to the last minute whether he would be allowed to go, he planned to sell American audiences an image of a principled democrat who had an informal, spontaneous style in any situation, including official ones. He designed this tactic to counterbalance the image of Gorbachev, who on his foreign trips always followed state-visit protocol. A person who was close to Yeltsin at the time told us that Gorbachev's phenomenal success abroad had made Yeltsin extremely competitive. Yeltsin sensed injustice and political blindness in Western Gorbomania; by the fall of 1989 he was firmly convinced that Gorbachev was no democrat either in his convictions or in his actions.

Yeltsin considered himself a faithful advocate of democracy and consequently—albeit naively—he believed that in America he would be greeted
as a soulmate.

In part, his calculations proved right. He was successful in public, in
jammed university auditoriums, and at street encounters. His official
sponsor, James Harrison, went as far as to claim that "Yeltsin was a
sensation. In nine days he became known to most Americans. His political instinct is impeccable, as he showed in dealing with most diverse
audiences—from the President of the United States to Cuban-Americans
in Miami, from pig farmers in Indianapolis to Texas tycoons in Dallas."

In nine days, Yeltsin, accompanied by two interpreters and four aides,
visited eleven cities. He structured his meetings after his tried-and-tested
Moscow format: a brief introductory speech followed by questions and
answers. In all his speeches, he outlined the main points of his opposition
platform, which could be summarized as follows. Gorbachev—Yeltsin's
strategic ally but tactical opponent—had driven perestroika aground and
it had to be salvaged. The United States could help in an active way. The
Soviet Union was on the edge of disaster; 48 million people lived below
the poverty line; Communism—in his own words—was a pipe dream; and
the leadership had one year at the most to prevent a revolution "from
below."

Yeltsin had said essentially the same thing at Moscow rallies. By introducing Americans to his country's real problems, he hoped to dampen
their euphoria over Gorbachev's triumphs.

Yeltsin as the opposition leader also favorably impressed the American
foreign-policy establishment. After his speech at the Council for Foreign
Relations, attended by many prominent scientists and public figures,
David Rockefeller called him "a charming and impressive person, who
clearly is a highly skilled politician." Perhaps Yeltsin was just the person,
he added, "to start a whole new trend of Russian history" by putting it
on the track of democracy. George F. Kennan, former Ambassador in
Moscow and perhaps the oldest American Kremlinologist, declared that
Yeltsin as a politician was "not to be underestimated." Former Secretary
of State Cyrus R. Vance called him "a modern politician" and wondered
how one like him could have emerged from Moscow.

Much as Yeltsin valued meeting American financiers, economists, and
foreign-affairs experts, the main purpose of his visit—meeting the President—was constantly on his mind. Only this meeting would be an ade-
quate recompense for the ordeals and humiliations to which he had been
subjected in Moscow before departure; only this meeting would confirm
his official status as the leader of the Parliamentary opposition—though
deep inside he knew that he was leading a *popular* opposition to the
Kremlin. Even while visiting America for the first time, Yeltsin did not

lose sight of the political combat at home; moreover, he factored America into that struggle.

Yeltsin had no illusions that the meeting would be easy to obtain. Even in Moscow, as he tried to arrange it with top US Administration officials, he did not get a definite answer. He was assured he would meet Senator Claiborne Pell, Democrat from Rhode Island, and Senator Bill Bradley, Democrat from New Jersey; the latter had lately become actively interested in the Soviet Union. Yeltsin decided to use his own diplomacy to coerce the American President into a meeting. Just as he had broken into Soviet politics through the back door, now, too, he was going to crash the White House despite Bush's resistance.

Yeltsin hit the ground running. He had barely landed on American soil when he tossed Bush a rather crude teaser, telling reporters that Bush would be the very first to hear Yeltsin's proposals on how the US could help perestroika. While the White House hesitated, delaying daily the decision whether the Soviet opposition leader should be received, Yeltsin pushed on. The next day, at a press conference at a private home, he said several times that he had many things to tell the President.

Still, the White House, with its touching loyalty to Gorbachev, hesitated. They did hear Yeltsin say in an interview on PBS that a year from now a revolution "from the bottom" would break out in Russia; that he had concrete proposals on how to prevent it, and he would be willing to discuss them only in a private meeting with George Bush.

On the third day of his visit he spoke at Columbia University—where we saw him—and several times he brought up his desire to meet the President. Some of his comments seemed far-fetched or non sequiturs. When asked if he had a hobby, Yeltsin said that he had abandoned volleyball for tennis and added, "I would be happy to meet President Bush on a tennis court."

One of his closest associates at the time described him to us with rough affection. "He's an obstinate, bullheaded Ural peasant. He pushes straight ahead and doesn't flinch till he gets what he wants. In 1989 we told him, 'Boris Nikolayevich, you're like a battering ram; we're going to smash this wall with your help.' He only said, 'You could come up with a more human image.' "

To befuddled White House officials, Yeltsin demonstrated his obstinacy in scoring political points. When, on the fourth day of his visit, a limo brought him from Baltimore to Washington, he was sure he was on his way to meeting George Bush. Upon his arrival he was informed he would be seen only by Scowcroft; he pouted and would not leave the car at the White House parking lot.

"We talked him into the West Executive basement lobby," recalls a top Bush aide, "and then he had another fit and refused to go upstairs to

Scowcroft's office unless he could see the President. He was in a very strange mood."

Yeltsin ultimately prevailed and a compromise was struck. He would not be admitted to the Oval Office, but Bush would drop by Scowcroft's office to meet the Soviet guest. Only then, according to *The New York Times'* Maureen Dowd, did Yeltsin agree to go upstairs to meet the National Security Advisor.

Bush ended up spending all of fifteen minutes in Scowcroft's office. Then Yeltsin talked to Vice President Quayle for ten minutes, and spent an entire hour with Secretary of State Baker. Although no photographers were allowed in the fifteen-minute meeting, and Bush himself would write off the Soviet visitor as a "jolly fellow," Yeltsin would later affirm that he had the feeling of a mission well accomplished. He had succeeded in lending an official status to his unofficial trip and thus earning the title of Leader of the Soviet Opposition. The main objective—the political one— was achieved.

Delighted by the White House meetings that according to him "were extremely important in emphasizing the significance of his trip," Yeltsin continued on his travels, surprising America and being surprised by it. Later, in Moscow, he said that his impressions "surpassed all expectations" and that "the entire trip served to destroy my clichés and stereotypes of America." Early in the morning of September 13, he left to deliver a lecture in Philadelphia, blissfully unaware that the same day's *Washington Post,* in its "Style" column, published a piece—a crass caricature—subtitled "Yeltsin's Boozy Bearhug for the Capitalists."

"Boris N. Yeltsin," it read in part, "Soviet politician of the people, imbiber nonpareil, radical legislator and member of the Supreme Soviet, *nyetter* within the system, came swaying and galumphing and bassooning and mugging and hugging and doom-warning through the greater Baltimore-Washington corridor yesterday. It was the third day of his will-he-ever-sleep, I'll-take-America-by-storm tour."

Maintaining this derisive tone, the author, Paul Hendrickson, related the main stages of Yeltsin's political biography and the key moments of his American visit, calling it "his American blitzkrieg." He added a few tidbits of his own: Yeltsin, a long-time lush, had sneaked late at night into the bar of his Baltimore hotel and put away a bottle and a half of Jack Daniel's all by himself. As a result of this late-night revelry, the Soviet Senator showed up the next morning at Johns Hopkins with a nasty hangover: "He clasped his hands over his head like a boxing champion. He tilted. He rocked. He swerved. He careened . . . He looked like a man asleep on his feet."

Further, the article said, on Monday Yeltsin was scheduled to tape an interview for *Nightline,* but at three in the afternoon one of his aides called the studio to cancel for reasons of fatigue. In fact, the *Post* reporter wrote, Yeltsin was bending his elbow in a Manhattan bar.

All of this was later proven to be a fabrication, or, according to Yeltsin's companions on the trip, "a ridiculous journalistic escapade." It would also become the opening shot in the disinformation campaign waged against Boris Yeltsin by the American media. As Pavel Voshchanov, Yeltsin's press secretary during the trip, explained later, originally Yeltsin's companions decided not to tell him about the *Washington Post* canard. The group swung across the US at a breakneck pace as Yeltsin tried to pack into nine days the program originally planned for two weeks. Suddenly, Voshchanov says, a local paper published a piece with the same "drunk" story, adding new details: now it turned out that Yeltsin had begun his binge in New York and, together with his companions, had not been sober for four days straight.

Today Voshchanov thinks that concealing the piece from Yeltsin was a tactical error. *The Washington Post*'s lampoon of Yeltsin as a boozer had snowballed, generating additional unsavory tidbits. At any press conference he ran a risk of being caught off guard if asked about his alleged alcoholism. Lev Sukhanov, his closest aide on the trip, told us that owing to lack of information, Yeltsin had run into a minor jam. Their small group visited a pig farm outside Indianapolis. Afterward, host Jim Hardin invited the Soviet guests over and apologized for not having any of "your favorite Jack Daniel's." Later, in the car, Yeltsin asked his aide, "Lev, I didn't get it—who's the Jack he was talking about?"

His aides realized they had to tell him. They placed the translation of the *Post* piece in front of Yeltsin when they were aboard a private plane going from Indianapolis to Dallas. According to Voshchanov, "he remained silent throughout the flight. Only as he was getting into the car, he said, 'It's all hogwash!' "

Yeltsin gave it no further thought. By then he was already aware of the US yellow press, which no self-respecting man should be bothered by, and had assigned Paul Hendrickson's shoddy attack to the realm of fantasy. Besides, according to Sukhanov, Yeltsin had assumed that a democratic press would treat him, a guest and an advocate of democracy, favorably, so there was a brutal gap between his anticipation of journalistic reality and reality itself. Later it would be noted by *The New York Times'* conservative columnist A. M. Rosenthal that, "I don't know whether he knows it, because everybody was polite, but within the Bush-Quayle-Baker team, he went down like a lead *pirogi.*"

Although, according to Voshchanov, "all the American papers later published retractions of their pieces on the drunkenness of the Soviet delegation headed by Yeltsin," the reputation so cavalierly launched by *The Washington Post*—that Boris Yeltsin was a buffoon, a Russian bear, a yokel, and, worst of all, a lush—was still very much alive when Yeltsin returned to America two years later.

In June 1991 Yeltsin visited Washington in his new capacity—the democratically elected Russian President. This time he did not have to pout his way into the White House. He was given a lavish reception that included an hour and forty minutes with George Bush in the Oval Office and a joint press conference in the Rose Garden.

This time the newfangled Russian President, who had rushed to be "certified" by the US Administration even before his official inauguration, behaved in a markedly different fashion. Gone was the impulsive, spontaneous, small-town pol with his uncurbed passion for glad-handing and back-slapping; now he was reserved, subdued, and thoroughly statesmanlike. Yet the reporters still dwelt on his alleged predilection for alcohol as a sine qua non of his nature. *The New York Times'* Maureen Dowd alone wrote twice about Yeltsin's excessive fondness for Jack Daniel's and there were similar remarks in *The Washington Post.* Yeltsin, learning from bitter experience, would not touch even water at receptions—so as not to be photographed with a glass in his hand.

During his first trip, on its last day, at the Miami airport, Yeltsin signed a contract with sponsor Harrison according to which the honoraria from his lectures, ultimately more than $100,000, would be used to buy disposable syringes to combat the spread of AIDS in the USSR. The Esalen Institute, Yeltsin's official American host, undertook to purchase the syringes and deliver them overseas. Later, Yeltsin would remark on the irony: the morning he signed the contract, *Pravda* reprinted a piece from an Italian paper. The reporter wrote that Yeltsin had spent almost all his earnings on VCRs and round-the-clock boozing.

When Yeltsin rushed back to Moscow on September 18 to attend the Central Committee Plenum, he landed in the middle of a political scandal. *Pravda* had reprinted the piece by Vittorio Zucconi, the Washington correspondent of *La Repubblica,* without commentaries and in its entirety. Zucconi described in juicy detail the revelry that, according to him, Boris Yeltsin plunged into during his nine-day tour of America.

Zucconi claimed he had decided to write the piece after reading *The Washington Post*'s account of Yeltsin's Baltimore Binge. The Italian characterized Yeltsin's tour as "a holiday, a stage set, a bar counter 5000 kilometers long." Elsewhere, he informed his readers that "Yeltsin brought the bodily smells and the physical vigor of the homeland of Mother Russia to the corridors of American power. He now has everything he dreamed about: whiskey, dollars, knickknacks, and *Rambo* videocassettes." According to the article, Yeltsin had downed at least four bottles of Jack Daniel's and two bottles of vodka, as well as countless cocktails at receptions in his honor.

As for Yeltsin's promise to donate his American earnings to the Soviet AIDS fund, accountant Alfred Ross (who turned out to be Zucconi's invention) said, "Soviet AIDS patients should not count on that money. If he goes on spending like this, by the time he leaves America he will have nothing but debts."

Later, the Soviet papers wrote that the article had hit Moscow like a missile, initially confusing many of Yeltsin's supporters. Even his closest aides admitted that these lies, reprinted in *Pravda,* could seriously damage his reputation. The Soviet people did not trust *Pravda,* but Western papers were taken seriously.

Yeltsin's reaction was unequivocal. "Garbage!" he told Associated Press. "It's a simple lie, slander, and revenge for the fact that the Americans received us with admiration."

Deputy Victor Yaroshenko, who remained in America waiting for the syringes, declared at a press conference in New York that "this was a blatant political provocation against Boris Nikolayevich Yeltsin, aimed at discrediting one of the leaders of the left-wing opposition. The provocation caused a profound political crisis in the country, which has not abated yet. And, contrary to the expectations of the organizers of the provocation, it will boomerang and come to haunt them."

Which is what happened. Hundreds of copies of *Pravda* were publicly burned in Pushkin Square. An investigation conducted by a number of correspondents for other papers showed that most of Zucconi's assertions were not supported by witnesses. Some were obvious lies. *Pravda* published an apology—an act unprecedented in its history. *La Repubblica* followed by admitting "distortions." In Zelenograd, outside Moscow, a ten-thousand-strong rally was held in support of Yeltsin.

As had happened with previous attempts to slander Boris Yeltsin, this one only enhanced his popularity. But he did not need any more: his approval rating was already sky-high. It also turned out that, instead of the alleged shopping spree, Yeltsin had spent on himself all of $24: a few gifts for his grandchildren. On September 24, Soviet TV ran a brief story on Yeltsin receiving the first shipment of disposable syringes at the Moscow airport. Right there, on the tarmac, he handed the syringes to the Public Health Minister, whom he had begged to come to the airport to see for himself how the American honoraria had been spent. As Yeltsin put it, "The provocation failed."

His relief was premature. Hardly had another paper printed convincing evidence that Boris Yeltsin "in no manner abused the Soviet citizens' pride abroad"; hardly had the wind carried away the ashes of the copies of *Pravda* burnt by enraged Muscovites, when Soviet TV showed an hour-and-a-half feature on Yeltsin's visit to the United States.

Having failed to expose the drunkard Yeltsin in the print media, his enemies decided to present visual—indisputable—evidence. The highlight of the program was Yeltsin's speech to professors and students of Johns Hopkins. Appearing bedraggled on the screen, Yeltsin mumbled in a hoarse, incoherent voice, drawling his words unnaturally, gesturing abundantly and out of sync with his speech. The viewers could not help avoiding an impression that Yeltsin, indeed, was tipsy. Yet most of them, it turned out, simply refused to believe what they saw, suspecting yet another, more sophisticated, anti-Yeltsin canard.

Later, in an interview in *Ogonyok* magazine, Yeltsin would attribute his appearance during the lecture to an insanely busy schedule, jet lag, fatigue, and lack of sleep. This would be confirmed by Johns Hopkins president Steven Muller; Yeltsin's American interpreter, Harris Coulter; and his official host, James Harrison, who was with Yeltsin around the clock. Moreover, a source from the Ostankino TV studio would reveal that the tape had been tampered with by "experts" who made slow-motion and sync "adjustments" to both the audio track and the images. This was confirmed by a comparison of two tapes, one shown on Soviet TV and the other at Johns Hopkins. Incidentally, Yeltsin did stumble a few times.

For the moment, Soviet viewers, while smelling a fraud, still saw People's Deputy Yeltsin looking inebriated, and they impatiently awaited more explanations.

Meanwhile, the person who had caused all the brouhaha had vanished. Yeltsin's supporters, accustomed to his prompt counterstrikes in response to the clumsy attempts to discredit him, were initially puzzled and confused. There was no word from him in the media. No public appearances. He did not even show up at the Supreme Soviet, they noted with concern. Rumors began spreading around Moscow, one more sinister than the other. There had been an assassination attempt, he had been hurt in a car accident, he was dead. In the provinces, which lagged behind Moscow in information and were still wondering about Yeltsin's showing up "drunk" on TV, appeared a version of his suicide. Later, he would ironically sum up his fate as published by the Soviet Rumor Agency: "They say I've had a heart attack—two heart attacks—a stroke; they say I've had accidents, I've drowned—that I died, period."

Two weeks later, when passions reached their apogee, Yeltsin reported back. In an interview published by *Komsomolskaya Pravda* on October 15, he offered the following—false, it would later turn out—explanation of his sudden disappearance: "I must have caught a cold during my American trip. Right now the fever is down and my physician said that starting October 16, I can go back to work. On Monday, I will attend the session of the Supreme Soviet."

The session was broadcast on TV, and the viewers finally saw Yeltsin, right in the front row. Then, Gorbachev suddenly interrupted a routine discussion of a new law and invited Minister of the Interior Vadim Bakatin to step up to the podium. What happened was unexpected both for Yeltsin and for millions of TV viewers. Yeltsin could never have thought that the nation's highest legislative body would spend the entire hour discussing his "personal case," his "private life." It was the first time they heard from an official source the sensational tale of the attempt on Yeltsin's life and his swim in the Moscow River.

The Minister's statement, replayed the same day twice on TV, went as follows: On September 29 two militiamen assigned to guard duty outside the Uspensky dachas (where nomenklatura lived) reported to their superiors that they had been approached by Boris Yeltsin, soaking wet, who told them that an attempt had been made on his life. Two men had thrown a bag over his head, shoved him into a car, driven him onto a bridge, and pushed him off it into the water. When his wife and daughter came to pick him up, Yeltsin asked the militia officers not to report this to anyone. Bakatin said that Yeltsin had fabricated the story and later retracted it.

Bakatin's speech was followed by a new political scandal. Now millions of Russians were shuffling the contradictory and unconfirmed data to determine whether there had indeed been an attempt on the life of People's Deputy Boris Yeltsin. The next day Yeltsin issued a written statement in which he accused Gorbachev of personally arranging this farce in order to remove him from the political arena.

Two years later, Gorbachev's involvement in the Yeltsin affair appears indisputable. He personally interrupted a session of Parliament and suggested that the country's highest legislative body discuss the private life of one of its members. In doing so, he knew perfectly well that the circumstances (of which he was aware) would prevent Yeltsin from giving a full explanation in public. It was at his, Gorbachev's, directive that the next day's *Izvestiya* printed the full transcript of the report. All of this took place with the elections to the Russian Parliament and local Soviets approaching. For the unpredictable Yeltsin, the elections were a chance to further enhance his political position, and Gorbachev was frightened by this.

Yet in the meantime, as Yeltsin would later admit, the plot against him worked. His popularity took a dive. Taking the floor after Bakatin, he did not provide the rebuttal that his followers expected; to the contrary, his evasiveness only served to befog the situation. His attempts to clear himself appeared unconvincing and even insincere: one sensed a thickly veiled mystery. Since Bakatin's version mentioned that Yeltsin was seen carrying a bouquet of flowers around the government dachas, many believed that a love affair was involved, and that Yeltsin's rival had pushed him into the river. The theory blossomed with colorful detail, while Yeltsin's obstinate silence, combined with a hint at a political provocation, merely added to popular curiosity. The Russian people were dying to know: what really happened to their hero on a late September evening at the Uspensky dachas? Scores of reporters, both Soviet and foreign, have spared neither time nor effort nor fantasy trying to solve the mystery.

We can offer our own version, compiled from both first- and second-hand sources. When we arrived in Moscow in October 1991 to research parts of this biography, we found ourselves willy-nilly in the role of detectives. We discovered that even now, Yeltsin's unfortunate promenade in Uspensky is surrounded by a wall of silence. But we found a talkative retiree, who lives in Uspensky full time and wishes to remain anonymous, "not out of fear, of course, but out of respect for Boris Nikolayevich's secret—it's up to him to disclose it when he sees fit."

> It was Prime Minister Ryzhkov's birthday, and they celebrated it at the dacha—that's a fact. Naturally, you can't celebrate without Gorbachev: he's General Secretary, after all. I don't think they would have invited Yeltsin—he was already an outsider, he would not belong at the table. On the other hand, Ryzhkov and he go back a long way, to Sverdlovsk days. Yeltsin can't easily forget a friend's birthday. And he decided to surprise Ryzhkov and show up uninvited. First, he liked surprises; second, he did not want to make a fuss about his coming.
>
> His arrival took everyone by surprise. Don't forget that *Pravda* had just published a fabrication about him, and there was this rigged TV program, where he looked tipsy and kept mumbling. So he was very jittery, seething—inside, of course. And they had a fight—even came to blows. Well, as you know, they're in different weight categories . . . So Gorbachev took his revenge by sending his personal bodyguards after Yeltsin. And that is how Boris Nikolayevich went for a swim.

Going through the newspaper archives, we found an interview that Yeltsin gave on November 25, 1989, to *Soviet Youth,* a Latvian paper. The interviewer refers to a story of a quarrel between Gorbachev and Yeltsin, followed by a fight between them, all at the Ryzhkov dacha. Allegedly, others had to use fire extinguishers to separate the opponents. Yeltsin laughed but did not deny the story.

The theory remains neither confirmed nor denied.

At the time Yeltsin took a dip in the ice-cold water, Valentina Lantseva, along with Sukhanov and Tanya Pushkina, worked under him at the Supreme Soviet's Committee for Construction and Architecture. She recalls Yeltsin's adventure:

He was sick for two weeks with bronchitis. His wife nursed him back, as usual. It was all because of that "swim," and after that, too, he spent so much time shivering until his wife and Tanya came to pick him up by car. He was hurt badly when he was thrown into the river—the left half of his face was one big bruise, and all along the left side of his body he was black and blue . . . How they humiliated him—him such a big man, so proud and strong. Really well-trained boys—all ganging up on one person. Clever, huh?

When he came back to work—on his first day he looked like a shaggy dog. He looked at all of us askance—by us, I mean his "team," ten people or so. He was so afraid that we would believe all these dirty lies, all that slander, in the papers and on TV. Finally he just shook his head—he had made up his mind. He called all of us inside, locked the door, and told us the whole story. He warned that it should not leave that room until the time came to make it public.

We realized that Lantseva was not going to share with us her boss's two-year-old secret, and asked her about the "romance" theory—Yeltsin wandering around Uspensky with flowers in his hand.

"Unfortunately this was no romantic story," she said. "Unfortunately." In her tone of voice we heard the same disapproval of Yeltsin's sexual indifference and lack of sensuality that we heard from other women who had worked with him. Lantseva also mentioned that "half the guards who dunked him are now working for him."

We were offered a chance to get to the bottom of the story, but owing to lack of time and the need to research other aspects of Yeltsin's life—less sensational but more important—we had to pass it up. To those still intrigued by the Uspensky incident we offer as clues the following facts at our disposal:

• That evening Prime Minister Nikolai Ryzhkov was celebrating his birthday.

• Yeltsin was not visiting a mistress.

• Yeltsin was about to surprise Ryzhkov on his birthday.

• Yeltsin was attacked not on the way *to* the dacha (as he later claimed) but on his way *from* it.

• Yeltsin was pushed off the bridge into the river by at least four men.

• As a result of the incident, Yeltsin's masculine pride was deeply humiliated.

One cannot accuse the Party PR people of fertile imagination. A year and a half later, during the presidential campaign, they sent cameramen after Yeltsin in the hope of obtaining some kind of compromising footage. Again, they got the same type of material as before: drinking and swimming. This is what happened, according to a man who accompanied Yeltsin on the trip:

When we were in Novokuznetsk, in Siberia, we were received by a rival of Yeltsin's, who showed us unexpected hospitality. The tables groaned with food and there was a bottle of brandy per person. We were surprised by his generosity until we learned that afterward he collected the empty bottles and declared that they had been consumed by Yeltsin alone. We laughed about it, but that's not all. Indeed, Boris Nikolayevich drank that night a bit more than usual. He sent the reporters away and dragged us to the river for a swim—no matter how we tried to talk him out of it, he would not listen.

It could not have been more than six or seven degrees above [Centigrade], a strong wind—Boris Nikolayevich strips down and goes into the water. He must have been dying for a swim. Meanwhile the cameramen got there, too, on their own, and shot the whole scene from the bushes: how he walks in and out of the water naked. Those guys were pulling no punches. And what were they trying to prove? Aren't we all naked underneath?

In the final analysis they decided not to use it. They were afraid it would boomerang. What if the voters *liked* Boris Yeltsin in the buff? Can you imagine those guys, sitting in the Kremlin projection room, watching a movie of Yeltsin naked and trying to decide, Should we run this stuff on TV or not? Aren't they something else?

Returning to the end of 1990: Yeltsin found himself on the sidelines. It was with good reason that he accused Gorbachev of using "unprincipled moral and psychological methods to remove opponents instead of political means." Yeltsin's advisers noted with dismay that the story of an attempted assassination alone had damaged their boss personally. In its wake he was disheartened, taking only a peremptory part in Parliamentary politics, which took a further toll on his political reputation. One interviewer asked him, "Are you still confident about yourself—sure of your strength?"

Yeltsin admitted, "I'm letting a lot of punches get through—bad ones, too. But, as fighters say, I'm absorbing them better. Now I'm working at full steam."

This is vintage Yeltsin: in order to rise, he first needs to touch bottom. He uses defeat to charge himself with energy. In the pitch dark he is able to see his path even more clearly.

Yeltsin is a rare psychological type. His early corporal and psychological traumas were an introduction to what would happen later in life. He nearly drowned in a baptismal font, was almost blown up by a grenade, had his nose broken, miraculously survived a harebrained march through the taiga followed by typhoid, was expelled from school, and acquired a serious chronic heart disease. His Moscow adventures oddly echo the dramas of his childhood: his ejection from the Kremlin is not unlike his expulsion from school, while being thrown off the bridge is reminiscent of his near-drowning during his baptism. Each of these events might seem like an isolated incident, but taken together they show us a man apt to get into extreme situations. On the one hand, he is what Russians call "thirty-three disasters," or accident-prone; on the other hand he was definitely born under a lucky star, for he managed to wriggle his way out of every calamity that befell him. Hence his behavioral pattern: hyperactive, risk-taking, sacrifice-prone, courageous, and high-achievement-oriented. His proclivity for self-sacrifice and his chronic misfortunes become a sort of inevitable compensation for a high-pressure life-style. With time, such conditions become par for the course for his type; accordingly, his survival skills improve. Dr. Dmitri Olshansky compared Yeltsin to an unstoppable tank. He cited the 19th Party Conference, when Yeltsin walked from the "bleachers" through the entire auditorium with his delegate's ID held high—and no one could stop him!

"Psychologists divide people into 'failure-evading' and 'success-oriented,' " Olshansky wrote. "The Soviet system creates the former, with a heightened sense of caution and fear of losing one's position. Yeltsin belongs to the latter type—with all of the attendant pluses and minuses."

Another event took place at the same time. "The sickly child of Soviet democracy," as it was called by essayist-politician Leonid Batkin, suffered a grave loss: on December 14, 1989, Academician Sakharov died. Several hours before his death he spoke at a meeting of the Interregional Group. By then the Group had scored enough political points with its radical proposals at the Congress of Deputies and at the Supreme Soviet, and they were no longer hesitant to identify themselves as the opposition. Sakharov's last speech—in a way, his political testament—was dedicated to exactly that subject: "I would like to define opposition. What is it? We can no longer share responsibility for the actions of our current leadership. By dragging out perestroika for years, it is leading the country into the abyss . . . The plans of transition to a market economy will turn out to be unrealizable, while the frustration level is already growing nationwide. This frustration will make evolutionary development impossible. The only path, the only possibility for evolution, is the radicalization of perestroika."

Sakharov's death left Yeltsin the biggest name inside the opposition. Earlier he had been elected Acting Chairman of the Interregional Group for its first year. Sakharov would become one sooner or later, too, though the Academician was not fond of routine work and preferred to address *urbi et orbi* with issues of international import. Sakharov's death increased Yeltsin's responsibility to his supporters and to the people, especially since many already perceived the Group as a shadow government. Yet the system did not have any legitimate levers to move Gorbachev's throne an inch.

The Yeltsin camp realized that the Congress of People's Deputies and its appendix, the Supreme Soviet—those ugly offshoots of glasnost and perestroika—had outlived their political usefulness, though they helped untie people's tongues and raised their political awareness. But now these two bodies, linked too closely to and controlled by Gorbachev, were obstacles to further democratization. Yeltsinites searched for new political arenas, especially since new elections were coming up—to the Russian Supreme Soviet, to the legislative bodies of Moscow, Leningrad, and other cities and regions.

"What about the rumor that you're planning to run for President of the Russian Federation?" Yeltsin was asked.

"It's a rumor, pure and simple. There's a lot of rumors circulating about me, and"—Yeltsin could not resist a dig at the hoopla over his Uspensky adventure—"not all of them get an airing at the Supreme Soviet . . . In any event you can't run for President in this country—we don't have a direct election for the job. We can talk only about running for the Republican or Moscow City Council. I know there are plans to nominate me, but I have not decided yet whether I'll agree or not."

Yeltsin did not dissemble: he could have run for the Moscow City Council and then tried to become Mayor—or for the Russian Supreme Soviet, which would then elect its chairman from its own ranks. Yeltsin's advisers could not agree on which path he should take.

Chairman of the Russian Supreme Soviet was a titular job, just as Russia was a Republic in name only. Russia was the most politically marginal of the fifteen Republics, since it was popularly perceived as the Soviet Union and never as a political entity in its own right.

Now, the Mayor of Moscow was something else. As democratization proceeded, the job acquired new importance: the head of the capital could become a powerful, independent leader. The objection to taking this path was that Yeltsin had already been head of the capital, albeit in a somewhat different capacity: as the First Party Secretary. The move had a soupçon of repetitiveness, and its opponents, including Lev Shemayev and Lev Sukhanov, quoted Heraclitus: You can't step into the same stream twice. (They were not making fun of Yeltsin's aquatic adventures.)

A two-step game plan was worked out: the Russian Parliament as minimum; the Russian Presidency as maximum. The plan presupposed the overhaul of the central power structure as well as a change of the status of Russia, which was even more important.

Let us move on from Gorbachev's parliaments to Yeltsin's Russia.

YELTSIN'S RUSSIA
(Spring–Summer 1990)

IN THE spring of 1990, we became personally involved in the story of
Yeltsin's Russia. We suddenly found ourselves transformed from sideline
observers, an ocean away, into participants in a historical event taking
place in the midst of the disintegrating Russian Soviet Empire. The
feeling that overcame us when we returned to the country that we had left
thirteen years earlier—forever, we thought—is best described by the poet
Fyodor Tyutchev:

> *Happy is he who visited this world*
> *In its fatal moments.*

The country in which we arrived that spring was radically, unrecogniz-
ably different from the one we left in the spring of 1977. The formal
pretext for the visit was an international conference on Nabokov, held at
the Moscow Tchaikovsky Conservatory, located not far from the Kremlin, on Hertzen Street. The street was ravaged with ditches, as workers
were laying new underground pipes. When we came back a year later, the
street looked even worse, which did not seem to upset the Muscovites,
who cheerfully considered it impassable for tanks—the capital was awash
with rumors of an inevitable military-police coup. By then people were
already so blasé about such rumors that when the coup finally did take
place on August 19, 1991, it caught everyone unawares.

After listening awhile to the presentations of our fellow critics, we
finally couldn't stand it anymore. After one of us delivered his report, we
fled the conference hall to plunge into the tempest of street rallies. Our
sentimental journey to revisit the home fires suddenly turned into a
political one—though not altogether devoid of sentiment.

The country we had left was a broken-down, frightened, politically
backward place, where even a modest, innocent undertaking like our

184

independent press agency could have sent us, had we stayed a bit longer, far eastward; instead of being thrown out of the country, we could have landed in jail or exile, if not worse. We endured KGB blackmail, anonymous phone threats, constant tailing, even a murder attempt. Someone dropped a cement slab off the roof onto Elena Klepikova. Had it landed a few inches closer, Elena's present coauthor would have cursed forever the day he conceived the idea of an agency and got his wife into it.

The hardest part for us, though, was the reaction of our friends to our activity, illegal at the time. Our two closest friends—a well-known writer and an equally well-known poet, both quite decent people, sworn liberals who became political activists in Gorbachev's era—both denounced us independently. They did not betray us nor make their denunciation official, yet they told us directly that we were creating problems for our friends and compromising them politically. The main reason for the short life of our little agency and our emergency departure from the USSR was not blackmail on the part of the authorities, or the anonymous threats, but our isolation among our Moscow friends. We are not writing this to reproach people whom we still love and remain friends with; rather, we are doing it with a sense of understanding. Indeed, we were morally responsible to them for our dissident activity, which was risky, and not just for us.

Such was the atmosphere of terror and repression that reigned in those days. One day a friend came over to tell us that he had heard our *New York Times* interview read over the Voice of America. He had been hurt by one of our remarks: "Each person has his norm, his quota of fear, just as each person can sleep only so many hours, then wakes up. I have had my quota of fear and I have used it up."

"That may be so, and your quota may be exhausted, but—trust me, I'm older than you—soon enough you'll have new fears," our friend said.

We did not wait around to see if he was right: soon enough we had to leave the country. At the time we were convinced—on the basis of our own experience and the thousand years of Russian history—that Russia would never be free—at least not in our lifetime; it would never shake off State terror and the collective burden of fear. This was historical determinism, if not fatalism, on our part: what had not happened in the past could not happen in the future. Our skepticism was reinforced by the failure of Russian democracy: a pathetic few months of political freedom between the two revolutions of 1917. We even thought that it was shameful to be optimistic.

And now, back in our Motherland, we found it in the throes of birth—freedom was being born where tyranny had reigned for a millennium. Gorbachev may have been Liberty's midwife, but he quit early, and later did all he could to destroy the delicate child. After he announced glasnost from the Kremlin, he glibly thought that democracy could be managed—by himself, from the same Kremlin. That somewhat puerile assumption—was it hope?—was most clearly debunked by the wave of street rallies that occurred throughout the country. The gatherings and demonstrations were the first, and the most vivid, manifestation of grass-roots democracy. We encountered a country of slogans—and they were thrilling. Using Gorbachev's glasnost as a platform, people expanded its limits to demand his own resignation—they saw him and his Kremlin team as the chief obstacle to real democracy.

On May 1, 1990, Red Square was the site of the traditional May Day celebration. At ten o'clock, the Spassky Tower clock struck ten times. The Soviet leaders, headed by Gorbachev, climbed atop Lenin's Mausoleum, and, still in a festive mood, waved greetings to the well-organized columns of demonstrators, who carried red flags, multicolored balloons, and official placards.

Then, from various parts of Moscow, a very different type of demonstrator began to converge on Red Square. They were well-organized, too, not by the authorities but by the radical Moscow Electorate Club, which had just helped elect democratic candidates to the Russian Parliament and City Hall. The club was the largest contemporary political organization, not counting the Communist Party, which long ago had turned into a gang of careerists. The Moscow Electorate Club sent the disgruntled citizens, armed with anti-government slogans, into the streets of Moscow at election time. Now, encouraged by that experience, having honed their skills at rehearsals, the club decided to put on a show for the bigwigs.

At twelve minutes to eleven, the official demonstrators left Red Square, followed by the unofficial ones, several hundred thousand strong. From the Mausoleum, Gorbachev could see the future political parties of a free Russia. Among the demonstrators were columns of Liberal Democrats, Anarcho-Syndicalists, and the Christian Democratic Union. A giant crucifix floated along Red Square, perhaps meant to symbolize the agonies endured by the Russian people at the hands of Bolshevik impostors.

The hot spot of the day was Lithuania, subjected to the Kremlin's economic blockade and military threats. Hence, many slogans and placards were dedicated to this Baltic David, the first to challenge the Goliath of the Empire:

Long Live Lithuania!
Down with the Lithuanian Blockade!
The Lithuanian Blockade Is the President's Shame!
For Our Freedom and Your Freedom!
Free Lithuania Now!
Today Lithuania, Tomorrow . . . ?

Waving yellow, green, and red Lithuanian flags, the demonstrators helped put to rest the imperial ambitions of the Russian people. For by now the Russian people had achieved a level of political maturity at which they understood that the Empire was a burden they could no longer carry—and who could? For in order to create, and then, for many centuries, to maintain, reinforce, and expand the Empire, the Russian people had to sacrifice their own well-being and freedom—far too high a price to pay for an ugly, disparate conglomerate about to disintegrate. As the Russian historian Vasily Klyuchevsky wrote in the late nineteenth century of Russia's increasing territorial acquisitions, "While the State swelled in size, the people swelled with hunger."

Russian flags outnumbered Lithuanian ones, but they were not official red flags, with hammer and sickle and a narrow blue stripe on the left—they were pre-Revolution white, blue, and red tricolors, introduced by Peter the Great (missing only the two-headed eagle, the symbol of monarchy). Demonstrators also carried large pictures, including those of Yeltsin. Like the white-blue-red tricolors, Yeltsin's pictures symbolized popular opposition to the Kremlin usurpers, from Lenin to Gorbachev. The slogans, both written and shouted ones, told the story:

Politburo, Resign!
Down with Marxism-Leninism!
Down with the CPSU! [the Communist Party of the Soviet Union]
Bolsheviks Must Give Up Power!
Give the President Another Capital!
Gorbachevism Will Not Pass! CPSU Is Kaput!
The KGB Are the Cannibals of the Kremlin!
Will Swap: A Leader's Mummy for Disposable Needles!

The demonstrators' main target was not the mummy of Lenin in the Mausoleum but the live people on top of it—primarily Gorbachev. Drowning the festive tunes blaring from loudspeakers, the chorus of demonstrators shouted: *"Down! Down!"* Down with Communist ideology, Down with the Party power, and Down with the nomenklatura, led by Gorbachev. Yet, as a popular Latin doggerel says, "People are booing at me, but I applaud myself."

During the demonstration, Gorbachev's facial expressions ran the gamut. At first he smiled as though nothing had happened, and waved at the demonstrators who were yelling for his resignation. Was he once again putting on a brave front? Or did he not realize right away what was going on? Gradually his face darkened, then he grinned and whispered something to his colleagues. He leaned forward, and, supporting himself with one hand, stared at the demonstrators. Was he trying to get a better view of the placards? Remember some of the demonstrators' faces? He was no longer smiling; his fingers beat a nervous, impatient, helpless tattoo, on the edge of the podium. He had no reason to be afraid: the square was surrounded by troops, and this act of civil disobedience was, though sudden, not unexpected. To Galina Starovoitova, a well-known democratic activist and a deputy in the Parliament, the sight of the soldiers with machine guns on that day was a reminder of the Tiananmen Square bloodbath: "Shouldn't we all have learned from the Beijing events?"

She did not have to travel to faraway China for parallels. Closer to home, on April 9, 1989, troops had attacked a peaceful demonstration in Tbilisi and massacred twenty Georgians. Of course, such events should teach a lesson, but perhaps one of a different kind than Starovoitova expected.

Again, Gorbachev consulted his colleagues in a whisper. Next to him, Prime Minister Nikolai Ryzhkov tried to persuade him to do something. Then Gorbachev leaned over to talk to someone unseen by the camera—perhaps Raisa, who was also on the podium, albeit keeping a low profile in order not to further irritate the crowd. Allegedly—we quote the rumor told us by the Moscow actor-director Sergei Kokovkin—Ryzhkov was the first to realize what was happening, and egged Gorbachev on: "How can you tolerate this, Mikhail Sergeyevich?" Raisa Gorbachev was simply frightened, and, perhaps recalling the bloody fate of the Ceausescus, said it was time to leave. Gorbachev, ever obedient to his wife, agreed. One way or another, the decision was taken, and the Kremlin leadership, pursued by whistles and boos, departed hastily in what was more of a rout than a dignified exit. The crowd yelled: "Shame! Shame!"

Was it on that spring day in 1990 that Gorbachev abruptly decided to change his relatively liberal policy? In any case, the next fall he began to pick a new team, which in August 1991 would launch a coup and take over Moscow for sixty-three hours.

A few days after the May Day demonstration, Gorbachev would label its participants riffraff and accuse them of an attempt to storm the Kremlin and the Lubyanka—KGB headquarters.

"It is a signal that we should take seriously," he said, also mentioning that the demonstrators carried placards that said, "Down with Lenin" and "Down with Gorbachev."

But it was not the demand for his resignation that most angered the Kremlin leader: "This riffraff carried the flags of anarchists, of Tsarist Russia, and portraits of Nicholas the Second, Stalin—and Boris Yeltsin!"

True, the anti-Gorbachev demonstrators represented a crazy quilt of political views. But neither the Tsar—murdered by the Bolsheviks—nor the tyrant Stalin, who had passed away peacefully, posed any threat to

Gorbachev's power. The reference to them was calculated to further compromise Boris Yeltsin, whom Gorbachev was taking more and more seriously. He was not Gorbachev's full-fledged rival yet, but an enemy, a magnet for hostile forces.

Recently Gorbachev had complained about the passivity of the masses; now it was time for him to lament the opposite—and he did, ranting about chaos and anarchy and bellowing for order and discipline. He still failed to realize that his revolution from above had played itself out and that the new revolution it had begotten defined itself as anti-Gorbachev from the start and promoted his opposite—Yeltsin—as its leader. Perhaps Gorbachev had already reached his limit as far as change was concerned and lacked sufficient energy and political instinct to grasp the upheavals taking place around him.

To him, the centaur-like Parliament—a democratic head with a totalitarian body—that he had created was as far as democracy should go. Inside the Parliament were raging debates, heated discussions, political conflicts, but Gorbachev had designed it skillfully so as to reduce risks to his position to practically nil. He knew how to manage the show, and, ultimately, was guaranteed a victory. But running the country was far more difficult. Gorbachev had managed the Stavropol Region and was still influenced by the paternalistic Stalinist notions on how things should be done. Gorbachev still thought of the Soviet Union as his bailiwick, but by now it was more like a ship heading into the tempest with its rudder smashed and sails torn.

From Estonia to Georgia, from Moscow to Siberia, from Armenia to Leningrad—people were awakening from a long slumber. To paraphrase a line from Rabelais's *Gargantua and Pantagruel,* the moans of the dead and of the still living that had frozen into the air in the course of decades were now thawing out and growing audible. Long ago Lenin thus defined a revolutionary situation: the people at the bottom do not want to live in the old way, while the people at the top are unable to. The situation at hand was rather a *pre*-revolutionary one: the top still wanted to carry on, but the bottom neither could nor wanted to. Gorbachev sided with the *apparatchiks,* atop the nomenklatura pyramid. Yeltsin, dropped off the pyramid, was now crawling back up, supported by the masses, who had chosen him as their leader.

Only recently glasnost had been compared to the taiga, to a Siberian forest: noisy at the top and quiet at the bottom. The joke was outdated; the noise now came from the bottom, while the top tried not to hear it, blocked it with earplugs, or jammed it the way they had until recently jammed the "enemy" voices of foreign radio stations. One recalls the uplifting march music blasting across Red Square, meant to drown out anti-Gorbachev chanting. It didn't work. Gorbachev panicked and fled the Mausoleum through the secret underground passage to his Bolshevik refuge—the Kremlin.

What happened to him at this turning point of the revolution that he himself had started? The leader found himself in the rear, overtaken by events he himself had brought about, and now he was trying to put a brake on them in order to remain at the helm. Besides the personal fear of losing power, Gorbachev must have also felt the pressure from the *apparat,* for whom this erosion of power was a more tangible reality than for him. However, the *apparat* still had the KGB—the most effective self-defense tool—at its disposal. In this situation it was easier for the opposition to make demands than for Gorbachev to respond to them. The members of the opposition in Gorbachev's Parliament were responsible only to their voters and were not, like Gorbachev, burdened with obligations to the nomenklatura, the generals, and the KGB. Nor, unlike Gorbachev, did they have anything to lose. They had an easier time in every respect than he did.

Ultimately, Gorbachev turned out to be a spineless wonder, a weather-vane with a highly developed sense of which way the wind was blowing and how strong it was. However, his political instinct was one-sided: a child of the nomenklatura system who intrigued his way to power with the help of the KGB, he was sensitive to the breezes blowing through the Kremlin and oblivious to any other kind. Loss of grass-roots support was a blow to his vanity, but could not compare to the loss of power. Had true democracy been in place at the time, had his power depended on the popular will, he might have initiated more significant political and economic reforms. For the moment, the question of whether he maintained power or not was not determined by the people, but by the pillars of his authority: the nomenklatura, the Army, and the KGB. For Gorbachev to openly challenge them would have been tantamount to lopping off the branch he was sitting on.

Even if everything had depended on him alone, it is unlikely that Gorbachev would have allowed the people to decide the question of who was to exercise power. It would have been too dangerous in view of the dismal economic results of his five-year rule. And the masses now had a new tribune, one who understood their outlook and their needs, and who was in tune with the times.

The political evolution of the masses in turn favored the political growth of Yeltsin himself. Simultaneously, Gorbachev was gradually turning from an *apparat*-style reformer into a conservative, stifling the revolution he himself had begun or perhaps was forced to begin. He relied more and more on the conservative alliance of the Party and the police rather than on the people, who frightened him, as May Day showed. Nevertheless he could not totally ignore their voices, and as a result both the nomenklatura and the masses were less and less content with him.

His last dependable source of support for his eroding power base was the intelligentsia, which defended him furiously from the complaints of the *apparat* and the criticism of the masses.

It is ironic that the intellectuals regarded both the reactionary Yegor Ligachev and the radical Boris Yeltsin as enemies, perhaps Yeltsin a bit more so, since, unlike Ligachev, he was loved by many. We argued endlessly with our Moscow fellow writers, who damned Yeltsin while defending Gorbachev from Yeltsin's and our criticism.

It was about that time that a booklet reprinting a chapter on Gorbachev from our book *Behind the High Kremlin Walls* came out in Moscow in at least five pirate editions. With little political literature around, the booklet became a bestseller nationwide. We saw it all over Moscow: on Gorky Street, Pushkin Square, and Red Square; in underground passageways and subway stations. One vendor we saw held up a homemade advertising poster, AMERICAN WRITERS VLADIMIR SOLOVYOV AND ELENA KLEPIKOVA AGAINST MIKHAIL GORBACHEV, while his partner cried out our biographical data. We were, according to him, former Central Committee members who had worked for British Intelligence and defected on a trip abroad. We read in a Moscow paper that the vendors had been arrested and fined, and copies of the booklet confiscated, but by the time we got to Moscow it was being sold freely, with impunity, for three rubles.

At a Komsomol congress, Gorbachev was asked in the lobby whether he had our booklet. He said he did, but would not comment. Some people said jokingly, others seriously, that we could become the first victims of the new law that threatened criminal prosecution for insulting the President—Gorbachev's attempt to protect himself from criticism. If that were not enough, a few months before our arrival in Moscow, Vladimir Solovyov had published an op-ed piece in *The Christian Science Monitor* bluntly entitled "Gorbachev Must Go." Our Moscow friends knew the article from foreign-radio broadcasts and were almost unanimously indignant—just as they were about our interest in Boris Yeltsin.

It took us but a few days in Moscow to realize that Gorbachev's bet on the intellectuals, with their widespread authority and influence, had paid off handsomely: they remained loyal to him even in his bleakest days, a loyalty that further alienated them, along with Gorbachev, from the Russian people. Only a year or so earlier, the Moscow intelligentsia marched in the vanguard of perestroika, claiming to be the brains and conscience of the nation—claims that had collapsed.

The intellectuals could not grasp the quickly changing situation, they underestimated Yeltsin, and, most important, they never understood that the masses were not satisfied with the glasnost circus, that they needed the bread of perestroika as well. We found the Moscow intellectuals' opinion that man does not live by bread alone to be hypocritical. The people and the intellectuals were not on an equal footing, and one could understand the popular anger not only against the Partocracy but against the intellectuals as well. Like their idol, Gorbachev, the intellectuals lagged behind the onrush of Russian history. They were paying the price for their alienation from the masses and their indifference to social needs. The people found glasnost wanting not only because it failed to deliver "bread" but also because it was merely the first stage of democracy. Now they were in a hurry to get on to the next stage—freedom.

The intellectuals were apprehensive about this freedom, as it endangered their privileged social position. They were in no hurry to share the freedom they had been given by Gorbachev—or the material well-being. There is of course more than crass self-interest to their pro-Gorbachev position at this key junction of Russian history; we wrote about it earlier in this book.

Yeltsin is again being accused of neo-Bolshevism. Considerably distorting Yeltsin's remarks, the well-known Soviet political writer Andranik Migranyan wrote, "At this coil of our developmental spiral we again run into the psychology of *lumpen* socialism, described by Marx . . . In my mind, Yeltsin is the kind of neo-Bolshevik leader whose speeches focus on the same leitmotif that Bolsheviks have belabored both before and after the Revolution: return the loot to the people . . . The public mood that has turned him into a populist leader is a very dangerous one . . . The path to the redistribution of available material goods leads to the dead end of future reinslavement. Pretty soon it will turn out that there is nothing left to redistribute. This will be followed by terror and repression."

Another intellectual, Leningrad poet Alexandr Kushner, frightened by the gathering momentum of the revolution from below, informed impatient Soviet citizens that "we need an evolutionary, a long process of familiarization with democracy. A lot of people in our country are chomping at the bit to accelerate the process and refuse to support Gorbachev. Instead, they are promoting others, in my mind, rather dubious characters." This cautious poet dared not mention Yeltsin by name, but it is clear whom he meant.

Gorbachev himself, with his arrogant, snobbish attitude toward his subjects, was so used to doling out freedom piecemeal that he could not even conceive of men and women deciding for themselves what kind of freedom they needed and in what amounts. Freedom is real only when it is embodied in a legitimate public institution independent of the generosity of the "good tsar"; when the *vox populi,* even if it is not *vox Dei,*

Yeltsin at the Construction Ministry, 1989, his career in shambles after being deposed as Moscow Party Chief. *Photo by Yuri Feklistov.*

Beginning the long road back: campaigning for the new Congress of People's Deputies, 1989. *Photo by V. Kiselev, from* Rossiya *weekly.*

Two victories: voting at the People's Deputy election, March 27, 1989; and crossing Red Square after being elected Chairman of the Russian Supreme Soviet, May 29, 1990, despite a massive anti-Yeltsin campaign. *Photos by Yuri Feklistov.*

Yeltsin among supporters, 1990. *Photo by V. Kochetov.*

Yeltsin leaves the auditorium at the 28th Party Congress, July 12, 1990, after shocking the nation and the world by resigning from the Communist Party. *Photo by V. Kiselev, from Rossiya weekly.*

Talking with automobile workers, February 1991. *Photo by Yuri Feklistov.*

The country's leader and his wife, Naina, at a church service—the first time since the Revolution—Easter 1991, at Moscow's Yelokhov Cathedral. *Photo by Yuri Kozyrev, from the family album.*

Taking the oath as Russia's first democratically elected president, July 10, 1991. *Photo by Yuri Feklistov.*

A rare shot: Gorbachev and Yeltsin laughing together, summer 1991, shortly before the roof fell in. *Photo from the Presidium of the Russian Supreme Soviet.*

Plotters: Yeltsin with one of the future leaders of the August putsch, Minister of Defense Marshal Dmitri Yazov, leaving Lenin's Mausoleum, June 1990 (*Feklistov*). Soviet Parliament Speaker Anatoli Lukyanov (left) and Vice President Gennadi Yanayev, who became President for three days (right). *Photo by Victor Solyaninov, from* Rossiya *weekly.*

Yeltsin speaking from a balcony of the Russian White House during the putsch. On the right, Secretary of State Gennadi Burbulis, a bodyguard, Vice President Alexandr Rutskoy (holding the flag) and Prime Minister Ivan Silayev. *Photo by Yuri Feklistov.*

Tanks in Red Square, facing St. Basil's. *Photo by Gennadi Shalayev, from* Rossiya *weekly.*

Father Gleb Yakunin, a key Yeltsin supporter. The story goes that the rain he had prayed for kept the Alpha troopers from landing on the roof of the Russian White House during the putsch. *From* Rossiya *weekly.*

translates into the expression of popular will and political action, be it reflected in economic reforms or presidential elections.

We came to Moscow just in time for the presidential election—not the Soviet, but the Russian. Gorbachev skillfully mined all the roads leading to his throne—there was no constitutional way to compete with him for the job of Soviet President. He refused to submit his candidacy to a popular vote, instead manipulating the obedient Kremlin Parliament. By now all the public-opinion polls were unanimous: Boris Yeltsin was the most popular politician in the country. The readers of *Sobesednik (Interlocutor)* magazine, in response to the question "Whom do you trust the most?" selected Yeltsin: 1420 votes. He was followed by Leningrad mayor Anatoly Sobchak (350), then his Moscow colleague Gavriil Popov (215), with Gorbachev closing the list with 115 votes. Gorbachev led in the list of the most disappointing politicians, with 1535 votes. Yeltsin would clobber Gorbachev in an election if given the chance.

Alas, he was not. Nor would he be in the immediate future, it seemed. Then he found a loophole. He entered the race for the chairmanship of the Russian Supreme Council—until then a figurehead position, something of a middle ground between the Speaker of Parliament and the President. It held no power, because, even though Russia occupied three-quarters of the Soviet territory and contained more than half of the country's population, it was the least autonomous and most deprived of the fifteen Republics, for it was identified with the entire Empire. In running for the job of Russian President, Boris Yeltsin promoted the concept of an independent Russia.

This was brand new. It was assumed that Russia was interested in retaining its imperial gains and that the Russian people were the carriers of the imperial idea; after all, many Russians believed that although the Empire yielded neither profit nor an elevated standard of living, it nonetheless endowed them with the prestige of being a superpower and gave them the leading position in the community of nations. The Russian philosopher Pyotr Chaadayev once remarked, "If we did not sprawl from the Bering Strait to the Oder, we wouldn't be noticed." The writer, statesman, and Arctic explorer Fridtjof Nansen (d. 1930) calculated that every seven years from 1500 to his day Russia had gained an amount of territory equal to that of his own country, the Kingdom of Norway.

We remember our schooldays. The teacher's pointer proudly roamed the map of the world, and we learned by heart that the Soviet Union took up one-sixth of the earth's land surface. It could accommodate 2.3 times the area of the United States or 40 times that of France—to say nothing of swallowing 92 Great Britains. Those tremendous figures had to arouse patriotic pride in a child (at least in one of us—the male half). It was not just government propaganda; it was national sentiment. In the USSR, geography was a substitute for history, politics, ideology; geographic patriotism led to geographic imperialism and vice versa.

Consequently, the desire to hang on to or expand the Empire characterized not only Russian statesmen, but also its best and in many ways most progressive minds in other fields. With rare exceptions, every great Russian writer was a sincere imperialist in his political (more precisely, his geographic) outlook. Gogol wrote rapturously that his country sprawled over half the world. Pushkin, in an ultrapatriotic, saber-rattling poem, glorified Russian suppression of a Polish uprising and their capture of Warsaw. Griboyedov, besides writing a comedy, drafted colonialist treaties for the government; while implementing one of them as Russian ambassador to Teheran, he was killed by a raging mob of Moslem fanatics. Dostoyevsky had passionate visions of the capture of Constantinople. On his deathbed, poet and diplomat Fyodor Tyutchev eagerly asked for details of the conquest of Khiva, a Central Asian khanate adjacent to Afghanistan.

Inevitably, a tandem of xenophobia and agoraphilia was developed. One of the Tsar's ministers defined it in a cynical epigram: "We need Armenia," he declared. "We do not need the Armenians."

Gorbachev, too, held to this traditional concept. He dared to pull the troops out of Afghanistan and vacate Eastern Europe, but was appalled at the Soviet Republics' pressure for independence. "We are on the edge of an abyss. Another step and we will collapse into it."

It was this anxiety about the fate of the Empire—the greatest Russian political achievement of the last few centuries—that reinforced the position of the nomenklatura, who now used imperialism in their battle against the reformers. True democracy, which would entail the inevitable disbandment of the ancient Empire and the formation of over a dozen independent states on its territory, would mean the destruction of the work and sacrifices of generations of Russians. Yes, the Russian people may have paid in slavery for the existence of the Russian-Soviet Empire, but it brings this political child that much closer to a Russian heart, maintain the chauvinists: the Empire is as dear to most Russians as democracy is to most Americans.

Against this traditional background Yeltsin's position appeared not merely radical, but revolutionary. Just as in the past century the specter of Communism haunted capitalist Europe, now the specter of separatism roamed the Communist Empire, frightening not only the reactionaries but many reformers as well, inducing them to turn conservative. They remained reformers on economic and even (within Russia) political issues, but took a defensive, Tory position regarding the Republics that wanted to break out of the Union. They favored pulling the troops out of Afghanistan and Eastern Europe, but not out of the Baltic countries, or the Caucasian or the Central Asian Republics—and they could not even conceive of losing the fifty-million-strong Ukraine, the country's breadbasket. No one would take the responsibility for surrendering what their ancestors had gained.

This imperial syndrome blinded many people to the historical significance of the Soviet retreat from Afghanistan. It was a turning point in Russian and world history. An empire cannot be static: it must either expand, as Russia did in the last centuries, or shrink, and the latter is a surefire sign that the end is near. The conquest of Afghanistan was the last-ditch expansionist effort of the last world empire. But Russia had by then gobbled more space (along with heterogeneous native populations) than its imperial stomach could digest. Thus, the Soviet abandonment of Afganistan was caused not by the Afghans' ferocity and dedication to freedom, or by sophisticated US weaponry, but for the most part by the condition of the invaders: after centuries of chronic territorial gluttony it was time for the Empire to go on a diet. Aside from the benefits reaped by much of the rest of mankind—primarily by the invaded and neighboring nations—it was in the interest of the Russian people to shrink geographically, to surrender their disastrous acquisitions, for dubious foreign-policy objectives had strained, then exhausted the country's resources. The shaky legs of the Russian colossus could no longer sustain its horrendous weight. Our friend Artyom Borovik, one of the first Soviet journalists to report the Afghanistan War truthfully, compared it to the attempt of an impotent man to have sex.

One needed a truly revolutionary mentality to sense the direction of the quake at its initial tremors, and that is what Yeltsin had when, at the height of his election campaign, standing to lose favor with much of the Russian vote—still a prisoner of the imperial viewpoint—he spoke out for tiny Lithuania.

How did it all come to focus on Lithuania? We can draw parallels with the decline and fall of other empires. What was the beginning of the end of Habsburg Spain? The destruction of the Armada? No, it was Spain's loss of one of its provinces—the Netherlands. Here, any of the fourteen non-Russian Soviet Republics could have stood in for the Netherlands, but it fell to Lithuania to spearhead the centrifugal movement inside the crumbling Empire and be the first to feel the lash of the Kremlin, which announced its economic blockade.

Yeltsin's position on the issue has been unfailingly principled and uncompromising, as evidenced by dozens of his statements, for example: "I am against the blockade . . . When Lithuania decided to declare independence, it met with a full-court press, so to speak. But we have learned the hard way: force is met with increased resistance, and you cannot resolve such issues by force . . . If people have set their heart on self-determination, you cannot hold them back."

It is important to emphasize that this did not come from a moralizing sage—Yeltsin was no Sakharov—but from a pragmatic politician. We do not know if Yeltsin realized at the time that the Soviet people's path to democracy can lie only over the corpse of the Empire or if he gained this understanding a few months later. But it was after Lithuania declared independence in March of 1990 and found itself under the Kremlin's pressure and blackmail that Yeltsin realized: the imperial nation—the Russians—would not be able to combine freedom for themselves on the one hand with tanks and guns for the conquered nations on the other. Not within one empire, and not for long. Massacres of peaceful demonstrators in Tbilisi and Beijing confirmed his suspicions—blood could flow in any Russian town or city, Moscow included. To Gorbachev, with his traditional imperialist psychology, the disintegration of the Empire was inconceivable—a catastrophe. Yeltsin saw it as an inevitable step in the historically correct direction: from an anomaly of an empire to a normal civilized country; from Kosmopolis to Russia. He realized that the path was long, hard, and painful, strewn with obstacles and snags. Yet it was the only way. For his election campaign—the third one within just one year, and he had two more ahead of him—he borrowed, ironically enough, his program from the nations that demanded independence from Russia. But he formulated the question somewhat differently, demanding autonomy for Russia proper, thus defining the common enemy: the Kremlin as the symbol of usurped central authority: "Of course Russia should become an independent Republic so as to be no longer automatically associated with the central power. We need to revive spiritual and cultural traditions, to divide the territory into economic zones, to put these zones on a regimen of economic independence and self-sufficiency . . . the same goes for our autonomous regions. I think that the Russian Federation should join the United Nations."

The improbability, the audacity of this statement are obvious when we compare it to the article "Will the Russian Federation Leave the USSR?" published in the radical Baltic paper *Atmoda*. It was written by a Muscovite, a geographer by profession—which is interesting in the context of this chapter. He wrote the article in a polemical, provocative mode:

> We must get rid of the imperial paranoia that combines megalomania with persecution mania . . . Once Moscow rids itself of the burden of governing huge, unfamiliar territories, it will be able to attend closely to its own environs—first of all, to pull the Russian villages, with their less-than-fertile land, out of the dirt and save them from extinction . . . Russia's sudden secession from the Soviet Union would be shock therapy for the Union . . . One can debate the future of

the USSR, but nobody and nothing threatens the existence of Russia. After any changes in the existing territorial and political structures, it will still remain a great country, spanning ten time zones, and it will still take the Rossiya Express train a week to reach Vladivostok from Moscow. Is it large enough for you, comrades superpower advocates?

I would advise M. S. Gorbachev to support the progressive forces, form a new party, and run for President of Russia . . . Liberation of the Motherland from the role of international policeman is as important as liberation from a foreign yoke. Otherwise, I think, this inevitable historic mission will sooner or later be performed by another leader, similar to Kemal Atatürk, who headed the Republic of Turkey after the fall of the Ottoman Empire.

The article's author was not only an impeccable diagnostician and analyst, but also a prophet, who foresaw the appearance of a Russian Kemal Atatürk on the political arena. Well, not quite. The article was published on February 12, 1990; Yeltsin's statement, quoted earlier, was made on January 24, three weeks earlier. Yeltsin was already outracing the most courageous, the most daring creators of hypotheses and predictions. He set himself an extraordinary task: to head a country that did not yet exist, a country he still had to construct on the ruins of the Empire with which Russia was customarily (and with good reasons) associated: "I want to see an independent Russia—a federation that would deal as an equal with Britain, France, Germany, and America."

Yeltsin raced in an endless, exhausting, electoral marathon. First it was the contest for USSR People's Deputies, then for the Union's Supreme Soviet, and now for the Russian Supreme Soviet, since there was no constitutional provision for the direct election of the Russian President. His candidacy was promoted in Moscow, Leningrad, in the Urals, in Siberia—he could have run from any district, but he picked Sverdlovsk, so as not to hurt the feelings of his hometown.

He no longer concealed his political ambition: "At almost every meeting where I was nominated candidate, the voters handed me a mandate: do not concede the battle for the job of the Chairman of the Russian Supreme Council; that is, do not do what you did at the first congress of the People's Deputies of the USSR. At one of the meetings I vowed not to do that."

Now it seemed that Yeltsin regretted not having challenged Gorbachev when the All-Union Congress had elected him President. But more likely it was bravado, calculated to irritate or to humble Gorbachev; at the All-Union Congress Yeltsin did not have a chance, of course, and he admitted as much a minute later in the same conversation: "The composition of the All-Union Congress of Deputies is rigged in such a way that the advocates of decisive democratic reform constitute a minority. I hope

that the Congress of Russian Deputies will have a different balance of
forces—fifty-fifty, perhaps. Then, by taking more democratic, radical
decisions within Russia we could push the center in the same direction."

Yeltsin accurately estimated the balance of forces in the future Russian
Parliament. Unlike the All-Union Parliament, the Russian one was
elected by direct secret vote, with several candidates for one seat, and with
no special seats assigned to the nomenklatura. The latter, of course, did
not give up its plotting and pressure, especially in the remote areas—after
all, this was the first free election on Russian soil since the Bolsheviks
closed down the Constituent Assembly—the Russian Parliament—in
January 1918.

Sverdlovsk voters elected Yeltsin to the Russian Parliament with 84.2
percent of the vote, which he considered a mandate to continue his fight
against Gorbachev: "The people made it clear that their lives are getting
worse every day. They blame it on Gorbachev's policies. They feel less
and less confident about the future. The five years of political half-
measures and compromise only made the situation more precipitous."

Of all the elections in which Yeltsin ran in fourteen months, the one in
May, for Chairman of the Russian Supreme Soviet, was the most difficult
and unpredictable. Besides the fifty-fifty composition of the Russian Parliament, the authorities launched a vigorous anti-Yeltsin campaign: in the
media, still obedient to the Kremlin conductor's baton; at the officially
sanctioned meetings and rallies; and, finally, inside the Russian Parliament proper. It was the Parliament that was to elect the President of the
Republic from its own ranks.

Finally, aware that the government's official propaganda lacked clout,
the Soviet papers used the foreign media in the campaign, expecting their
readers to find foreign voices more convincing. Campaign organizers
cleverly cut and spliced the reviews of Yeltsin's autobiography from
French, British, Swedish, Dutch, Japanese, and other papers (it was
published much later in the USSR). "A smug Siberian poseur," "a sly,
vain man with a huge thirst for power and skill in achieving that objective," "boastful, authoritarian, and overconfident"—this was Yeltsin's
image after the Soviet editors processed the reviews in *The Financial
Times, The Economist, Le Monde, L'Humanité,* and other foreign publications.

Still, the Kremlin was not confident about the effect of a print campaign, and resorted to mudslinging, a tested method of downing political
opponents. They did virtually everything to bar Yeltsin from the Russian
presidency: as Yeltsin put it, "another stage in the campaign of harassment."

At the time, Gorbachev was getting ready for a tour of the United
States and Canada, but his mind was clearly elsewhere. He suddenly

showed up, uninvited, at the Russian Congress, and erupted in anti-Yeltsin rhetoric. Moreover, he summoned 250 Communist deputies and demanded that they submit to Party discipline and vote against Yeltsin. Note that he was not promoting a vote *for* other candidates such as Krasnodar Party Boss Ivan Polozkov or Gorbachev's ex–Minister of the Interior, Alexandr Vlasov; the vote he was promoting was *against* Yeltsin. Gorbachev did not care who chaired the Russian Parliament—anyone but Boris Yeltsin! Provincial deputies staying at the Rossiya Hotel, across the street from the Kremlin, found in their rooms flyers "exposing" Yeltsin; other deputies found the same flyers on their seats in the conference room: Yeltsin "is selling out the country," "is tempted to escape to the West," "makes a fool of himself in front of other nations," "advocates private property," "will bury Russia," and the like. Such a massive offensive might have worked earlier, but now it was backfiring—at least for some deputies.

In the first round the votes split almost evenly: 497 for Yeltsin and 473 for Polozkov. In the next round Yeltsin picked up a few more votes—now he had 503, which was still not enough to be elected: winning required a minimum of 531.

At that point the Kremlin made a desperate last-ditch attempt to stop him. They replaced the ultraconservative Polozkov with Alexandr Vlasov, a moderate *apparatchik,* hoping he would draw the votes of the deputies scared off by Polozkov. But the Yeltsin supporters were alert, too, and mobilized the voters to put pressure on their deputies. A stream of telegrams from the provinces, nonstop phone calls, threats of strikes, demonstrations in front of the Kremlin—it was an exciting spectacle to witness. No longer was it a contest of two rivals for the post of Russian leader—it was the first head-on confrontation between the Kremlin and the people on such a gigantic scale. On its result rode not just the fate of Boris Yeltsin, but that of the entire country, and Russian democracy.

What was it that struck us—now tourists in our own country—the most? Official glasnost lagged hopelessly behind the unofficial one, the glasnost of street rallies. The election of the leader of Russia stimulated the people's political activity—for the first time in seventy-three years, since the Bolshevik takeover, they realized that their voices counted for something—moreover, that they were the masters of their destiny. Far after midnight, when we came back home from the Red Square rallies, we could no longer watch TV or read the papers, even the most radical ones—the comparison between what they said and what we had seen was too glaring.

To be precise, the rallies were not held on Red Square proper, but in the narrow space approximately one hundred yards long between St. Basil's Cathedral and the Rossiya Hotel, in the path of the deputies returning to the hotel from the Supreme Soviet sessions. At the entrance they were ambushed by several thousand demonstrators who, during those few days, were getting a crash course in democracy. And not just demonstrators: there were passersby, rubberneckers, militiamen posted to maintain order, KGB provocateurs, and plainclothesmen. Everybody was getting an education outside the Rossiya—including the deputies themselves. Once, Athens was called "the school of democracy"; now Moscow claimed the title.

An All-Union Congress of Deputies was taking place the same time as the Russian one. At the former, Prime Minister Ryzhkov made a speech proposing a price hike, which caused immediate panic in the capital and nationwide: people lined up to buy everything available, and by the end of the day the stores were stripped. We looked in on a few; there was not one customer, and the salespeople idled amidst empty shelves. That was mentioned, too, outside the Rossiya, but only in an incidental manner. Political debate replaced routine concerns; thus it was the Russian Congress and not the All-Union one that served as a whetstone for honing political consciousness.

The crowd included Yeltsin's opponents, too. One strapping young fellow yelled that Yeltsin wanted to revert to the scattered fiefdoms of ancient Rus, which made Rus an easy target for the Tatar-Mongol hordes. The Germans, to the contrary, were uniting, he added. We approached Sasha Balamutov, a graduate student at the World Literature Institute; judging by the sign he held, he was anti-Gorbachev, i.e., pro-Yeltsin. One of us voiced a doubt: could Yeltsin, after taking power, turn into another Gorbachev?

"But he himself proposed that the Russian President be reelected every two years."

"What if the same thing that happened to Yeltsin the Moscow Boss happens to Yeltsin the President? What if the *apparat* chokes him again?"

"Things are different now." Sasha nodded toward the demonstrators.

Unlike the hysterical loudmouths—there were plenty of those in the pro-Yeltsin crowd, too—Sasha did not idealize Yeltsin: "We should not idolize live people. It's just that right now Yeltsin is the only person not afraid to challenge Gorbachev. Without their confrontation, we are finished. Why can Lithuania confront the central authorities and Russia can't?"

He followed with a fable about a tree that had rotted to the extent that the worms that had gnawed through it became scared for their lives and tried to save the tree in order to survive. Sasha compared Gorbachev to one of these wise worms and designed his sign accordingly: a picture of Gorbachev with a caption, "Who Will Protect Perestroika From Its Architect?"

Someone informed Sasha that the sign constituted lèse-majesté—it violated the new law about insulting the President. The numerous militiamen would not interfere, but a man in gray started pushing Sasha off the sidewalk onto the lawn. He grabbed the sign, then started to drag Sasha away. The crowd immediately surrounded them: "He is KGB! The KGB is against perestroika!"

The simpleminded agent gave himself away: "Not true! We're all for it!"

Or was it an act of arrogant defiance, based on the spell that his organization has long exercised upon the Soviet citizens? In any event, he overdid it. We did not even realize what had happened. But once everyone started shouting that a KGB man had been spotted, we saw that it was no longer Sasha who was being threatened, but a representative of Authority.

The crowd was getting wilder, yelling at the agent. He put his hand to his ear, the gesture of a Russian criminal: *Yell at me all you want—I can't hear you!* Just as the crowd was upon him, he pulled out his walkie-talkie and was rescued by the militiamen.

Sasha Balamutov returned to the crowd, his sign shaking in his hand. The crowd was not really bloodthirsty—it was too early for that—though one of the demonstrators yelled, "If you don't elect Yeltsin, we're gonna go for the cobblestones—won't be the first time!"

"Are you in favor of throwing rocks, too?" we asked Lieutenant Colonel Sergei Yushenkov, a Russian deputy.

"I'm against it, but it doesn't depend just on myself. See how far people have been pushed? My voters write me they're ready for the barricades. I'm against barricades and rocks, but political strikes are an acceptable and necessary weapon. If Yeltsin is not elected, they are inevitable."

Another Russian deputy, Oleg Rumyantsev, confirmed: "The country is ready for a general strike."

The demonstrators—representatives of Moscow, Leningrad, Ural, and Siberian workers—agreed: if Yeltsin loses, the factories stop. To say nothing of the miners: they had been for Yeltsin for a long time.

When we went to visit our old friend Boris Nikolsky, now an active liberal deputy, at the Moscow Hotel, which housed All-Union Congress deputies, we discovered that hard-currency prostitutes, too, were for Yeltsin: they staged a lie-in in front of the hotel, protesting a new doorman who would not let them through to their foreign clients. They told us that all their hopes lay with Yeltsin.

The amount of blind, idiotic hatred that went into anti-Yeltsin plotting, including bribery (according to two deputies) was astonishing. Had Yeltsin lost, Gorbachev, not Yeltsin, would have felt the impact of strikes and protests. What kind of regime was it, to lose even the elementary instinct of self-preservation? Our view was cynical: Boris Yeltsin was their last resort, a shield—at least a temporary one—against the wrath of the masses, who considered him the bone in the throat of the Kremlin gang. Gorbachev had exhausted the trust of his subjects. Another few months and his former comrades would leave. Some would depart of their own free will; some would be kicked out by him personally as he feared for his power and veered to the right. Here was something remarkable: the common people recognized Gorbachev as a bankrupt politician well before the intelligentsia did.

The election of the Russian President was a standoff. The will of the Kremlin met its match—the will of the people, whom the Kremlin was not used to taking into account. After yet another vote, the deputies, weary and confused, strolled back to the hotel along the narrow passage that the demonstrators left for them. Some paused to read the signs and talk to people—they were either pro-Yeltsin or undecided. Others walked faster, afraid to look back; the demonstrators tapped them for the enemy and yelled in chorus:

"We're the millions! The people made their choice!"

"Don't sell the people out!"

"Yeltsin is not against the Party! It's the Party who's against the people!"

A man standing next to us scanned the deputies' faces as if trying to forecast their votes in the next round. "I don't like their faces," he said hesitatingly.

Another one called out to a delegate: "Nice suit, comrade!" He clearly supported Yeltsin's position on privileges.

The slogans were naive—but we were moved to tears:

Tormented Russia Believes Only Yeltsin!
Boris, We're with You!
Only Yeltsin's Hands Can Unshackle Russia!
From Sea to Shining Sea the People and Yeltsin Will Triumph!
For the People, Only Yeltsin Can Be the Leader!
With Yeltsin, Russia Will Flourish!

A small group of five- and six-year-olds outside the hotel entrance also carried placards:

Either You Elect Yeltsin or It's Civil War!
Don't Be Vlasovites—Vote Yeltsin!

The kids may have known who Yeltsin was, but did they realize that his new nomenklatura opponent bore the same last name as General

Andrei Vlasov, who, with his army, went over to the German side during World War II and whose name was synonymous with treason? We rather doubted they did.

A muscular man passed by with a sign: "I'm for Exploitation! Just Pay Me Four Times as Much!"

"And where will he get health?" complained an old woman next to us. "They'll drive Boris Nikolayevich to the grave, like they did Sakharov."

There were political thinkers, too: "You can't create a special people for Gorbachev: he'll just have to deal with this one."

Although the crowd was not generous to Gorbachev, it still held Yeltsin's open enemy, Ligachev, as a symbol of out-and-out reaction.

"Have you heard this one?" An ordinary-looking fellow gathered a crowd. "Ligachev is a jail warden. He roll-calls former radicals: 'Sobchak!' 'Here!' 'Popov!' 'Here!' 'Yeltsin!' Silence. Ligachev goes again, 'Yeltsin!' Silence again. Third time, 'Yeltsin!' Finally Yeltsin speaks up. Ligachev goes, 'Too late—you should've kept your mouth shut before.' "

Only once did the crowd grow aggressive: when they found a young man in a black shirt with a picture of St. George piercing the dragon—a symbol of Pamyat. He was booed and pushed away.

Although it was the election of a Russian leader, there were many Caucasian and Central Asian faces among the demonstrators. Besides signs demanding independence for Lithuania, we spotted the blue flag with a trident—the symbol of Rukh, a Ukrainian separatist organization.

Suddenly a rumor spread that Yeltsin was leaving the Kremlin, and we joined the others in a mad scramble to the Spassky Gate. The rumor was false. While most of the crowd went back to the Rossiya for their evening vigil, we decided to wait for Boris Nikolayevich. The last time we saw him was nine months earlier in New York, when he spoke at Columbia. Finally he showed up—tall, broad-shouldered, with the build of an ex-athlete. Yet it was obvious that despite his famed stamina he was dead tired. His face was swollen; his eyes were tiny slits; his movements were slow and wooden.

He paused and fielded a question. "If Gorbachev cannot have good relations with Russia," he said, "what will he lead then? Russia can survive without the Soviet Union, but what is the Soviet Union without Russia?"

With a visible effort he forced himself into the narrow door of a modest Moskvich sedan, and, with a groan, plopped himself onto the passenger seat.

On our way home we saw that the large recess in the wall of the GUM department store, the one facing Red Square, was packed with armed soldiers; then we saw trucks, also filled with soldiers with guns, next to the main entrance to the Rossiya. Was the Kremlin getting ready for Yeltsin's victory or his defeat? The latter was more likely. The authorities knew what they were doing: they expected disorders in case of Yeltsin's defeat, and were prepared to use the military to squash it. In the meantime they continued to do everything possible to defeat him.

The next day, in the third round of voting, Yeltsin received 535 votes against Vlasov's 502—four more than he needed. On May 29, 1990, Boris Yeltsin, fifty-nine years old, became the Chairman of the Russian Supreme Soviet. It was the Russian people's mandate for their national hero.

Yeltsin's victory took place the day after Gorbachev had left on yet another foreign tour. He spent his last pre-departure hours working for Yeltsin's defeat.

Yeltsin strode across Red Square, surrounded by the adoring crowd. He owed his election to the people, and now he was accountable only to them—not to the Party, not to the Kremlin, not to Gorbachev, of whom he was now safely rid—is that what populism is all about?

The TV evening news focused on Gorbachev's travels. Our hostess, as if apologizing for the dichotomy between the TV coverage and reality, said, "Mikhail Sergeyevich is sort of like our Elizabeth the Second, but Boris Nikolayevich is our Margaret Thatcher."

Immediately after he was elected, Yeltsin declared that, regardless of the Kremlin's actions, Russia would establish bilateral relations with Lithuania. This spelled the end of the economic blockade, whose main lever was oil.

Perhaps it was Yeltsin's decisiveness concerning Lithuania that led the Kremlin to try again to gag him by canceling his previously scheduled TV appearance; Yeltsin called it a "well-planned, organized political provocation." He was no longer an opposition leader—he now led an enormous country, and Gorbachev had to take him seriously. The decision was rescinded; he was allowed on the air.

Of all the commentaries on Boris Yeltsin's victory, the best came from the Baltic paper *Atmoda* and the Moscow paper *Kommersant,* the two most autonomous publications of the moment. The *Atmoda* article was titled "Boris Yeltsin—a Politician in a Nonpolitical Land." It was a good definition of Yeltsin but a bad one concerning the country: the paper seemed to identify the Soviet Union solely with its intelligentsia, who still claimed to be its only rightful representatives.

"Criticizing Yeltsin is considered reactionary," the piece said, "or elitist. Democratic intellectuals look down on him. But with Yeltsin's stature, they will find it hard to do this for long." The writer insisted that Gorbachev was "clearly becoming the leader of the nomenklatura, defining himself in traditional leadership terms."

The *Kommersant* piece was titled even more equivocally: "Boris Yeltsin and Mikhail Gorbachev: *Sic Transit Gloria Mundi.*" This was not quite accurate either: worldly glory was deserting only Gorbachev, not Yeltsin. However, Soviet readers hardly needed explanations: they knew whose political star was ascending and whose was descending. The article, however, advocated a compromise along the lines suggested by our hostess, with whom we had watched TV. There was an epigraph, too, taken from Russian history. It was from Count Alexei K. Tolstoy's verse drama about Tsar Fyodor Ioannovich (Ivan the Terrible's son), who was incapable of ruling, and Boris Godunov. Before Godunov crowned himself Tsar, he ruled the country for many years in Fyodor's name:

> *Oh Mighty Lord, thou hast no choice:*
> *Boris alone can rule thy kingdom.*
> *Just he—leave him*
> *The burden and the onus of the crown.*

Kommersant wrote further:

Last week Mikhail Gorbachev publicly flayed "political frauds" three times. The last assault, on May 28, addressed to Communist members of Parliament, was framed in words that many deputies found to be impolitic. The President of the USSR staked his own prestige on blocking Yeltsin from taking power, and Yeltsin owes his victory in a large degree to these efforts of Gorbachev's. It is not just his pressure on the deputies, which violated the principle of "You can bend 'em but you can't break 'em." But the liberals were alarmed by the authoritarian tendency recently gathering momentum, and by the growing dominance of emotional motives over rational ones in his behavior . . . Besides tactical errors, the President is looking at a debacle on a major scale. His centrist tactic—"beat up on the left till it goes right and beat up on the right till it goes left"—is increasingly showing its lack of internal substance. While both the left and the right are proposing some sort of way out of the crisis, the President's center offers little but criticism of both the left and the right. Considering the crisis that is rapidly turning into a catastrophe, such a position seems to be an unaffordable luxury . . . And when this centrism displayed its internal emptiness, the Russian deputies chose a glimmer of hope over a complete absence of it. As if the Baltic front were not enough for Mikhail Sergeyevich, now he has got himself a second—the Russian—one.

So much pain could have been avoided if only the Kremlin, instead of panicking, had soberly assessed Boris Yeltsin's victory. It was a pseudo-defeat for Gorbachev, and it could have still been converted into a victory. Had Gorbachev's plots borne fruit, the country would have been paralyzed by a general strike, with mines and factories at a standstill, and political resistance would probably have grown into an anti-Gorbachev revolution. The *Kommersant* writer was right: Gorbachev had allowed his emotions to take over; he was no longer capable of assessing the situation in a calm, businesslike manner.

Through the film of smog, we could see the Kremlin from the window of our apartment. We could not tear ourselves away from the sight of its gold-domed, white cathedrals. In discussing Yeltsin's victory, we hoped that, when the last empire on earth fell apart and he became the leader of an independent Russia, he would at least be smart enough not to move into this mossy center of the autocracy, whose representatives have for centuries been ruling a huge country as though it were their private estate.

The day before, when we were in the Kremlin, standing outside the Uspensky Cathedral, we ran into Father Gleb Yakunin, a Yeltsin supporter. Yakunin is a remarkable man, whose gnarled hands bear the marks of hard Gulag labor, and who, as the Russians are fond of saying, has through suffering earned his right to tell the truth. He was surrounded not by believers, but by tourists, who mostly asked him about Yeltsin's election as Russian President, and his opinion of Father Alexei as the Patriarch of All Russia. It is high time the Kremlin was turned over to tourists and priests, we thought.

A month and a half later, the same Kremlin housed the 28th Congress of the Communist Party—the last one, as it later turned out. Had the delegates been told that the Party, after seventy-three years at the helm, had only one year to go, none of them—Yeltsin included—would have believed it. Even a few modest appeals to de-Particize the Army and the KGB brought howls of fury from most Communists, and, of course, the stormy indignation of Gorbachev, the Party's General Secretary. The Party was not about to share power with anyone—least of all with the people. The fate of the country was being decided by the Party elite, as the conservatives and the reformers engaged in petty infighting at the Congress. And then, this closed-room, all-in-the-family, ill-concealed lovefeast was exploded by a three-minute speech by Boris Yeltsin.

Although he warned of the possibility of a "Rumanian scenario" if the Kremlin made no concessions, he could hardly have predicted the dizzying speed of the events the next summer. One thing he knew, not just from the debacle of Communism in Eastern Europe, but from the popular mood that he sensed so well, was that the Party was a dinosaur. It was not in his power to decide the Party's fate, but he could well decide his own fate within the Party, and he felt obliged to do so according to his conscience, his principles, the radical change in circumstances, and the popular mandate he held. By his own confession, the decision was preceded by three nights without sleep.

On July 12, 1990, Boris Nikolayevich Yeltsin, a Communist for almost thirty years, rose to the podium of the Party Congress and removed the prepared notes from his pocket. The audience caught its breath—what was Boris up to this time? In the eyes of the Party elite, he was still merely a provincial clown who provided a moment of comic relief for them between the main acts of the Party Circus. They expected anything, but not what followed. As the leader of the highest legislative authority, Yeltsin declared, it was his duty to submit to the will of his voters; therefore he was resigning from the Party. And, to remove the slightest trace of doubt, he did just that: he descended from the podium and, pursued by the agitated murmurs of the stunned audience, walked down the long aisle—calmly, without looking back. And then he was gone.

Thus did the Communist Party lose one of its 18 million members. Yeltsin had once again played the skunk at Gorbachev's garden party. By shedding his role of Party clown, Yeltsin exposed the Kremlin forum as the true clown act: a political farce. (He had been beaten to it by a member of his family, his son-in-law Valery, who was the first one to lay down his Party card; Yeltsin's wife was still hesitant.)

Turning his back on the Party boosted Yeltsin's popularity even higher. In August the new master of Russia (6,592,500 square miles) met the old master of the Kremlin (69 acres) for a five-hour tête-à-tête. Gorbachev had Yeltsin vow that never, under any circumstances, would he seek the position of President of the Union, even if the people demanded it.

"Even if you let me run as an alternative candidate, I'll turn it down—categorically!" Yeltsin said.

Only then did Gorbachev sigh with relief.

In the same month of August the Russian President, now a former Party member, left on a working tour of his country. In twenty-two days, traveling by plane, helicopter, and train, he covered tens of thousands of miles, crossing ten time zones. He visited the Volga and the Urals, Siberia and the Far East—three autonomous Republics, four regions, and twenty-seven cities. The trip was filled with sixteen-hour working days—nothing like Gorbachev's two- or three-day sightseeing junkets with Potemkin villages flanking the route. Yeltsin passed up the prestigious locales and went where even the local bosses, to say nothing of Moscow ones, would not set foot: construction sites, empty food stores, fishermen's shacks, and slumlike workers' barracks.

"Why did he have to tour all of Russia?" a Moscow paper demanded rhetorically. "What is the purpose of these plane-train treks all the way to the volcanoes of Kamchatka, when there are so many urgent problems, when so many projects can no longer wait for his signature?"

But it was just like 1986, when, having become the Moscow Boss, he rode the subways and buses all over town, dropped in on cafeterias and stores, and stood in long lines: he wanted to experience and understand the life of the citizens for whom he had assumed responsibility. The intent was the same, but the scale had changed: now he wanted to know how all of the country lived. He had done it as a young man, riding atop train cars in the company of petty criminals, since he had no money for tickets or even for food.

He returned from his 1990 tour with a firm conviction: things had to change. In his own words, "I saw too many tears and heard too many people talk—it will stay in my soul for many years. I will not rest till we put this mess in order."

Was this rhetoric, albeit spoken from the heart, or did Boris Yeltsin indeed have a specific plan to eliminate poverty, injustice, and disorder?

We read many of the speeches he had made during this marathon trip. Here are some excerpts:

"We will not follow the All-Union path, in which conflicts are choked, then extinguished altogether. But if you want to rule your own land, go ahead; if you want to share power—pass some to the center," he said in Tataria, where nationalism was on the rise. One should remember that the Russian Republic includes hundreds of different peoples, many of whose nationalistic aspirations tend to become heated in conjunction with the separatist sentiments found in the other fourteen Republics of the Union. The subject of Tataria's sovereignty came up in practically every conversation: "I believe that the people of Tataria are entitled to decide what kind of autonomy they need."

He said the same in neighboring Bashkiria. Even in Kamchatka, as he met with the representatives of the smallest ethnic group, he reiterated his position: "Of course, ethnic minorities should be given autonomy, self-sufficiency. But it should be limited to what they can utilize," he cautioned. "If they can't—if they number only seven hundred people—if they take possession of their land, with all its natural wealth, they won't be able to properly exploit this wealth. We talked to the representatives of the Karyak Territory for a long time yesterday. Of course they demand sovereignty, but they also want the entire supply and distribution system of the Kamchatka Region. It doesn't work like that. You want total control, then take total responsibility."

In another speech he said, "We must work to put an end to the rigid vertical pressure exerted on everyone and everything by the *apparat* and the State. We will do this with our horizontal agreements. We must tear down the bureaucratic system of distribution that takes from everyone everything they produce and then doles it out. This is what power consists of. And we must deprive the *apparat* of this power. We are moving in this direction. On the Russian Federation level we are cutting the number of ministries in half. Half the staff, half the number of ministers' deputies, half the expenses."

Wherever Yeltsin went, he asked his hearers to allow him to implement a three-year program to resolve the present crisis: two years for privatization and stabilization of the economy and the third for raising the standard of living. All of this would be possible only if the iron fist of the Kremlin were unclenched.

What most impressed Yeltsin was that his audience placed political demands above economic ones. "Give us freedom!" they cried. In the past few years they had gone through a school of democracy that made Gorbachev's glasnost pale in comparison. Unlike the eremite of the Kremlin, Yeltsin went to this school with his people.

IN OUR youth, we—and thousands of other Russians—had read a book considered to be the key to Russia's thousand-year history. Generations of Russians had read it from cover to cover. Some hated it, from Nicholas the First to Solzhenitsyn to Stalin (who predictably banned it). Others, like Hertzen, loved it, though they could not help being pained by its merciless description of Russia. The author, the Marquis Astolph de Custine, visited Russia in 1839 and wrote his impressions of the trip. His book is to Russians what de Tocqueville's *Democracy in America* is to Americans.

Other people, too—foreign diplomats and reporters, especially in Stalin's time—read it in order to understand what kind of a country they had ended up in. A 1951 translation was made by the wife of a US ambassador in Moscow; a 1979 edition bore a foreword by former Ambassador George Kennan: "De Custine's 'Russia in 1839' turned out to be a magnificent—perhaps the best—book on Stalin's Russia and a pretty good one on Brezhnev's . . . How can one explain this strange anomaly: that the nightmare of 1839 becomes reality in 1939 and half-reality in 1979?"

De Custine's book described the total subjugation of an entire immense nation. It was not merely about the indentured serfs, whom he called "the slaves of slaves," since their masters were slaves too, albeit of an aristocratic sort. De Custine claimed that every single Russian man and woman was intoxicated with servitude, boasting of it, and that Russian political absolutism accorded perfectly with the spirit of the nation, which consisted of mute obedience: "They move and breathe by command, consequently everything is grim and looks forced . . . Russian rule is that of the military camp, substituted for the orderliness of a civil community; it is a state of siege become everyday social normalcy."

The author offered no comfort; since the Russians were born to and for slavery, whatever they did, they could never leave their prison.

We recall the shock of recognition and the pity for our country that overcame us when we read the book. We thought that this was the

definitive work on Russia, that de Custine's pessimism concerning Russia
had been confirmed by history.

And now we are strolling about the streets of Moscow. We stand in
lines, we hear loud, heated remarks, frank and uncomplimentary, about
the Kremlin, we watch demonstrations and rallies, we learn about the
political demands of striking miners. Can these be slaves? Not only de
Custine but even Chekhov was wrong: one should not squeeze the slave
out of oneself drop by drop. One should pour it out by the bucketful,
which is what was happening before our eyes, on an individual and a
national level. One cannot squeeze the slave out of oneself drop by drop,
for by the time one drop has fallen, others will have formed.

It was a century and a half after de Custine before the absurdity of
slavery became fully apparent. The philosophical Frenchman had a keen
eye, but suddenly his conclusions were outdated. Only the Communist
masters were still slaves, in Pasternak's words, "the martyrs of dogma,"
clinging to their privileges. Against the background of the slaves liberat-
ing themselves, the tired slavery of their masters stood out particularly
vividly; in political and social consciousness, the masters were quickly
lagging behind their slaves.

It was this incompatibility between the self-liberating slaves and the
ones still in thrall of their slavery that inspired a certain optimism in
foreign guests like us: sooner or later, free Russia would reject its outdated slaves, who are still clinging to their slavery, considering it their
privilege and prerogative.

For the first time, the Marquis de Custine's book failed to inspire close
associations and was perceived more in its contrast than in its analogy.
This brilliant, intelligent, talented, perhaps great book has finally become
a historic one; it has become associated with the precise period when it
was written and which it described. It acquired heuristic value, losing its
urgency. There was nothing left to read between the lines there. Thank
God—the Marquis was finally out of date; his conclusions did not apply
to Yeltsin's Russia.

THE TEMPTATION OF
DICTATORSHIP
(November 7, 1990–August 18, 1991)

Order leads to all the virtues;
but what leads to order?

—George Christoph Lichtenberg

Twice a year the Soviet leadership would climb the Lenin Mausoleum on Red Square to beam at the happy Soviet citizenry marching below. In 1990 Gorbachev did not beam long on either occasion. On May Day the demonstrators booed him and called for his resignation until he left the podium in embarrassment. And, on November 7, Bolshevik Revolution Day, two shots echoed across the square.

Alexandr Shmonov had planned to assassinate Gorbachev for a long time, and was thoroughly prepared. In 1987 he purchased a shotgun and joined the Hunting and Fishing Club. He took a course in skeet shooting, and hit eight targets out of fifteen at the graduation test. Shmonov sawed off the stock and made himself a special holster that he fastened to his body with leather straps. He filed off the sight so that it would not get snagged by his clothes as he took out the gun. He repeatedly rehearsed the shooting; how he would pretend to be taking out his handkerchief, then replacing it, while in fact preparing to bring the shotgun into position to fire. He protected himself against the unlikely possibility of having to pass through a metal detector by making a "We Support Democracy" placard mounted on a metal rod—"Look, that's what is making the buzzing." With both barrels loaded, he was now ready. When Shmonov pulled out the gun and aimed it, less than 150 feet separated him from the podium where Gorbachev stood, so the target was within easy range. With his marksmanship and his careful preparations, how could he fail?

At the interrogation he explained he had spent too long aiming. Suspecting Gorbachev would wear a bulletproof vest, he wanted to shoot him in the head. The delay enabled a policeman to run up and seize his arm. Both shots went too high.

Why did Shmonov want to kill Gorbachev? His justification was not convincing: he claimed he wanted to show that there were people ready to die for democracy. The psychiatrists who examined him were divided: some considered him insane, while others said he was sufficiently sane to be held responsible for his acts.

Whether Alexandr Shmonov spends his immediate future in jail or in an asylum, the question stands: did he act alone or were certain powers aware of his intentions? And was the purpose of the attempt to kill Gorbachev or merely to scare him?

Whatever the answer, the latter objective was achieved. When Gorbachev heard the shots, he did not flee the podium, but from that day on, his policies took a gradual but inexorable turn to the right: from glasnost to a crackdown, from the self-proclaimed "new thinking" to the old order. Although Muscovites tend to see elaborate conspiracies everywhere, and are skeptical about what are probably easily explained cause-and-effect events, we cannot discard the hypothesis that the attempt on Gorbachev's life was a fake one.

When asked whether the affair should be taken seriously, Yeltsin said, "Not really—unless it was prearranged." Yeltsin himself had survived car accidents, a plane crash, and even an involuntary dip in the Moscow River, and now took such incidents with a sense of humor. "I must have more lives than all the Moscow cats put together."

Someone may have counted on Gorbachev's unstable psyche as well as on his developing a "Holiday syndrome": if, on one national holiday you are booed off the podium, and on the second someone tries to kill you, what will the third be like? If the attempt on his life was staged, it had to be the KGB. One can draw a straight line from November 7, 1990, the date of the attempted assassination, to August 19, 1991, the date of the coup attempt. Although in the case of the latter, the conspiracy was obvious, there are also certain connections that we will consider later.

Gorbachev's holiday misfortunes cannot alone explain the changes in his political course. He himself denied he was personally effecting them: when Yeltsin phoned him and reproached him for his rightward tilt, Gorbachev answered pompously, "I am not the one who is moving to the right, Boris Nikolayevich, our society is."

This answer was not just Gorbachev's absolutist arrogance: *"L'état, c'est moi."* Nor can one attribute the answer to his being misinformed, though by then he, like Brezhnev once upon a time, was growing increasingly dependent on his advisers. His answer contained a grain of truth.

Yeltsin realized it as early as 1987, and it had led to his break with the Kremlin, but two or three years later it began to dawn on the entire society: perestroika was at an impasse. The crises grew nationwide, embracing all social strata; discontent increased; the State was in serious danger. The recipes for salvation varied.

The confused upper classes, from the Kremlin nobility and Party nomenklatura to the intelligensia, the KGB, and the generals, were terrified of democracy long before the country got a real taste of it, appalled by what had not even happened yet. The first breath of freedom was like a bone caught in the throat. It could neither be swallowed nor spat out.

This was the general reason for the emergence of the "iron hand" that would return the country to law and order. In essence it was a throwback to Stalin's day, though few longed for full-fledged Stalinism. Under Stalin no one was safe, including the political and social elite, who now wanted history to revert to a tried-and-true autocratic model.

They longed for absolutism, but of an enlightened, or at least reasonable sort, and their dreams focused on one person: Gorbachev. His followers split into two camps. Some insisted that he remain on a democratic course, while others wanted him to assume emergency powers. The curious thing about this long, embittered schism was that none of the participants could conceive of any major political changes independent of Gorbachev, even though at the time his popularity was plummeting while Yeltsin's was soaring.

The first clamor for dictatorship came as early as the summer of 1989 from two political observers, Igor Klyamkin and Andranik Migranyan. They contrasted Yeltsin, whom they labeled an "ideologue of *lumpen* socialism," a "neo-Bolshevik," and a "demagogue," with Gorbachev—"a serious reformer who cannot count on widespread popularity." It followed that it was necessary to "form a Committee of National Salvation while temporarily suspending the activities of all other institutions of power."

This was precisely the sort of committee that was later set up by the putschists. It lasted three days. In the summer of 1989, the idea of an emergency committee at first seemed extravagant, facetious, provocative. Nonetheless it quickly penetrated the public consciousness. Tatyana Karyakina, a democratic economist, said, "Perestroika will triumph if Gorbachev remains strong." Émigré Arvid Kron exclaimed breathlessly (in a Soviet paper, but from the safe distance of Paris): "Let us shake hands with the hand of iron!" Finally, outpacing the events, Radio Liberty commentator Boris Paramonov declared a state of emergency in the USSR to be inevitable.

Historical quotations and literary analogies were quickly dusted off and cited. Some pundits pointed out that it had taken the Western democracies centuries to take shape. Others reminisced about France, with its two centuries of revolutions and dictatorships, interludes of mob rule, and flipflops from republican governments to monarchies and back. Pyotr Stolypin, Russia's Prime Minister in the early 1900s, was remembered, too, more for his arbitrary acts than for his reforms. Some even reproached him for being too liberal: he was the product of the *apparat* (meaning the imperial court) rather than the Revolution, and only the children of revolutions could be true dictators—like Napoleon. Some, citing Max Weber, claimed that neither a viable economy nor a true democracy (in some remote future) was possible without a charismatic dictator—by which, of course, they meant Gorbachev, whom *Time* had just crowned as Man of the Decade.

Others, fearful of a rightist putsch, demanded an immediate preemptive democratic one. Perhaps it was this fear that motivated the open letter signed by fifty-three well-known and respected public figures, from Patriarch Alexei the Second to actor Nikolai Gubenko. Entitled "With Hope and Belief," it was an appeal to the President "to introduce a state of emergency and direct presidential rule in the areas of major conflict."

Appeals from liberals increasingly resembled ones from conservatives. Each wanted an infallible leader to help them against the other side. The liberals were more coy about it as they pursued a political goal that the reactionaries went for directly. "The path of democracy lies through dictatorship," "Democracy is needed to reinforce the power of the leader," "Dictatorship is the bulwark of democracy"—such were the shadows of 1984 projected into the Soviet newspapers of the year 1990.

We encountered these opinions galore each time we went to Moscow. We could observe them growing among the intelligentsia, with whom we socialized for the most part. In a house on Malaya Bronnaya Street we met people—well-known Soviet writers—who were convinced that they were slightly ahead of their time.

They referred us to Sumgait, an Azerbaijani town, where an anti-Armenian massacre had just taken place. We agreed: Tanks in the streets would have been preferable to babies thrown out of windows, castrated men, and women raped with waterpipes. They predicted that Moscow would be a Sumgait on a grander scale. They had come to the capital from their dacha to see us, and spent the evening worrying about their daughter, who had stayed behind—houses next door had been burglarized, they said. As they talked about the anarchy to come, it was clear that they were taking their cues from fear; angst formed the basis of their political philosophy.

Chaos and anarchy could not be stopped, they said, for the pace of the disintegration of the State exceeded that of the birth and formation of democratic institutions intended to channel the popular will into constitutional outlets rather than into violence. They threw in a quote from Pushkin: "God save us from seeing a Russian riot, devoid of sense or mercy."

The intelligentsia had been given their circuses and were better supplied with bread than the *plebs,* too—the latter wanted to eat and drink, while the supply of both bread and vodka was waning. Despair, hunger, and thirst will, our hosts went on, pit bloodthirsty mobs against those with power and property. They might be stopped with tanks—perhaps even tanks would not suffice, but they are a hope, anyway. And let them come too soon rather than too late, as happened in Azerbaijan—before, not after, the killing begins. Neither Yeltsin not Gorbachev will save us; the name of the person does not matter, but he will be the first to realize that our only salvation lies with those tanks. It is a pity that blood will be shed to bring these truths home to those who are capable of assuming responsibility for the safety of the State. But blood needs to be shed so that the new order will be accepted as the only road to salvation.

These opinions go back to late May 1990—about the same time, if the reader recalls, that the election of the Chairman of the Russian Parliament was being held. In one round of that election Yeltsin ran against Ivan Polozkov, who managed to garner almost half the vote (473 against 497 for Yeltsin). The *apparat* took a major gamble with Polozkov—he was not quite an *apparatchik,* but was nonetheless a champion of law and order by any means. Not for nothing did he appeal to the imperialist mind-set of the imperialist nation, to its obsession with defense, to popular egalitarianism, at the same time inflaming hatred of democracy, the free-market economy, and the "cooperators"—budding Soviet capitalists. A columnist for the *Baltic Times* wrote, "This is no longer a stake in an *apparat* game—this is a recipe for civil war. The Yeltsin-Polozkov contest is a genuine split into two camps, who are now facing off. By picking Polozkov as its top candidate, the Politburo has undercut all the appeals to unity that had come from the Party leadership."

What unity were they talking about? What about another gathering that took place about the same time—the Peasants' Congress? Two speakers received more applause than anyone else—Yeltsin and Zigachev, two antagonists. Dictatorship or democracy! No compromise, no golden mean, no third—middle—way!

Gorbachev's love of concessions and tendency to hesitate helped him remain the favorite of both the left and the right. Both appealed to him to define his ideological stand, to get off the fence and take sides. They all tried, including Yeltsin.

"Whose side are you on, Gorbachev?" he kept addressing the Soviet leader. "We would like to see complete steps being made, forward and left, and we would like these steps to be taken by Gorbachev himself. So far he has been taking half-steps. He stays on the fence. Now, I think, he must realize that there is just one chance left. If he does not take it, it will spell disaster for the country, for the people, and for him personally. We sense a tiny shift to the left, but at this point it is not enough. Time is running out fast; we are facing an avalanche that can land us in real trouble. To save the day, we must take urgent measures *now.*"

This warning of Yeltsin's, like many others both before and after it, went unheeded. When we returned to Moscow a year later, in the spring of 1991, the political polarization seemed even more dramatic. The country was fed up with Gorbachev's pussyfooting, middle-of-the-road leadership that no longer suited anyone but, perhaps, Gorbachev himself. The policy of, as the Russians put it, sitting "between two chairs" did not work for the country, though it worked quite well when it came to holding on to his job. When he sensed he was losing the support of the Partocracy, Gorbachev could always turn to the democrats for support, and vice versa. Thus Gorbachev left himself considerably more room for maneuvering than he would have by taking a decisive step in one direction or the other.

In despair, society rejected Gorbachev's palliatives; seeking a panacea for its ills, it was looking for that Man on Horseback.

In a meeting in Aksakov Lane, we were told, "Yeltsin is our magic wand." A little farther down the street, on Malaya Bronnaya, the magic-wand savior was presumed to be a certain Mr.X with an opposite, anti-democratic program. Part of society saw Gorbachev as Mr.X: after all, he had already proven his protean ability to change, so why couldn't he turn from a democrat into a dictator, given the gravity of the situation? On the one side, ideological proteanism; on the other, a democratic, Western implant—let it be an iron hand, but not Stalin, please.

Whether Gorbachev was motivated by tactical considerations or by his customary smug affection for the status quo, at first he rejected the suggestions of his supporters: "Again we hear people saying that our country needs a savior. I think we have already seen saviors—and we don't need that kind. A power structure that would make the people the player—that, I think, is our salvation."

However, as early as the spring of 1990, five years after taking power, Gorbachev changed his viewpoint—again—and took the most determined, and at the same time the most risky step in his political career: using a formal Parliamentary majority, he amended the Soviet Constitution and assumed emergency powers. Since he did it during the Empire's most profound crisis, when his popularity was at its lowest, and when the Gorbophiles' appeals for him to become Leader Maximus were drowned by appeals, from both the right and the left, for his resignation, it was easy to see this act as a legalized coup d'état, a veiled power grab—just at the moment when power was slipping out of his hands.

Had Gorbachev, before constitutionally expanding the President's functions and authority, put up his candidacy to popular vote, it might have looked different. But he did not do it—because of Yeltsin. He was afraid of losing to his chief—most likely, his only—rival, whose popularity was growing in direct ratio to his falling one. In any event, the initiator of the peaceful revolution in the Communist world made an about-face: While East European and (future) Baltic countries moved quickly and decisively toward decentralization, de-Partization, and democratization, Moscow saw a determined step toward the centralization of unelected power, toward its concentration in one hand—a potential step to dictatorship.

This about-face—from calling on the people to move to political center stage to usurping even more power—took a mere few months. Did Gorbachev, a lover of eclectics in politics, believe that it was possible to combine grass-roots democracy with dictatorship in the Kremlin? More precisely, *of* the Kremlin? Perhaps in our native country, that Looking-Glass Land, the path to democracy could *only* lie through a dictatorship. Or was it the other way around: a procrastinated democratization inevitably led to dictatorship?

In addition to such rhetorical questions, essential ones arose, too, and they were increasingly acute. We summed them up in the spring of 1990 in a piece called "Gorbachev's 'Coup': A Dangerous Return to Autocracy."

1. What can Gorbachev do as a dictator that he could not do in his previous two capacities—as the Party's General Secretary and Chairman of the Supreme Soviet?

2. How will this dictatorship be established? The legislative act of the Parliament is not enough. More important, by what means will it be retained? Since the end justifies the means, will it again be the military, the police, and the punitive organs? And if so, where is the guarantee that Gorbachev will not be their puppet?

3. Where is the guarantee that, over the years, Gorbachev will not turn from being a sensible politician into a tyrant? Historical examples abound—Deng Xiaoping and Nicolae Ceausescu are two modern ones. Montaigne was right in saying that a political leader must not be judged until he dies.

4. Finally, where is the guarantee that Gorbachev will stay at the helm for a long time, and that he will not be replaced by another dictator with an agenda different from, if not opposite from, his? Establishing the institution of autocracy is a dangerous precedent, especially in view of the Russian tradition of authoritarianism and the Soviet one of totalitarianism.

Gorbachev will be more vulnerable than when he was neither a true dictator nor a true democrat. He will have far less room for maneuver and intrigue, but much more personal responsibility. In short, it seems to us that his highly developed instinct of political self-preservation didn't work this time. The return to the Russian tradition of autocracy will hardly be a political advantage for Gorbachev. Nor will it be of use to his country, exhausted by endless experiments.

Now the Russian Parliament and its Chairman were the only counterweight to Julius Gorbachev Caesar. Soviet journalists, given to historical analogies (although ex-Soviets, we are no exception), were busy drawing comparisons between Gorbachev/Yeltsin and Caesar/Pompeius. The battle between the Kremlin and the Russian White House became a "ukase war" between Gorbachev and Yeltsin. By neutralizing each other, the ukases lost their potency. It was what the Chinese might call a war of paper tigers. Now Moscow had two Presidents, and each wanted full authority. It was like a tennis game at 40–40; the deuce went on midst un-Wimbledon-like bitterness and compromise, with each side gaining an advantage, but never locking in the game, till August 21, 1991, when a failed putsch rocked the capital and violently rearranged the balance of forces.

A year earlier, in the fall of 1990, Gorbachev and Yeltsin, having rested in the summer, set out to prepare for the battle. Gorbachev took his planned regrouping and consolidation of Kremlin forces off the drafting board and put it into practice. He again changed the Constitution, acquiring additional authority as well as the unrestricted option to declare a state of emergency, to proclaim the rule of the President, and to personally promulgate ukases and laws. In short, he set out to create a Super-Presidency. Father Gleb Yakunin, a liberal deputy, commented, "Gorbachev is trying on the Emperor's crown."

His Kremlin court underwent rapid unheavals. He distanced himself from Alexandr Yakovlev, the man who had inspired him to launch glasnost and perestroika. Prime Minister Nikolai Ryzhkov discreetly left the stage. Gorbachev fired Minister of the Interior Vadim Bakatin, who had bitterly opposed the use of his troops to suppress nationalist movements.*

On New Year's Eve, 1990, without waiting to be dismissed, Eduard

---

*Bakatin had once been ordered to report to the Supreme Soviet a mysterious incident in the Moscow suburb of Uspenskoye, when Boris Yeltsin, returning from a meeting with voters, found himself taking a swim in the river. Bakatin performed his task reluctantly. He was nervous, his hands were shaking—in short, he looked like a man who was carrying out orders without losing sight of his conscience, which in turn meant that at some point he would stop carrying them out. After the coup, he was appointed KGB Chairman.

Shevardnadze left his position as Foreign Minister; he did so with pa-
nache, slamming the door after warning Parliament that preparations for
a coup d'état were under way:

"The reform has gone to hell. Dictatorship is coming; I state this with
conviction. No one knows what kind of dictatorship it will be and who
will come—what kind of dictator—nor what the regime will be like.

"I wish to make the following statement: I resign. Let this be—do not
say anything, do not curse me—let this be my contribution—my protest,
if you will—against the onset of dictatorship."

Shevardnadze's warning was unexpected and sensational, but vague:
He knew more than he was willing to reveal; than he dared reveal,
perhaps. Something held him back. It could hardly have been cowardice.
Perhaps it was unwillingness to violate the code of male friendship, which
is important in his native Georgia. Or perhaps his suspicions were still
unformed. That would remove the criticism that he failed to give full
information about the preparations at the time of the warning. Nevertheless, it is possible that his warning led to the postponement of the coup.

Only a month after his resignation, Shevardnadze privately criticized
Gorbachev about the massacre launched by Soviet tanks in the Lithuanian capital.

Gorbachev replied, "How can you think that? How could it occur to
you that I would allow something like that to happen?"

But Shevardnadze no longer believed his former boss.

In Moscow, we heard another explanation for Shevardnadze's resignation. Unlike Yeltsin, he did not rebel, but fled Gorbachev's sinking ship
like the proverbial rat. We detected a note of envy in these words, spoken
by a man who was still aboard ship. Eventually he changed sides, too, and
by the time of the putsch was already on Yeltsin's team. As the joke goes:

"Hey, minority, where are you going?"

"To join the majority!"

But at that point, Gorbachev's partisans, their ranks now thinner,
regarded Shevardnadze's resignation an act of betrayal. Now completely
isolated from the people, alone among democrats, his former comrades,
Gorbachev hastily staffed a new Kremlin team.

Minister of Defense Dmitry Yazov gained influence, while KGB Chairman Vladimir Kryuchkov became Gorbachev's éminence grise. Kryuchkov also recommended KGB man Boris Pugo to replace the liberal
Bakatin as Minister of the Interior. Soon, in January 1991, Pugo would
order his hoodlums to fire on peaceful demonstrators both in Lithuania
and in his native Latvia, as if proving his ethnic evenhandedness to his
bosses. Gorbachev rejected "500 Days," a radical program of transition
to a free-market economy developed by Stanislav Shatalin, and appointed Valentin Pavlov Prime Minister. (That appointment seemed to

have been made to draw popular hatred away from Gorbachev and direct it at Pavlov.) Finally, Gorbachev appointed Gennady Yanayev, a nonentity, his Vice President. Now even the puppet Parliament, heretofore obedient to Gorbachev, was up in arms and would not confirm Yanayev. Gorbachev whined, cajoled, threatened, blackmailed, and, violating every rule, forced a second—successful—vote.

His five protégés—Yanayev, Yazov, Kryuchkov, Pugo, and Pavlov—would form the nucleus of Putsch '91.

Yeltsin warned the people that 1991 "will be the year of decision: either democracy will be suffocated or we—democrats—will not merely survive but triumph."

In January there was a massacre at a peaceful demonstration in Vilnius: fifteen dead in one night. Yeltsin, shattered, called Gorbachev several times. He pleaded, he begged, but Gorbachev was stolid: hesitations were over; he had made his choice. He turned a deaf ear to Yeltsin's entreaties and arguments. Perhaps Gorbachev thought that the entire society, and not just he, was veering to the right—who knows?

Yeltsin despaired: "It was Gorbachev who was removed from reality, because society had become even more politicized, but on the democratic side . . . My impression was that the leadership had decided that the democratic path was too hard, so they decided to turn to the hand of iron."

The Lithuanian incident caused a change in Yeltsin's tactics. Now he realized that a compromise with today's Gorbachev—the man who had dismissed Yakovlev, Bakatin, and Shevardnadze, and brought in Yanayev, Yazov, Kryuchkov, Pugo, and Pavlov—was no longer possible. Even if it had been possible, compromise would have been dangerous. It was time to part company.

At this crucial moment, Yeltsin acted according to his conscience, not just tactical considerations. He made several appeals to Russian soldiers not to fire on Lithuanian civilians. Here is part of one such appeal.

I address you, soldier; you, a member of our young generation. Dictatorship is at the gate, and you are the one who opens that gate, with your machine gun atop the tank! Didn't you, too, dream once of freedom? Didn't you ever yawn at "political education" classes? Did you believe what Brezhnev, Chernenko, and others told you? They are the ones who have sent you to Vilnius! They are the ones who have betrayed you. In turn, you are about to betray your generation. Do you think that smashing unarmed people with rifle butts makes you a Rambo, a hero on the side of law and order? No! Again, you're a pawn in their dirty game; a grain of sand in the sand castle of our Empire . . .

You can obey an order. But how? If there is an order to clear the square, this does not mean smashing people's heads with shovels. If there is a command, "Fire!", you can fire over their heads. You will not be court-martialed, and you will earn the respect of your people and your country—Russia . . .

Yours is the choice of a lifetime: are you on the side of freedom and truth, which will prevail anyway, even if all of us, like in Rumania, have to lie down to block the tanks—or are you on the side of jails and lies? Are you with your generation or not? Answer! DO NOT SHOOT!

But Yeltsin did not confine himself to personal appeals: He stepped up the recruitment of his own armed supporters—Army, police, KGB—something he had planned long ago. He no longer ruled out the possibility that the democratic forces of Russia might have to fight an armed battle against the *apparat,* the KGB, the Kremlin, and Gorbachev himself. If Gorbachev was capable of inciting pogroms in Kazakhstan, Georgia, Azerbaijan, Lithuania, and Latvia, he would surely resort to force in Russia if he thought he had to.

The direct appeal to Russian soldiers and the creation of a Russian army were extremely dangerous. By calling on Russian soldiers not to shoot down Baltic civilians, Yeltsin seemed to be shedding his populist label, throwing away the support of an important segment of the Russian population that still cherished pro-Empire sentiments. A number of "patriotic" writers, including such well-known names as Valentin Rasputin and Vasily Belov, published an open letter to Yeltsin, which undoubtedly reflected the mood of anxiety afflicting part of Russian society:

Your appeals and musings on our glorious Russian military traditions, which sounded in your address to the soldiers and which urged them to violate their military oath, are another proof of your disregard of Russian history and your penchant for political games. Your statement about creating a Russian armed forces is a direct call to civil war. Finally, in the middle of a political and economic crisis, your approval of strikes must be considered irresponsible, leading to further anarchy and to the ruin of the national economy . . . None of your statements fit the traditional popular concept of national honor and dignity, so we must hope that the Russian people will be able to decide for themselves what is honorable and what is not.

Only a callous politician, indifferent to the fate of his Motherland, could dispense, left and right, free economic zones and sovereign areas within Russian territory, thus practically dismembering the Russian State and the indivisible Russian national body. Your actions in their totality amount unequivocally to the disintegration of the USSR and the destruction of Russia: You did not create them, and it is not your place to decide their destiny. Don't you understand that the destruction of the territorial integrity of the Union that you encourage, deliberately or unwittingly, will not stop at the Russian border? By wrecking the Union, you and your cohorts are destroying Russia.

By the early '90s, ideological chaos had reached its apogee; even Yeltsin's supporters were split along ideological lines. It was not a matter of persons grouping around ideas, but, rather, of ideas grouping around persons. Boris Yeltsin was of course the principal magnet, emitting a powerful field that drew in various, sometimes quarreling, factions. The anti-Kremlin opposition was so fragmented that had it not been for Yeltsin, it would have instantly fallen apart.

By contrast, the Kremlin had failed to produce a charismatic leader; Gorbachev's magic worked only at a considerable distance—namely, abroad. Nonetheless, with all his popularity, Yeltsin still took a big chance by voicing decisively his anti-imperial views, and it did lower his rating. (Paradoxically, Alexandr Nevzorov, host of the famous TV program *600 Seconds,* a man with big political ambitions, praised the Imperial Soviet Army on his program and lost a lot of fans.)

Apparently a part of the Russian population that was once infected with imperialist, chauvinist sentiments had for some reason lost them during glasnost, often along with their ethnic identification. This to some extent explains the meager number of Pamyat supporters. Yeltsin's principled stance on the Baltic issue would scare away some and induce others to pause, reflect, and perhaps even change their viewpoint—among the Russians, his appeal was that strong. True, he was a populist, but he went further: he saw as his mission the reeducation of some of his supporters in the spirit of democracy and internationalism. As he changed himself, he reeducated other, well, less conscientious, citizens. People listened to Yeltsin and heeded his words—unlike Sakharov's, for example—because they accepted Yeltsin as one of their own. In addition to entailing risk, his highly moral position embraced a long-range stratagem.

Gorbachev was up in arms against both Yeltsin's humanitarian appeal to the soldiers and to the decision to create a Russian army, denouncing them as "flagrant violations of the Soviet Constitution and politically intended acts of provocation toward the Supreme Soviet authorities, ones that not only do not encourage the cohesiveness of our society, but to the contrary aggravate the present ambience of confrontation . . . They should be rejected and denounced . . . Yeltsin must acknowledge this in the spirit of self-criticism and rescind such appeals. Let us hope that he has not yet completely taken leave of his senses."

It should be noted that as a longtime veteran of fighting the Kremlin, Yeltsin planned for all eventualities. He was a principled, implacable enemy of the KGB, but took a more conciliatory stance toward the Army, and did all he could to bring it over to the side of the democrats. He emphasized the importance of propagandizing in the Army, which both he and his emissaries did regularly, overtly and covertly.

Yeltsin used the services of his secret backers in the Air Force as early as during his election campaign of '89. He had to attend a campaign rally in Perm, in the Urals. Since the local Party Bosses, following Kremlin orders, were commanded to do everything to prevent him from appearing on the ballot, he had to catch them off guard and arrive unexpectedly. After the last Perm flight left Moscow, Yeltsin flew to Leningrad, where his well-wishers quickly took him to a military airfield and put him on a transport plane. Holding on to a missile for support inside the plane, Boris Yeltsin flew to Perm and made it in time for the meeting.

Looking ahead, it is interesting that of all the branches of the Soviet Armed Forces, Yeltsin would have the closest links with the Air Force. He would show it by picking an ex-pilot, Alexandr Rutskoy, as his Vice President; later, during the August putsch, Air Force General Yevgeny Shaposhnikov would openly take Yeltsin's side and threaten to bomb the Kremlin—the den of the conspirators. Immediately following the collapse of the putsch, Shaposhnikov would be promoted to the rank of Marshal and appointed Minister of Defense.

Yeltsin of course flirted with other branches of the military. During his marathon cross-country travels in August 1990 following his election to the Russian presidency, he visited border guard posts, military academies, the "closed" military town of Petropavlovsk-Kamchatsky, Navy ships, and even a nuclear submarine. He donated $50,000 out of his foreign book royalties for the Cadet Museum in the city of Tula. He vowed to open up and declassify Petropavlovsk-Kamchatsky. He decided to reduce the duration of submarine missions, which used to last ninety days, and to improve the physical and social condition of military families. These were not preelection promises, it was a postelection program. This was how Yeltsin summed up his impressions: "The midlevel officers favor radical transformation, a true reform in the Army—not the kind the generals have in mind."

A few days after Yeltsin's return to Moscow, someone put paratrooper units in Ryazan—a mere 100 miles from Moscow—on a state of alert, and the soldiers, armed with sappers' shovels and wearing bulletproof vests, were on their way to Moscow. Yeltsin immediately summoned the commanders of the various military districts to his office and explained to them that nowadays the legitimate power in Russia was held by the Russian Parliament—not by the Kremlin.

Yeltsin's quarrel was not with the Army, but with Gorbachev's generals and marshals. It was Gorbachev's chief military adviser, Sergei Akhromeyev, whose body was found hanging from a noose in the wake of the putsch, who spoke out most stridently against Yeltsin. In early 1991 *Soviet Russia,* a newspaper that regularly attacked Yeltsin, published Akhromeyev's polemical article in which he enumerated the major heretics: Boris Yeltsin, Moscow mayor Gavriil Popov, Leningrad mayor Anatoly Sobchak, historian Yuri Afanasyev, and others:

They have openly linked themselves with the nationalist and separatist movements in the Baltics. The Chairman of the Supreme Soviet of the largest Republic [i.e., Yeltsin] openly confronts the policies of the USSR President . . . It is typical of Boris Yeltsin to trample the Constitution. He acts as if it did not exist . . . The struggle for power, launched recently by Boris Yeltsin and the Interregional Group's leadership, logically leads to the necessity of having their own army. Are other Republics expected to set up their own armies as well? Then the USSR will cease to exist as a state.

Who is, then, really planning a coup d'état? Generals and admirals who guard the Constitution—or those who collaborate with separatist forces of certain Republics toward the dismemberment of the Soviet Union? Who is really to blame for the crisis and instability in the country?

More fuel for the blaze was added by the Interregional Group's counterweight in the Supreme Soviet, the Soyuz (Union) conservative bloc. Soyuz considered both the Interregional Group and Baltic separatists the lackeys of the CIA. As its name shows, Soyuz took an openly imperialist position in favor of the preservation of the Soviet Union, though there is not a single Russian among its leadership: the Latvian Victor Alksnis, the Jewish Yevgeny Kogan, and the Ukrainian Nikolai Petrushenko.

This is not surprising, for the imperial idea is supranational. Disraeli was the jingoist mastermind of the British Empire, Napoleon was a Corsican, and Catherine the Second was German. Soyuz's popularity kept growing. According to polls, it was supported by 22 percent of the population, while 56 percent said that only a strong hand could pull the country out of its economic and political morass. By 1991 the number of Soyuz-affiliated Parliamentary seats increased from 461 to 560.

Whether speaking from the podium or giving interviews right and left, Colonel Alksnis was direct and outspoken: "Call me a reactionary, I don't mind," he said. He was called far worse, but that did not bother him. Unlike his superiors, men such as Marshal Akhromeyev, Colonel Alksnis did not care for Communist Newspeak and called a spade a spade. According to him, Gorbachev had two choices: either declare a state of emergency now or resign and let others do it:

"If we do not halt the swelling anarchy, millions will take to the streets and smash everything in sight, from McDonald's to museums. That's when a really monstrous dictatorship could emerge; you never know who will take over . . . Time has run out for Gorbachev. He must either take charge or leave. There's nothing left to wait for."

When Gorbachev talked about the country turning right, did he mean

Soyuz? In any event, Alksnis and his supporters were already acting as a detonating fuse for the coup being planned, or perhaps, already under way.

In effect Gorbachev announced the state of emergency on February 1, 1991. Although he used a euphemism, "combined Army and militia patrols in the major cities, including the capital," he fooled no one. Here is an excerpt from the order, issued jointly by Minister of Defense Marshal Dmitry Yazov and Minister of the Interior Colonel General Boris Pugo:

> Develop and implement joint administrative and practical measures aimed at the reinforcement of public order and the prevention of lawbreaking . . . Should a serious tactical situation emerge, Soviet Army and Navy personnel with light arms will be assigned for joint patrolling for the following time periods: for mass civil rallies, twenty-four hours; for preparation and implementation of planned public demonstrations, as well as for holidays, for nighttime; for weekends only if the need arises. Standing reserves of patrolmen with armored personnel vehicles, as well as units in each garrison, a company or a battalion strong, will be kept in a state of alert, with arms and ammunition . . .

Unlike the no-nonsense Alksnis, the Kremlin still used Newspeak. Nevertheless they gave themselves away. A state of military emergency was decreed for "mass civil rallies"; that is, for anti-Kremlin, pro-Yeltsin rallies and demonstrations. The Kremlin was moving from a passive defense to an aggressive one. It was really a putsch, but a slow, gradual, veiled one. In this extraordinary situation, Boris Yeltsin took an extraordinary gamble.

After long negotiations and delays, he finally got a chance to be on TV. On February 19, 1991, the Chairman of the Russian Parliament addressed the Soviet people with an unprecedented appeal in which he called Gorbachev a liar who was leading the country to dictatorship, and demanded his resignation. The country listened to Yeltsin with bated breath:

> . . . In the first two years after 1985, Gorbachev extended some degree of hope to many of us. Then he launched an active policy—sorry, I have to use this word—of deception. He made promises that, I guess, he did not have a clear idea how to implement. Once people were filled with hope, he changed course. Lately this became especially apparent when he paid lip service to the notion of perestroika, but in fact acted to preserve the system, maintain rigid central power, and keep autonomy away from the Republics—most of all, from Russia. I'm talking about the monetary manipulations,* Pavlov's unprecedented price

*Large 50- and 100-ruble notes were taken out of circulation.

hike,* being prepared now; a rightward tilt in his policies; the use of the Army against civilian populations; the increase in interethnic conflicts; the failure of the economy; low living standards for our people; and so on. These are the results of six years of perestroika—this is what really counts.

Now we are witnessing a rollback: we see attempts to restore administrative-command methods by reinforcing the administrative-command center. Our leaders show no desire to look at what is really going on.

After I was elected Chairman of the Supreme Soviet, the voters voiced their demands that I work with the central leadership. I'll tell you frankly: God knows I tried. On a number of occasions we got together, for five hours at a time, to discuss our problems. But unfortunately the result was the same.

It does not look like the center will allow the Republics to act autonomously. I have analyzed the events of the last few months thoroughly, and I must state the following: in 1987 I warned that it is inherent in Gorbachev's nature to strive for absolute personal power.† He has gone far in that direction; he has brought about a dictatorship under the pretty name of "President's Rule." I dissociate myself from the President's position and his policies and I call for his immediate resignation, with the power passing to the collective body—the Federation Council.**

I believe in Russia, and I call on you, my esteemed fellow citizens, fellow Russians, to believe in our Russia as well. I have made my choice, and now each of you must make his choice and define his position. I want you to hear me and understand me. I repeat—I have made my choice, and I intend to follow this path. I need your support, the support of all the people of Russia—and I am counting on it . . .

Yeltsin spoke for forty minutes, preceding *Vremya* (Time), the main evening newscast. He had been trying to get on the air for a long time. Naturally, the Kremlin, forced to give him a nationwide audience, hedged its bets by flanking Yeltsin with two Party media hacks, who opened the program by attacking him with abrupt, hostile questions. Only after he answered them did Yeltsin read his statement demanding Gorbachev's immediate resignation. In chess terms, he had prepared the end game. Right after his speech, he left Moscow for, as they say, a "destination unknown," using distance to cushion himself against the new barrage of assaults; had he been in Moscow, it would have been more painful.

In the months following Yeltsin's speech, the barrage of anti-Yeltsin criticism in the Kremlin-controlled media continued unabated. Yet in the middle of all this a defiant article in his defense was published in *Kuranty* (Chimes), the official organ of Moscow's liberal City Council, written by Yuri Vlasov, an Olympic gold-medal weight lifter who had made his

---

*Named after Prime Minister Valentin Pavlov and effected on April 2, 1991.
†Yeltsin's speech at the October Session of the Central Committee, described in Part One.
**The council consisted of the fifteen leaders of the Republics, including Yeltsin.

name a year earlier when he spoke out against the KGB in the Soviet Parliament. In the article, the ex-athlete politician gave a penetrating analysis of the roots of the Gorbachev-Yeltsin conflict; the title itself showed the author's position: "The Real Target Is the People—Not Yeltsin."

> By now the battle lines are drawn on a strictly personal basis. They are attacking not the Russian Parliament—which, without its Chairman, they could overrun—but the leader of the opposition—to be precise, the leader of the popular movement. This is their last-ditch effort, for Boris Yeltsin's victory will consign Communists all across the land to political limbo . . . Russia in its entirety, embittered and humiliated, has closed ranks behind Yeltsin, who speaks its language . . . The people, not Boris Yeltsin, are now the real target, which is why people have risen to his defense. Besides, they have no other protector on Yeltsin's scale. Were he without this ally, were he a rank-and-file ambitious politician, he would have been swept away long ago. Today this cannot happen; today he *is* the people. And he senses his responsibility . . .
>
> Democracy has been placed in an extraordinary position. In normal societies, it was formed through decades, it developed its own leaders, spokesmen, journalists; it created its ethic, its environment; it learned how to get rid of fellow travelers and windbags; it developed a language of communication with working people and created its own media; but it did not groan as it was being gagged and slandered by its enemies.
>
> Our democracy is only one year old. Its destiny has been to race in a year the distance it took others decades to cover. Without respite, without grass-roots efforts by its parties, without consistent promotion of its views in the media, it has been cast into the fiercest baptismal fire, as it must represent the interests of the left wing of the people, who are truly enraged . . . One can only sympathize with Boris Nikolayevich Yeltsin, upon whom history has placed such a tremendous burden.

We returned to Russia in the spring of 1991. If we had not recognized it the year before, it seemed as nothing to the country we discovered now. Russia had changed in one year more than in the previous thirteen—events outpaced one another, political stage sets were changed daily, the attitudes of the masses were in a state of flux—metamorphoses were everywhere. But the Kremlin stubbornly ignored all this. The idea of Russian state sovereignty itself was born out of despair: if the Kremlin did not want to give up its power, or at least share it with the people, then a huge country—even without the other fourteen Republics—would be declared independent of the Kremlin. Just as mad old King Lear lost his kingdom after dividing it among his daughters, Gorbachev lost power immediately after the Russian Parliament adopted its Declaration of State Sovereignty. Now he was the leader of a country that existed nowhere but on maps.

"Gorbachev is the last President of the Union," Lev Shemayev, a Yeltsin supporter, told us. "You can't preside over something that doesn't exist. For the time being, every day he is at the helm is a catastrophe."

"A catastrophe for whom?"

"For all of us. For them it means millions, represented by a different type of property. That's why they are clinging to Gorbachev. What happens now is that State and Party property is converted into shareholder property of the same nomenklatura who used to own it. This is the thing: the officials got a one-time shot to make a killing. They have a clear advantage over anyone else. If today a State factory belongs to a ministry—that is, a huge group of nomenklatura on different levels, all feeding at this trough—they will simply form an association or a company and transfer the property into the hands of a limited number of people who will get, so to speak, a head start on the road to capitalism by controlling the majority of the stock. The nomenklatura is only too happy to make the leap into the market economy . . . No, they won't allow Gorbachev to be overthrown, either by the Union or by Russia, until they have pumped property from one form into another, until they have laundered their money."

Shemayev was a politician, Yeltsin's "campaign proxy" (in the campaign he was Yeltsin's stand-in in the district where Yeltsin ran), and the cochairman of the Democratic Russia coalition movement. Here, also, was an opinion from a more objective source: journalist Victor Yaroshenko, who sided neither with Gorbachev nor with Yeltsin—not an easy task, he admitted.

He recalled a popular slogan: "Hey, Party, we want to steer, too!"

They won't let us behind the wheel, though they seem to be pulling over to the curb. They won't give up till they are finished transferring the property, converting it into their personal possession, or at least getting their hands on the majority of the stock. Only when they feel that they and their children are guaranteed financial security will they give it up. There you can have your wheel—you can steer all you want. Otherwise, "What was the point?", they'd say. They demand a tacit social contract from the democrats: you will let us go quietly, with our pockets full, while we will peacefully—without jailing or shooting you—allow you to set up a democracy. Considering their real capacities and capabilities, this isn't such a bad deal . . .

Maybe—but those pockets got fuller all the time. Russia was being devastated by the transfer of the Communist Party's funds abroad. About 10 percent of the Soviet gold reserve was smuggled into Switzerland; then the ingots were forwarded to London in two shipments—

altogether, according to conservative estimates, about 10 million troy ounces, with a total value of some 4 billion dollars. Furthermore, this is only a part of the mysteriously vanished Party cashbox, which was valued at 12 billion dollars. The person in charge of this Golconda was Nikolay Kruchina, Gorbachev's old friend and protégé, who fell—or was pushed—out of a window after the putsch.

The Party quickly set up a fire sale of devalued—"wooden," Russians call them—rubles. They are sold abroad at a fraction of their value, while inside the country the mint is working around the clock, printing more money. In December 1990, 100 billion rubles were sold for 5.5 billion dollars. Another 25 billion were sold in January; 15 billion in May. The largest deal took place on the eve of the coup: 140 billion rubles were sold for 4.5 billion dollars as the ruble kept plummeting in the black market.

Curiously, the same amount—140 billion rubles—was cited by Valentin Pavlov, the future Prime Minister and a putschist (if a reluctant one), who was then Minister of Finance. He declared that Swiss, Austrian, and Canadian banks were trying to destabilize the Soviet economy by buying cheap rubles. At the time, the statement caused much laughter, yet what if Pavlov—just like Shevardnadze with his warnings of the coming coup—knew more than he revealed?

A month after the putsch, Moscow requested all the world governments to freeze the Party's deposits in their countries' banks. The Party's conspirators, covering their paper trail, apparently had more expertise in finance than in warfare.

Meanwhile the battle between the two leaders continued unabated. Of course, the concept of power-sharing between the Russian and Soviet Presidents was nonsensical. Power-sharing was equivalent to a power vacuum, and Moscow was not big enough for two Presidents; they canceled out each other's actions.

The ranks of Gorbachev's supporters thinned quickly. According to a poll taken that spring by *US News & World Report,* only 14 percent of Soviet voters said they would vote for Gorbachev in a national election, and 70 percent would vote for Yeltsin. Many Gorbachevists now adopted a more ambiguous position, criticizing both rival leaders or drawing an equation between them. Eduard Shevardnadze called on both Gorbachev and Yeltsin to stop "presidential warfare."

We had a long talk with journalist Artyom Borovik. Before he became editor of the Moscow tabloid *Top Secret,* he worked at the progressive weekly *Ogonyok.* He spoke to us about the generation that included his ex-boss, *Ogonyok*'s editor, Vitaly Korotich, as well as Yevgeny Yevtushenko and other writers who were closely linked to Gorbachev's era:

"These people have a bad case of split personality. I knew Korotich very well; you could say I examined him under a microscope. I owe him a lot, but he is of that generation, flesh and blood. In one brain hemisphere they have the Communist enthusiasm of the '30s and '40s; in the other, the late '50s. This is the generation that wept at Stalin's funeral and then welcomed Khrushchev's thaw. Gorbachev, too, has two people in him: a totalitarian and a democrat. He is a bit of both."

"What about Yeltsin?"

"I don't think he's very different from Gorbachev. His personality is structured the same way. He just placed a strategic bet on democracy. There is no doubt that there is a dictator in him as well."

"Perhaps it is the difference in their situations? Have them switch places: then Yeltsin would have to maneuver between different groups of the ruling establishment while Gorbachev would go into the opposition."

This did not take into account their individual qualities. Under no conditions would Gorbachev have dared to rebel the way Yeltsin did.

"No matter how we dislike Gorbachev, he delivered the first blow against the wall," Artyom said.

"Remember when Lenin was interrogated at a police precinct? 'Your struggle is in vain,' the police said. 'You're facing a wall.' 'But it's a rotten wall,' he responded; 'one touch and it will crumble.' The wall that Gorbachev faced was no sturdier."

Artyom disagreed: "This system could go on for another hundred years."

Now, after the system collapsed in August 1991, it is hard to say who was right.

No one doubts that Yeltsin is the child of the "command-administer system," as Russians say nowadays, but so much greater is his courage in breaking away from it. Of course, if we compare democracy to the Promised Land of Exodus, former slaves might not enter it at all. God had a purpose in having the Jews roam across a relatively small piece of land: the generation of Egyptian slaves had to die out before people returned to their homeland. Even Moses, who led his people out of captivity, could see the Promised Land only from the distance and had to die without setting his foot in it.

Thus we found another comparison for our hero—one from the Bible.

A few days after Yeltsin appealed to Gorbachev to resign, he was answering questions in public:

"Don't you think that, in order to stabilize the situation, not only Gorbachev must resign, but you as well?"

Yeltsin reflected, then said unflappably, "It's possible."

"You wrote in your book that you disliked taking orders. Do you think your nature contributed to your appeal for Gorbachev's resignation?"

"We're not talking about the relations between Gorbachev and Yeltsin. We're talking about the system still in place. We're talking about defending Russian sovereignty. If Russia remains trampled upon, it will never overcome its backwardness. This is something you must understand. It is not a personal conflict between Gorbachev and Yeltsin. It is on a higher level."

Everything was intermingled here: personality and the State; matters private and political. Any label applied: politics, career, destiny. Trying to distinguish among them would amount to splitting hairs. Napoleon once said, "What are you talking about—'destiny'! Politics are destiny." That applies equally to Gorbachev and Yeltsin.

"Boris Nikolayevich, a hypothetical situation: One night someone rings your bell, you open and see Mikhail Sergeyevich and Raisa Maksimovna on your doorstep. Your reaction?"

"First, I'll ask them in. Well, the women will go to the kitchen, they have their own stuff to talk about.* As for us, I'd tell him, For three years, I've been asking—begging—you to let the forces on the left prop you up. Then we would have not let the right-wingers develop into such a menace—and they are the ones who are now muscling you out. Today you would be removed by the right, not the left. On the other hand, you recently called the left the right, and the right the left, so no one can figure out anymore whom you consider what. But it is obvious that Polozkov criticizes you worse than I do. I'm not claiming your job nor am I offering myself as your alternative. But I'll stand firm on this: let Russia breathe freely; give it autonomy. Russia has everything at its disposal to solve its problems if the doomed system gets out of its way."

They were undoubtedly obsessed with each other, though by then Gorbachev was more obsessed with Yeltsin than vice versa. Those who met Gorbachev in the spring of 1990 later told us that he had raved like a lunatic about Yeltsin—the latter was an idée fixe, a thorn in his side. Whatever the subject was—ethnic problems, literature, the economy— Gorbachev invariably turned the conversation to Boris Yeltsin, that disturber of the peace—including Gorbachev's personal tranquillity. His guests were expected to nod sympathetically.

A Moscow friend of ours said that after meeting Gorbachev he felt sick for a few days: "He lives in another world. Does he really think that Yeltsin is the root of all evil? The country's going straight to hell, life's

---

*At the advice of our translator, keenly attuned to American gender-related political discourse, we felt we should comment on this remark. To be sure, Yeltsin is a product of his times, with a he-man mentality. Yet this remark was a veiled barb aimed specifically at Raisa Gorbachev, who irritated many—not just Yeltsin—by her heavy-handed interference in politics. We are convinced that if Raisa were President, Yeltsin would not think twice about sending her husband to the kitchen (the very word "kitchen" is symbolic here and tells you something about the size of Soviet apartments—though Yeltsin's apartment was so modest that he could have meant a real kitchen).

getting worse every day, with no light at the end of the tunnel—Yeltsin is to blame for that, too? I shudder at the thought: a national leader with an idée fixe!"

"Did you tell him that?"

After a pause he said, "I don't want you to believe I'm a coward. And I know times have changed. But it was impossible to disagree with him. Remember the old slogan: 'He who is not with us is against us'? He perceives any objection on any issue as switching to the enemy side. If you have a different opinion, you are spying for Yeltsin. I was not alone there—no one disagreed with him, though all were baffled by his verbosity. He talks nonstop, he has grown very nervous."

In point of fact, Gorbachev was right to blame Yeltsin for his troubles. The people were pinning all their hopes on him. He epitomized the popular rebellion against the Party, the Kremlin, against Gorbachev; Yeltsin was not merely a leader, he was the personification, the symbol of the revolution. What really stood behind the envy that Gorbachev, a target of popular curses, felt for Yeltsin's record popularity? It was an impostor's fear of a man chosen by the people—a personified fear of the people and their will.

From the Russian point of view, Gorbachev was by then a political cadaver who would not step into his grave, but clung to the power that had come his way as a result of Kremlin machinations blessed by KGB Chairman Yuri Andropov, his fellow Stavropolian and his mentor. Accordingly, Gorbachev pinned all his hopes on that organization, which had survived glasnost and perestroika better than most. Alas, even the KGB was no longer happy with Gorbachev. Who was? Neither left nor right; neither workers nor middle class; neither generals nor politically-oriented intellectuals. The intellectuals, from economists Nikolai Shatalin and Grigori Yavlinsky to Georgi Arbatov, who had served every Kremlin Boss, jumped Gorbachev's ship en masse and swam to Yeltsin's. As for the pro-Gorbachev establishment intelligentsia, its influence waned as political freedoms spread; it failed the test of democracy.

Gorbachev tried to please everybody; it was his undoing. We, two Russian-born foreign tourists, recognized Russia as a polarized society in which one needed to define oneself, to state one's intentions unambiguously. But Gorbachev flirted with everyone and played everyone off against everyone else; he frightened conservatives by playing up to liberals, and vice versa. The tactic worked until both sides saw that Gorbachev was blackmailing them, siccing them on each other, thus hoping to hold on to the Kremlin throne.

All the questions that he had once been asked—Who are you? Whose side are you on? Where are you leading us?—were suddenly no longer valid. What can you ask of a sixty-year-old man made of Silly Putty? No one demanded anything of him anymore; he no longer suited anyone but the bunch of yes-men around him. And he kept threatening the people—with a civil war, among other things. In Moscow, the meaning of that threat was an open secret: if the masses, represented by their democratically elected leaders, attempted to take power by legitimate means, the KGB and the Army would march out against them, even though it would touch off civil war.

Yeltsin saw through this threat, and, acting against his own previous convictions, now insisted that the bugbear of civil war was being used to "scare the population again, to distract them from vital issues, to justify the use of violence against them, and to put pressure on the democratic movement." More pointedly, he added, "I don't believe a civil war is possible. No matter how much the President and his comrades are raising the level of tension, I have an absolute belief in the common sense of the people."

No matter what one thinks of Gorbachev, it is difficult to deny that his political style was closer to Orwell's model than Brezhnev's or Khrushchev's were. The favorite of the *apparat* and the KGB, the last scion of the Brezhnev-Andropov Kremlin, Gorbachev accused the legitimately elected democrats of attempting to seize power—how Orwellian can you get? As early as in October 1989, Gorbachev declared that Yuri Afanasyev, one of the most radical democrats, was "cooperating with Yeltsin to set up a power-hungry fascist clique," and has been recycling that charge ever since. His authoritarian regime developed more sophisticated camouflage: Gorbachev moved from Communist slogans to democratic lingo. He emoted, orated, feinted—it was hard to tell what sort of audience he had in mind, since everyone in the country had figured him out long ago. It was a one-man show in a practically empty theater. Meanwhile, the wings were filled with fidgeting stand-ins, from Yeltsinists in their Russian-flag tricolors to "black colonels," which is what the Russians, alluding to the Greek junta, called the right-wing military.

The one-man show, with its protagonist who was alternately a democrat and a dictator, and a starving audience, went on for too long. It was one thing to watch it all from overseas; it was something else to see it from the inside—from Russia itself. With each visit we felt more strongly that the curtain was about to fall, that Gorbachev would not hold out and die peacefully in his job of a Kremlin god, the way his predecessors had and the way he dreamed he would, too. His reliance on the punitive organs and the military was misplaced: what could they gain from supporting a loser? They would score more points by removing him. Gorbachev was so discredited nationwide that he cast a dark shadow on all those who still supported him—and that included Yeltsin, whenever he agreed to a temporary compromise. To say nothing of the eternal *Quis custodiet ipsos custodes* problem: who will guard the guardians?

Antonio Gramsci, an Italian Marxist theoretician, summed it up: "The old is dying and the new cannot be born. In this interregnum there arises a rich diversity of morbid symptoms."

It was a bad time to visit Moscow: an uncomfortable pause, a black hole in time; not yet democracy, no longer totalitarianism. One could speak out but not act. Now, the endless rallies that we had praised on our previous visit seemed tiresome and repetitious: the same political format, the same slogans, the same cast of saints and villains; even the extras at these overrehearsed crowd scenes looked suspiciously familiar. How long could they merely protest? Wasn't it time to work, to get cracking, to leave street-rally democracy behind and move on to normal, multiparty democracy, Western-style? But the Kremlin still hated liberty, and Russian history was spinning its wheels. The Kremlin was a fortress under siege, the last bulwark of Gorbachev's power. Nonetheless, Boris Yeltsin and the people, by voting in representatives without real power, were doomed to practice political masturbation.

Taking their cue from the Kremlin, Russian Communist members of Parliament demanded an emergency session, hoping to use it to overthrow Yeltsin, who perceived it as more than a personal attack—it was an attack on Russian sovereignty. "I'll fight God himself for Russian sovereignty," he said; yet at closed-door meetings he discussed resignation as an alternative.

The Kremlin, still in control of the media, launched another offensive against Yeltsin, on an unprecedented scale—up to accusing him of working for the CIA. In response, Yeltsinites rocked the country with a wave of rallies. Miners went on strike, now adding political demands to economic ones and demanding Gorbachev's resignation. The Kremlin was faced by a united internationalist front: Lithuania sent Russian miners forty trucks of food. These were the "horizontal" links that Yeltsin had talked about: voluntary ties that would replace the "vertical" ones imposed by the Kremlin. "We don't need a mere reformist policy," said Yeltsin at the time. "We need an emergency policy. Only by joint effort can we break this unfavorable chain of events, so rare in history."

Yeltsinites announced a rally in support of their leader to take place in Moscow on March 28. The Kremlin declared it illegal. Defying the threats, the organizers stood firm: the rally would be held as planned. All of a sudden, the formerly vacillating Gorbachev displayed a rare decisiveness: he sent troops into Moscow, thus occupying his own capital. Fifty thousand soldiers with tanks and armored personnel carriers—Moscow had never seen anything like it. The stage appeared to be set for another massacre, one like Beijing, Tbilisi, Baku, and, recently, Vilnius.

The rally did take place. Hundreds of thousands of Yeltsin backers took to the streets. They were barred from the center of town as the Kremlin girded itself with a ring of steel. Paradoxically, this barrier of soldiers and armor demonstrated both Gorbachev's force and impotence; his decisiveness and hesitancy. Not one shot was fired, no one died, and the next day all the military hardware was gone.

Five months later the real putsch would take place in similar throes of indecision. This time it would take two days longer and people would die. Was Gorbachev's occupation of Moscow a dress rehearsal for the putsch of August 19–21, which took place in his absence?

Explaining his decision to summon the troops to the capital on March 28 to Alexandr Yakovlev, Gorbachev claimed he had received information that democrats were "arming themselves with hooks and ropes" to storm the walls of the Kremlin.

In any case, the Muscovites were not daunted by the display of force. The emergency session of the Russian Parliament, convoked to overthrow Yeltsin, backfired. In attempting to break the Kremlin's manacles, he managed to increase his authority. Not only that, but in Gorbachev's referendum on the future of the USSR, the citizens of its largest Republic decided to hold a direct election for the Presidency of Russia. If Yeltsin won, he would no longer have been elected just by the deputies of Parliament, but by the people. Thus Yeltsin reinforced not his power but its legitimacy. Five other candidates for the post declared themselves, including Gorbachev's Prime Minister, Nikolai Ryzhkov; his ex–Minister of the Interior, Vadim Bakatin; General Albert Makashov, the commander of the Volga-Ural Military District; and Russia's fascist Vladimir Zhizinovsky. The election was set for June 12.

Meanwhile, on April 23, 1991, at the high point of the miners' strike, which demanded Gorbachev's resignation, he and Yeltsin signed a peace agreement at Novo-Ogarevo, Gorbachev's dacha near Moscow.

Lev Shemayev, Yeltsin's active supporter, denounced the agreement as "a sellout of the workers, the miners in particular. What happened? Yeltsin personally urged the miners to come out and act decisively—and now he is throwing them to the wolves. With his TV speech, he prodded all of us to come out and fight for Gorbachev's resignation—where does this leave us now? This is a horrible blow for Democratic Russia."*

The Novo-Ogarevo agreement was called "9 + 1": it was signed by nine Republic leaders, including Yeltsin, but not by the split-away leaders

---

*Democratic Russia was an umbrella coalition of democratic political groups.

of the Baltics, Moldova, Georgia, and Armenia, plus the President of the Union. Gorbachev made considerable concessions by giving the Republics an increased independence from the center; in exchange they recognized the center—Gorbachev himself—as a kind of Higher Coordinator among themselves.

"What a smartass," we overheard someone saying in a trolleybus the next day. "The Party and the KGB saved him from Yeltsin, and Yeltsin saved him from the Party and the KGB. What a slippery SOB! You just can't beat him, he can outfox anybody."

Paraphrasing Martin Luther, one could compare Gorbachev to a drunkard: "You support him from the left, he falls to the right; you support him from the right, he falls to the left."

And in the line outside a newspaper kiosk—the most politicized line in the country—we heard a much cruder metaphor: "He's like a turd in a hole in the ice: now he floats to one edge, now to the other."

We asked Shemayev to comment on these expressions of the *vox populi*. What he said reflected his party line, that of Democratic Russia, more than his personal opinion:

"Somehow it never floated to our edge. What can I tell you? It's the same thing all over again—Gorbachev has scammed Yeltsin, and in a big way, too. I know Boris Nikolayevich well: he's psychologically unstable, he's no good in close combat. And Gorbachev takes it into account in his preparations. Judge for yourselves: Gorbachev suddenly sends an invitation to meet in the morning for a confidential talk, which turns out to be a conference with ten leaders, and goes on for ten hours—a marathon! Boris Nikolayevich can improvise only with large audiences. He gave us an account of the meeting today at Democratic Russia—we're very unhappy with it. He said there were some *tough paragraphs* in the draft joint statement, but he managed to get them taken out. So, even as he was defeated, he felt like a winner."

"Perhaps that was exactly what Gorbachev planned?"

"What do you think! Gorbachev is a superb strategist, far superior to our man. He has conducted this operation brilliantly; it was not just a lucky break, it was an effective strategy! And then the next day he followed up with a little farce at the Central Committee's Plenum by submitting his resignation from the post of General Secretary—naturally, the Plenum rejected it. Gorbachev simply outplayed Yeltsin."

"What kind of game is it between them?"

"One is struggling to hold on to power, and the other one to take over. As a player, Gorbachev is superior, of course. And with the fate of the country at stake—if there's one thing that Boris Nikolayevich is lacking, that's willpower."

One should keep in mind Shemayev's personality. Lev Shemayev is well known in Moscow, and, to some, notorious. He is a man of rare courage, and in the fall of 1990 was one of the three activists (another one was Deputy Oleg Rumyantsev, whose remarks are scattered through this book) to lie down in the path of the tanks, preventing them from entering Moscow. Yet there is something theatrical about him, an affectation that verges on parody; on the other hand, parody follows the original like a shadow. After all, Shemayev is a partisan activist, not a statesman. His time was also running out. He criticized Yeltsin for not having become the Party leader: "Boris Nikolayevich is sort of *neformal,** while the opposition to Gorbachev has already taken a formal shape. This is where his hesitations are rooted. He always flies solo. Also, he does not quite understand the program of Democratic Russia."

Despite criticism, Shemayev continued to emphasize his loyalty to his leader—perhaps for lack of another one. He compared Yeltsin to Lech Walesa, termed him a populist and a far-from-ideal leader, but who else was there? According to Shemayev, the only alternative to Yeltsin could have been Academician Sakharov, whose death was a catastrophe for the democratic movement.

One of us objected, saying that Sakharov would have made a figure-head President; he had been canonized even when he was alive—but politics are made for politicians.

Shemayev, an adoring fan of Sakharov's, persisted: "Yeltsin met Sakharov only a few times, and realized instantly that there was no contest—he could not keep up with Sakharov. I think Sakharov could be the country's President—an intellectual President." His expression was almost dreamlike.

"Whom would you vote for, Sakharov or Yeltsin?"

"I did not have a choice: I was Yeltsin's campaign proxy. And now my job is to get him elected President."

Or, perhaps, both Yeltsin and Gorbachev needed a breather before the presidential election and therefore decided to make a truce—a tactical alliance that delayed the coming battle without canceling it, a time-out both of them needed to regroup their forces.

The election was Yeltsin's foremost concern. He was willing to support Gorbachev; in exchange the latter would agree not to resort to dirty tricks during the campaign. From the four previous campaigns, Yeltsin realized only too well what Gorbachev was capable of. Yeltsin was tired of *that* kind of struggle. Besides, as Pushkin put it, "Deceiving him is not hard, for he is glad to be deceived." Although Yeltsin was well aware of Gorbachev's capacity for sudden maneuvers and about-faces, he simply

---

*A colloquial term for members of all (but especially radical) non-Communist—i.e., "nonformal"—parties.

preferred to believe him. In Moscow, their compromise was called a Munich Agreement.

The day of the election dawned with Yeltsin needing at least 50 percent of the vote to avoid a runoff. The nation held its breath—but it wasn't even close. On the first ballot, Yeltsin won just under 57.4 percent of the total vote, and became the first democratically elected Russian President in one thousand years. As if to get even for the debacle of his first trip to the US, immediately upon being elected Yeltsin crossed the ocean again. This time President Bush received him as a fellow President rather than a gate-crasher.

On July 10, 1991, in a somber, pompous inauguration ceremony, Boris Yeltsin was blessed with a sign of the cross by Patriarch of All Russia Alexei the Second. Gorbachev congratulated him, too, though in a somewhat backhanded manner: "Someone might say, 'So what—one more President in this country,' " joked Gorbachev as he opened his speech. "But," he quickly continued, "I believe this is a very important event, not only for Russia, but . . . for our multinational Motherland."

The joke was a little ambiguous: indeed, two Presidents in one country is one President too many. A country needs only one President: an elected one. And who needs a President of the Union, when the Union itself is in a shambles?

But Yeltsin was still euphoric, and the next day he made a generous announcement: he would support Gorbachev's candidacy at an All-Union election, provided that Gorbachev stayed the course and stuck to the Novo-Ogarevo agreement.

One of the items of the agreement was a democratic election of the President of the Union. Without Yeltsin's support, Gorbachev did not stand a chance of winning; it is doubtful that he had any even *with* such support.

Again, many of Yeltsin's supporters were unhappy, saying that the victory had made him mellow and overly generous—which is, indeed, typical of him. Oleg Rumyantsev, Deputy from Russia and the leader of the Social Democrat Party, viewed Yeltsin's statement of support of Gorbachev's candidacy for President as a mistake: "The April truce was a sound decision: it helped us elect a Russian President. But if we sign an agreement between democratic Republics and the Communist center, all the fruit of our democratic revolution will come to nothing."

While seemingly making concessions to the democrats, Gorbachev at the same time relied on the support of the loyal team of Kremlin brigands he had picked in his "reactionary" period: Yanayev, Yazov, Kryuchkov, Pugo, and Pavlov. Despite their boss's flirting with Yeltsin, all of them remained in place. Nor had anything changed in the makeup of the Kremlin power base—the KGB, the Army, the Party—at least on a high level. Progress and reaction in Russia kept running on parallel tracks, canceling each other out. In the summer of 1991, the paradox became glaringly evident.

Before Gorbachev went to crash the meeting of the Big Seven in London, he held almost daily meetings with the radical economist Grigori Yavlinsky, a Yeltsin supporter, leading everyone to believe that this time Gorbachev would definitely parade decisive evidence of the country's move to a free-market economy in front of the Western leaders. Nothing of the kind. After chatting up Yavlinsky for a week, Gorbachev brought along to London his orthodox Prime Minister, Pavlov, whose presence filled the conservatives' hearts with joy. As we know now, Gorbachev left London empty-handed.

Two weeks later, when President Bush visited Moscow, he witnessed yet another—after a brief respite—confrontation between the two Presidents, of the USSR and of Russia. Although it was more of a spat over protocol, one could sense that Yeltsin was irritated with Gorbachev, who had not stuck to his promises. Formally, Gorbachev was in the right. He invited Yeltsin, along with other Republic leaders, to meet President Bush. But Yeltsin refused to play the role of an extra. He was too big now, even physically, to just be part of Gorbachev's entourage.

Boris Yeltsin and George Bush ended up meeting face-to-face.

On the day Gorbachev and Bush were signing a disarmament treaty, six Lithuanian customs agents were found at their border post, machine-gunned point-blank. Someone was showing the American guests, the Lithuanian insurgents, and the world who was in charge.

The massacre took place eighteen days before the putsch.

Weary from diplomacy, Gorbachev went on vacation to his luxury dacha at Foros. The word dacha, often used to describe the tiny sheds that Muscovites build outside the city, does not begin to describe Foros. It is a small resort town, with its own harbor, airfield, and a TV tower; with a guesthouse, servants' quarters, and barracks. When Gorbachev came to power, he inherited another dacha, in Oreanda, from his predecessors, but that one turned out to be too close to the polluted waters of Yalta harbor, and he had to build himself a new one, in which he would be sitting out the putsch in Moscow.

Paradoxically, we see events better from a distance than from close up. It is a political myopia of sorts: we pre-sense and predict what has already been going on for a long time, and we take the current present to be a sudden future. Essentially, a clairvoyant is a person who traces tomorrow inside today, who hunts down the signs in today that lead to the developments of tomorrow. This was the nature of the warnings of the coming right-wing coup in the USSR. The preparations were in full swing; they took place in plain sight. What do you call tanks on Moscow streets and executions in Lithuania—a rough draft? A rehearsal? A test of force? A training session?

The danger of a right-wing uprising took shape visibly, but, instead of the expected one-acter, the audience got a complex, multiplotted Shakespearean drama in five acts. An epilogue would follow soon enough, though it would differ from the one expected by the audience.

The traditional concept of a small gang of villains who plot and bring about coups d'état needs at least a partial revision. Our "villains" were attuned to the public mood and used some of its elements to justify their acts. The last empire in the world was in its death throes; ideas of law and order were in the air; for, as a nineteenth-century Russian anarchist said, anarchy is the mother of order.

Unlike in France, Vendée was everywhere; it could not be localized; like cancer it attacked from right and left, from top and bottom. Vendée infected Gorbachev himself, who was well aware of his political fiasco. One could have made demands on him three or four years earlier, but now it was too late: the time for reform was hopelessly lost.

"Gorbachev may find himself—perhaps he already has—in a situation in which he has no other choice but to head a plot aimed at himself. Not against himself personally, but against his political course, which has not justified itself."

Lest we be accused of hindsight, we have enclosed this statement in quotation marks. It comes from an article we published two years before the putsch.

The self-occupation of the country was proceeding apace, and the dictatorship grew into a temptation that was increasingly hard to resist. It was a path of least resistance—of resistance overcome by force. It was easy to picture a person voting with one hand for Yeltsin and with the other for dictatorship. And what if Yeltsin himself were a dictator—wouldn't that make it all the more attractive?

This is speculation, of course; Yeltsin had already gained power democratically and did not need to win it again with a coup.

In late July, conservative papers published an "Address to the People":

Beloved Russians! Soviet citizens! Countrymen!

A great, unspeakable calamity has befallen our land. Our Russia, our great State, handed to us by all of history, by nature, by our glorious ancestors, is perishing, crashing, sinking into darkness . . .

What has happened to us, brothers? The sly, cunning rulers, the clever, shrewd heretics, who mock us, who hurl blasphemy at our beliefs, who take advantage of our naive goodness—how did they seize power, steal our wealth, take away land, houses, and factories, carve up our country, pit us against one another, poison our minds, wean us from our past, rob us of our future, doom us to abject penury and slavery under the yoke of our powerful neighbors? How could it happen that, at our mighty rallies, in our irritation and impatience, in our yearning for change, in our dreams of prosperity for our land, we allowed these people who hate our land, who pray to foreign idols, who seek advice and blessing from their foreign masters—how could we allow them to seize power?

Brothers, we are late to awaken, late to come to clearly see our troubles. Our house is afire on all sides, and it is not with water that we will have to put out this fire, but with our own tears and blood. Shall we again allow civil discord, civil war—for the second time in this century? Shall we again cast ourselves into the maw of destruction, letting the millstones shatter the bones of the people— the backbone of Russia?

Young and old, let us awaken, let us come to our senses, let us stand as one for our country. Let us say No! to its invaders and despoilers. Let us put an end to our retreat; let us stand firm in our last line of defense.

We are launching a popular movement, and we summon to our ranks all those who have recognized the horrible affliction that has fallen upon our home- land . . .

Russia—our only and dear Motherland—cries out for help!

It is doubtful that this highly emotional appeal to save Russia by violently returning it to the old days deserved to be mentioned had it not been for its twelve signatories. Besides such well-known nationalist writ- ers as Valentin Rasputin, Yuri Bondarev, and Alexandr Prokhanov, it was also signed by two Afghan War generals, Deputy Minister of the Interior Boris Gromov and Deputy Minister of Defense Valentin Varen- nikov. The last-mentioned participated in the future coup, along with two other signatories and future junta members: Vasily Starodubtsev and Alexandr Tizyakov. The "Address" was less a theoretical justification of the necessity of a coup than a poetic and emotional appeal for it.

Yet all the parties in the coming catastrophe had committed errors. However unusual it may sound for conservatives, in this case they overes- timated the power of the written word (they were *Russian* conservatives, after all) and the propaganda potential of their artfully written appeal. But Yeltsin and the democrats miscalculated, too, thinking they were dealing with a crude, run-of-the-mill sample of chauvinist propaganda. Yeltsin called it "the cry of Yaroslavna," referring to the medieval Rus- sian epic in which the heroine bemoans the defeat of Russian warriors by the Polovets tribe. Coming from him, the comparison sounded somewhat sarcastic. Gorbachev, in Foros, continued to do nothing.

On August 16, Yeltsin, who opposed vertical links—from the Kremlin downward—went to Kazakhstan to set up horizontal ones.

With both Presidents absent, KGB Chairman Vladimir Kryuchkov held a secret meeting with the Minister of Defense, the Minister of the Interior, the Prime Minister, the Vice President, and the Speaker of

Parliament. The same day—August 18—the plotters' messengers flew to the Crimea to meet with Gorbachev. They found him incoherent. In the evening, among the military stationed in Moscow, there were persistent rumors of Gorbachev's serious illness.

Alexandr Yakovlev, the coauthor of perestroika, phoned Gorbachev in Foros on the evening of August 18. A day earlier, he had left the Party, publicly sounding a warning of the coming coup.

They fell on deaf ears. Everyone had already sounded them, including Shevardnadze the preceding winter—still, nothing happened. Maybe nothing would. Besides, it was August, a time for vacations, and a weekend, too, and it was hard to reach Moscow on the phone.

Although he had lost all of his Kremlin jobs, and now his Party card, too, Yakovlev nevertheless maintained a sort of relationship with Gorbachev. When he tried to talk to him seriously on August 18, Gorbachev would not listen. He merely complained to his ex-comrade of sharp pains in the lower back: "Must be arthritis . . ."

The next day Gorbachev's ailment was officially confirmed by his Kremlin courtiers, who referred to it as the reason for his inability to carry out his presidential tasks—and took over the ship of State.

Thus began the Three Days That Shook the World.

GORBACHEV VS. GORBACHEV
(August 19–21, 1991)

In revolts, as in novels, the ending is the hardest part.

—ALEXIS DE TOCQUEVILLE

"Who then are you?"
"Part of the power that would
Alone work evil, but engenders good."

—GOETHE, *Faust*

WE ARE writing this chapter in Moscow, amidst the participants and witnesses—who almost became victims—of the three-day spectacle that had finally jolted Russian history out of its ancient rut. Being here both helps and hinders our work, for the same reason: we are overwhelmed with testimony and hypotheses. The trial of the conspirators is yet to come. Alexandr Obolensky, a deputy in the Parliament disbanded immediately after the putsch, claims that the truth about it will not be known for generations—if ever. Many crucial junctures in Russian history have vanished into the fogs of the past, too: was Emperor Peter the Third killed in a drunken fight by the lover of his wife, the Empress, who would soon be known as Catherine the Great, or was he assassinated at her behest? Did Alexander the First know that the plotters—whom he supported—planned to kill his father, the Emperor Pavel? Did Lenin die a natural death or was he murdered at Stalin's orders? And how did Stalin himself die? He was planning a purge of his inner circle—did they preempt him? None of these questions have ever been fully answered. Would this also

be the lot of the question of Gorbachev's participation in the anti-Gorbachev plot?

Lev Sukhanov, Yeltsin's aide and confidant, told us that Gorbachev
himself insisted that the trial be held behind closed doors. Anticipating
events, Gorbachev also claims that some of the plotters would try to
blame everything on him. The word from the Russian White House is
that such claims stem from fear of being exposed. Yeltsin finds it particularly suspicious that Gorbachev, right after his return to Moscow, replaced the plotters with their First Deputies: Leonid Shebarshin as KGB
Chairman, Mikhail Moiseyev as Defense Minister, and Vasily Trushin as
Minister of the Interior. All of them had been involved in the coup, and
Yeltsin insisted that these three generals be removed the very next day.
One day would have been enough to shred the documents compromising
Gorbachev in all three ministries.

As we arrived in Moscow, the mysterious epidemic of alleged suicides
of high officials involved in the coup was continuing. It began with the
deaths of Minister of the Interior Boris Pugo, one of the chief plotters,
and his wife. They died the day after the coup's failure, minutes before
Yeltsin's four emissaries arrived to place Pugo under arrest. The quartet
included the famous economist Grigori Yavlinsky, a brilliant theoretician
but a man somewhat removed from reality, who was later interviewed by
the *Moskovsky Komsomolets* daily. The interview was entitled "Shot by
His Own Hand or by Someone Else's?"

According to Yavlinsky, the former minister was lying in a track suit
in a double bed and still seemed to be breathing. But Yavlinsky's attention was first drawn to Pugo's wife, who sat on the floor, leaning against
the bed. She bore numerous wounds, and her face was covered with
blood. Yavlinsky could not determine whether the wounds had been
caused by stabbing or shooting. Most of all he was surprised that the
medical team paid no attention to the dying woman, tending exclusively
to Pugo. Later on, it turned out that the ambulance personnel, summoned
by phone, had not even been allowed into the courtyard of Pugo's building. Where, then, did the medical team who treated the couple come
from? Pugo died on his way to the hospital; his wife, a few days later in
the intensive care ward of the Kremlin Hospital in Kuntsevo. Another
odd fact: Pugo's personal bodyguards had been withdrawn a few hours
before the deaths.

Yavlinsky left Pugo's apartment without waiting for the experts. At the
time, he registered some details that would later come back to him: three
empty shell casings on the floor, for example. (Later, Moscow police
sources revealed that there had been three bullets shot through Pugo's
head; those who arranged the "suicide" did not bother with plausibility.)
The light-gray handgun that the Pugos had allegedly used to kill them-

selves was placed neatly on the bedside table that neither the dying Pugo nor his wounded wife could reach. When a man shoots himself, the gun falls out of his hand—how can it be otherwise? Nor did the bloody mess on Mrs. Pugo's face look like a gunshot wound. Her movements were uncoordinated, she seemed incoherent—but Yavlinsky did not try to make out her words. At the time he was simply too shaken by what he saw and could not absorb any extra impressions, to say nothing of analyzing them. Much later, the question arose that no one could answer: even if we assume that Pugo killed himself, why would he kill his unfortunate wife, too, and so cruelly? Or was she a witness of her husband's murder?

The next day, the body of Marshal Sergei Akhromeyev, Gorbachev's military adviser, was pulled out of a noose in his Kremlin office. Suicide again. Along with Minister of Defense Yazov, Akhromeyev was Gorbachev's main liaison with the Army, and, as soon became known, participated in the plotters' most important councils. No one who knew him could recall any suicidal bent on his part; it was even harder to believe that the old soldier would have chosen the rope—if anything, he would have honorably shot himself. Artyom Borovik, who went to the Marshal's funeral, told us that none of the guests believed in the suicide version—least of all the widow.

Pugo and Akhromeyev's deaths were followed by a series of defenestrations of ex-Party executives. Nikolai Kruchina, the Central Committee's financial manager and Gorbachev's assistant in the Kremlin since the early days, was the first, supposedly leaping from the eighth floor. We were already in Moscow when he was followed by Georgi Pavlov and Dmitri Lisovolik, also Central Committee executives. We saw Kruchina's house and his landing spot—the flight trajectory looked too much like an arc, making one wonder if Kruchina had been assisted. A woman passing by commented, realizing what we were after: "He knew too much."

Each of these men indeed knew too much: about the coup preparations, about the Party riches smuggled abroad in rubles, dollars, and bullion.

When Kruchina's First Deputy was asked whether he was frightened by the suicides of his former colleagues and bosses, he replied, "If they tell you I threw myself out of my eighth-floor office—don't believe it."

We have not met one single person in Moscow who believed these were suicides—perhaps a few were, but certainly not all of them. Some fear for the lives of other conspirators, especially those now in jail. A career criminal, placed in the same cell with Vladimir Kryuchkov, tried to talk the former KGB Chief into hanging himself: "They're gonna sentence you to death anyhow." Equally worrisome is the fate of Anatoly Lukyanov, ex–Speaker of Parliament and Gorbachev's close friend since the university—on the second night of the coup, he claimed his ex-boss had been involved. Lukyanov became paralyzed on his left side, and after a brief stay in the prison hospital was transferred back to solitary. Since officially he did not belong to the junta, he was the last to be arrested. Telman Gdlyan, an ex–KGB investigator, considers the delay deliberate. Someone hoped that Lukyanov would panic and kill himself: "He can spill beans that would be more scary that the coup itself."

One of Gorbachev's aides, who chose to remain anonymous, told us that to his boss, Lukyanov is the most dangerous witness: if Lukyanov was capable of betrayal, Gorbachev must think, then he could stoop to slander, too. (Those outside of Gorbachev's inner circle understandably account for his fear differently.) Lukyanov's relatives said that he had taken extra security precautions in the few days between the debacle and his arrest, and was relieved to finally be arrested. His wife, however, does not believe he is safe in jail and told his investigator that she was "afraid of a catastrophe."

To the plotters, the only good witness was a dead witness. But such quick disappearances were too obvious an indication of foul play. Many Muscovites are convinced that a gang of hired assassins is operating, and prison walls are no obstacle. Naturally, those who know too much are prime targets. Of the dead, Pugo knew the most; what about those still alive? Again, Lukyanov is believed to head the hit list: the only way he can save his life is to tell the real story of the Three Days That Shook the World before he is done in. Others believe he can save himself only by remaining silent.

The putsch unfolded in three places and had three main characters: the putschists, Yeltsin, and Gorbachev. One character is collective: the putschists, who early in the morning of the 19th announced their takeover. Although in those three days they moved within a small area in the vicinity of Red Square—KGB headquarters, in Lubyanka; Army headquarters, near Arbat; and the Rossiya Hotel, across the street from St. Basil's—they operated primarily from the Kremlin, reckoning that holding the citadel was synonymous with holding power.

Yet by then a new power center had emerged and gained strength: the Russian White House, which housed Yeltsin and the Russian Parliament. Although Yeltsin had an office in the Kremlin, to the Kremlin Bosses this did not mean much: only a few months previously he was admitted through the Kremlin gate after several minutes of having the picture on his pass checked against an original, although by then one had to be from Mars not to know Boris Yeltsin's face. It was this battle between the Kremlin and Yeltsin's White House that had determined the preceding year of Russian history, and the putsch was the culmination of this conflict. And, if the Russian White House was run by Yeltsin, then the

Kremlin in those three days was commanded not by Gorbachev, but by his closest and most loyal assistants. He had handpicked them personally, had them confirmed in their jobs over parliamentary resistance, and, as he once said, "at this difficult turn in life [I] trusted them completely."

Accordingly, Gorbachev left the Kremlin and calmly headed for the Crimea, where he walked and swam until he was afflicted by ennui and back pain—radiculitis. It was then that he became the third leading character in our story.

Of the three, our hero is the easiest one to follow, minute by minute— he was in the view of the entire world. This absolves his biographers of the necessity of re-creating in detail what has been repeatedly described in the media. By now, everybody knows the main events: the sudden declaration of the coup, the farcical news conference, the angry crowds, the defiant speech by Yeltsin on top of the tank—"The reactionaries will not triumph!" he shouted—the hastily erected barricades by the crowds in front of the Russian White House, the refusal by key Army and KGB units to storm the barricades, the stream of interviews and telephone calls emanating from the White House to the rest of the waiting world, and Yeltsin's dramatic announcement to the Russian Parliament that the coup leaders were fleeing Moscow. At one point we thought we were losing our wits: one day, leaving the Russian White House, we saw Yeltsin speaking from the tank again—but it was an American actor in an American TV production!

When the state of emergency was announced, and power was seized by the GKChP (an acronym equally unwieldy in Russian—in fact, some jokers claimed that the difficulty of pronouncing it was the main reason for the coup's defeat), the real Yeltsin was in his dacha in Usovo, outside Moscow. The dacha is normally guarded by six to eight men with machine guns.

"I knew Yeltsin's every step," recalled Major General Victor Karpukhin, the commander of the Alpha Group entrusted with storming the White House and arresting Yeltsin.

Indeed, shortly before the coup Yeltsin was placed under intensive surveillance. His every move was monitored. The KGB went as far as to bug the telephones of his daughters and his tennis coach and even installed a hidden camera in Yeltsin's favorite sauna. After the coup's defeat, the investigators found a tape with Yeltsin's most private conversations in the safe in the office of Valery Boldin, Gorbachev's Chief of Staff. We do not know whether Gorbachev himself had a chance to listen to the tape.

"I monitored his every movement," General Karpukhin went on. "We could have arrested him at any time. He's got lousy bodyguards."

"Was there an order to kill Yeltsin?"

"No. Just to arrest him and hold him in isolation."

After the coup and Gorbachev's disappearance became known, Yeltsin's supporters began arriving in Usovo: his Prime Minister, Ivan Silayev; Speaker of the Russian Parliament Ruslan Khasbulatov; State Adviser for Defense Colonel General Konstantin Kobetz; and St. Petersburg Mayor Anatoly Sobchak. Later Sobchak would say that a platoon could have arrested the entire Russian leadership.

In Usovo, they composed the appeal to Russian citizens. They disagreed about the location of the center of resistance. Some thought it should have been right there, in their dachas in Usovo; others insisted they should go to the White House. Both options were fraught with risk. There was little hope of making their way to Moscow: all roads were jammed with tanks.

Then Khasbulatov said he was going straight to Moscow with the appeal. "You figure out the rest . . ." And he left in a private unmarked car, to avoid identification.

Sobchak insisted that they follow Khasbulatov: "We're still a presidential cortège . . . We'll put up the State flag and take off. We should not lose any more time."

Casting the crucial vote, General Kobetz supported Sobchak.

It was then, as she helped Yeltsin into the car, that his daughter Tanya said to him, "Don't worry, Dad. Now it all depends on you alone."

Twelve minutes after they were gone, the dacha was overrun by a KGB Special Unit that came to arrest Yeltsin. Perhaps the commander of Alpha told the truth—the delay was deliberate: "I did everything in my power to do nothing," he said. "I talked to the KGB leadership only on the radio. They really were on my back, forcing me to report my actions every minute. I told them I could not arrest him in the village: there would be witnesses, innocent people would be hurt. Although I want you to know that my boys are so well trained that no one would have noticed a thing. We had the entire village surrounded; all the roads were blocked off—yet we let the two Government limos leave."

One cannot rule out that the commander was trying to score a few points after the coup's failure. Or perhaps Boris Yeltsin is just lucky; a fairy-tale hero does not burn in fire, does not sink in water, and, even beaten, turns up a winner.

If that is the explanation, the trip from Usovo to Moscow was pure luck. A state trooper car was in front of them, forcing other cars, tanks, and armored vehicles to let them pass. Yeltsin's car, as befitted the President, was flanked by security. And still he could have been taken with ease.

Why wasn't he captured several hours—even a day and a half—later in the Russian White House? Everything was ready for the storming, including special KGB plane No.762612, assigned to fly Yeltsin to an unidentified destination.

General Karpukhin, the commander of Alpha, again:

"Were you ordered to storm the White House?"

"Yes. The evening of the 19th, there was a closed-door meeting at the Ministry of Defense, chaired by General Ochalov. Moiseyev and Akhromeyev were there, too, and Yazov came by a few times. I was ordered to lead the putsch. Under my command were a Ministry of Interior division, an OMON division [special counterterrorist troops], and three special KGB units—a total of 15,000 men."

"Were you monitoring the events taking place outside the White House?"

"Of course. We filmed everything. We had agents both among the defenders and inside the Parliament. At night, General Lebed and I toured the barricades. They were toys; we could have easily smashed them."

"What was the battle plan?"

"At three A.M. the OMON troops would clear the square. They would disperse the crowd with tear gas and water cannons. Our units would follow, from the ground and from the air, by using helicopters, grenade launchers, and other special means . . . Then we would take the building . . .

"My boys are practically invulnerable. The whole thing would be over in fifteen minutes . . . It was all up to me. Thank God I could not bring myself to do it. It would have been a bloodbath. I refused."

His second-in-command, Colonel Sergei Goncharov, agrees: "We could have taken the White House in fifteen to thirty minutes. But—I'm horrified even to think about it—the losses among the defenders would have been sky-high."

The commander of paratroopers, Colonel General Pavel Grachev, who, following a personal call from Yeltsin, crossed to his side the first morning of the coup, confirms that General Karpukhin was not in a rush to follow the junta's orders. "I'm not going to storm the building," he told Grachev over the phone. Yet the putschists themselves did not seem too bent on having their orders followed. Says Grachev: "The time to move the troops in was set on midnight of August 20. The assault was to start at three A.M.

"Now, the interesting part. Just before that all the putschists went to bed. We did not move in our paratroopers at midnight; an hour passes, another—no one calls. My deputies were cracking jokes: they must have gone to sleep, setting us up again, saddling us with responsibility."

What was going on here? Did it mean there was never a final order to storm the White House? Moreover, the State Commission to investigate the KGB actions during the coup never found this kind of an order in the KGB files. What happened?

The putschists may have had a change of heart after Air Force Commander General Shaposhnikov delivered an ultimatum, threatening to bomb the Kremlin if the White House were stormed. Or perhaps they had not expected passive resistance from their subordinates who had been charged with launching the coup proper—the same formerly rock-solid Alphas, who now were playing for time. Perhaps the putschists had blown their chance—they should have had Yeltsin seized in the very first hours. Later, with the White House surrounded by thousands of volunteers, it was too late, for Boris Yeltsin could have been captured only over the bodies of his defenders, and it appeared that no one wanted to pay such a price. Marshal Yazov was shaken to learn about the three slain demonstrators, so the first victims apparently served to prevent further bloodshed. The conspirators may have hesitated not because they were irresolute or incompetent but because they were neither tyrants nor hangmen; they were bureaucrats, not Stalinist killers. It must be noted, though, that they made the distinction between shooting demonstrators in distant Tbilisi or Vilnius and ones in Moscow, on their own doorstep.

They tried to set up emergency rule quietly and bloodlessly; instead they ran into unexpected resistance from Yeltsin and his supporters, both within and without the White House. They encountered, in addition to barricades, a human wall of dedicated men and women. After it was all over, the rightists circulated rumors that the White House had been defended by capitalist fat cats who shoved vodka and cash under the noses of tank drivers, and hard-currency hookers who offered to sleep with the soldiers.

"So what?" said our old friend, the poetess Yunna Moritz. "The soldiers were freezing their butts off in the tanks. The girls just tried to help them get warm."

Another poet, Eduard Limonov, who cannot stand Yeltsin and calls him a "crazy chieftain," described the scenes outside the White House: "It was kind of a pop musical, with tanks and democratic crowds as extras . . . The profiteers defended *their* regime. Hundreds of mafiosi roared on their bikes among the tanks, throwing wads of bills at the soldiers: 'Go away!' Someone brought a bevy of brave, gorgeous hookers and unleashed them on the barricades, from where they offered their bodies to the Taman Division tank drivers. If the putsch had been made by real putschists, this would have been the death toll for both rackets— prostitutes and mafiosi—but it was made by straight-up family men who did not even think to turn off the White House phones."

Spontaneous movements apart, democrats did conduct a well-planned campaign to subvert troops sent to the White House. According to Art-yom Borovik, Yeltsin supporters had not waged enough propaganda in the Army, a shortcoming that would cost them dearly should another coup occur. For example, they failed to win over General Varennikov, who found himself among the putschists through a misunderstanding.

We disagreed with Artyom, citing facts to the contrary, which the reader knows from previous chapters—Yeltsinites conducted work in the Army consistently and intensively. Later on, during the investigation, Marshal Yazov would complain he had no one to rely on: the Tula Division commander turned out to be a personal friend of Yeltsin's, other division commanders were turned around by Yeltsin personally during the putsch, and many others were hesitant. What kind of war was it when carnations were pushed into gun barrels, elderly women treated soldiers like their sons, and young women offered their bodies? Out-of-town soldiers, who had arrived in Moscow armed with tourist maps and did not know the Kremlin from the White House, were disarmed by Musco-vite hospitality.

One should add here Yazov's own order not to use firearms. And is it possible that Yeltsin exaggerated the danger to the White House in order to mobilize his supporters? Some Muscovites suggested that Yeltsin skill-fully cast himself as the sacrificial lamb and dramatized the putschists so brilliantly that when they saw the villain roles in store for them they turned away in horror.

Marshal Yazov, too, complained that "torrential rain and politicized crowds" would have caused excessive bloodshed.

General Kobetz, who headed the round-the-clock defense of the White House, agreed in a way. For rain, he said, he thanked God and His personal White House emissary—Father Gleb Yakunin, a dissident priest close to Yeltsin:

> Our major task [Kobetz said] was to prevent the advance unit of the 103rd KGB Paratrooper Division from breaking through and thus setting the scene for the A [Alpha] Group to storm the building. Our second task was to prevent a firefight. You understand that if shooting had broken out, we would not have lasted more than fifteen minutes. It would have been a sea of blood, no one would have surrendered—still . . .
>
> Shaposhnikov helped: he refused to provide them with helicopters. Gleb Yakunin must have helped by praying for our victory. God provided, too: in that kind of weather, helicopters could not have taken off anyway . . . It was raining heavily and the visibility was so poor that they could not have stormed us from the air. Definitely, it was divine intercession.
>
> Since the 103rd unit did not break through, the A Group could not storm either. They would have simply been unable to get through that crowd. It was

no disorganized mob—they were carefully divided into squads, platoons, and companies, and each unit knew its task. We even found time to train them, to let Alpha through first and then press them with bodies and disarm.

Perhaps the Alpha commander overestimated his team's professional capacity. According to another Alpha officer, Lieutenant Colonel Mikhail Golovatov, they did not even have a plan of the White House. The only thing they knew was that Boris Yeltsin's office was somewhere on the fifth floor. "We were supposed to find our bearings within two to three minutes and then carry on with our assignment."

We assume Golovatov never visited the White House, or else he would not have been so confident. We went there every day, the way people go to work, yet finding the section of the fifth floor that houses the offices of Yeltsin, Burbulis, and Sukhanov was always a headache. First you go up to the sixth floor, walk along a lengthy corridor, cross the dining room to another corridor, then go down to the fourth, take another long corridor, and only then do you make it to the staircase that you climb to the "Yeltsin" section of the fifth floor. The White House was deliberately designed as a maze: even if the troopers had found Yeltsin's floor, how would they have gotten out?

Besides, Yeltsin was not in his office during the siege. Kobetz twice begged him to leave the White House for a safer place. Yeltsin hugged the general and declared, "I'm staying here to the end."

The victory in this confrontation went to the more determined side—the defenders. They were prepared to fight to the bitter end; they would rather die than surrender. The plotters, by contrast, were not ready to shed blood, theirs or anyone else's. According to the brave General Kobetz, "The coup was made by people who were not sure of themselves." Further, he added, he preferred "to die right here rather than surrender."

Burbulis: "The feeling that the bullet meant for you has been stopped by your courageous fellow citizens while you yourself are unable to do anything to correct this injustice—that's the toughest."

Yeltsin felt similarly, and at the funeral he begged forgiveness from the parents of the three slain young men for having been unable to defend them.

Yeltsin addressed people, gave orders, and made appeals: In Gorbachev's absence he declared himself the Supreme Commander of the Armed Forces and proclaimed the putschists to be criminals. Gearing for defeat, he found time to form two backup governments in exile: One was to be headed by Russian Foreign Minister Andrei Kozyrev, the other by Russian Vice Prime Minister Oleg Lobov. The future leaders quickly left town: Kozyrev for America and Lobov for the Urals, where he set up headquarters in Point X, an underground military bunker in the woods outside Sverdlovsk.

Yet Yeltsin spent most of the three days on the phone, talking to President Bush and Prime Minister John Major, to his supporters, to hesitating generals, and to the confused plotters—"He spent hours with his phone glued to his ear." And not just Yeltsin; Gennady Burbulis and Ivan Silayev, General Kobetz and Father Yakunin—everyone was on the phone, putting out feelers, collecting information, cajoling, encouraging, threatening, blackmailing . . . Phones defeated tanks; words prevailed over bullets.

From the very onset, in his first address to the Russian people, Yeltsin demanded that Gorbachev be given an opportunity to address them. Shevardnadze demanded it, too, but he, who knew Gorbachev better and longer than Yeltsin, phrased it differently: he "demanded that Soviet President M. Gorbachev make a public speech on TV and give his opinion of the situation"—thus obfuscating whether the demand was addressed to the putschists or Gorbachev himself.

On August 22, the day after the failure of the putsch, three plotters—ex–Prime Minister Valentin Pavlov, ex–Defense Minister Dmitri Yazov, and ex–KGB Chairman Vladimir Kryuchkov—stated at the interrogation that on the eve of announcing a state of emergency the plotters had sent a delegation to see Gorbachev at Foros. The delegates found him rather incoherent and under medical care. All three insist that there was no anti-Gorbachev conspiracy, but, rather, a secret general agreement. According to Kryuchkov, Gorbachev told them they "could give it a shot," but he was in poor health, he claimed, and had to excuse himself. Pavlov recalls that "this was not the first time the President delayed his reaction. He always needed to go through it two or three times in order to make a decision." This was not Gorbachev's first cop-out; his role in the bloody events in Tbilisi, Baku, Vilnius, and Riga is still unclear.

Once Gorbachev's closest comrades declared a state of emergency on the morning of August 19, 1991, the media began to speculate that he had been arrested, that his Foros dacha was blocked, and he was cut off from the nation and the world.

We have at our disposal the unique testimony of Ivan Kolomytzev, the head of the Crimean KGB—someone required by his job to be omniscient. His interview appeared a few days after the coup failure in *Southern Courier,* a Crimean paper. For reasons unknown, it never reached the Moscow papers. Part of Kolomytzev's job was taking care of Gorbachev in the Crimea, be it routine protection or making a possible arrest.

The news of the coup, however, reached Kolomytzev the same way it reached other Soviets—through the TV news. Naturally, he was nervous: he had never received any special instructions through secret channels. He immediately called his boss, the Chairman of the Ukrainian KGB, which included the Crimean KGB; the latter had not received any orders from Moscow either, and told Kolomytzev to keep guarding Gorbachev, but with increased vigilance and combat readiness.

Exhausted by mounting uncertainty, Kolomytzev placed calls to other units responsible for protecting the President. His friends in the Border Guards told him that they had received no new orders: in other words, business as usual. The Special Section of the Navy had no new information either. Sailors from the Coast Guard calmed Kolomytzev down: they were watching Gorbachev through binoculars, they said; he was taking his usual walks on the beach. Later, they told Kolomytzev that Gorbachev was taking long swims, which was rather frivolous of him considering his complaints of radiculitis. However, he continued risking his health, and after taking a swim with his bodyguards, went for another one, with his granddaughter. This was later confirmed by other witnesses, including Gorbachev's closest aide, Georgi Shakhnazarov. The coup did not seem to disrupt Gorbachev's vacation with his wife, his daughter, his son-in-law, and his granddaughters. All his servants and bodyguards were at his side; according to his later confession, he had ordered the guards to shoot any intruder without warning.

The *Courier* interviewer was surprised. "You mean the President and his guards were never arrested?"

That's the thing: Gorbachev could have been arrested only by Kolomytzev's officers, but, according to Kolomytzev, "from the moment the Emergency Committee was established, we never got one order from Kryuchkov or his deputies."

The reporter reminded him that Gorbachev's dacha had been blocked, allegedly by different units. By whom, specifically?

By no one, it turns out. "I sent one of my officers there; he did not see anything. We called the Border Guards: they reported no additional units invading the perimeter. Our active unit at the gate [of the dacha] did not register anything either."

Kolomytzev rejected outright the rumor that the Sevastopol KGB regiment allegedly had participated in sealing off the dacha. There was no such unit, he stated. "I'm in charge of the entire Crimean KGB, and I'm telling you that the only personnel I have is the city KGB section and no other troops."

What about the naval blockade of the dacha?

"As for the Navy," the talkative KGB man went on, "I called Rear Admiral Prokopchuk, the Special Section Chief for the Navy, on the very first morning, August 19, to ask him if he had any orders through the chain of command of military counterintelligence, and what he knew about the commander of the Navy's plans and intentions. He told me he had the same information as I did, and had received no special directives. I asked him if he had been ordered to place his forces on any kind of alert; he said he had received no such orders. My colleague, the Special Section Chief for the Navy, stated officially that he had received no report of it either, on paper or in reality."

All this information comes from Ivan Kolomytzev, who collected it through his agents in the Navy, in the Border Troops, and among the guards—through the so-called special sections. Information does not get any more reliable than that.

To be on the safe side, the pedantic Crimean KGB Boss added that he had no information on goings-on behind the closed gate—that is, on the dacha grounds proper; he had his agents there, too, but he could not get in touch with them. We know already, from the Gorbachevs themselves, that the guards remained loyal to the President. Several days after the putsch, a major in charge of the dacha guards said unequivocally on the *Vzglyad* (Glance) TV program that "there was no house arrest."

The loyal officer, Ivan Kolomytzev, was worried about loss of contact with his agents inside Foros. Having ascertained that Gorbachev was not under arrest and the dacha was not sealed off either by land or by sea, Kolomytzev nevertheless put his subordinates on combat alert—just in case the situation in Moscow heated up and the President decided to go there in person and influence the course of events. Kolomytzev expected the free, healthy President to do just that, and kept his "boys" ready to lend him a hand. Consequently, he was worried about the lack of contact with the dacha—for the first time the Crimean KGB had no idea what was going on there. It was just not possible that at a time like this Gorbachev would do nothing but go for walks and swim! Were these walks or swims diversionary tactics, aimed at misleading someone?

Kolomytzev could not make contact even with the guards in Miskhor, the town next to Foros. Finally, he sent a unit to Foros, but the guards, still loyal to Gorbachev—thirty-two soldiers headed by General Medvedev—would not let other friendly troops inside. A major interagency conflict had broken out, and, from Kolomytzev's point of view, there could not have been a worse time for it.

Finally, what happened to communications? Kolomytzev found out that the KGB's automatic special channel in Yalta was turned off, and switched over to the manual mode: it was up to the operator to let the calls through or not. The local KGB was barred from calling Foros. And who decided whether the calls would reach Foros or not? In the manual mode, it could be reached only through ATS-1, the emergency Kremlin exchange. What about Foros—could its inhabitants make outside calls if they needed to?

All Kolomytzev's testimony is confirmed not only by indirect sources, but also by the sources even more direct than he. Here is the secret log of the KGB Special Section in charge of Government Communications:

AUGUST 18

17:55. As ordered by Comrade A. G. Beda [KGB head of Government Communications], channels of communication with Yalta and Foros from Kiev, Simferopol, and Sevastopol are switched to the manual mode [i.e., through an operator].

20:00. All channels switched to the manual mode.

AUGUST 19

15:14. Com. Beda orders to disconnect all of Comrade Yeltsin's telephone lines.

15:25. As per Com. Beda, Comrade Yeltsin's lines have been disconnected.

22:02. Received a call from Bush in Washington to connect him to Gorbachev. Call reported to Com. Volkov [Beda's deputy].

22:17. From Com. Volkov: Offer Bush to connect him to Com. Yanayev, the acting president, instead.

22:21. American side rejected the offer to talk to Yanayev. Would talk only to Gorbachev. Reported to Com. Volkov.

AUGUST 20

13:42. A call from Bush in Washington to connect him to Yeltsin. Reported to Com. Volkov.

13:44. Mr. Mitterrand in Paris would like to talk to Mr. Gorbachev. Reported to Com. Volkov.

14:07. From Com. Volkov: In response to Bush's request, no connection.

14:07. From Com. Volkov: In response to Mitterrand's request, offer instead to connect to Com. Yanayev.

14:17. We explained to Washington again that we are looking for Com. Yeltsin and his line.

14:40. Mitterrand has personally reached the Moscow operator and asked if she had any information about Gorbachev. After the negative answer, Mitterrand hung up. Reported to Com. Volkov.

16:55. Another request from Washington to connect to Com. Yeltsin. Reported to Com. Volkov.

AUGUST 21

13:04. Following Beda's order, Com. Yeltsin's line turned back on.

Although this log of the Kremlin's special communications speaks for itself, two facts are of interest here. One, there was an order to turn off all Com. Yeltsin's lines, reversed after the coup failure. No such orders were given regarding Com. Gorbachev's lines.

Second, even with his phone lines dead, Yeltsin still managed to spend hours on the phone. He talked to his family, persuading them not to come to the Russian White House; to St. Petersburg's mayor, Anatoly Sobchak; to ex–Foreign Minister Eduard Shevardnadze, to whom he complained: "I have *almost* all the lines turned off, I can't reach the rest of Russia."

Almost is the operative word here.

Moreover, when Comrades Beda and Volkov refused to patch President Bush through to both Yeltsin and Gorbachev, Bush and Yeltsin had already established a telephone link. According to Yeltsin's aides, he had rarely talked as much on the phone as he did in those three days. Thus, contrary to the KGB log, not *all* Yeltsin's lines were switched off.

We have no information that there was no telephone communication between Foros and the outside world; we know only that one of the phone systems was switched to the manual mode. What about the others? The communications system at the Soviet President's disposal is of course more diverse and effective than one available to any of his subjects, including the out-of favor Yeltsin.

In the story of her Foros woes, Raisa Gorbachev mentions the arrival of the plotters at the dacha around five P.M. on Sunday, August the 18th. According to her, by then all the telephones at the dacha were already dead, including the "red" one: the line of the Supreme Commander of the Armed Forces.

"Everything was turned off, including TV and radio," Raisa Maksimovna complains, obviously dramatizing the situation: after all, theirs was a regular TV that could receive the signal with an indoor or outside antenna. A talkative and careless woman, she let her tongue slip later in the same interview—several times.

First she spoke of some "demands that Mikhail Sergeyevich was constantly passing on to Moscow." So he did have a channel of communication with the capital after all. Second, she mentioned the putschists' press conference on TV, evidently forgetting that their TV had been spitefully turned off. She is a bit like Lady Macbeth who on one occasion mentions having breast-fed her children, while on another we learn she had no children. In commenting upon this contradiction, Goethe believed that Shakespeare cared more about the power of each speech and hardly thought that someone would pore over the text.

The Soviet First Lady got caught before she came to talk of her children. The interviewer was surprised: "Did you see the press conference on TV?"

"Yes," she said without batting an eye. "By the evening of the 19th, after our persistent demands, they turned it back on."

This brings up a number of questions. The main one is, if the people closest to the President—his servants and his guards—remained loyal to him, who, then, were the mysterious "they" at whom the demands were aimed? By the way, Gorbachev, more careful and calculating than his wife, does not mention the TV's being turned back on either in his memoirs or in his press conferences; instead, he insists that they learned all the news from foreign Russian-language stations. They listened to them on a shortwave radio that he managed to put together with his son-in-law.

By the way, Yakovlev, Shakhnazarov, and Gorbachev's aide, Arkady Volsky, managed to reach Gorbachev on the phone on the evening of August 18, when all the lines to the dacha were allegedly turned off. Oddly, Gorbachev did not mention the plotters' visit to them. "I kept picking up one phone after another," he said to his wife at five P.M. that day. "All lines dead. Even the red one."

"The tension around us mounted," said Raisa Gorbachev concerning the second day of their captivity. "We were in complete isolation. No one was allowed either in or out of the dacha."

According to the KGB, who were monitoring the dacha from land, sea, and air, the Foros citadel was not all that impregnable; in particular, on August 19, 117 vehicles went through. Nor was the link to the world outside broken on the following days.

"We had a line to the Crimea," confidently states Gorbachev's Party Deputy Vladimir Ivashko, who talked to Gorbachev on the phone in those days. In the White House we were told that Yeltsin, too, had been able to reach the dacha on the phone on August 19, but his timing was not good: he was told that the President was resting.

There is information about many other calls. For example, when Foreign Minister Bessmertnykh was invited to join the junta and refused, Kryuchkov immediately picked up the phone and called to tell someone about it. He sounded as if he was reporting it to his boss. The rest of the junta were at his side. Who could have been on the line but Gorbachev? Perhaps it was Bessmertnykh's refusal—and his subsequent blabbing of its circumstances—that cost him his job.

On August 21, when the putsch was running out of steam, Yuri Golik, then the Chairman of the Soviet President's Committee on the Coordination of Law Enforcement Agencies, summoned other committee members, including Kryuchkov's First Deputy, Yevgeny Ageyev, who was involved in the coup and would later be arrested. The committee decided to open a criminal case against the junta. That shocked Ageyev so badly that he immediately rushed to report it to someone on the phone. His boss, Kryuchkov, and other plotters were already aboard the plane on their way to Foros; and whom else would Ageyev report to—another deputy?

Yuri Golik himself believes that "the so-called Emergency Committee"—the junta—"is but the tip of an iceberg. Someone was leading the plotters and withdrew into the shadows for reasons we do not know; but the engine of the plot, however rusty and out of tune, was puffing along and could not be stopped. Then the junta attempted to take the initiative. Or perhaps they just hoped to wing it. There was no way to back out of it."

But we are slightly ahead of our narrative. Going back to Gorbachev's telephonic woes in Foros, we already mentioned in the introduction the letter that Valentin Zanin, director of the Leningrad-based Signal Company, had written three days after the putsch's failure.

"I have acquainted myself with the explanation that M. S. Gorbachev gives in the papers," Zanin wrote, "and I must say that it is impossible to cut off the Soviet President's communications in this manner. I am in the business of manufacturing communication systems, and it is impossible to isolate a President who is alive and unfettered without disassembling, removing, and carting away the main equipment—tons of it—which, according to reports, was not done. Thus we are talking about voluntary failure to communicate."

Besides his written statement, Zanin added the following orally: "You should realize that this is no dacha, or, in any event, it's more than just a dacha. It is one of the main control panels of the country, housing numerous communications systems that function autonomously. If you turn off the power, a local generator will be turned on; if it breaks down, you can turn on an accumulator. If the accumulator is disabled, you can feed the communications system from a manual mechanism. There is another system that I cannot mention here. All the President needs to secure connections with the country is a pen and a piece of paper. If Gorbachev is telling the truth, then I, as well as many other designers of such systems, as well as whole groups of people who worked on them—should be fired immediately, or perhaps even criminally charged, because millions—perhaps billions—of rubles have been spent on creating these systems."

This statement was rebutted by Nikolai Andreyev, Chief of the KGB's Eighth Directorate—a person who should really know whether Gorbachev's Foros communications were switched off or not. "It is possible to turn off communications on Gorbachev's Crimean dacha," Andreyev said, glossing over the issue whether it had actually been done.

The discussion became irrelevant to the core of the issue. Indeed, the KGB might have additional capabilities unknown to the engineers who designed the Foros system. Yet it would seem like the simplest thing in the world for Gorbachev's KGB subordinate to confirm his boss's statement in plain terms. Andreyev did not; he merely said that the KGB had the capability to do so. By dodging the direct question, he indirectly yet unequivocally let on that the connection had not been switched off.

The contact was alive, the dacha was not blocked off, Gorbachev was not arrested—unless he had himself arrested. Later, at an investigation, ex–Defense Minister Marshal Yazov would say, implicitly on behalf of the entire junta, "If betraying the President is equivalent to betraying the Motherland, I have not committed such a crime."

Thus, in Foros, the first two days of the coup—August 19 and 20—passed amidst the usual calm. The President walked, swam, played with his granddaughter—his usual leisure activities, watched by the Navy observers. What they could not see was Gorbachev working. We have information that 117 vehicles arrived in Foros on August 19. Unfortunately, we do not have a similar number for the next day, but, judging by observations, Gorbachev was not exactly a hermit on that day either. We have enough evidence to suggest that the telephone line between Moscow and Foros was quite busy—perhaps no less than Yeltsin's, though Gorbachev's communications were less diverse without international calls.

On August 21 things in Foros changed radically. No more walks on the beach, no long swims, no playing with the granddaughter—at least none of these activities were recorded by curious Navy personnel with their binoculars. It was a boring day for them. The Special Sections—i.e., the KGB—were not entertained, either: there was no information on the President's moves. Whatever was taking place, it was inside the dacha, unseen by the snoops. For the Gorbachevs it was the most unsettling day of the putsch—perhaps of their entire lives.

For us, outsiders, it was the most mysterious day.

As we know from Gorbachev's words, up to the 21st his wife carried herself well, even assuming the leadership of Fortress Foros—he called her "our Minister of the Interior." We do not know what sort of duties this job involved, but with no direct evidence we must reject the suggestions that Raisa Gorbachev was the chief conspirator—the person behind the coup. This hypothesis, circulated widely in Moscow's political and artistic milieu, owes more to suspicions and prejudice than to fact.

Raisa Gorbachev had never been popular with her subjects, serving as something of a scapegoat for the general crisis. She undoubtedly knows more about the events in Foros than she reveals—Gorbachev himself said that he had no secrets from her. We also know about her habit of interfering in politics, for which she was often attacked by Yeltsin. Finally, her Lady Macbeth–sized ambitions are no secret; if we consider that on August 20 the Union Treaty was scheduled to be signed, leading to a long-awaited nationwide presidential election six months later, we would be hard put to say which would be a steeper comedown: for Gorbachev to become a regular citizen or for his wife to lose her First Ladyship.

We do not discount these speculations; but they are not sufficient evidence for accusations. Nor do we wish to delve into the Gorbachevs' family life. Is he indeed under her thumb? Is she indeed his evil demon? Which of them did what in Foros is another question. We are more interested in the role of Foros in the August putsch.

One could say that in the first two days the Gorbachevs behaved either courageously or followed their calm, unworried routine—it depends on one's general concept of the Foros situation. The level of anxiety there rose only on the third day—right after the defenders of the Russian White House spent their sleepless, anxiety-ridden night. Their fortress was not stormed, whether owing to weather conditions or because in the last analysis the attackers rated Yeltsin's political chances higher than Gorbachev's. It was only after the tide turned and the fate of the coup became more or less clear, when, after aimlessly circling Moscow streets and boulevards, the tanks and armored troop carriers began moving out of Moscow—only then did Foros grow really agitated.

Raisa Maksimovna was the first to break down, depriving Fortress Foros of its "Minister of the Interior": ". . . when we realized that the putschists were being defeated, we decided to take no action that might lead to a shoot-out that in turn would pose danger to Mikhail Sergeyevich's life," she recalls. In another interview she describes her own condition on that day: "On the 21st, I felt much worse . . . I felt that a tragic ending was near. I had an acute hypertension crisis, with partial loss of speech."

What was wrong? Why were the spouses frightened by the failure of the coup rather than by the coup itself? Was it still the case of Caesar laughing and Pompeius crying? This time, though, it was Pompeius laughing.

What "tragic ending" was Ms. Gorbachev talking about? On the 21st it became clearer every minute that the farce was inexorably moving to a happy ending. In the wee hours, Burbulis called Kryuchkov, who assured him there would be no storming: "You can go to sleep." The Moscow City Government declared the curfew illegal. Defense Minister Yazov signed an order for the troops to return to their bases, and by eight in the morning, accompanied by applause and booing, the tanks began moving out of the capital. At 10 A.M. the Russian Parliament opened its session, and Yeltsin made a speech. At 2:20 P.M. Yeltsin declared that the plotters were heading for the Vnukovo airport, and from there on to Foros. Yeltsin's emissaries, headed by his Vice President, Alexandr Rutskoy, and Prime Minister Ivan Silayev, also flew to Foros. The dacha denizens awaited their visitors with anxiety.

The most striking feature of this flurry of activity is that both sides—the plotters and the democrats—took the same route to Foros (at least they used different planes). Yeltsin's people were flying to bring the President back to the capital. What was the Gorbachevites' mission? To report? To beg forgiveness? Forgiveness for what?

Foros is the central mystery of the putsch. That is where it sprang into action—the talk between the putschists and Gorbachev in the evening of August 18. And that is where it died—they went back to inform Gorbachev that the coup had failed. In the interim were the three days of intense phone calls between the Kremlin and Foros. Upon returning to Moscow, Gorbachev carelessly said, "I will never tell the whole story." He also claimed to have called the plotters "assholes."

We tend to believe he did. The question is, *when* did he call them assholes, and for *what?* Was it when they reported that a putsch was about to begin—or when it became clear that it had failed? Why did Gorbachev consent to see them on August 18, then conduct regular negotiations with them on August 19 and 20, then refuse to see them on August 21, preferring to see Yeltsin's team instead? Was it Gorbachev who betrayed the plotters or did the plotters betray Gorbachev? Where was the control center of the coup, in the Kremlin or in Foros?

Even if Gorbachev had not been the secret mastermind of the plot, on August 21, when it ran out of gas, he had more than enough reasons to be scared. Consider this:

One. The junta was made up of his protégés and friends, who were his sole power base and the entire national leadership (with or without him): Vice President, Prime Minister, KGB Chief, Defense Minister, Minister of the Interior, and, perhaps, Speaker of the Parliament. Even if Gorbachev had not been involved, he was fully responsible for the people whom he had promoted to power and who were accountable to him. Let us recall that in the early '60s the entire British Government had to resign just because Defence Minister John Profumo had shared a call girl with a Soviet agent. And what about Watergate, which pales next to Forosgate? Should the sympathies of the reader of this chapter still lie with Gorbachev, let him or her imagine that a coup was attempted in the United States, headed by the Vice President, the Secretary of State, the Secretary of Defense, the FBI and CIA Directors, and the President's Chief of Staff—and the President himself is under suspicion. Could the President avoid impeachment?

Two. The idea of emergency powers and emergency rule, briefly implemented during the putsch in a halfhearted (and half-assed) manner, had been long cherished by Gorbachev himself. It was his obsession, as was pointed out in the previous chapter (incidentally, written before the putsch). It is hard to trace back the exact date of its genesis in his panicked mind. With the decline of his popularity and the rise of Yeltsin's, with the threat of direct presidential elections becoming more real, the idea ripened in his mind into something concrete and inevitable: objectively, as the only way of preventing the country from falling into anarchy and ruin; subjectively, as the only way for him personally to stay in power. This motivational duality distinguished Gorbachev from the official plotters—they had only the objective reason.

In order to get to the bottom of the August events, it is not enough to de-heroicize Yeltsin and his comrades. We must also "rehabilitate" the putschists, at least terminologically, from villains into ordinary mortals. Whatever epithets were thrown at them by the outraged Soviet media and politicians, in their own minds the conspirators were either "the saviors of the Motherland" (if they acted of their own free will) or "sacrificial lambs" (if they had been forced to follow orders). The group probably included both categories. Pugo, Kryuchkov, and Yazov belonged to the former, while Yanayev, who could not keep his hands from shaking at the press conference; Pavlov, with his soaring blood pressure; and, finally, Lukyanov, who broke down under pressure and later, in jail, became partially paralyzed—these were more likely to think of themselves as lambs.

When Gorbachev's Deputy, Vladimir Ivashko, learned of the coup, he called Lukyanov early in the morning of the 19th. "I think they're bluffing," Lukyanov said, and only a few hours later declared that Gorbachev was involved in what he termed as the "lowlifes' plot." Whatever the investigation reveals, in the last moment Lukyanov managed to slip away from the "bluffers" who, he thought, included his old friend Gorbachev: he was not a part of the official junta and did not show up at the press conference. Prime Minister Pavlov claimed he had been dragged in against his will, while Vice President Yanayev—who had been a Soviet President for three whole days—claimed he had been subjected to pressure for several hours and threatened with a "tribunal." All these statements were made *during,* rather than after, the putsch, and show that at least some of its participants were thoroughly lost. They had been shanghaied into the adventure and qualify as scapegoats.

If this is indeed the case, and some of the putschists were lured into the plot against their will, then others decided to take the plunge, thinking that it was no putsch at all—doesn't a real putsch have to be against a legitimate government? But they *were* the government—Ministers of Defense and the Interior, KGB Chief, Prime Minister, and so on—perhaps up to the President himself. At least some if not all of them thought, like Lukyanov, that Gorbachev was on their side and was staying out for purely tactical reasons. Didn't Yanayev say confidently at the August 19 press conference that Gorbachev "upon recovery will resume his duties"? Moreover, Yanayev solemnly declared that "we will follow the course he started in 1985." Really, who was grilling this three-day-wonder for information? They just asked about Gorbachev's fate—and Yanayev volunteered that he and other junta members were loyal to the country's President. Committed by the State's top officials, who, on top of it, swear loyalty to the country's leader, promise to continue his policies, and return him to the throne—what kind of a coup could that be?

The list of rebuttals is growing: no one sealed off the Foros dacha, no one turned off its communications with the world, no one arrested or dethroned Gorbachev. Thus, there was no coup in the strict sense of the word. If there was one, it was, rather, preemptive, in view of the pending presidential election that Gorbachev did not have a chance of winning.

Of course, his comrades were motivated not only by loyalty to him and the desire to keep him in power; more important to them was the idea of order, the desire to save the country from disintegration and self-destruction; one might even call it responsibility to the people. The "overt" plotters can be viewed as idealists—dreamers—utopians; it is harder to fathom Gorbachev's chief motivation, if he was indeed part of the conspiracy. Was it concern for the nation or for his own power? In any event, it was not a coup against Gorbachev; it was a coup against freedom, and Gorbachev had headed it long before August 1991.

If we consider as rehearsals the massacres in Georgia, Azerbaijan, Lithuania, and Latvia, and the occupation of his own capital to prevent pro-Yeltsin rallies, then the August events should be regarded as a logical consequence of Gorbachev's policy of further bolstering his power. If Tbilisi and Baku were rehearsals, what was the August coup d'état? History will show whether it was a first night that bombed or a dress rehearsal that would be followed by a real opening, in which the director would eliminate the glitches.

In this regard, a surprising speech was made by Gorbachev's personal aide, Georgi Shakhnazarov, on the afternoon of August 21 at the emergency session of the Russian Parliament. The so-called plot had failed by then, and the plotters had embarked on their mysterious mission to Foros.

Speaking on Gorbachev's behalf, Shakhnazarov denounced the methods employed in proclaiming the state of emergency. "Such measures must be taken within the framework of the law," he said. "Today our task is to save the country." He compared the situation to a plane in a dive: "It is extremely hard to pull the plane out of it. We need emergency measures to set the country on an even course. We will undoubtedly need a committee that, acting with the approval of the Russian Supreme Soviet"—Gorbachev-Shakhnazarov's only concession to the audience—"will take upon itself the task of bringing the situation under control."

Shakhnazarov, who had no status, prestige, or power of his own, supported the idea of a state of emergency and a Committee of Salvation as both vital and inevitable. It was the methods of Kryuchkov, Pugo & Co. that were branded as false. If that indeed reflects Gorbachev's point of view, it means that the disagreement between him and the Eight were tactical—for example, the timing and the ritual of introducing emergency rule—rather than strategic. Perhaps that was the reason he called his subordinates assholes.

For example, Prime Minister Pavlov, shortly after his arrest, admitted on his way to jail that he had no idea what had happened. Gorbachev, he claimed, had promised to hold a session of the USSR Supreme Soviet on September 16 and officially announce the state of emergency, then suddenly changed his mind and adjourned the session to August 26. But this was exactly the date on which Lukyanov was convoking the Supreme Soviet in his August 19 directive, published in the papers, along with the reason for the session: "the introduction of the state of emergency." Does it mean that the emergency session had been agreed on with Gorbachev even before the "coup"? (In the light of all the doubts we have cast in the course of our investigation, we are now forced to put the word in quotation marks.)

The Russian Parliament deputies told us that after Shakhnazarov's speech the audience exploded. Another Gorbachev aide we spoke to was angry with Shakhnazarov for a different reason—his indiscretion had put the President on the spot. But it is clear even without Shakhnazarov's speech or Pavlov's confession that the idea of the state of emergency had not come out of the blue on the eve of August 19, but had been brainstormed, developed, formulated, and implemented in bits and pieces for at least the two preceding years. And Gorbachev himself was behind it. No one else could implement the idea by transforming his presidential powers into emergency rule. That was one of the reasons for Gorbachev to be alarmed: even if we assume that he was not directly involved in the "coup," its failure brought to light all of his previous schemes and intentions with striking clarity.

Three. For Western viewers, *Three Days in August* was an exciting, made-for-TV thriller, with colorful heroes and villains, with a cliff-hanger plot and a happy end. For the Soviet people, it was a radio show: Radio Liberty, BBC, Voice of America, and the Deutsche Welle covered the situation nonstop, live, and in Russian, interspersing the reports with rumors and commentaries. Like the rest of the Soviet people, the Prisoner of Foros was glued to the radio. That is where he heard the "mad theory"—that the anti-Gorbachev plot was spearheaded by Gorbachev himself. It was one thing when the theory was proclaimed by people like Georgian President Zviad Gamsakhurdia; or Sakharov's widow, Elena Bonner; or by world chess champion Gary Kasparov—no love lost there. But it was a different story when it was announced with conviction by people like his buddy Anatoly Lukyanov and his ex–Foreign Minister Shevardnadze—ones who were close to him and knew him well. Whether their suspicions were founded or not, their very existence had to alarm Gorbachev. For, if proven, his participation in the plot meant high treason.

Four. Raisa Gorbachev described her husband's and her own torments on August 21: "The BBC reporter said that Kryuchkov had agreed that a delegation would fly to the Crimea—not just to meet Gorbachev, but to see that he was indeed in poor health, that he was disabled. I thought that that lie could be followed shortly by certain actions intended to turn it into reality. I felt that a tragic ending was near. I had an acute hypertonic crisis, with partial loss of speech."

Here, we should believe Raisa Gorbachev: the report of the Moscow delegation flying out to the Crimea—two delegations, they soon learned—sent the Gorbachevs reeling. The question is, What specifically did they fear?

Raisa hints that they thought the purpose of the Moscow delegation was to kill her husband—to "disable" him in the fullest sense of the word. That was nonsense, of course: just as no one arrested Gorbachev in Foros, no one planned to murder him there, either—especially not after announcing the trip to the entire world. The Gorbachevs knew this better than anyone else: they had obedience-trained Kryuchkov & Co. for many years. Besides, it was the same trip to Foros that Yeltsin had demanded from the beginning—to examine Gorbachev the pseudo-patient and give him a chance to speak to the Russian people. Now, finally, Kryuchkov agreed to the trip. Gorbachev should have been excited about his coming liberation. Instead, he panicked.

Was he afraid that the doctors would not find any back ailment and that he would be exposed as a malingerer?

Or else, having learned there were two planes on the way—one filled with the plotters, the other with liberators—he did not know how to receive either one? Whose side to take?

Or he did know whom to back—he had waited three days to pick a winner—but now he was afraid that the plotters, whom he had betrayed, who now were like puppets without their master, would denounce him to the liberators?

Was he afraid of falling into a trap he himself had set for others?

Was he afraid that his alibi—his self-isolation at Foros—would not convince his rescuers, even with evidence like an appeal to the people that he had taped, and the seventy-two-page memoir he had slapped together?

On the other hand, were Yeltsin's emissaries really coming to free him or to arrest him along with other conspirators?

Too many questions. And the answer to all of them was the white-knuckle fear that had spread across Foros.

THIS CHAPTER contains more questions than answers.

The Gorbachev drama has had a happy ending: finally free, he returned late at night to a liberated Moscow.

The plotters have been arrested, and Gorbachev is testifying, either as a victim or as a witness—it is not clear which.

He has set up his own presidential commission to investigate the "coup" and insists that the trial be held behind closed doors, lest State secrets be divulged.

In the Russian White House, the subject is taboo. Even talkative Sukhanov refuses outright to discuss those three days, though he spent them at Yeltsin's side. We feel we have run into a wall. But there is plenty of curiosity: the putsch chapter, yet unwritten, was the main reason Yeltsin asked to see our manuscript. Perhaps they wanted to appear disinterested, so as not to inadvertently influence the investigation, but finally one of Yeltsin's supporters, unable to hold back, remarked on the "mad theory." "In America, your guys know everything better than we do. Bush knows everything. He knew from the start that the coup was doomed. Just be patient—it's not time yet."

So our plot has a happy ending without a real *dénouement*. It's not time yet.

We know who the hero of August was—Boris Yeltsin. His triumph over the conspirators exceeded even his election victory and endowed his reign with an extra dose of legitimacy. Henceforth his real inauguration date would be the 19th of August, when he made his speech from the tank, instead of the official July the 10th. The country had voted for a President and a knight in armor had shown up in addition.

Who, then, was the villain, if villain there was?

Whatever his name, he was, without realizing it, "part of the power that would alone work evil, but engenders good." A midwife to history, a catalyst to dissolve stagnation, a street sweeper for the nation, he ended up by wrecking everything he had launched a coup to retain: the Empire, the ideology, the Party, the KGB.

Out of the events of August grew a profusion of theories and hypotheses. We will limit ourselves to facts and questions.

Meanwhile Russian history continues to race away at breakneck speed, perhaps toward its finale.

Anxiety over the future is displacing the euphoria of victory. The hero of the August revolution has no respite in which he can bask in his triumph. He is being overwhelmed by an avalanche of worries and by accusations of self-betrayal. The world is waiting for him to perform tremendous deeds, but fears that a new coup may succeed thanks to the apparently never-ending economic and political chaos.

Vladimir Solovyov presented the hero of our book with a copy of his futurological novel, *Operation Mausoleum,* a description of a successful coup d'état. He inscribed the book: "To Boris Nikolayevich Yeltsin, who prevented this work of fiction from becoming reality."

Solovyov paused and added: "For now." And signed his name.

THE MINEFIELD OF POWER
(Fall–Winter 1991)

*"Hannibal, you know how to win, but will you be able to take
advantage of your victory?"*

LIVY

*Those who give the first shock to the system are the first to be
overwhelmed in its ruins.*

MONTAIGNE

THE MAP in Yeltsin's office was dotted with colored pins. The President
used them to indicate crisis areas, social disturbances, or ethnic conflicts.
It did not seem to ruffle him that one could barely see the map for the
pins; he seemed to welcome the challenge in a boyish manner—or else he
hadn't played enough war games as a child, and was catching up. We
heard people sneer, "He's only good to jump from the bridge in a sack
or to orate from tanks." A newspaper cartoon showed Yeltsin asking his
assistants to move his desk atop an active volcano.

In peacetime a map dotted with pins reminds one of playing with toy
soldiers, but the era of the downfall of the Soviet Empire could hardly be
called peaceful. Russia may have been experiencing a vivid, monitory
memory of the excesses of the past, and was without question in a deep
recession; nonetheless blood continued to flow and chaos continued to
spread. With the Party disbanded and the KGB bridled, the only systems
that once embraced and held together this vast space like hoops around
a barrel were gone or almost gone. In other words, the situation was
custom made for Boris Yeltsin, who loved nothing better than emergen-

cies—the more horrendous the better. He now saw himself as being involved in a war—against economic collapse, panic, famine, decline, death. The situation was so hopeless that Russian analysts were said to fall into two categories: pessimists and skeptics. Against this grim background, Yeltsin's optimism—things will get worse but then they will get better—appeared to be either sophistry or bluff.

"I have never looked for the easy way out, but now I can see that the coming months will be the toughest of my life," he admitted.

They were delivering his lunch to his office, "Just to save him time standing in line," his friend and assistant Lev Sukhanov explained. "But it's from the same cafeteria as everyone else's." Sukhanov, our guide to the corridors of the new power, had been with Yeltsin for four years, since the Construction Ministry. Yeltsin had him take a personal loyalty oath then. It looked old-fashioned and cartoonish, if not outright paranoid, yet one could understand Yeltsin: he had, after all, been betrayed by his closest comrades in the Moscow Party Committee. He developed a deep-rooted fear of betrayal—call it persecution mania, but that's how it is: once burnt, twice shy. At that time Yeltsin trusted no one but his wife. It's a miracle he did not collapse altogether.

Yeltsin was fortunate with Sukhanov. Lev was as loyal as a dog. Neither flattery nor hypocrisy is meant by this, since Sukhanov is a proud man, too, and apprehensive about outsiders discovering this canine quality—an adoration shared by many of Yeltsin's assistants, regardless of their gender. Yeltsin's Secretary of State, Gennady Burbulis, reputedly an independent-minded intellectual, even walked a bit like Yeltsin. In short, as we can testify, once you were around Boris Yeltsin, it was hard not to fall under his spell.

In Sukhanov's office, we talked uninterruptedly, despite the constant ringing of the phones, one louder than the other as though they were vying for his attention. Suddenly he grabbed one of them marked PRESIDENT—he recognized it by its pitch, just like another phone that says, ATS-1: the Kremlin line. Yeltsin had two offices: one in his White House, the other in the Kremlin, next to Gorbachev's. We voiced our doubts: should a democratically elected leader settle into the citadel of an eight-hundred-year-old absolutism? Wasn't it dangerous? Yeltsin's younger daughter, Tanya, explained: "The White House is his real office. The Kremlin is just for show—to receive foreign guests and hold other official ceremonies."

Yeltsin and Sukhanov were close enough friends to argue, and sometimes yelled at each other. Sukhanov often chided Yeltsin in an admonishing manner. In the rapidly changing structure of presidential authority, Sukhanov now had a direct superior, Victor Ilyushin, but Yeltsin summoned Sukhanov to confirm that he, Sukhanov, was still accountable to him, Yeltsin, personally and to no one else. "For you, my door is always open." They took vacations together, too—when we arrived in Moscow, both were in Sochi, on the Black Sea.

Yeltsin took flak from all sides for that vacation, especially since he was rumored to have fallen prey to the memoirist bug—the epidemic was raging through Moscow. Shevardnadze, Yakovlev, Raisa Gorbachev, Anatoly Sobchak, even the brand-new KGB chief, Vadim Bakatin—all had slapped together memoirs and sold, or were trying to sell, them abroad. Moscow was awash in rumors of skyrocketing advances. Gorbachev's led the list: a half million dollars for seventy-two pages about his stay in Foros during the putsch. The prevalent opinion, however, was that the latest oeuvre from the President of the nonexistent Soviet Union was more of a political maneuver and an exercise in self-justification than a straight business deal. On the other hand, the new dispensation was devoid of privilege, of former means of making a profit, and now one had to look for ways to make money on the side. That's how Bakatin put it: "How could I build my dacha without the book advance?"

A midlevel *apparatchik*—now an ex-*apparatchik*—hoped for a six-figure advance for his memoirs. Even the lowest possible six-figure number, $100,000, was equivalent to 10 million rubles, for which in Russia you can buy a lot more than for a hundred thousand dollars in America. Besides, publication in the West was proof of the author's democratic evolution.

From talking to Yeltsin's inner circle and members of his household, we formed an impression that he was concerned less with the prizes in the publishing sweepstakes or with an author's laurels than with one-upping Gorbachev. When Yeltsin learned that Gorbachev had parlayed his three-day imprisonment into half a million dollars, the real hero of those three days was outraged. Allegedly it was then that he agreed to his London agent's suggestion that he write his own memoirs to counter Gorbachev's. A different point of view? Absolutely! A different concept? No doubt! But a different advance, too—if Gorbachev got six figures, Yeltsin needed seven. The two Presidents were still competing—now as authors. It was a curious turnabout: if Yeltsin used to be Gorbachev's idée fixe, now Gorbachev seemed to become Yeltsin's, as well.

"Forget about Gorbachev, for Chrissake!" Valentina Lantseva, Yeltsin's talkative assistant, pleaded with her boss. "You *must* stop this love-hate relation with him."

"Stop teaching me how to live," Yeltsin shot back.

Valentina would not give up. "Enough writing! You're no writer! You wrote one book—that's enough! Let the writers write."

Actually, said Yeltsin's press secretary, Pavel Voshchanov, his boss needed a respite badly, and that was why he went to the Black Sea, not to write. Tanya echoes him: "Father was so sick after the putsch." Another source from Yeltsin's circle: "He crawled back into his den to lick his wounds." After Yeltsin's first hundred days in power, the reporters made wisecracks: "His hundred days minus two weeks." Finally, Gorbachev's assistant: "Out of his Hundred Days, he worked only three."

By his Hundred Days "anniversary," Yeltsin had returned to the capital, but he did not show up at the charity concert in his honor. Instead he sent his Vice President, Alexandr Rutskoy, an Afghan veteran, and Speaker Ruslan Khasbulatov. And what was there to celebrate? Yeltsin's putsch heroics had been long forgotten, his aides were fighting among themselves, and the anniversary was used to launch new attacks on him. Here are some quotes from the media:

"Of course, it is not every hundred days that we have a putsch. Such an event makes everything else fade away. Yet even with the greatest effort we cannot recall a single fruitful achievement of the Russian President since the Great Victory . . . It is time he used his powers; it is time he did something with his credit."

"Trust has a short shelf life—we doubt it will last another hundred days."

"The euphoria of victory is over. Now we can see that we have rid ourselves of a stabilizing force that penetrated the entire society. With all its reactionary nature, the Party was such a force . . . We are approaching a period with many destructive factors and not one stabilizing—conservative—one. We had great hopes for Yeltsin, for the structure of his presidential power. Alas, today the structure is not there . . . In his two-week vacation he lost the momentum, the time to take decisive steps . . . Unfortunately, he has failed to create a working structure of executive power . . . Perhaps Yeltsin works on a purely subconscious level and we should look for explanations for his actions in Freud rather than in our minds."

"In practical terms, he follows his every victory with a period of depression, rendering himself unable to capitalize on his winning . . . At the moment when he needs to convert and to collect the prize, he falls into apathy, alternated with senseless moves."

"Our President's very world view will not make it possible to conduct the necessary reforms. Yeltsin does not have an economic program nor can he have one. By nature he is a populist, a not entirely rational man; he does not perceive the world in entirely rational terms and basically cannot be guided by a program or any consistent measures . . . Such reforms are psychologically alien to him, which is really very important. He will not be able to hold on to his power in a situation where he is required to take stern, logical, thoughtful measures; where he cannot afford to veer left or right—on both sides he faces the end of the reform and an economic catastrophe."

These quotes are from liberal, democratic-minded media sources.

We arrived in Moscow in the middle of Yeltsin's Black Sea time-out. All our attempts to get hold of him in Sochi ended in failure. We should not complain: even his closest comrades, Ruslan Khasbulatov and Alexandr Rutskoy, could not reach their boss.

"Did you really try?" Yuri Petrov, Yeltsin's Administrative Director, snapped at them. He is one of the most influential members of the "Sverdlovsk mafia" in the Russian White House. He took over the Sverdlovsk Region after Yeltsin moved to Moscow, and, when Yeltsin fell in 1987, Petrov was exiled as Ambassador to Cuba. Understandably, upon becoming Russian President, Yeltsin instantly offered a high-ranking post to the man who had suffered because of him.

Another Sverdlovsk Party functionary, Victor Ilyushin, is Yeltsin's Chief of Staff. Yet another, Alexei Tsaregorodtsev, has taken a similar position with Vice President Rutskoy. According to some, Yeltsin charged him with keeping an eye on the indomitable ex-soldier. Also from Sverdlovsk Yeltsin brought Lyudmila Pihoya, Gennady Kheril (who died recently), and Gennady Burbulis, whose job title in an American table of organization would be Secretary of State, though neither he nor anyone else had a very good idea of what his duties were. " 'Secretary of State' is a political figure, while 'Council of the State' is a consultative organ," he tried to explain—perhaps more to himself than to others.

Besides the Sverdlovsk mafia, Yeltsin's close circle contained many other out-of-towners, and a Russian Henry Higgins could have had a field day sitting in the White House and studying the dialects of this huge country, which more and more resembled a runaway train. Against this crazy-quilt background, Lev Sukhanov took pride in his Moscow ancestry and showed us from the window a hillock from which he used to snow-sled as a child. He must have been looking far ahead. . . .

Fears that Boris Yeltsin's hometown chums would wield excessive influence over him were unfounded. Sverdlovskites are human too, and, as such, turned on one another with a vengeance. Which is not surprising: what does a former *apparatchik* like Petrov have in common with a refined philosopher like Burbulis?

Burbulis called Russian society "deranged." It seemed like a good description of the bedlam that we witnessed in the Russian White House. After a few days, nothing could surprise us. So what if Speaker Khasbulatov called Burbulis and Yeltsin's chief legislator, Sergei Shakhrai, "kids who have to grow up to be in politics." Another Yeltsinite labeled the entire Russian Council of Ministers "a bunch of amateurs in power." Yeltsin himself was compared to a two-headed eagle (the symbol of Russian monarchy): one head does not know what the other is thinking, and sometimes the two scrap. That is what happened when he went on that unfortunate vacation.

Burbulis, Yeltsin's Kissinger, did his best to distance himself from the infighting that was shaking the foundations of the new democratic power. Perhaps because he did not wish to soil his hands, he was being muscled aside by ex-functionaries, the graduates of the Party School of Intrigue, who had turned democratic. Their numbers were not confined to Sverd-lovskites, of course. During the coup the philosopher rose to the occa-sion: the White House defenders heard his calm voice regularly on the radio. He personally talked twice to KGB Chief Vladimir Kryuchkov, one of the chief plotters, and finally persuaded him to order the 103rd Tank Division to stop advancing. However, in the current infighting against the ex-*apparatchiks* Burbulis was faring less well, for he lacked experience, or perhaps even political vanity—being a rather abstract-minded person, a little removed from reality. He was working on general strategy issues—the theory of power rather than its practice. Paradoxi-cally, those who were working on practical issues were trying to trap him on theory.

In the bitter quarrels among the freshly liberated Republics, Yeltsin was regularly accused of superpower nationalism and imperial chauvin-ism. Burbulis's statement that Russia would become the successor state of the Soviet Union brought even more criticism than Voshchanov's about a possible revision of Russia's borders in regard to the other Republics.

International public opinion sided unequivocally with the non-Russian Republics, especially after hearing the rumor that Yeltsin discussed with Russian generals a possible preventive nuclear strike against the Ukraine. The tale was nonsense, of course, though a war between Russia and the Ukraine cannot be ruled out. After talking to Russian leaders, we felt that the issues were far more complicated than they had seemed from over-seas. It is of course simplistic to put a larger State automatically in the wrong. Also, Russia no longer saw itself as big; if anything, it was feeling slighted, slandered, swindled out of its resources by other Republics, as though someone had punched holes in its map, since after the departure of the Republics of the Union, Russia proper had been falling apart, too. Chechens, Tatars, Bashkirs, Yakuts, and other ethnic groups were voic-ing their wish to leave as well. They compared Russia to a rotting *ma-tryoshka* doll; time to flee, they figured, before the rot reached them.

"One look at the map is enough to see the territorial losses," said Galina Starovoitova, the only woman in Yeltsin's council. "We are left with the same ports that Peter the Great had at the beginning of his reign."

Yeltsin's adviser Sergei Stankevich complained, too: "Immediately after the coup, the Republics went about developing their statehood, and took a rather peculiar position: whatever is on our territory belongs to us, and whatever is on Russian territory is common property and should be divvied up."

Finally, Oleg Rumyantsev, the leader of the Social Democratic Party, who had been assigned the task of writing the new Russian Constitution: "Russia is much larger than this chopped-off intestine of the Russian Federation, ridden with holes. The Soviet Union was a form of existence of Russia. So it is only natural that the Russian Federation is an inheritor of the Union . . . We never had any problems with the Crimea, but now I suppose we will."

The Crimean Peninsula, home of the Soviet Black Sea Fleet as well as the nearby cosmopolitan city of Odessa with its large Odessa Region, with a sizable Russian population, was handed over to the Ukraine by Khrushchev's arbitrary decision. While it was within the Soviet Union, it did not matter; now the situation has changed. The best way out would be a referendum: the citizens should decide whether they want to be in the Ukraine, in Russia, or independent of both. Unfortunately, neighbors rarely coexist in a rational manner. One does not need a crystal ball to predict future wars on the territory of the former Soviet Empire: the new countries have little experience with statehood, and possess grandiose nationalist ambitions and phobias in excess of their size.

It is doubtful that the Commonwealth, hastily hammered together as a replacement for the Union of Soviet Socialist Republics, will be a panacea for these inevitable conflicts. Its creation—most likely Yeltsin's act of political improvisation—was a fig leaf, a move designed more to create an effect; to quote the diplomat-poet Tyutchev, it was "a shroud over the abyss." The agreement, the "December Surprise," will go down in history as an act of destruction rather than construction—the death sentence of the world's last Empire and its last rulers. Boris Yeltsin, the sponsor of the initiative, again acted in his customary role of a destroyer.

What links these newly born states? Is it the instinct of economic survival? Fear of universal chaos? Or is it hatred for the center, still exploiting them even as it agonizes in its death throes? Once the center is gone, it will take one of the principal—if not the only—sources of unity with it, and nationalistic egoism, however suicidal its potential consequences, will triumph.

The dispute among the former Soviet Republics is reminiscent of a deathbed argument among heirs. The legitimacy of Russia's claims to inherit the Union mantle is being put to debate. It was one of the members of the Union, but this claim can be made—in theory, at least—by any other Republic. The issue of whether one single Republic can be the heir is made especially vital by nuclear weapons: can Russia control them if they are on the territory of another Republic—the Ukraine, Belorussia, Kazakhstan? Burbulis's statement about inheritance rights was what one might call *ultima ratio regum*—force, the ultimate argument of kings, albeit a verbal one; more of a warning than an ultimatum.

The most striking reaction to his statement came, however, from those who were essentially in agreement with him; his White House colleagues gloated over his mishap. The reasoning was the same as with Vosh-chanov's statement about borders: for the moment, one should keep quiet about certain things.

Burbulis's reception room was equipped with a number of phones. As deputies and ministers waited for their turn, they called their associates and friends. We eavesdropped on a few conversations:

"There's more people who voted for Yeltsin—millions—more than yours, who voted against him."

"I believe the Ministry should occupy itself with the harvest and not with politics."

"You know, Sasha, we can't go on like this. We waste hours on unimportant subjects. We've got to think of something. We don't know how to work yet. We need some kind of protocol."

"You can't hold Yeltsin responsible for everything—he's been President for only three months!"

In the reception rooms were nickel-plated samovars and large gift-shop teacups with views of the Kremlin. In the offices, the large pictures of Lenin on the walls had been replaced by smaller pictures—cheap reproductions of landscape paintings in gaudy gilded frames. Infighting broke out the moment the democrats moved in, over offices and reception rooms—some offices had them and others did not. The next battle took place in the garage—over government limos. "They were like kids!" Lantseva exclaimed. "They all wanted low-beam lights on their cars. They're such beggars—they just want to grab something. They're so poor."

The fifth-floor bathrooms were spacious, blue-tiled affairs with huge mirrors, but no toilet paper—just like any Moscow public toilet. "There was some in the morning," the cleaning lady complained, hinting transparently that the advisers, deputies, and ministers stole this luxury item for use at home. "There's never enough for them."

The dining room had no waitresses: for most White House employees it was self-service (exception was made for the likes of Yeltsin, Sukhanov, or Burbulis). In the cafeteria, you could buy bread, sausage, meat pies, and apples to go—the deputies did not go home empty-handed. The prices were moderate, though not subsidized, as in the good old days of perks and benefits. The food was average: reasonably tasty, though nothing fancy. The master of the Russian White House was no gourmet: he ate whatever they set in front of him without noticing what it is. To him, food was a body function, an unavoidable distraction.

Of course, as the Russians never tire of quoting, man does not live by bread alone. Although, if the conditions in the White House had been better, perhaps its employees would have been less motivated to engage in interoffice wars. While Yeltsin was away for two weeks, the battles took on global dimensions: everyone against everyone else. This was no longer a struggle against Yeltsin; it was jockeying for a position to influence him. "A minefield of power," Burbulis called it. He had somehow succeeded in alienating everyone from Speaker of the Parliament Khasbulatov to Yeltsin's Chief of Staff, Petrov. Burbulis was dubbed an *éminence grise* and "the iron chancellor," while the State Council that he headed was "the generator of insane ideas." Local political observer Andranik Migranyan—he who first called for an "iron hand" a few years earlier—called the White House infighting "a struggle for powerlessness."

Another remark we heard: "Fish begins to rot at its head, and right now the White House is the center of instability."

"Well, *our* fish rots from all sides. It would be odd if the White House were an exception."

Immediately after the coup's failure, Yeltsin banned the Communist Party, which constituted its base, and closed down several newspapers that not only supported the coup but seemed to be directly implicated. Carried away by the euphoria of victory, democrats occupied several buildings that only the day before had belonged to Communists. Yeltsin began getting anonymous letters: citizens were already reporting on others' lack of dedication to democracy. The question, *Where were you and what did you do on August 19 to 21?* became a loyalty test for the new dispensation. Add Yeltsin's two or three careless gestures toward the former Republics, and all of these things unleashed a new panic: "Witchhunt!", "Redistribution of property!", "Rob the robbers!", "The last rows occupy the boxes and call it revolution!", "The democrats are the Communists of yesterday and the dictators of tomorrow!", *"Demokratura!" ("democratia" + "dictatura")*, "The revolution is prepared by idealists, carried out by fanatics, and its fruits are enjoyed by villains!" Finally, a cry for help: "Stop the revolution—it has already won!"

Some would say that it never began.

While everyone feared revolutionary rioting and demanded that it be guarded against, the rioting was in fact limited to the removal of the few monuments to Lenin's less popular comrades. Then, to universal surprise, it came to a stop. The parallels to the horrors of previous Russian upheavals and pogroms were the result of "parallelomania," and had little to do with reality. If Trotsky was right in saying that youth are the barometer of revolution, then, having defended the White House from the Party's tanks, the youth—artists and hookers, Afghan vets and Moscow yuppies—quietly drifted home. There was no looting, no pogroms—no incidents at all. To paraphrase a nineteenth-century Russian statesman, No mighty cataclysms, no mighty Russia. The nation had simply used up its quota of revolutionary unrest for this century; the previous storms had been so dreadful, so destructive, that the fear of revolution was attributable to the survival instinct of the Russian masses—if not on a national level, then at least on an individual one. Staying alive was more important than revolutions and coups, which is why both were so muted.

The same goes for Yeltsin's dictatorial ambitions. After the failure of the coup, the Soviet media compared him to every historical figure they could think of, from Napoleon to Napoleon the Third; from Pinochet to Jaruzelski. "Boris does have a bit of a tsar in him," his own aides admitted. Perhaps, but for the moment, the taking of power was directly followed by its paralysis. It was a lack of genuine thirst for power: as if the process of fighting for it were more important to him than its fruits, and, once he reached the top, he was lost. According to the philosopher Berdyayev, no one understands revolutions—even "velvet" ones like Boris Yeltsin's—less than the revolutionaries themselves.

If we compare Yeltsin and Gorbachev in Machiavellian terms, Gorbachev is a fox, who avoids the traps with remarkable shrewdness but is afraid of wolves. Yeltsin is a lion, who, to the contrary, has no fear of wolves—he has proven that he can scare them off—but he may not see the traps in his path. The first trap into which he stepped a few weeks after the coup was the power games played by his supporters. He came back from vacation looking darker than a raincloud; everyone grew silent, afraid to bother him with the accumulated problems. Those who did were shooed away. We went through it, too. "Don't you see the mood he's in?" his assistant explained to us. "It shows in his face!" We could not ask Yeltsin our questions in person: he referred us to his family or assistants.

Every Sunday the Yeltsin family got together at the dinner table: Boris, his wife, the two daughters with their husbands, and three grandchildren. Tanya dutifully described the conversation for us:

"Dad, Solovyov and Klepikova want to know your military rank."

"Well . . . colonel."

"What about Gorbachev?"

"Why don't they ask Gorbachev?"

"They think he's a general!"

"Hah! General! He's a colonel—just like me! You can't give civilians ranks above colonel in times of peace. If war breaks out, God forbid—that's different."

We passed little notes to Yeltsin through Sukhanov and Voshchanov, and, later, the manuscript with the finished chapters. Yeltsin stayed up late in the Kremlin, reading his biography. "It's even better when viewed from the outside," he remarked upon finishing it.

When he came back from Sochi, he was upset because he realized—he could not help but realize—that his staff's inability to share him peacefully was his own fault.

Like Gorbachev, Yeltsin had a huge staff. But, unlike Gorbachev, who kept them in the background, and, when time comes, parted from them easily, Yeltsin took pride in his advisers and liked showing them off—especially the ones who crossed over to his side from Gorbachev's. Yet the same advisers had to wait for months before he could see them. Moreover, Yeltsin was incapable of letting go favorites whom he no longer needed. He did not replace people; he collected them, inventing new sections and duties for them, creating one advisory group after another. Phantom jobs, excessive favoritism, advisers saved for a rainy day—how could such a bloated staff not develop frictions that, in their boss's absence, would mushroom into conflicts?

Individual rivalries were complemented by professional ones: Engineer Lev Sukhanov was retained for his devotion; Sverdlovsk's Victor Ilyushin was a *landsman,* just like Yuri Petrov; Moscow's Mayor Gavriil Popov was introduced into the inner circle after the sleepless night of August 21, which the two spent in heart-to-heart talks, awaiting the storming of the White House. Enmity developed not merely between individuals, but between entire bureaucratic structures—new against old, Council of Ministers against Council of State, Council of State against President's Chancellory, and all of them against the Parliament, which they dreamed of dismissing or at least suspending. State Adviser Sergei Stankevich, voicing not only his own opinion, but Yeltsin's as well, believed that "a period of radical reform has never been a period of Parliamentary democracy."

As they quarreled and plotted against one another, the White House democrats feared a new putsch, which would succeed by virtue of learning the lessons of the failed one. Our friend Artyom Borovik, an expert on the Army, considered a Roman scenario plausible, i.e., one carried out by troops back from Eastern Europe and the former Republics. Besides, as political anarchy and economic chaos increased, so did nostalgia for the good old days; Communist rule was likened to the golden Confucian age. After the putsch, the Communists went underground, but democracy allowed them to return a few months later to exploit the public mood of depression and panic—both unfortunately well-founded.

Another overheard White House remark: "The only hope is that most professional bureaucrats followed the new power. That's why the nomenklatura putsch failed—because most of the nomenklatura had already gone over to the democrats."

That may have been true, but it may also have contained dangers of its own: the old *apparatchik* in his new office together with the luggage of his old habits, which were already corrupting the new power and eventually even determining its future nature. Then the democratic victory may indeed turn into no more than a change of a store sign under the same ownerships—"commutants," as they are derisively called in Moscow.

Yeltsin was a wreck: he feared he was facing a replay of what happened during his rule over Moscow, when he had to change his subordinates several times—in vain. Mistrustful of the provincial Soviets, he sent out his own emissaries to replace their chairmen—what the Bolsheviks called *komissars*—in effect introducing a version of presidential rule. This upset him particularly: in the Krasnodar Territory he had to replace, one after the other, two legitimately elected and apparently democratic bosses who had made a mess of it and appoint Vasily Diakonov, an economist. And would he fail, too?

For Yeltsin, no news was good news indeed. But news kept pouring into his office, the control room of the former Soviet Empire, from all sides, and it was more and more troubling. In anticipation of new purchase prices, unwilling to sell too cheap, peasants were throwing grain into ravines, where it rotted—even cattle would not eat it. In the northern Caucasus ethnic groups were killing one another. For surpassing quotas, workers were promised payment in hard currency; they were even issued checks, but the banks would not cash them—a breach of trust in the new leadership. Amateurishness and sabotage were everywhere. The new system was not firmly established yet, and the old one no longer worked. Yeltsin was getting it from all sides. The electorate was disenchanted, his ratings were plummeting, and Moscow journalists were falling back on the famous quote from Schiller: "The Moor has done his duty—the Moor may go."

Meanwhile, as our and Yeltsin's publisher, Alexandr Rekemchuk, put it, "Gorbachev is beginning to stir in his feathered cradle." Gorbachev sat out the putsch in Foros and returned to Moscow as a stranger, an outsider. He was said to be in quiet opposition to Yeltsin, but general confusion, uncertainty over tomorrow, democrats' mistakes and the growing popular disgruntlement with them were giving a flicker of hope to this discredited leader of a nonexistent country. He was inching toward the sidelines, like a substitute player warming up.

It was hard to say whether the change in him was real or superficial, but his style and appearance were different now: he looked modest, grim, and preoccupied. The soliloquies of yesterday had given way to serious attention paid to others, whose circle was widening: foreign guests, Soviet businessmen, local malcontents. He seemed to have a soft spot for those who for one reason or another had not been received by Yeltsin. From time to time, Gorbachev gently corrected Yeltsin's errors and lectured him in an avuncular manner when the latter forged ahead too rashly. Gorbachev had formed his own circle of advisers: Eduard Shevardnadze, Alexandr Yakovlev, Anatoly Sobchak, Gavriil Popov, Academician Velikhov, the new KGB Chief, Vadim Bakatin. Something funny was going on with the KGB: it had been formally disbanded and four new bodies had been created on the old base—all of them under Gorbachev. The Alpha Brigade, whose superbly trained thugs never got to storm the Russian White House, has been preserved, but taken out of the KGB structure and subordinated to both Presidents—Gorbachev and Yeltsin—at the same time. It did not make sense. And the coexistence of two Presidents—of two capitals—in one city: did that make sense?

Gorbachev was out of business, and his forced idleness freed his hands for mischief as never before. He lured Yeltsin's advisers and friends over—his former Prime Minister, Ivan Silayev; Economist Grigory Yavlinsky; Mayor Gavriil Popov—to consult him, and was routinely flirting with others—the phones in the White House offices were ringing more and more often. "Damn!" Yeltsin's Vice President, Alexandr Rutskoy, stormed out of his office, late for the meeting with his boss. "Every time Gorbachev calls, he blabs on for a half hour!"

Meanwhile, the edifices of the Union were crumbling one after another. Yeltsin refused to finance Gorbachev's ministries; even the Foreign Ministry fell under the ax and was reduced to one-tenth of its budget and staff. Gorbachev no longer had a country; his power no longer had a political base. All he had left was his personal staff, his bodyguards, and his monthly salary of 4000 rubles.

When we were in Moscow, the Russian Parliament decided to make Yeltsin's salary equal to Gorbachev's. A couple of days later, Gorbachev ordered that billions of rubles more be printed. The Mint worked around the clock seven days a week, spending hard currency to buy paper and ink in order to print nonconvertible Soviet currency. The new slang word for a hundred-ruble bill was "paper." Yeltsin viewed Gorbachev's order as another stab in the back. The Fifth Floor of the White House debated separating the Russian banking system from the Soviet one and confiscating the national gold reserves. The battle between the two Presidents entered a decisive stage.

Gorbachev's only assistant who agreed to be interviewed, anonymously (we mentioned him earlier), was still loyal to his old boss. Nonetheless he was looking for a new job. According to him, Gorbachev's

Nobel Prize was spurring Yeltsin on to new efforts. "Otherwise why would he go to Nagorny Karabach to negotiate the Armenian-Azeri conflict? Russia has plenty of its own conflicts to settle."

For this unsuccessful peacemaking mission, which Yeltsin had undertaken together with the Kazakh president Nursultan Nazarbayev, he got a blast of criticism from friends and foes alike. Those closest to him chided him for not having given himself enough time to recover from a heart attack. Yeltsin's attitude to his health has been discussed in this book—some call him a masochist, others a fatalist, and even claim a suicidal bent.

Yeltsin was a psychological puzzle, and visiting journalists got a feeling that the nation had placed its President on the couch, publicly musing over his psyche and running him through a battery of tests. Historical analogies were drawn endlessly—primarily with other revolutions. "Yeltsin is our Danton." Who is Robespierre, then? we wondered. "Why, Burbulis, of course." As during any other revolution, people were living from day to day and preferred not to plan too far ahead. For example, it was impossible to make an appointment with anyone in the Russian White House, including its master, two or three weeks in advance: "Maybe half an hour today. You've got to wait. Don't you see how bad your timing is? Boris Nikolayevich is just back from Sochi, and he's got a mini-putsch in his own team going on."

While Gorbachev was a regular social butterfly—to Madrid for Mideast talks, then to Paris for a rendezvous with Mitterrand—Yeltsin's image of an open, sociable man had changed to one of a hermit, distanced from public and media, with rare sorties outside his circle.

"His mentality is an example of Party puritanism," we heard people say about him.

"Now that he's lost his chief enemy, he can either remain a fighter or lose his passionate temperament; his policies are listless and incoherent."

"Yeltsin has three souls: a nomenklatura one, a populist one, and a reformist one."

"He always thrived on his defeats, turning them to work for him. Psychologically he's not equipped to be a victor: that's why he's so confused. While he has the blues, the power is paralyzed."

"Unlike Gorbachev, whose brilliance consists in his command of textbook moves and playing percentages, Yeltsin has never mastered even a beginner's textbook. He is best at wrecking his opponent's tactics; if he wins, he does it by playing against the rules rather than by following them. He's instinctive and irrational, he grasps an extreme situation instantly, but becomes paralyzed by day-to-day politics. He needs to explode a situation in order to act calmly and confidently. The worse off he is, the more effectively he acts: when they send a tank to storm the

White House, he turns it into his podium to demoralize the attackers. But the better off he is, the worse he feels—like now, for example."

This is what we read and heard about him in the fall of 1991. The nation's curiosity about its first democratically elected leader peaked in this headline in the *Kommersant* weekly: BORIS NIKOLAYEVICH: EXCUSE ME, BUT WHO ARE YOU?

It is a legitimate question; the country was curious not only about its leader but about itself and its future. The growth of skepticism about Yeltsin was the result of a general mood of depression: the public, befuddled by its sudden gift of freedom, yearned to concede responsibility, dump it in the lap of its still charismatic leader. Perhaps this was the essence of the Yeltsin phenomenon: all questions about him and claims on him stemmed from quasi-religious faith in him. But this faith also had a certain logic to it: if he could overthrow the old system, then by God he should be able to create a new one! His original vocation was being brought up as people hoped he had not forgotten his construction skills while battling the Kremlin. The revolutionary had to become the builder; the destroyer of the false utopia had to create a new reality. In economic terms the country had to leap into capitalism—but did it have either the strength or the fulcrum for such a leap?

Perhaps Yeltsin indeed lost time by taking a vacation. Perhaps it would have been better to ram through the unpopular but inevitable reforms in the very wake of the putsch, when he was riding the crest of his popularity. We believe that the effect of the Black Sea respite was to transform the heroic rebel leader into a head of state. The change was not a cosmetic one: all Yeltsin's external mutations were accompanied by internal ones. He had already proven his capacity for change like no other political leader in the world. Ultimately, the Motherland could be saved in different ways: from the top of the tank or from behind a desk. One thing seemed clear: the street-rally period of Russian history was over.

Yeltsin did not return from Sochi physically rested, but he was nonetheless raring to go, to sink his teeth into the business of running the country. His first measures were decisive and uncompromising: he put forward a shock therapy program for the quick, painful, and unavoidable transition to a free-market economy. He signed decrees taking over the remaining structures of the Soviet Finance Ministry, including its authority to control foreign currency, raised the minimum wage, assumed control over Russia's most valuable commodities, including oil, diamonds, and precious metals, and announced plans for sweeping denationalization and the lifting of price controls from most products.

In doing this, he confounded the expectations of many, who thought he would follow in Gorbachev's footsteps and opt for the role of a referee in affairs of state; or that, like the Queen of England, he would reign instead of rule. He went in the opposite direction and, by assuming additional prerogatives—a Prime Minister's on top of a President's—increased his authority and his responsibilities. It was our impression that, unlike the power-hungry Gorbachev, Yeltsin did not value or enjoy his power very much: He was, however, politically ambitious, which was not the same thing. In 1987 he left the Kremlin's Mount Olympus of his own free will, and in 1991, when his enemies, prodded by Gorbachev, called for an extraordinary session of the Russian Parliament, Yeltsin held in his pocket a statement on his voluntary resignation as the Chairman of the Republic's Supreme Council. Had Parliament disagreed with his proposal to hold a direct Russian presidential election, Yeltsin would have undoubtedly resigned.

This does not mean, however, that Yeltsin planned to rule the country by periodically blackmailing it with his resignation. Although he paid a heavy price for power, he neither saw it as an end in itself nor assigned it any intrinsic value. His risk-taking, his rigidity, and his fatalism certainly presented an element of danger for the country, the cripple that he had inherited. At such political altitudes, the fearless are no less dangerous than the cowards. Besides, as we mentioned, he was not sensitive to nuances; he perceived the world as an entity, not the sum of its parts: (Curiously, Yeltsin claims Chekhov as his favorite author. It happens quite often: love is dictated by contrast, not by resemblance, and literature compensates for individual shortcomings as well as those inherent in life itself.)

Yeltsin's history of fighting for power did not prepare him for wielding this power. He was fatigued, perhaps exhausted. Would he have enough skill and energy to accomplish the feats that the people who elected him expected? The tragedy of the nation, and of Boris Yeltsin personally, was that he was totally alone, without political alternatives. The entire burden of state affairs lay on his shoulders. He represented the last hope of a people who had lost the faith and strength to endure any more political or economic experiments. Everyone expected a miracle from Yeltsin because no one believed in a steady, natural pattern of historical evolution. In Moscow one got the impression that not just the Soviet Empire, but all of Russian history was coming to an end. Hence the infantile, primitive attitude toward a democratic leader. He was their lord, their father. Having exhausted the last of their self-confidence, the Russian people called on Boris Yeltsin to accomplish what they were unable to do by themselves.

Yeltsin had stepped up to the captain's bridge of a sinking ship. That is why, regardless of how we feel about him personally, we dare not, in all sincerity, close this book on an optimistic note.

*

THE SOVIET Union is dead, the Commonwealth is born, and Yeltsin now sits in Gorbachev's old office in the Kremlin. But already the Commonwealth disagrees on more subjects than it agrees on, and, at home, voluble disputes with Popov, Khasbulatov, Sobchak, and Rutskoy spotlight massive cracks in the brotherhood of August.

Can Yeltsin survive? Can the Commonwealth? No other world leader is facing a challenge as colossal, as superhuman, as Yeltsin's: to prevent the total collapse of his country. In the last months of 1991 Yeltsin relieved Russia of the crushing burden of ideology, of the empire and totalitarianism; but the tasks of economic transformation, of raising the living standards, and of making the Russian people believe in their future again, will take more than a few months—they will take years to accomplish. Yeltsin came to power several years too late, robbed of this time by Gorbachev. And now Yeltsin really has to race against the clock—does he still have enough time?

Things have come full circle. In the beginning of this book Gorbachev kicked Yeltsin out of power, seemingly forever—with all that has happened since, hard to believe it was only four years ago! Now, as if taking revenge for past humiliation, Yeltsin has muscled Gorbachev out of the Kremlin. Gorbachev is Yeltsin's past; but does Yeltsin have a future? And what about Russia? With the loss of the Empire, it has lost its statehood, too, since through the last centuries the Empire was the only form of statehood that Russia knew—does Russia have a future?

We may cast doubts, we may criticize, we may pose question after question without hoping to get answers. But one thing we are convinced of: whatever obstacles, losses, and dramas Russia faces on its new democratic course, it has no alternative. Just as there is no alternative to the man who has set Russia on this course—Boris Yeltsin.

Moscow–New York–Moscow

The private Yeltsin: at home, on the tennis court, and with his grandson—also named Boris Yeltsin. *All photos by Yuri Feklistov, from the family album.*

Yeltsin and Gorbachev at the session of the Russian Supreme Soviet a few days after the putsch. *From* Rossiya *weekly.*

At the wake for the victims of the putsch, September 1991. *Photo by V. Kiselyov, from* Rossiya *weekly.*

NOTES

To KEEP the narrative flowing, we chose not to use footnotes or numbers to refer to sources. Therefore, in these notes we describe the quote and its source in more detail. If a Russian source exists in English, we opted for the original, to avoid the distortions and losses inevitable in a translation. That includes Yeltsin's own memoir, *Confession on an Assigned Theme* (PIK Publishers, Moscow, 1991). In many cases, instead of quoting, we retell Yeltsin's reminiscences and supplement them with details from his interviews or from our own interviews with his friends and relatives. The latter are referenced in the text itself rather than in the notes.

INTRODUCTION and PART ONE: A POLITICIAN IS BORN

The conversation with Artyom Borovik is quoted from *Novoye Russkoye Slovo (NRS)*, a New York–based Russian-language daily (June 21, 1991). Also from *NRS* is the quote on the technical communication between Foros and the outside world (August 30, 1991), and Alexandr Podrabinek's comment on the putsch (September 12, 1991), though originally both appeared in *Moscow News* and *Express Khronika,* respectively. The interview of Yeltsin during the putsch was taken by Diane Sawyer and broadcast on ABC on August 20, 1991. The statement of Acting Soviet President Gennady Yanayev appeared in *Izvestiya* on August 20, 1991.

A BULL IN A CHINA SHOP

Yeltsin's answers at the meeting at the Political Enlightenment House are quoted from our own typed transcript of the meeting. Excerpts appeared in *Le Monde* (July 16, 1986), *Russkaya Mysl* (Paris, July 25, 1986), and in *NRS* (August 1, 1986). Quotes from *Confession on an Assigned Theme,* in the order of appearance—pp. 88–89, 93, 119–120, 123, 91, 8–11. The speeches at the meeting with Pamyat are also quoted from our own complete typed transcript of the meeting. Excerpts appeared in *NRS* (August 13, 1987) and the *NY Times* (July 26, 1987). Yeltsin's answers on the "Jewish Question" appeared in *Komsomolskaya Pravda* (March 11, 1991) and *Forbes* (August 1991), and were broadcast on Rossiya Radio

(January 11, 1991, 14:00). The quoted article by David Remnick appeared in *The Washington Post* (May 31, 1991). Boris Paramonov's article "Shit" appeared in *Nezavisimaya Gazeta* (July 27, 1991). Yeltsin's summary of his Moscow activity as a Party Boss is quoted from his interview with *Moscow News* (August 24, 1986 and October 18, 1987). The recollections of Mikhail Poltoranin appeared in *Corriere della sera* (May 12, 1988).

CRIME AND PUNISHMENT, KREMLIN STYLE

Speeches at the Central Committee Plenum are quoted from *Izvestiya TsK KPSS,* No.2, 1989. Quotes from *Confession on an Assigned Theme* are from pp. 138–139, 144, 153–154, and 140. Yeltsin's speech at the November Plenum of the Moscow Party Committee is from *Izvestiya* (November 14, 1987). False versions of Yeltsin's speech are quoted from our own copies of Samizdat publications, as well as from *Le Monde* (February 2, 1988), *NRS* (February 4, 1988), and *Russkaya Mysl* (February 5, 1988). Marshall Goldman's article and a report from Moscow are from the *NY Times* (November 22 and November 16, 1987, respectively). Comparison of Yeltsin and Trotsky was made by *The Los Angeles Times* (November 13, 1987). Chekhov's and Hershensohn's negative comments on the Russian intelligentsia come from *Vekhi* (Landmarks) collection (Moscow, 1909, pp. 81 and 89). Yeltsin's comment on criticism in his interview to Diane Sawyer was broadcast by CBS on June 24, 1987. Comments of Georgi Arbatov and Gennady Gerasimov on the Yeltsin Affair appeared, respectively, in *NRS* (November 10, 1987) and the *NY Times* (November 20, 1987).

JOSEPH AT THE BOTTOM OF THE WELL

Beginning with the story of the gravely ill Yeltsin being hauled to the Plenum of the Moscow Party Committee, all excerpts from Yeltsin's speech at the Superior Komsomol School—320 questions and answers—are quoted from our own typed transcript (55 pages). Excerpts, with some distortions and misquotes, were published in the Soviet out-of-town papers (in Ufa, Sverdlovsk, Kursk, Kazan, Yakutsk, etc.); we used *Molodaya Gvardiya* (Perm, April 12, 1988) and *Komsomolets Tajikistana* (January 22, 1989), as well as *Russkaya Mysl* (Paris, January 6, 1989). *Confession on an Assigned Theme* is quoted from pp. 24–25, 24, 29–30, and 155–165 (his battle at the Party Conference), and p.170 (his conversation with Gorbachev). The story of being threatened with a special gadget was told by Yeltsin several times, for example in his interview to Radio Liberty (October 19, 1989). The story of three Yeltsin brothers sharing one coat comes from Andrei Goryun's booklet *Boris Yeltsin—Lights and Shadows* (Sverdlovsk, 1991, first booklet, p.5). The interview with Mikhail Poltoranin appeared in *Corriere della sera* (May 12, 1988). Yeltsin's comments on preparations for the elections, about Central Committee Member Tikhomirov and Gorbachev's rightist tilt were in an interview, "42 Questions to Boris Yeltsin," published in *Sovetskaya Molodezh* newspaper (Riga, January 3, 1990).

PART TWO: THE PRINCE AND THE PAUPER: PARALLEL LIVES OF MIKHAIL GORBACHEV AND BORIS YELTSIN

Naturally, it was *Pravda* that defined Yeltsin as the main political figure opposing Gorbachev (May 3, 1991). Yeltsin's mother, Klavdiya Vasilyevna, is quoted from her interview in *Sudarushka* newspaper (reprinted in *Vechernyaya Moskva* on October 2, 1991) and from the above-mentioned Goryun booklet. From the latter we also borrowed the stories of young Yeltsin reading Lenin, of his biographical questionnaire (that Goryun saw personally), Yakov Olkov's reminiscences of student Yeltsin and Rosa Alexeyeva about the Yeltsins' family life, the story of Yeltsin's crush on a coed, of a broken telephone cable, as well as Yelokhin's story and Goryun's personal recollection of seeing Yeltsin speak in Sverdlovsk. In describing Yeltsin's life in the barrack we used an interview with him in *Time* (March 20, 1989), and his *Confession,* which we used for other stories as well (pp. 121, 23, 79–80, 36, 74, 22–23, 30, 71–73, 26, 70, 51, 54, 58–59, and 103). For information on Yeltsin's parents and grandparents, we used *Rodina* magazine (No.1, 1990). The Lvov episode: *NY Times Magazine* (September 23, 1990). All the information on Gorbachev's career comes from our book *Behind the High Kremlin Walls* and from our booklet *Mikhail Gorbachev: The Way to the Top,* which appeared in a pirate edition in Moscow in 1989. Yeltsin's remarks on the meaning of life come from Leningrad's *Smena* newspaper (April 29, 1989). The interview with Yeltsin's college professors appeared in *The Washington Post* (March 31, 1991). The meeting in the Moscow market comes from Mikhail Poltoranin's article in *Moskva* magazine (No.12, 1990). The story of the never-opened Brezhnev Museum is told by Yeltsin himself in the already mentioned "42 Questions . . ." (*Sovetskaya Molodezh* paper, Riga, January 3, 1990). The letter to the editor suggesting that Yeltsin be cursed for having destroyed the Ipatyev House was printed in *Sovetskaya Rossiya* (April 1, 1990). Yeltsin's remarks on Party finances were printed in *Sovetskaya Rossiya* (February 23, 1991). Residential housing construction in the Sverdlovsk Region is described in Yeltsin's book *The Mid-Urals: Frontier of Creation* (p.72). Yeltsin is quoted on social inequality in "USSR Today" (Radio Liberty, August 7, 1989). Sergei Demyanenko's description of Yeltsin in Sverdlovsk comes from *Nezavisimaya Gazeta* (October 5, 1991).

PART THREE: THE SCHOOL OF DEMOCRACY

MR. YELTSIN GOES TO WASHINGTON

The story of Yeltsin's initial failure to be elected to the Supreme Soviet and of accepting Kazannik's seat is derived from the Soviet and international media of the period; specific remarks come from Yeltsin's numerous interviews, including the already mentioned "42 Questions to Boris Yeltsin." Sakharov's activity at the Congress of People's Deputies and his selected remarks come from his *Gorky, Moscow, and Everywhere* (Chekhov Press, NY, 1990, p.193, 170–171, etc.). Yuri Vlasov's speech is quoted from *NRS* (June 17–18, 1989). The story of the Interregional Deputy Group involves recollections of its two cochairmen, Yeltsin and Sakharov, as well as its Managing Secretary, A. Murashov (*Ogonyok* No.32, August 4–11, 1990). From the same source comes Sakharov's definition of opposition. The details of Yeltsin's rejection of a trip to Germany come from an interview with him in *Ogonyok* (reprinted in *NRS*, October 17, 1989); from the same interview comes the description of his pre-departure humiliation and of the political importance of meeting with President Bush, as well as Yeltsin's explanation of the Johns Hopkins episode and his reaction to the Pravda article. *Neues Deutschland*'s reaction was reported by the *NY Times* (September 19, 1989). The conversation with Jack Anderson was reported at Yeltsin's press conference (*NRS*, September 12, 1989). Yeltsin on the need of Russia learning from America: *Izvestiya* (September 15, 1989). Yeltsin's reference to American forecasts and Sovietologists' calculations come from *Confession* (p.5) and our own notes of his speech at Columbia on September 11, 1989. Alferenko spoke on the difficulties in organizing the trip in *NRS* (September 25, 1989), James Harrison on the objectives of Yeltsin's visit: *NRS* (September 25, 1989). Regarding Yeltsin's request to see American leaders: *NY Times* (September 9, 1989). Yeltsin's dismissive evaluation by American politicians were reported by *Time* (June 11, 1990). Harrison's evaluation of Yeltsin's visit: *NRS* (September 21, 1989). Comments on the visit by David Rockefeller, George Kennan, and Cyrus Vance were reported in *The Washington Post* (September 12, 1989). Yeltsin's persistent signals to the hesitant Bush: *NRS* of September 12 as well as our Columbia University notes on September 11. Yeltsin's twenty-minute interview with Jim Lehrer was broadcast on PBS on September 11, 1989. The scene that Yeltsin threw in the US White House en route to Scowcroft's office was reported by the *NY Times* (June 23, 1991). Yeltsin's impressions of America: *Argumenty i fakty* (No.38, 1989) and *NRS* (October 17, 1989). Paul Hendrikson's piece appeared in *The Washington Post* on September 13, 1989. Pavel Voshchanov told about scandals during the trip and about Yeltsin's expenses in *Komsomolskaya Pravda* (September 27, 1989) A. M. Rosenthal wrote about Yeltsin's visit in the *NY Times* on September 19, 1989. Quotes about Yeltsin's 1991 visit are from the *NY Times* (June 20 and 22, 1991) and *The Washington Post* (June 20, 1991). Zucconi on the sources of his scandalous article: *Washington Post* (September 20, 1989). Excerpts from Zucconi's article are quoted from the *Pravda* reprint on September 18, 1989. Yeltsin's reaction to Zucconi's piece was reported by the *NY Times* on September 19, 1989. Victor Yaroshenko's statement at a press conference in NYC is quoted from *NRS* (September 25, 1989). The information about the tampering with the videotape comes from *Teatralnaya Zhizn* magazine (No.1, 1990). Yeltsin commented on rumors about him in an interview printed in *NRS* (November 2, 1989). The Uspensky Incident, Yeltsin's comments, and his accusations of Gorbachev: transcript of Supreme Soviet session in *Izvestiya* (October 17, 1989); David Remnick's article in *The Washington Post* (October 18, 1989); *Soviet Media News Digest* (Radio Liberty, October 19, 1989); Yeltsin's "statement" in the Latvian paper *Sovetskaya Molodezh* (October 20, 1989). A reporter's question and Yeltsin's answer comes from *NRS* (November 2, 1989). Dmitri Olshanski's article with Yeltsin's psychological evaluation was printed in *Rossiya* (October 23–29, 1991). Yeltsin's remark on his possible nomination for Moscow City Council or Russian Parliament comes from his interview to *Vecherny Leningrad* (November 3, 1989).

YELTSIN'S RUSSIA

The quoted interview with Vladimir Solovyov and Elena Klepikova was published in the *NY Times* on May 4, 1977. The information about the proliferation and banning of our booklet, *Mikhail Gorbachev: the Path to the Top,* comes from *Dom Kino* (December 1990), *Pravda* (April 9, 1990), and *Express Khronika* releases, reprinted by *NRS* (February 9 and March 28, 1990). Gorbachev spoke about the booklet in the lobby at the 21st Congress of Komsomol in the spring of 1990. Vladimir Solovyov's article "Gorbachev Must Go" appeared in *The Christian Science Monitor* on January 9, 1990. Andranik Migranyan's article "Populism" appeared in *Sovetskaya Kultura* (No.75, 1989), and his "Long Way to Europe House" in *Novy Mir* (No.7, 1989). The interview with Alexandr Kushner was published in *Kontinent* (No.66, 1991). The public opinion polls are quoted from *Sobesednik* (No.48, 1990). Yeltsin's remark about Russia's independence is from *Literaturnaya Gazeta* (January 24, 1990). "Will the Russian

Federation leave the Soviet Union?" was published in *Atmoda* (February 12, 1990). Yeltsin's evaluation of the composition of the Congress of People's Deputies and suggestion regarding the struggle for the chairmanship of the Russian Supreme Soviet are from *Literaturnaya Gazeta* (January 24, 1990). Yeltsin's remark that the Soviet people's life has become worse is from *NRS* (March 6, 1990). Articles on Yeltsin are quoted from *Atmoda* (April 29, 1990) and *Kommersant* (April 27, 1990). Yeltsin's story about leaving the Party is from *Sovetskaya Molodezh*, a Riga paper (August 3-4, 1990); one about his talk with Gorbachev, from *Komsomolskaya Pravda* (August 8, 1990). The tour of Russia and Yeltsin's remarks on the road: *Izvestiya* (August 26, 1990), *Sovetskaya Kultura* (September 1, 1990), *Soyuz* (August, No.32-33, 1990), and the *NY Times* (September 3, 1990). Yeltsin's press conference on the results of his tour appeared in *USSR Today: Soviet Media and Features Digest* (Radio Liberty, September 1, 1990). The Marquis de Custine is quoted from the Russian edition: *The Marquis de Custine. Russia Under Tsar Nicholas* (Terra, Moscow, 1990).

THE TEMPTATION OF DICTATORSHIP

Yeltsin talked about the alleged attempt on Gorbachev's life in *Moscow News* (December 2, 1990). Igor Klyamkin and Andranik Migranyan's "Do We Need an Iron Hand?" appeared in *Literaturnaya Gazeta* (August 12, 1989). Commentary on the *apparat*'s games and civil war was in *Baltiyskoye Vremya* (June 4, 1990). Yeltsin on Gorbachev's half-steps, *NRS* (May 17, 1990). Quotes from our own piece in *The Chicago Tribune* (March 14, 1990) and *NRS* (July 28, 1989). Shevardnadze's speech, *Komsomolskaya Pravda* (December 21, 1990) (see also the Russian publication of his book, *My Choice,* Moscow, *Novosti,* 1991). Yeltsin's warning about the "decisive year" comes from his March 9 speech to the leaders of Democratic Russia (typed transcript in our archives). Yeltsin's address to Russian soldiers in Lithuania, *Moscow News* (January 27, 1991), *Atmoda* (January 15, 1991), and *Komsomolskaya Pravda* (January 19, 1991). Open letter to Yeltsin from Russophiles, *Literaturnaya Rossiya* (January 2, 1991). Yeltsin told the story of flying aboard a military plane many times—e.g., the already mentioned "42 Questions to Boris Yeltsin." Yeltsin's flirting with the military is derived from the already mentioned accounts of his three-week tour of Russia; the information on the coup in the making is from *Komsomolskoye Znamya* (September 30, 1990). Marshal Akhromeyev's article is from *Sovetskaya Rossiya* (February 12, 1991). Yazov and Pugo's joint order comes from a typed copy in our archives. Yeltsin's speech with the demand for Gorbachev's resignation was broadcast on Soviet TV on February 19, 1991, at 18:50 (typed transcript in our archives). Yuri Vlasov's article in support of Yeltsin was in *Kuranty* (March 26, 1991). Yeltsin on his relation with Gorbachev, *Komsomolskaya Pravda* (March 14, 1991). Yeltsin spoke on the threat of civil war and blackmail with this threat on Rossiya Radio, July 3, 1991, 23:41; also see *Ogonyok* (No.12, March 16–23, 1991). Yeltsin as Jacob, ready to fight God for Russian sovereignty: *Sobesednik* (No.6, 1991). Gorbachev's speech at Yeltsin's inauguration was reproduced in most Soviet and American papers on the next day, July 11, 1991. Oleg Rumyantsev's remark is quoted from *The Christian Science Monitor* (July 11, 1991). "Yaroslavna's Wailing" in its modern version was referred to in *Russky Vestnik* (July 31, 1991).

GORBACHEV VS. GORBACHEV

The August 19–21 events in Moscow and Foros are reconstructed primarily from personal testimony (references in the text), as well as reports, interviews, and commentaries in the Soviet media from late August to late December. We were generally guided by two booklets, whose authors had spent the days of the coup in the Russian White House. The two are *Black Night Over the White House*—a collection of leaflets and press releases put out during the coup by *Rossiya*, the paper of the Presidium of the Russian Supreme Soviet—and *Chronicle of the Putsch: Hour by Hour,* a collection of reports of the Russian Information Agency. Both appeared in Moscow a few days after the putsch's failure; it is one of many reasons why they are reliable, unembellished accounts. All the official junta documents are quoted from *Izvestiya* and *Pravda;* the interview with Yavlinsky was in *Moskovsky Komsomolets* (August 24, 1991); the deputy to the late Nikolai Kruchina is quoted from *Kommersant* (August 14–21, 1991); Telman Gdlyan, from *Argumenty i fakty* (No. 39, 1991); Anatoly Lukyanov's wife, from TASS (October 13, 1991); Alpha Commanders Gennady Karpukhin, Mikhail Golovanov, and Sergei Goncharov, from *Literaturnaya Gazeta* (August 28, 1991); Colonel General Victor Grachev, from *Izvestiya* (September 4, 1991); Army General Konstantin Kobetz, from *Moskovsky Komsomolets* (August 31, 1991), *Moscow News* (September 1, 1991), and *Sobesednik* (No.35, 1991); Anatoly Sobchak, from *Moscow News* (September 1, 1991); Eduard Limonov, from *Literaturnaya Gazeta* (October 16, 1991). Testimony of Marshal Yazov, Valentin Pavlov, and Vladimir Kryuchkov was broadcast on Soviet TV evening news, October 20, 1991. Shevardnadze's demand that Gorbachev speak in public is quoted from the earlier mentioned booklet *Black Night Over the White House;* his phone conversation with Gorbachev, from his book, *My Choice* (p.340). The interview with Crimean KGB Chief Ivan Kolomytsev is quoted from a special issue of *Yuzhny Kurier,* a local paper

(August 27, 1991); the Kremlin secret report log appeared in *Moscow News Fax Digest* printed by *NRS* on September 13, 1991; Georgi Shakhnazarov's speech in the Russian Parliament, in *Black Night Over the White House;* his interview regarding Gorbachev in Foros, in *Argumenty i Fakty* (No. 33, August 1991); interview with Vladimir Ivashko, in *Nezavisimaya Gazeta* (October 24, 1991); description of plotters' phone calls—possibly to Gorbachev—and Yuri Golik's comments, in *Nezavisimaya Gazeta* (October 24, 1991); Valentin Zanin's hypothesis of phone connection with Foros, in *Moscow News Fax Digest* printed by *NRS* on August 30, 1991; interview with Raisa Gorbacheva, in *Trud* (September 3, 1991), and on the Soviet TV evening news on October 6, 1991; Lukyanov calling the plotters "lowlifes" in *Literaturnaya Gazeta* (September 11, 1991); Pavlov's statement about two dates for convoking the emergency session of the Supreme Soviet—transcript of his testimony, and *Literaturnaya Gazeta* (October 16, 1991).

THE MINEFIELD OF POWER

This chapter is primarily a product of conversations inside and outside the Russian White House, both with and about the new faces in power. In two cases we quote copiously from the Soviet media regarding Yeltsin's "100 Days": *Komsomolskaya Pravda* (October 17), *Moscow News* (October 13), *Kuranty* (October 18), *Rossiya* (October 23–29), *Kommersant* (September 23–30), *Nezavisimaya Gazeta* (October 12)—naturally, all dates are in 1991.

BIBLIOGRAPHY

IN ENGLISH

Alexandrov, Victor. *The Kremlin, Nerve Centre of Russian History.* New York: St. Martin's Press, 1963.

Beichman, Arnold, and Michael Bernstam. *Andropov, New Challenge to the West,* New York: Stein & Day, 1983.

Bialer, Seweryn. *Stalin's Successors: Leadership, Stability and Change in the Soviet Union.* Cambridge University Press, 1980.

Binyon, Michael, *Life in Russia.* New York: Pantheon Books, 1983.

Carter, Paul A. *Revolt Against Destiny.* New York: Columbia University Press, 1989.

Cohen, Stephen, and Katrina Vanden Heuvel. *Voices of Glasnost: Interviews with Gorbachev's Reformers.* New York: W. W. Norton, 1989.

Conquest, Robert. *Stalin, Breaker of Nations.* New York: Viking, 1991.

Corson, William R., and Robert T. Crowley. *The New KGB: Engine of Soviet Power.* New York: Morrow, 1985.

Crankshaw, Edward. *Khrushchev, a Career.* New York: The Viking Press, 1961.

Custine, Astolph, Marquis de. *Journey of Our Time.* New York: Pellegrini and Cudahy, 1951.

Doder, Dusko. *Shadows and Whispers: Power Politics Inside the Kremlin from Brezhnev to Gorbachev.* New York: Random House, 1986.

Doder, Dusko, and Louise Brenson. *Gorbachev: Heretic in the Kremlin.* New York: Viking, 1990.

Dornberg, John. *Brezhnev: The Masks of Power.* New York: Basic Books, 1974.

Finder, Joseph. *Red Carpet.* New York: A New Republic Book/Holt, Rinehart, and Winston, 1983.

Fischer, Louis. *The Life of Lenin.* New York: Harper & Row, 1964.

Frankland, Mark. *Khrushchev.* New York: Stein & Day, 1967.

Gurevich, David. *From Lenin to Lennon: A Memoir of Russia in the Sixties.* New York: Harcourt, Brace, Jovanovich, 1991.

Habbs, Joanna. *Mother Russia: The Feminine Myth in Russian Culture.* Indiana University Press, Bloomington, Indiana, 1989.

Hough, Jerry F. *Soviet Leadership in Transition.* Washington, D.C.: The Brookings Institution, 1980.

Hyland, William, and Richard W. Shryock. *The Fall of Khrushchev.* New York: Funk & Wagnalls, 1968.

Kaiser, Robert. *Russia: the People and the Power.* New York: Atheneum, 1976.

———. *Why Gorbachev Happened: His Triumphs and His Failure.* New York: Simon & Schuster, 1991.

Kennan, George F. *Sketches from Life.* New York: Pantheon, 1989.

Kerbley, Basile. *Gorbachev's Russia.* New York: Pantheon, 1989.

Klose, Kevin. *Russia and the Russians: Inside the Closed Society.* New York/London: W.W. Norton, 1984.

Laqueur, Walter, and others. *Soviet Union 2000: Reform or Revolution.* New York: St. Martin's Press, 1990.

———. *The Long Road to Freedom: Russia and Glasnost.* New York: Scribner's, 1989.

Lewin, Moshe. The *Gorbachev Phenomenon:* A Historical Interpretation. Berkeley: University of California Press, 1987.

Murphy, Paul J. *Brezhnev, Soviet Politician.* Jefferson, N.C.: McFarland, 1981.

Nagorski, Andrew. *Reluctant Farewell.* New Republic/Holt, 1985.

Nixon, Richard M. *In the Arena.* New York: Simon & Schuster, 1990.

Openings: Original Essays by Contemporary Soviet and American Writers. Edited by Robert Atwan and Valery Vinokurov. University of Washington Press, 1990.

Owen, Richard. *Comrade Chairman: Soviet Succession and the Rise of Gorbachev.* New York: Arbor House, 1986.

Pipes, Richard. *Russia under the Old Regime.* New York: Charles Scribner's Sons, 1974.

———. *The Russian Revolution.* New York: Alfred A. Knopf, 1990.

Rositzke, Harry. *The KGB: The Eyes of Russia.* Garden City, N.Y.: Doubleday, 1981.

Shevchenko, Arkady N. *Breaking with Moscow.* New York: Alfred A. Knopf, 1985.

Shipler, David K. *Russia: Broken Idols, Solemn Dreams.* New York: Times Books, 1983.

Sinyavsky, Andrei. *Soviet Civilization and Cultural History.* Boston: Little, Brown, 1990.

Smith, Hendrik. *The Russians.* New York: Quadrangle, 1976.

———. *The New Russians.* New York: Random House, 1990.

Solomon, Andrew. *The Irony Towers: Soviet Artists in a Time of Glasnost.* New York: Knopf, 1991.

Solovyov, Vladimir, and Elena Klepikova. *Yuri Andropov: A Secret Passage into the Kremlin.* New York: Macmillan, 1983.

———. *Behind the High Kremlin Walls.* New York: Dodd, Mead, 1986.

Steel, Jonathan. *Soviet Power: The Kremlin Foreign Policy from Brezhnev to Andropov.* New York: Simon & Schuster, 1983.

Steel, Jonathan, and Eric Abraham. *Andropov in Power: From Komsomol to Kremlin.* Garden City, N.Y.: Anchor Press/Doubleday, 1984.

Talbott, Strobe, ed. *Mikhail S. Gorbachev: An Intimate Biography.* New York: Time, 1988.

Tatu, Michel. *Power in the Kremlin: From Khrushchev to Kosygin.* New York: The Viking Press, 1970.

Taubman, William, and Jane Taubman. *Moscow Spring.* New York: Summit Books, 1989.

Trager, Oliver, ed. *Gorbachev's Glasnost: Red Star Rising.* An Editorials on File Book. New York: Oxford, 1989.

Ulam, Adam B. *Stalin: The Man and His Era.* New York: The Viking Press, 1973.

Walker, Martin. *The Waking Giant: Gorbachev's Russia.* New York: Pantheon, 1986.

Willis, David K. *Klass: How Russians Really Live.* New York: St. Martin's, 1985.

Wren, Christopher. *The End of the Line: The Failure of Communism in the Soviet Union and China.* New York: Simon & Schuster, 1989.

IN RUSSIAN

Abalkin L. I. *Perestroika: Paths and Problems.* Moscow: Ekonomika, 1988.

Adjubey, Alexei. *Those Ten Years.* Moscow: Sovetskaya Rossiya, 1989.

Agursky, M. *Ideology of National Bolshevism.* Paris: YMCA Press, 1980.

Amalrik, Andrei. *The USSR and the West in the Same Boat.* London: Overseas Publications Interchange, 1978.

Arbatov G. A. *Prolonged Recovery.* Moscow: Mezhdunarodnye Otnosheniya, 1991.

Avtorkhanov, A. *The Origins of the Partocracy.* 2 Vols. Frankfurt am Main: Posev, 1973.

————. *The Technology of Power.* Frankfurt am Main: Posev, 1983.

————. *The Kremlin Days and Deeds: From Andropov to Gorbachev.* Paris: YMCA Press, 1986.

Batkin, Leonid. *History Resumes.* Moscow: Moskovsky Rabochi, 1991.

Bazhov, P. P. *Malachite Box. Selected Stories.* Moscow: Khudozhestvennaya Literatura, 1978.

Borovik, Artyom. *Afghanistan: Once More About the War.* Moscow: Mezhdunarodnye Otnosheniya, 1990.

Burlatsky, Fedor. *New Thinking.* Moscow: Politizdat, 1989.

Cherez ternii: perestroika, glasnost, demokratiya ("Ad Aspera: Perestroika, Glasnost, Democracy"). Moscow: Progress, 1990.

Chernaya noch nad Belym Domom ("Black Night Over the White House"). Moscow: Gazeta Rossiya, 1991.

Custine, Astolph, Marquis de. *Russia Under Tsar Nicholas.* Moscow: Terra, 1990.

Fedotov, G. P. *The New City. A Collection of Articles.* New York: Chekhov Publishing House, 1952.

Forbidden Laughter: Soviet Underground Jokes. A Collection. Los Angeles, 1978.

Gautier, Theophile. *Journey to Russia.* Moscow: Mysl, 1990.

Glasnost. Nasushchnye voprosy i neobhodimye otvety ("Glasnost: Vital Issues and Necessary Answers"). A collection. Moscow: Politizdat, 1989.

Gorbachev, Mikhail S. *Selected Speeches and Articles.* In 7 Vols. Moscow: Izdatelstvo Politicheskoy Literatury, 1986–90.

Gorbacheva, Raisa. *I Hope.* Moscow: Kniga, 1991.

Goryun, Andrei. *Boris Yeltsin: Light and Shadows.* 2 booklets. Sverdlovsk: Clip, 1991.

Gromyko, A. A. *Memoirs.* In 2 Vols. Moscow: Politizdat, 1988.

Gumilev, L. N. *Ancient Russia and Great Steppe.* Moscow: Mysl, 1989.

Heller, Mikhail. *Landmarks of 70 Years.* London: Overseas Publications Interchange, 1987.

Heller, Mikhail, and Alexander Nekrich. *Utopia in Power: A History of the Soviet Union from 1917 to Our Day.* 2 Vols. London: Overseas Publications Interchange, 1978.

Inostrantsy o drevney Moskve ("Foreigners About Ancient Moscow"). Moscow: Stolitsa, 1991.

Karamzin, N. M. *Legends of Old.* Moscow: Pravda, 1987.

Khronika putscha. Chas za chasom ("The Putsch Chronicle: Hour by Hour"). Moscow: Russian Information Agency, 1991.

Khrushchev, Nikita. *Memoirs.* In 2 Vols. New York: Chalidze Publications, 1979.

Klyuchevsky, V. O. *Collected Works.* In 9 vols. Moscow: Mysl, 1987–90.

Komarov, Boris (pseud.) *The Destruction of Nature: The Aggravation of the Ecological Crisis in the USSR.* Frankfurt am Main: Posev, 1978.

Kozlovsky, Vladimir (ed.) *New Uncensored Ditties.* New York: Russica, 1982.

Lenin, Vladimir I. *On Glasnost.* Moscow: Politizdat, 1989.

Ligachev E. K. *Selected Speeches and Articles.* Moscow: Politizdat, 1989.

Makanin, Vladimir. *He Who Lagged Behind.* Moscow: Khudozhestvennaya Literatura, 1988.

Mlynar, Zdenek. *A Cold Wind Blows from the Kremlin.* New York, 1983.

Nuikin, Andrei. *We and They.* Moscow: Avers, 1990.

Obratnogo hoda net: perestroika v narodnom hozyaystve ("No Way Back:

Perestroika in a People's Economy"). A collection. Moscow: Politizdat, 1989.

Osmyslit kult Stalina. Lichnost i vlast ("To Comprehend the Stalin Cult. Personality and Power"). A collection. Moscow: Progress, 1989.

Perestroika i sovremeny mir. ("Perestroika and the Modern World"). A Collection. Moscow: Mezhdunarodnye Otnosheniya, 1989.

Platonov, S. F. *A Time of Troubles.* Prague: 1924.

Pokrovsky M. N. *Collected Works.* In 4 Vols. Moscow: Mysl, 1965–68.

Sakharov, Andrei. *Memoirs.* In 2 Vols. New York: Chekhov Press, 1990.

———. *Gorky, Moscow, and Everywhere.* New York: Chekhov Press, 1990.

Shafarevich, Igor. *Does Russia Have a Future?* Moscow: Sovetsky Pisatel, 1991.

Shevardnadze, Eduard. *My Choice.* Moscow: Novosti, 1991.

Shturman, Dora, and Sergei Tiktin. *Soviet Union Reflected in Political Anecdotes.* London: Overseas Publications Interchange, 1985.

Soldaty Chernobylya ("Chernobyl Soldiers") A collection. Moscow: Voenizdat, 1989.

Solovyov, S. M. *Readings and Stories on Russian History.* Moscow: Pravda, 1989.

Solovyov, Vladimir. *Operation Mausoleum.* New York: Liberty Publishing House, 1989.

Solovyov, Vladimir, and Elena Klepikova. *Mikhail Gorbachev: the Path to the Top.* Moscow: a pirated edition, 1989.

———. *The Kremlin Plotters: From Andropov to Gorbachev.* Moscow: Tsentr Iskusstvo, 1991.

———. *Struggle in the Kremlin.* New York, Jerusalem, Paris: Vremya i my, 1986.

Sorokin, V. *The Line.* Paris: Sintaksis, 1985.

Surovaya drama naroda ("The People's Ordeal"). A collection. Moscow: Politizdat, 1989.

Tarakanov N. D. *Chernobyl Notes.* Moscow: Voenizdat, 1989.

Telesin, Yuli. *1001 Anecdotes.* New Jersey: Hermitage, 1986.

V borbe za vlast ("In the Struggle for Power"), Pages from Russian Political History. A collection. Moscow: Mysl, 1988.

Vekhi ("Landmarks"). Collection of Articles about the Russian Intelligentsia. Moscow, 1909.

Voinovich, Vladimir. *Moscow 2042.* Ann Arbor: Ardis, 1987.

Volkogonov, Dmitri. *Triumph and Tragedy.* In 2 Vols. Moscow: Novosti, 1989.

Voslensky, Mikhail. *The Nomenklatura: The Soviet Ruling Class.* London: Overseas Publications Interchange, 1984.

Yeltsin, Boris. *Confession on an Assigned Theme.* Moscow: PIK, 1990.

————. *The Mid-Urals: Frontier of Creation.* Sverdlovsk: Mid-Ural Publishers, 1981.

Yesli po sovesti ("Speaking Openly"). A collection of articles on the problems of perestroika. Moscow: Khudozhestvennaya Literatura, 1988.

Zavisit ot nas. Perestroika v zerkale pressy ("It Is up to Us: Perestroika Reflected in the Media"). Moscow: Knizhnaya Palata, 1988.

Zemtzov, Ilya. *Political Dilemmas in the Struggle for Power.* Jerusalem, 1983.

————. *Corruption in the Soviet Union.* In French. Paris: Hachette, 1976.

————. *Party or Mafia? A Stolen Republic.* Jerusalem, 1976.

————. *Soviet Political Dictionary.* London: Overseas Publications Interchange, 1987.

Zemtov, Ilya, and John Ferrar. *Gorbachev: The Man and the System.* London: Overseas Publications Interchange, 1987.

Zhaba, S. P. *Russian Thinkers on Russia and Humankind.* Paris: YMCA Press, 1954.

Zhvanetsky, Mikhail. *One Year for Two.* Moscow: Iskusstvo, 1989.

Zimin, A. (pseud.) *Socialism and Neo-Stalinism.* New York: Chalidze Publications, 1981.

PERIODICALS

IN ENGLISH

Christian Science Monitor
International Herald Tribune
New York Times
Newsweek
Time
U.S. News & World Report
Wall Street Journal
Washington Post

IN RUSSIAN

Argumenty i fakty
Atmoda (later renamed Baltiyskoye Vremya, "Baltic Times")
Chas pik ("Rush Hour")
Demokraticheskaya Rossiya
Express Khronika
Iskusstvo Kino ("Film Art")
Izvestiya

Izvestiya TsK KPSS
Kommersant
Kommunist
Komsomolets Uzbekistana
Komsomolskaya Pravda
Kontinent (formerly Paris, now Moscow)
Krasnaya Zvezda
Kuranty
Literaturnaya Gazeta
Literaturnaya Rossiya
Megapolis Express
Molodaya Gvardiya ("Young Guard")
Moscow News
Moskovskaya Pravda
Moskovsky Komsomolets
Moskva
Nash Sovremennik ("Our Contemporary")
Novoye Russkoye Slovo (New York)
Nedelya ("Week")
Nezavisimaya Gazeta
Novoye Vremya (New Times)
Novy Mir
Ogonyok
Oktyabr
Pravda
Rossiya
Rossiyskaya Gazeta
Russkaya Mysl (Paris)
Semya ("Family")
Sintaksis (Paris)
Smena ("New Generation")
Sobesednik ("Interlocutor")
Sovershenno Sekretno ("Top Secret")
Sovetskaya Kultura
Sovetskaya Molodezh ("Soviet Youth")
Sovetskaya Rossiya
Stolitsa ("Capital")
Strana i mir ("Country and World") (Munich)
Sudarushka
22 (Jerusalem)
Teatr
Teatralnaya Zhizn ("Theater Life")
Trud

Vechernyaya Moskva ("Evening Moscow")
Vek XX i mir ("20th Century and the World")
Voprosy Literatury ("Problems of Literature")
Vremya i my ("Time and Us") (New York)
Yunost ("Youth")
Zhurnalist
Znamya

INDEX